I0819515

Adirondack Photographers, 1850–1950

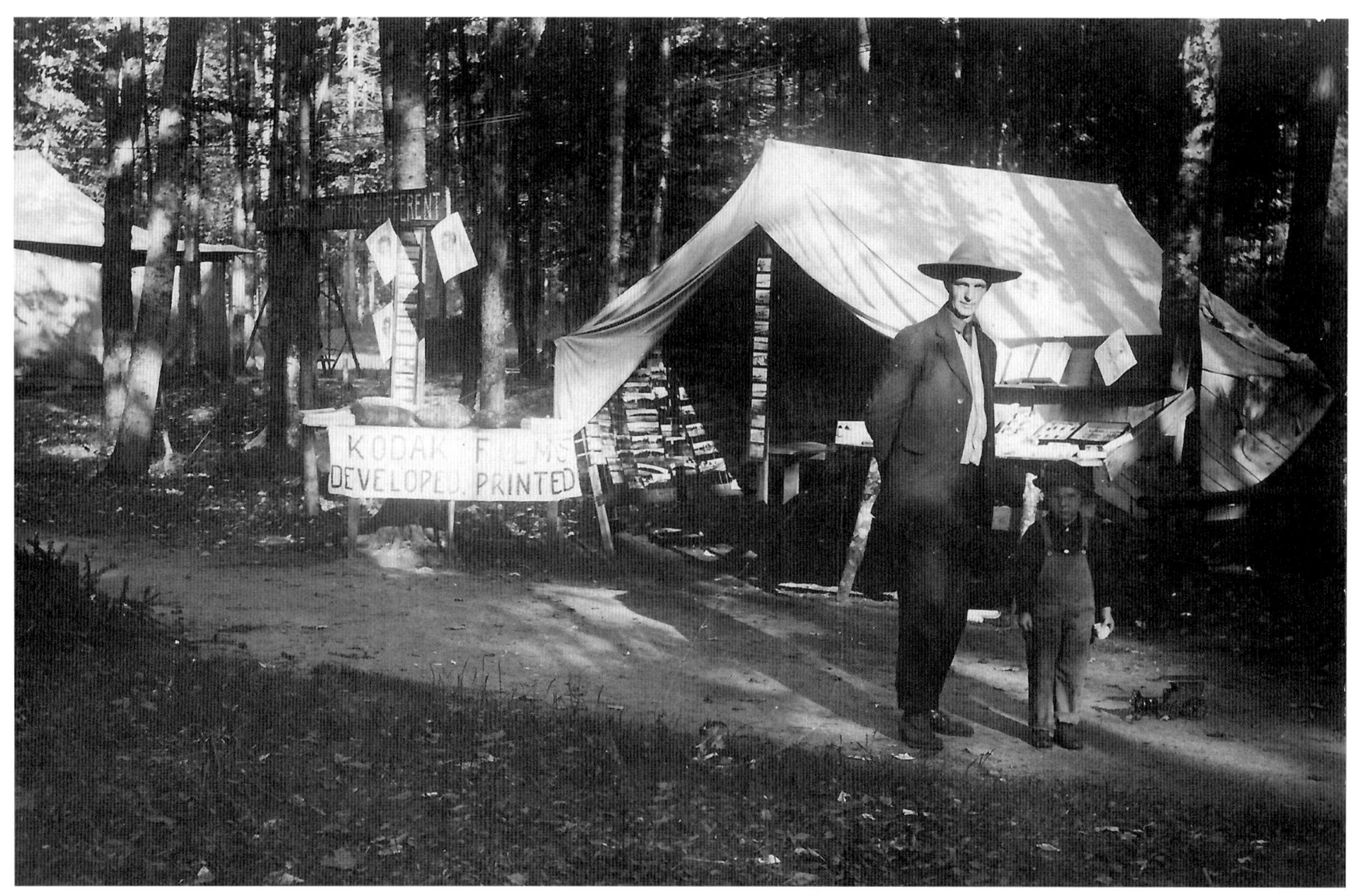

Frontispiece. H. D. Ross, woodland studio, Fulton Chain. RPPC, 1905–1910.

Adirondack Photographers, 1850–1950

Sally E. Svenson

SYRACUSE UNIVERSITY PRESS

All images not otherwise credited are from the author's personal collection.

First Edition 2023

23 24 25 26 27 28 6 5 4 3 2 1

∞ The paper used in this publication meets the minimum requirements of the American National Standard for Information Sciences—Permanence of Paper for Printed Library Materials, ANSI Z39.48-1992.

For a listing of books published and distributed by Syracuse University Press, visit https://press.syr.edu.

ISBN: 978-0-8156-1153-0 (hardcover)
978-0-8156-5585-5 (e-book)

Library of Congress Cataloging-in-Publication Data

Names: Svenson, Sally E., author.
Title: Photographers in the Adirondacks, 1850–1950 / Sally E. Svenson.
Description: First edition. | Syracuse, New York : Syracuse University Press, 2023. | Includes bibliographical references and index.
Identifiers: LCCN 2022038849 (print) | LCCN 2022038850 (ebook) | ISBN 9780815611530 (hardcover) | ISBN 9780815655855 (ebook)
Subjects: LCSH: Photographers—New York (State)—Adirondack Mountains Region—Biography. | Adirondack Mountains Region (N.Y.)—Biography. | Photography—New York (State)—Adirondack Mountains Region.
Classification: LCC TR139 .S89 2023 (print) | LCC TR139 (ebook) | DDC 779/.36097475—dc23/eng/20221017
LC record available at https://lccn.loc.gov/2022038849
LC ebook record available at https://lccn.loc.gov/2022038850

Manufactured in the United States of America

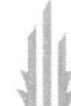

Publication supported by a grant from

The Community Foundation *for* Greater New Haven

as part of the Urban Haven Project

Contents

LIST OF ILLUSTRATIONS ❧ *vii*

AUTHOR'S PREFACE ❧ *ix*

Introduction ❧ *1*

Biographical Entries ❧ *21*

BIBLIOGRAPHY ❧ *181*

INDEX ❧ *191*

Illustrations

1. Beer Bros., Lake George, 1861–1863 ☙ 2
2. E. and H. T. and Anthony Co., Fort William Henry Hotel, circa 1865 ☙ 2
3. Adirondack exhibit at Sportsmen's Exposition, 1898 ☙ 11
4. S. R. Stoddard, *Au Sable Chasm, The Boat Ride*, circa 1880 ☙ 12
5. A. Knechtel, load of spruce near Elen Lake, Hamilton County, 1906 ☙ 14
6. H. M. Beach, *Steam Shovel Loading Ore—Benson Mines, N.Y.*, 1906–1916 ☙ 14
7. Kilburn Bros., *The Old Camp-Fire, Adirondacks*, 1882 ☙ 15
8. Tintype souvenirs from Sacandaga Park, 1900-1912 ☙ 17
9. J. J. Steffel, Camp Red Wing campers, Schroon Lake, 1946–1948 ☙ 18
10. A. N. Allen, advertisement, 1908 ☙ 22
11. A. Alletag, Camp Welcome, 1905–1909 ☙ 23
12. E. C. Austin, *Boulder Greens, Warrensburg, N.Y.*, 1937–1940s ☙ 26
13. H. K. Averill Jr., *Bartlett's Hotel, Upper Saranac Lake*, 1865–1875 27
14. G. W. Baldwin, *St. Regis Lake, Paul Smith's*, 1875–1880 ☙ 32
15. I. D. Barnum, *Ruins of Fort Ticonderoga*, 1868–1869 ☙ 33
16. H. M. Beach, *Observation Point, Lake Bonaparte*, 1906–1916 ☙ 35
17. E. O. Beaman, V. Colvin's Adirondack Survey, 1873 ☙ 37
18. M. Bourke-White, Camp Cedars, Forked Lake, 1933 ☙ 43
19. H. J. Brown, gem tintype, 1867–1873 ☙ 46
20. W. W. Brownell, Main Street, Lake Placid, 1897 ☙ 47
21. W. S. Carpenter, beaver dam on Indian Brook, Fourth Lake, 1919 ☙ 50
22. D. P. Church, advertising postcard, 1930–1940 ☙ 53
23. V. Colvin, Barton Garnet Mine buildings, 1895 ☙ 55
24. A. E. Coonrod, Frank Peterson's drive on the Boquet River, 1903 ☙ 59
25. E. N. Crane, *Looking North from D. C. Randalls*, 1899 ☙ 61
26. E. H. DeGraff, *Camp Kawanuta—Spider Pavilion, Old Forge, N.Y.*, 1909–1911 ☙ 64
27. C. Derby, portrait of Henry Martin, 1890–1900 ☙ 65
28. G. W. Dixon, lumber camp, 1890–1895 ☙ 67
29. F. O. Dodge, *The W. D. Watt Lumber Co. Stewerts Landing, Stratford, N.Y.*, 1910–1917 ☙ 68
30. Eastern Illustrating and Publishing, *E. B. Rogers Store and P.O., Vermontville, N.Y.*, 1914–1925 ☙ 70
31. C. R. Fay, *Big Clear Pond*, 1867 ☙ 72
32. L. H. Fillmore, *Steam Launch, Hague Regatta*, 1887–1898 ☙ 75
33. N. S. Foote, crossing log jam, 1914–1930 ☙ 76
34. S. H. Gottscho, *Adirondack Forest: "Still Life,"* 1942–1943 ☙ 81
35. P. R. Hastings, man working on railroad tracks, 1949 ☙ 85
36. F. A. Hodges, *Moonlight, Big Moose*, 1924 ☙ 87
37. J. F. Holley, portrait, 1890s ☙ 88
38. G. H. Houghton, Bartlett's, Upper Saranac Lake, 1864 ☙ 89
39. W. H. Jackson, *Mt. Ampersand and Round Lake, Adirondack Mountains*, 1900 ☙ 94
40. H. J. Kaiser, advertisement for Kaiser Stores, 1906 ☙ 97
41. E. E. Kellogg, *Boarding Steamer for Blue Mountain Lake*, 1911 ☙ 99

42. W. F. Kollecker, Fowler's Livery parade entry, Carnival, 1905–1910 ☙ *102*
43. H. L. Locke, *Camp Watokalo*, 1903–1911 ☙ *104*
44. G. F. Marvin, construction of railroad bridge over Ausable Chasm, Keeseville, 1889 ☙ *108*
45. H. K. Maxwell, Lake George from the air, 1921–1922 ☙ *109*
46. K. E. McClellan, *Lake Placid*, 1897 ☙ *110*
47. F. J. McCormick, women at Oval Wood Dish factory, 1920 ☙ *112*
48. A. L. Mix, double portrait, 1890s ☙ *114*
49. C. D. Moses, guides' camp, Upper Ausable Lake, circa 1901 ☙ *118*
50. W. T. Purviance, *Au Sable Chasm—The Long Gallery*, 1873–1874 ☙ *127*
51. O. D. Putnam, Johnsburg family, 1886 ☙ *128*
52. G. T. Rabineau, winter scene, Lake Placid, 1917–1931 ☙ *129*
53. G. H. Reising (as G. H. Rison), self-portrait, 1894 ☙ *130*
54. F. W. Rice, Wilmington landscape, circa 1896 ☙ *131*
55. F. Robbins, *Ausable Series: From Devil's Oven, Looking Out*, 1865–1867 ☙ *133*
56. H. V. Roberts, *In the Stillness of the Night*, 1907 ☙ *135*
57. Runions Brothers, portable photo gallery, Tupper Lake, 1890s ☙ *137*
58. A. W. Santway, *Along the Shore, Bear Mt. Camp*, 1916–1917 ☙ *139*
59. I. L. Stedman, skating on Mirror Lake, Lake Placid, 1910–1920 ☙ *145*
60. A. Stieglitz, *Music—A Sequence of Ten Cloud Photographs, No. II*, 1922 ☙ *148*
61. W. J. Stillman, untitled, 1859 ☙ *151*
62. S. R. Stoddard, Au Sable Pass from Beede House, 1887 ☙ *153*
63. A. F. Styles, *Iron Works, Port Henry, N.Y.*, 1865–1871 ☙ *157*
64. I. Sumy, newspaper readers on Chestertown post office steps, 1938 ☙ *159*
65. F. C. Thatcher, flying boat *Big Fish* at Lake George, 1921 ☙ *161*
66. J. A. Thatcher, Fort William Henry Hotel baseball team, 1890s ☙ *163*
67. A. C. Trumbull, *A Profitable Adirondack Industry*, 1902 ☙ *165*
68. F. A. Van Sant, men at Rogers Co. log slide, 1900-1901 ☙ *168*
69. L. Webster, portrait, 1868–1870 ☙ *170*
70. G. B. Wood Jr., Boquet River, 1882–early 1890s ☙ *173*
71. G. T. Woodward, President McKinley, Plattsburgh Barracks, 1899 ☙ *175*
72. J. S. Wooley, *Along the Shore, Lake George, Pilot Knob*, 1907–1920 ☙ *176*

Author's Preface

I fell in love with Adirondack photographs not long after arriving in the Adirondacks as a seasonal resident in 2002. In searching for images with which to illustrate a book on the rich history of the region's church architecture, I discovered compelling images in often unexpected places. Few of them came with much in the way of background, and my curiosity grew about the largely unheralded photographers whose work I was enjoying. This book is the somewhat overdue result.

The first step in compiling a record of the region's photographers was to identify them. I had no idea when I started out that the eventual list would be so long. It was surprising to find that a substantial number of Adirondack images are held by national archives as well as those of institutions in major cities outside the region, among them the Library of Congress, the Getty Museum in Los Angeles, and the New York and Boston public libraries. Within the Adirondacks, the most important publicly available collection is that of the Adirondack Experience in Blue Mountain Lake. Other regional entities—museums, colleges, local historical societies, libraries—hold compelling photographs as well. A few collections, or portions of them, are accessible online, but many are squirreled away—not always in optimum environments for their long-term preservation—in sometimes out-of-the-way locations. Ferreting out treasures has been a rewarding challenge.

Upstate New York is fortunate in having access to even the most ephemeral of early regional newspapers through two online reference sources: New York State Historic Newspapers and Tom Tryniski's Old Fulton New York Post Cards (commonly known as Fulton History). These sites made it possible to precisely date some visits by outside photographers to the Adirondacks as well as to uncover intriguing details about locally based practitioners. Both have been pivotal in compiling the biographical entries, and I am so grateful for their existence.

The most frequent recipients of my questions were staff members at the Adirondack Experience, where special thanks for their gracious responses go to past and present team members Doreen Alessi, Ivy Gocker, Hanna Person, Jerold Pepper, Laura Rice, and Angela Snye. Curators and staff at other regional archives—the Chapman Museum and the Hyde Collection in Glens Falls; Special Collections at the Feinberg Library, SUNY, Plattsburgh; and the Adirondack History Museum in Elizabethtown—have also offered valuable assistance. Michele Tucker, curator of the Adirondack Room at the Saranac Lake Free Library has been a steady source of information. I'm indebted, too, to past and present town and county historians who so generously responded to my queries: Stan Cianfarano (Warren County), Rachel Clothier (Corinth), Gail M. Cramer (Northampton, Northville), Dave Davidson (Day), Jean Dickerson (Lewis), Shawn Doyle (Richland and Pulaski), Priscilla Edwards (Edinburg), Mark Friden (Clifton), Laurie Halladay (Croghan), Mary Hotaling (Harrietstown), Carol Henry (Candor), Sharron Hewston (Jay), Jim Kammer (Raquette Lake), Jonathan Kopp (Tupper Lake), Donna Lagoy (Chester), Betty LaMoria (Moriah), Margaret Mannix (Lake George), Peg Masters (Webb), Aurora McCaffrey (Essex County), Pam Morin (Lake Luzerne), Richard Nilson (Caroga) Sandi Parisi (Warrensburg), Beverley Reid (North Elba, Lake Placid), Sally Rypkema (Hague), Betty White (Westport), and Deana Wood (Johnsburg). What an amazing service they provide.

Now for the blanket list of all those other people who have been helpful during the several years in which I have pursued this project: staff members and volunteers at large and small institutions, photographers' descendants, individuals. Many of them have, I'm sure, forgotten me, but I have not forgotten them. First, thanks to Edward Comstock Jr., who has fed me information from the beginning. Warmest gratitude, too, to Jaclyn Andersen, Rachel E. Andrews, Roger Bailey, Concetta Barbera, Maggie Bartley, Bob Bayle, Mike Beccaria, Barbara Bertucio, Mary Biddle, Bob Bogdan, William Bollman, Hallie Bond, Mazie Bowen, Mark Bowie, Kaitlin Buerge, Michael Burgess, Erica Burke, Meagan Carr, Moe Casey, Brian Castler, Nany Cohen, Kathleen Coleman, Matt Couture, George Davis, Gary Delemeester, Brenda Dentinger, Jill Foote Dignard, Prudence Doherty, Bill Dolback, Rachel Dworkin, Kelly Dwyer, Cecily Dyer, Barbara Edsall, Steven Engelhart, Daniel Fish, Alison Follos, Denise Fynmore, Jeanne Gamble, Glenda Gephart, Mary Gilbert, Sarah Gilmor, Ben Gocker, Rita Goldberg, Rebecca Grabie, Dana Grover, Todd Gustavson, Carol Haber, Gale J. Halm, Joan Hardekopf, Bill Healy, Mitchell Hemann, Charles Herr, Nicole T. Herwig, Bob Hindman, Jim Horton, Mary Hotaling, Bill Johnson, Kevin Johnson, Carol Johnston, Bill Keeler, Debra Kimok, Karen Klingenberger, Sarah Kozma, Wade LaPan, Paul Larner, Janet Lehr, Kate Lewis, Lisa Lincoln, Shana McKenna, Heather McNabb, Larry Miller, Christina Milliman, Deb Mohr, Marsha Morgan, Susan Navarre, John Norton, Mark Osterman, Mary Panzer, Keith Park, Moira Smith Park, Bambi Pedu, Jerry Perrin, Jesse Peers, Miranda Peters, Ed Pitts, Ron Polito, Gordon Pollard, Carole Poole, Justin Potter, Pam Pulley, Gregory Rami, Callie Raspuzzi, Kristy Rubyor, Alan Rumrill, Emma Sarconi, John L. Scherer, Tom Schmidt, Susan Scott, Don Seauvageau, Kay Schlueter, Molly Seegers, Donald Smith, Kenneth Smith, Conor Snow, Jeff Spencer, John Taibi, Phyllis Thompson, Kareen Tyler, June Venette, Marc Wanner, Jeff Ward, Joseph Watson, Donald

Wickman, Sarah J. Weatherwax, Caroline Welsh, and Gail Wiese. Finally, love and acknowledgement to my daughter, Alicia Svenson, who has been my tech adviser and tech support in the final stages of this project.

This book is hardly the last word on Adirondack photographers. New ones will be identified, and other researchers will update and expand upon details of the working lives and personal histories of those profiled here. My heartfelt appreciation in advance for their efforts to honor the diverse group of people whose visual contributions have enriched the ever expanding knowledge base of Adirondack history.

Adirondack Photographers,
1850–1950

Introduction

The new technology driving photography caught hold in the Adirondack region of upstate New York in the mid-nineteenth century as it did throughout the United States. A number of people, most of them young men (often from farming backgrounds), began to experiment with cameras and tried to earn their livings with local portrait work. From photographing individuals and families, many expanded their focus to include other groups as well as homes, workplaces, streetscapes, landscapes, and important events—from town festivals and commemorations to celebrity visits, train wrecks, floods, and fires. Even the smallest hamlet was likely to support a photographer. Occasionally it sustained more than one. Local photographers played a central role in chronicling community life, acting as visual diarists in their recording and preservation of regional history.

The development and evolution of photography in the Adirondacks was similar to that undergone in rural regions throughout the United States in most ways. It was dissimilar as well. For the Adirondacks was an early focus of tourism, drawing sophisticated summer vacationers from East Coast urban centers such as New York, Boston, and Philadelphia. By 1840 the town of Saratoga Springs, Saratoga County, some thirty miles to the south of the then loosely defined region, was recognized as the leading resort in America. In the 1820s its visitors began to travel by stage, and later by train, to the Warren County village of Caldwell (now the Adirondack town of Lake George), the southernmost settlement on thirty-two-mile-long Lake George. From there, steamboats carried them to other points of interest on the lake. The accessibility of Lake George and its reputation as "one of the most admirable sheets of water to be found in the whole world" soon made it a destination in its own right. Photographers based in and close to the metropolitan hubs from which tourists journeyed to the Adirondacks made numerous visits to the area, drawn by the developing taste of sightseers, on-site and armchair, for visual souvenirs. The Fort William Henry Hotel, based on Saratoga models, went up in Caldwell in 1854–55. By 1891 the shores of Lake George could accommodate four thousand overnight guests during the course of a summer season.[1]

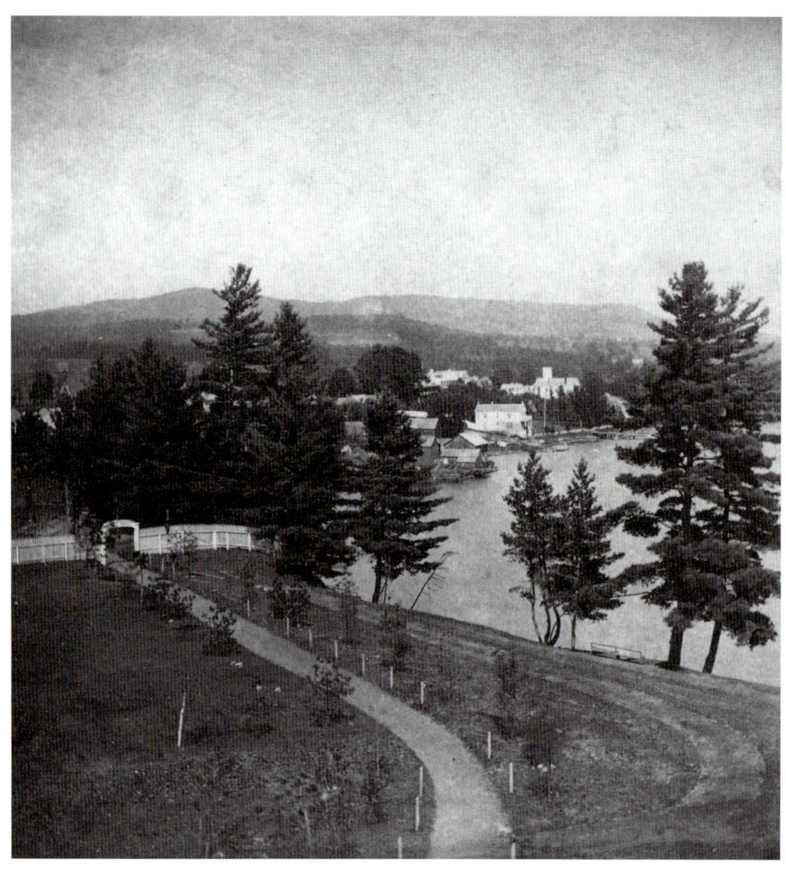

1. Beer Bros., Lake George.
One-half stereoview, 1861–1863.

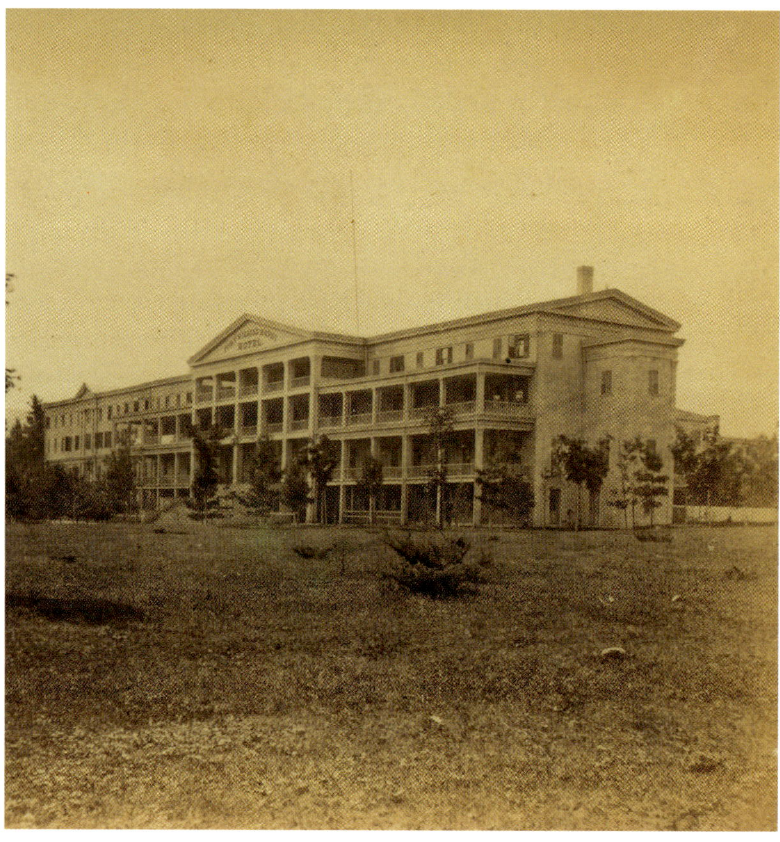

2. E. and H. T. and Anthony Co.,
Fort William Henry Hotel, Caldwell.
One-half stereoview, circa 1865.

DEFINITION OF "ADIRONDACKS"

The geographic boundaries of the Adirondacks as the term is used throughout this book conform approximately to the present-day borders of the New York State–designated Adirondack Park. This forested, lake-flecked expanse—about the size of Connecticut or Vermont—takes its name from the mountain range at its heart and is the largest publicly protected area in the contiguous United States. The park is an unusual composite of public and private lands, providing scenic home to modest hamlets, villages, and small towns. An early lumbering center, its core was set aside in 1885 as a forest preserve by the state in an effort to guard against over-logging, which it was feared might threaten its water supply; the park was incorporated in 1892. Its boundaries have little to do with political divisions, encompassing two counties in their entirety and small or sizeable segments of ten others. It continues to be primarily rural in nature.

WHO IS INCLUDED IN THE BIOGRAPHICAL DICTIONARY? WHO IS NOT?

Well over two hundred photographers operated briefly or long-term in the Adirondacks between 1850 and 1950. The following pages document career photographers who worked within and just beyond park borders as well as photographers from outside the region who catered to Adirondack tourist interests. They also profile individuals who integrated photography into other professional undertakings as well as talented amateurs who received some sort of public recognition.

For many who took up photography as a career, it represented a lifetime commitment. For others it was no more than an entry occupation—an early choice of livelihood for both skilled artists and technologically inclined tinkerers who later moved on to fields or geographic districts that more reliably met their personal and financial needs. A few photographers entered the commercial arena after mastering necessary skills in rehabilitation programs encountered while undergoing treatment for tuberculosis in and near the popular Adirondack "health resort" of Saranac Lake.

A compilation of individual stories, the biographical entries provide a fascinating account of the evolutionary course of photography over a one-hundred-year period. Additionally, they offer a place-based look at occupational and physical mobility in one small area of the United States. Extraordinary in this chronicle is the regular appearance of personalities important in the history of American photography in general. **Matthew Brady**, for example, grew up in the Adirondacks. Native sons **William Henry Jackson** and **Elias Olcott Beaman**, celebrated photographers of the Old West, also produced Adirondack images. Other profiled photographers developed wide reputations in specialized fields: from aerial to architectural to documentary photography. Talented amateurs **Alfred Stieglitz** and, to a lesser extent, **George Bacon Wood Jr.**, took photographs of the region, not for financial gain but as a means of personal expression, making important contributions to the Adirondack photographic legacy.

Photographers whose names appeared in early business directories but did not leave behind any identifiable images are largely excluded, as are photographers who produced a small number of images with local imprints about whom little relevant biographical information could be found. Not covered, either, are the many individuals who worked behind the scenes in regional photographic studios: from operators who staged setups and manned cameras in businesses owned by photographer-proprietors to retouchers and other studio employees who, like operators, never had their names on the finished photographs they were instrumental in producing. With few exceptions, no attention is given to large, city-based firms and small-town druggists, souvenir vendors, and stationery wholesalers and retailers inside and outside the park who published Adirondack images from negatives supplied by anonymous photographers. No attempt has been made to offer critical assessments of the work of the photographers included. Dates of Adirondack activity are approximate.

No one will be surprised at the paucity of women's names among the biographical entries. It was not until the 1890s that technological, social, and cultural changes led women to take up photography in any number. They were at first steered toward the domestic and feminine in subject matter, with the author of an 1897 *Ladies' Home Journal* article recommending studio portraiture—her own specialty—and noting other opportunities in "interior and architectural work, the copying of paintings, 'at home' portraits, outdoor pictures of babies, children, dogs and horses, and of country houses." (Photographic journals of the period enthusiastically endorsed women as receptionists to male photographers.) Between 1880 and 1910 the number of career women photographers across the United States rose from 271 to about 4,900, or 15 percent of professional practitioners. By 1920 they constituted 20 percent. Women were, however, responsible for a good deal of studio work in offstage roles—sometimes as operators or, more often, as retouchers of negatives and colorers of finished prints—specialties considered "traditional female" jobs and carrying considerable status in the community. A few women learned camera skills in helping to run studios with their photographer husbands, occasionally carrying on after their spouses' deaths—not infrequently as *Mrs.* followed by a husband's full name.[2]

A BRIEF HISTORY OF PHOTOGRAPHY

Many users of this book are no doubt thoroughly familiar with the early history of photography. The following section is intended for those who are not, on the assumption that dates of processes, formats, and trends in the field are useful to have at hand in interpreting the work of individual photographers.

First Photographs

Incredulity was the initial response to daguerreotypy, the earliest successful method of photographic reproduction to gain widespread public attention. "We have seen the views taken in Paris by the 'Daguerreotype,'" effused an editor of New York City's *Knickerbocker* magazine in 1839

> and have no hesitation in avowing that they are the most remarkable objects of curiosity and admiration, in the arts, that we ever beheld. . . . Let a reader suppose himself standing in the middle of Broadway, with a looking glass held perpendicularly in his hand, in which is reflected the street, with all that therein is. . . . Then let him take the glass into the house, and find the impression of the entire view, in the softest light and shade, vividly retained upon its surface. This is the Daguerreotype![3]

Producing unique positives directly onto silvered copper plates, daguerreotypy took its name from Louis Daguerre, a French diorama painter who announced the discovery in January 1839. Before the end of the year Americans were eagerly mastering the procedure. As early exposure times were long (up to ten seconds), the process was at first used only for outdoor views. But as rapid advances in technology and technique made it possible to capture images more quickly, the daguerreotype became primarily, but not exclusively, used for indoor portraits during the twenty years in which it was popular. The first daguerreotype studio opened in New York City in March 1840. The 1850 US Census enumerated 938 males over the age of fifteen across the country who called themselves daguerreotypists. Some practitioners preferred the term *artist*, pragmatically referring to themselves in terms of the profession they were, in portraiture, at least, beginning to supplant. Few stayed in business for long, and few signed their images.[4]

Itinerant daguerreotypists began visiting the towns and villages of the Adirondack region not long after the process was introduced. An early arrival, George Brown Jr., announced in February 1842 that he had taken rooms in a Plattsburgh, Clinton County, hotel and would "be happy to wait upon all who wish to procure correct Likenesses." "Messrs Ficket & Martin" engaged quarters "for a few days only" above a Keeseville, Essex County, jewelry store in 1846 and advertised "colored daguerreotype miniatures . . . in all sizes, from that of a sixpence to the largest ever taken in this place . . . put up in fine cases or lockets, and warranted to give satisfaction." Transient daguerreotypists were active throughout the Adirondacks during the following decade. They often worked from specially equipped portable wagons or "saloons": usually large, horse-drawn chassis topped by boxlike structures containing small chambers with side- or skylights to illuminate sittings, as well as developing rooms. Settling in small population centers, artists stayed long enough to exhaust the local market and then moved on.[5]

Philemon Tenney Gates of New Hampshire opened a permanent daguerreian gallery in Plattsburgh, Clinton County, in 1850. Locally born **Tarrant Putnam** offered daguerreotypy in Keeseville, Essex and Clinton Counties, the same year. Lifelong Adirondack resident **Horace S. Tousley** launched Tousley's Sky-Light Daguerreotype Rooms in Keeseville in 1851. Both Gates and Tousley advertised aggressively. Gates did what he could to discourage competition from itinerants, warning in 1853 against "pretended Daguerreians, that are impositions on the public. . . . Have your Daguerreotyping done by skillful and experienced STATIONARY ARTISTS, that can be referred to any future time." That year, at the peak of the art form's popularity, American photographers produced some three million daguerreotypes.[6]

The earliest challenge to the daguerreotype was the sharply detailed unique ambrotype on glass, which knew a brief vogue after its introduction in 1854. It was succeeded circa 1856 by the tintype (also called ferrotype or melainotype). A nonreflective single photograph on a thin sheet of iron coated with dark enamel, the tintype was cheaper to produce and more durable than the daguerreotype; it remained popular through the first two decades of the twentieth century. Both the ambrotype and tintype were, like the daguerreotype, primarily used in portrait work.[7]

By 1860 photographers were using a new collodion wet-plate process to produce well-defined negatives on glass that could be infinitely reproduced on paper at little cost. While effecting a revolution in photography, the procedure was cumbersome, and entailed pouring a light-sensitive syrupy liquid onto a blank plate that had to be exposed and developed in a darkroom in the vicinity of water before it dried. (Photographer **William Henry Jackson** estimated that half an hour was barely enough time to complete the process for each plate.) Outdoor photographers had to carry with them fifty- to seventy-pound loads of heavy paraphernalia to execute their work, but the method quickly displaced all forms of single-image capture and was used until about 1880.[8]

The carte de visite, a photo on a cardboard mount about the size of a calling card (4 x 2.5 inches), was launched in the United States in 1859 and spread rapidly. The cabinet card (usually 6.5 x 4.25 inches), introduced in 1866, was a larger and more refined version of the carte de visite. Like earlier photographic advances, both the carte de visite and cabinet card were primarily but not solely vehicles for portraiture. The cabinet card captured more than 90 percent of the portrait market by 1890.[9]

The stereograph, or stereoview, dominated landscape work in photography's early decades. The image was achieved with a specialized camera featuring two lenses spaced roughly 2.5 inches apart on the same horizontal plane. On glass or mounted on cardstock, the side-by-side images appeared as a single three-dimensional representation when viewed through a special apparatus known as a stereoscope or stereo viewer. European stereographs appeared in the United States from England in 1851 and were sold commercially by 1853. The Langenheim Brothers of Philadelphia produced a short American series in 1855. Public interest intensified with the invention by Oliver Wendell Holmes Sr. of a practical handheld stereoscope in 1859—the same year that the **New York Stereoscopic Company** was producing views from around Lake George and **Elisha M. Van Aken** was working in the region of Long Lake, Hamilton County. Before long, stereoscopes, along with a selection of views, adorned most middle-class parlor tables. Stereoviews attained their peak of popularity in the 1870s before being largely supplanted in the 1880s by individually mounted photographic prints.[10]

The gelatin dry-plate negative on glass, launched in 1871, represented a vast improvement over the collodion wet-plate process and greatly simplified the work of photographers. Some ten times more sensitive to light, dry plates could be prepared well in advance of use and developed at leisure, eliminating the need for cumbrous portable darkrooms when taking pictures outdoors. Dry-plate glass negatives were commercially manufactured from 1875 and quickly displaced collodion wet-plate negatives in photographic production.[11]

The Business of Photography

The ideal setup for a commercial photographer was a specially fitted-out studio or gallery—generally a leased space in a building shared by a variety of business enterprises. Before 1885, when electric lighting became economical, studios were likely to be found on top floors in buildings of more than one story in order to accommodate the skylights necessary to focus light on posing sitters. Small-town practitioners often operated satellite studios in addition to their primary galleries: portable buildings, rented interior spaces, or vacant ground in nearby population centers that they visited on a regular schedule. During the summer many regional photographers went on the road, setting up temporary quarters in county seats, seasonal resorts, and other venues, such as county fairs, where people congregated. Portraits, available in various sizes, could be hand-finished in an assortment of techniques: India ink, watercolors, crayons, oils. Negatives, as well as selected equipment, were generally passed on to succeeding photographers when studio ownership changed hands. Some retreating or retiring photographers sold negatives and copy-negatives to other photographers who substituted their own names on mounts for those of the original artists.

Backgrounds and accessories made their appearance in studios not long after the invention of the daguerreotype. Their importance escalated, with the trend reaching its zenith in the early 1890s when photographers who may once have owned a few accessories—a posing stand for holding the head still during an exposure, a chair, a table, a column, a rug, and a painted backdrop—now owned an extensive selection of fixtures. Some Adirondack photographers painted their own backdrops. Others ordered from specialist companies. In 1880 Plattsburgh photographer **William A. Bigelow** reported that he used "the latest styles . . . from Seavey," a reference to New York City–based Lafayette W. Seavey (1842–1901), the foremost photographic background painter of the late nineteenth century. Sixty other-odd background and accessory companies sold their wares via mail order and from displays at photographers' conventions. Traveling artists provided some backgrounds: William Blackburn (1860–1935), an eccentric English-born itinerant minister and scene painter from Oswego, Oswego County, was reported to be painting backdrops for Corinth, Saratoga County, photographer **Joseph K. Dunlop** in 1919. The taste for elaborate backgrounds and accessories faded with the close of the Victorian era. They were little used after the first decade of the twentieth century except in arcade photo booths at county fairs and amusement parks.[12]

Ink-stamped or printed information on the reverse sides of images or image mounts both identified and advertised their makers in the early years of photography. Like backgrounds, imprints evolved over time from small and simple to large and elaborate; by the late 1880s they might take over the entire back of a cabinet card. The printing of photographers' names on the front of mounts began to displace back imprints at around the same time. Commercially produced photographs in the North displayed federal tax stamps on mount backs from 1864 through 1866, levied to help support the Union's effort during the Civil War.[13]

Commercial photographers shared ideas and learned new techniques through books and specialized journals—to which many submitted photographic samples in the hope of garnering positive reviews on which to build business. They joined professional organizations that brought them together at conventions and, occasionally, participated in local camera clubs and photographic societies, often supported by well-heeled amateur photographers, that began appearing in population hubs from the mid-nineteenth century. A number of camera clubs sponsored juried exhibitions—sometimes with cash prizes—that raised the level of participants' aesthetic and technical sophistication.

The Advent of "Kodakery"

In 1888 the Eastman Kodak Company of Rochester introduced a portable, handheld camera for amateur photographers, or "Kodakers," that utilized flexible, rolled paper film and required little technological knowledge for its use. Enthusiasm for what became known as "snapshotting" skyrocketed, diminishing opportunities for professional photographers. As early as 1894 the *Elizabethtown Post* republished an article credited to the *New York World* on the countrywide decline in photographic portrait galleries. The availability of the new camera option had a similar dampening effect on landscape photography. As Vermont-based landscape specialist **Charles P. Hibbard** phrased it in 1896: "The amateur . . . and there are thousands of him in this section every summer, devastates this field of work."[14]

Commercial photographers responded to the contracted market by expanding their offerings and developing sidelines to meet amateur demand for cameras, photographic supplies, and black-and-white photo finishing. Some offered additional items—stationery, souvenirs, curios—creating something of a variety store atmosphere in their public rooms. They also began to use rolled film themselves. (Kodachrome color film would not be available until 1936.) Landscape specialists adopted larger camera sizes and made greater use of the newly popular panoramic format to differentiate their work from that of nonprofessionals. Despite their efforts, by the early twentieth century many Adirondack communities could no longer boast of having their own professional photographers, as practitioners abandoned small markets or left the business altogether.[15]

Magic Lantern Shows

Photography-based public performances given before audiences by live narrators were popular from the 1880s into the early 1900s. They were regularly offered by entrepreneurial individuals charging admission fees in meeting halls or churches with travel, science, and art as favored themes. Presenters utilized a two-lensed slide projector, or stereopticon, illuminated via kerosene, limelight, or electric light, to dissolve between sometimes hand-colored, glass photographic slides projected onto screens. Several Adirondack photographers presented their own travel-based shows.

Postcard Photography

An international craze for picture postcards gained momentum in the early twentieth century, opening a new field for photographers. Enthusiasm in the United States was generated by Congressional passage of the Private Mailing Card Act in 1898, which relinquished the government's monopoly on printing postcards and allowed individual publishers to enter the field. The format at first required that one side of a card be limited to address, leaving restricted room for a message and an image on the other. Regulations changed on March 1, 1907, permitting the image to appropriate the card face while address and message shared the back. The years between 1905 and 1920 have been called the "golden age of postcards." Official US figures for postcards mailed between July 1, 1907, and June 30, 1908, were 667,777,798, or more than seven cards for every American.[16]

Postcards generally celebrated specific events or places of local or tourist interest. The majority of cards were mechanically mass produced by large conglomerates from hand-colored images captured by nameless photographers. In out-of-the-way places such as the Adirondacks, small-town commercial photographers and a few amateurs offered black-and-white or sepia "real photo postcards" (RPPC), often in editions of one hundred or less and printed from negatives on photographic paper with postcard backs. In some localities, these were the only postcards available.[17]

News Photography

Photographs were used from the early-1860s as the basis for wood engravings published in magazines and newspapers. Appearing as drawings, these were copied from photographic images onto ink-receptive wood (and often embroidered upon by the transferring artists). The *Daily Graphic*, a New York City–based newspaper, reproduced an actual photograph for the first time in 1880. Halftone, a process employing discrete dots to break down photographs for printing, was used by newspapers from 1888 and solved the technical difficulties inherent in reproducing them. The career field in news photography dates to 1896 and the founding of a news bureau photography press agency: Underwood and Underwood. World War I established news photography as inseparable from news itself. The Associated Press (launched in 1848) began a picture service in 1927 and photo transmission by wire in 1935. The first images sent over the new network related to a small plane's forced landing in late December 1934 on Pine Mountain in Wells, Hamilton County. Many newspapers continued for several decades to use photographs provided by mail.[18]

News photography—or photojournalism as it is called when employed in its most sophisticated sense to tell a picture story in journalistic terms—differed from both portraiture and landscape photography. As Vincent Jones, executive editor of the *Utica Observer-Dispatch*, observed in 1949, "Your news photographer shoots from the hip when his instinct tells him that he's going to catch the story. His focusing may be a mite fuzzy, the 'composition' might draw reproving clucks from a board of judges—but he'll have the news for you. It may not be perfect—but it will be human, and thus eminently suitable for that most human and imperfect of institutions—the daily newspaper."[19]

Only **Dante O Tranquille** (who worked for the *Utica Observer-Dispatch*) covered the Adirondacks as a career news photographer during the one hundred-year period encompassed here. Other Adirondack newspapers routinely purchased images from local photographers but did not carry professionals on staff. It was only in the 1950s that a few regional newspaper employees developed reputations for combined photographic and writing skills.

ADIRONDACK THEMES

Every American town and city, every area of the country, had photographic subjects that spoke specifically to the interests of residents, or, as in the case of the Adirondacks, its multifaceted market of locals and visitors. Following are a few specific themes that, in addition to portrait work, resonated with photographers working in the Adirondack region between 1850 and 1950.

Tourism

The influx of summer visitors that began in the 1850s continued to soar as the nineteenth century progressed. While Lake George was still a center of holiday activity and photographic enterprise, vacationers increasingly penetrated the semi-populated Adirondack interior; by 1900 the region's summer population was estimated to be twenty-five thousand. Photographers played a crucial role in defining and marketing the tourist experience—both in promoting "consumable" destinations and mediating visitors' reactions to popular venues and landscapes. Images of important "sites," including the eighteenth-century forts of Ticonderoga and Crown Point on the Lake Champlain shoreline, were popular. Even more so were photographs of high-end hotels and modest hostelries throughout the region. **George W. Baldwin** displayed a collection of framed photographs focused solely on individual hotels and their neighborhoods in an 1898 exhibition jointly mounted by the

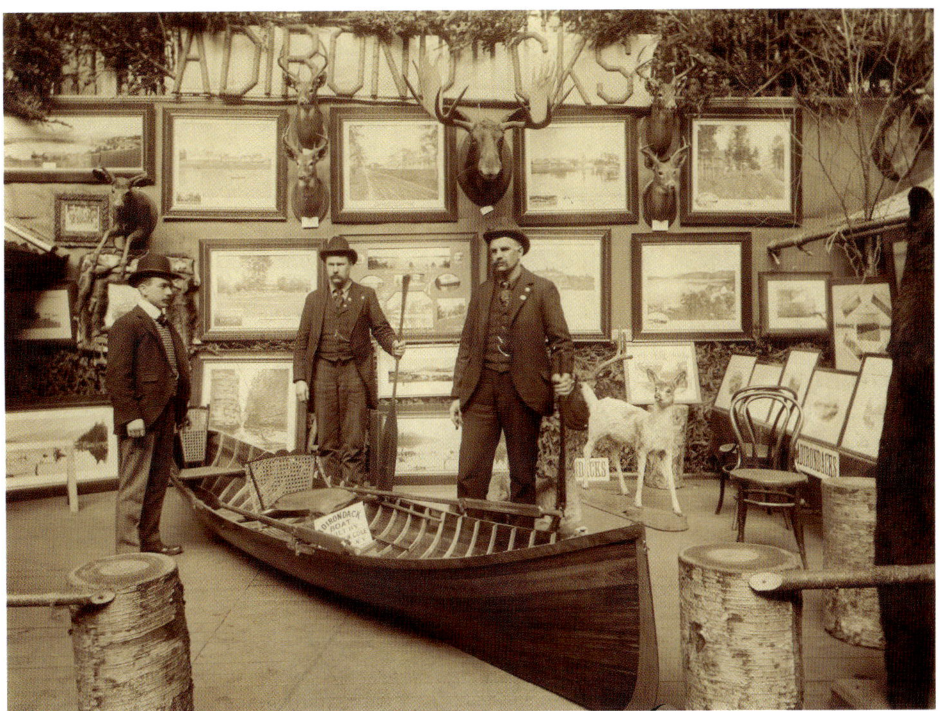

3. Adirondack exhibit at Sportsmen's Exposition, New York, featuring photographs by G. W. Baldwin, 1898. Courtesy of Adirondack Experience.

Adirondack Hotel League and the Adirondacks Guides Association at the Sportsmen's Exposition in New York City.[20]

Natural Features: Ausable Chasm

The Adirondacks' lakes and mountains were core subjects of early regional photography. But Ausable Chasm, located on the border of Essex and Clinton Counties near Keeseville, was the region's most extensively photographed natural setting into the first decades of the twentieth century. Initially described in 1763 by explorer and settler William Gilliland, the chasm's dramatic surface geology had been cut by the swiftly flowing Ausable River through a layered sandstone sheet on its plunge from the state's highest mountain, Marcy, to its Lake Champlain outlet. The gorge's reputation was

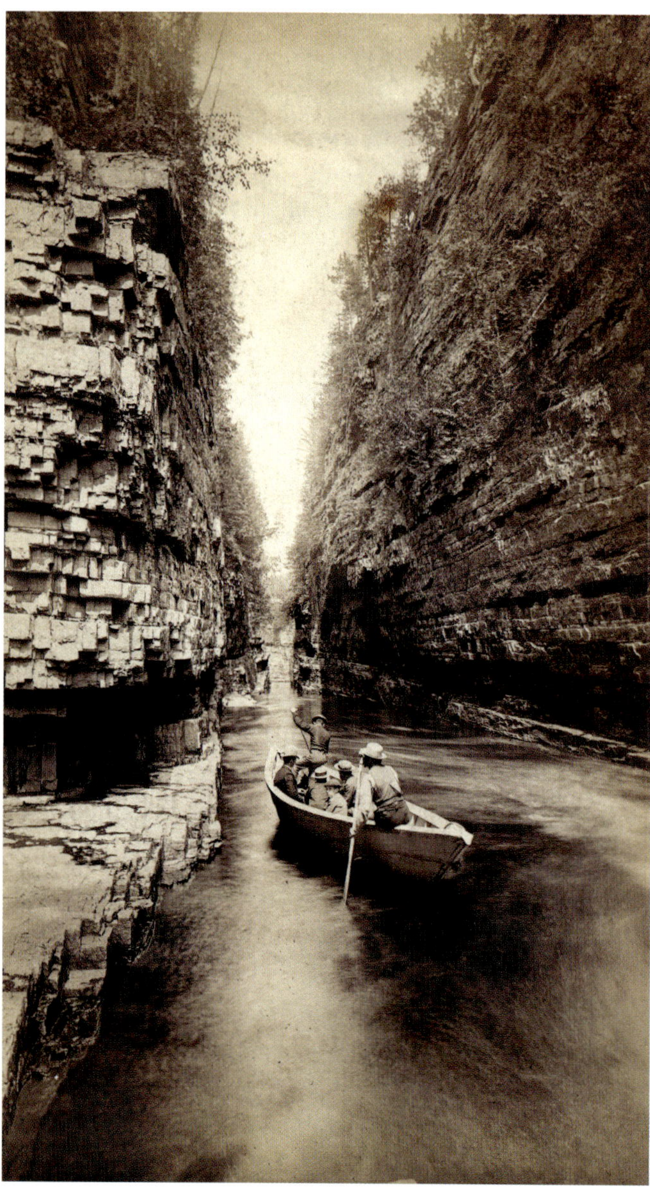

4. S. R. Stoddard, *Au Sable Chasm, The Boat Ride*, circa 1880. Courtesy of S. R. Stoddard Collection, Chapman Museum.

enhanced in 1851 when Fredrika Bremer, a celebrated Swedish literary figure and travel writer, praised its beautiful location and "rapid, though shallow little river, Au Sable, where the rocks present the appearance of regularly built, inaccessible fortress walls of a most remarkable character."[21]

Some twenty-five commercial photographers found Ausable Chasm a remunerative source of photographic focus before 1920. In some cases, it was their only Adirondack subject. One of the first to lug his equipment down one of the two flights of steep, ladder-like stairs built by the early 1850s for public access was **Henry Ketchum Averill Jr.,** who published a "splendid lot" of chasm stereographs in 1865. A trio of Philadelphia investors purchased the land bordering both sides of the gorge in early 1873 and developed the site as a full-fledged tourist venue, adding an interconnected series of pathways and staircases to ease entry. More than 2,600 individuals paid the entrance fee of fifty cents to explore the chasm between early July and mid-October that year; over 1,500 took the boat ride offered as part of the experience. **Seneca Ray Stoddard** and **George W. Baldwin** were the most prolific recorders of the site. Stoddard's 1877 catalog listed 103 stereoviews of the gorge, highlighting thirty images as "principal" or "most important." It also included a full-page chasm map designating individual sites by their popular names.[22]

Railroads

A profound agent of technological change, railroads served as the inspiration for many of America's finest photographers, commissioned by line owners to produce images meeting a variety of needs. At first their work was aimed at attracting financial backing and reassuring potential clients about the new technology with photographs of trains, tracks, bridges, and tunnels. Later, railroads looked to enhance ridership through documentation of scenic landscapes and other enticements along their routes. Promotional images for lines serving the Adirondacks appeared in general advertising and railroad-produced travel guides and posters. Large photographs were in demand for hanging in stations and railroad-owned hotels. In the 1910s the New York Central Railroad spent thirty thousand dollars a year on marketing the Adirondacks.[23]

Businesses

Adirondack mining operations—iron, garnet, titanium, graphite, wollastonite—and the harvesting and milling of wood products were frequently recorded subjects. Owners hired photographers to formally document facilities and processes. Employees recorded themselves as well. Lumberjacks proved to be particularly good clients of small-town image-makers, commissioning portraits—singly and as groups—when lumber camps broke up in the spring and workforces were homeward bound. A variety of local

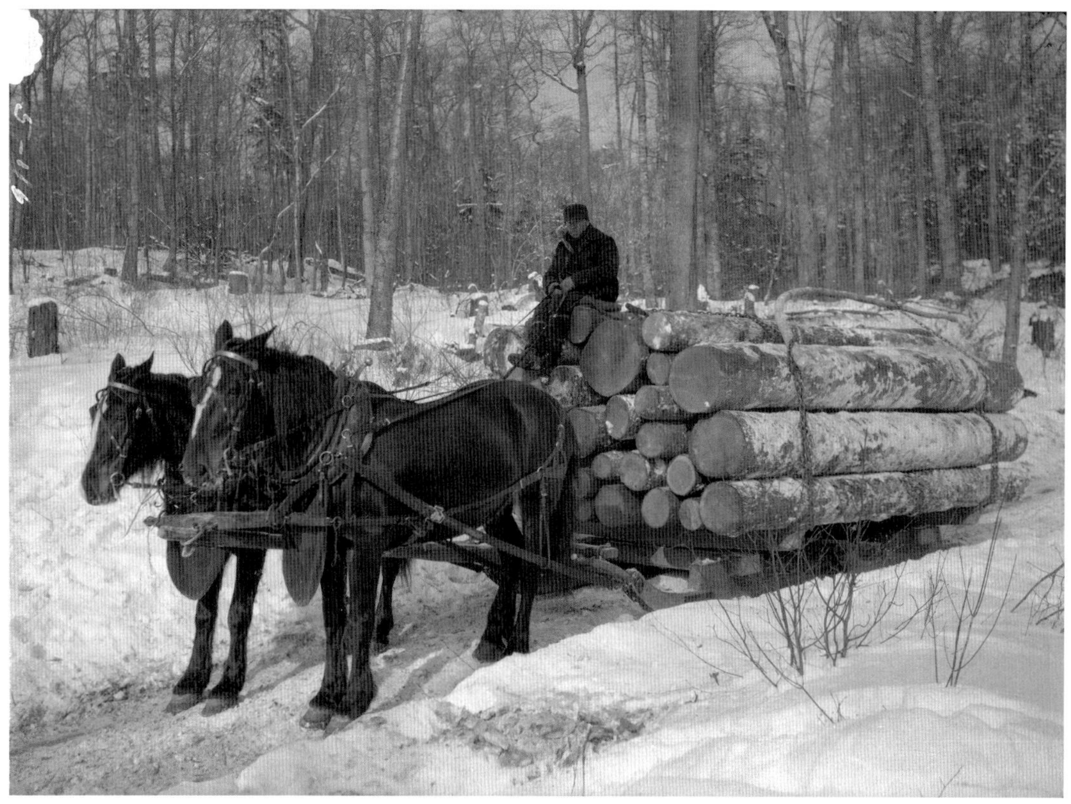

5. State forester A. Knechtel for New York State Forest, Fish, and Game Commission, load of spruce near Elen Lake, Hamilton Co., 1906. Courtesy of New York State Archives and New York Conservation Department.

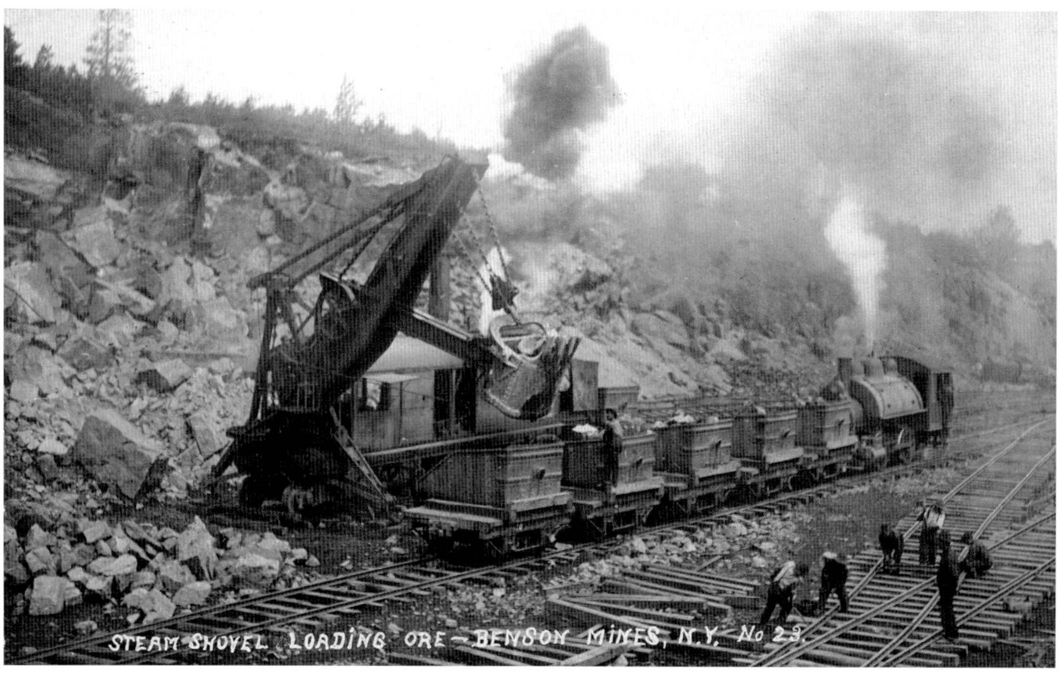

6. H. M. Beach, *Steam Shovel Loading Ore—Benson Mines*, N.Y. RPPC, 1906–1916. Courtesy of Mark Friden, Clifton Town Historian.

enterprises were automatically photographed in the course of recording community life.

Outdoor Recreation: Camping, Hiking, Hunting, and Fishing

Popular with full- and part-time Adirondack residents and visitors of all classes, these pastimes were assiduously documented by regional photographers, who often shared their interests and their adventures. Thousands of deceased members of the finny tribe lived a second life in recorded images; deer, bear, and other varieties of game were posed with those who dispatched them. A few locally based guides combined their occupation with photography, guaranteeing that their clients' sporting exploits would be professionally immortalized.

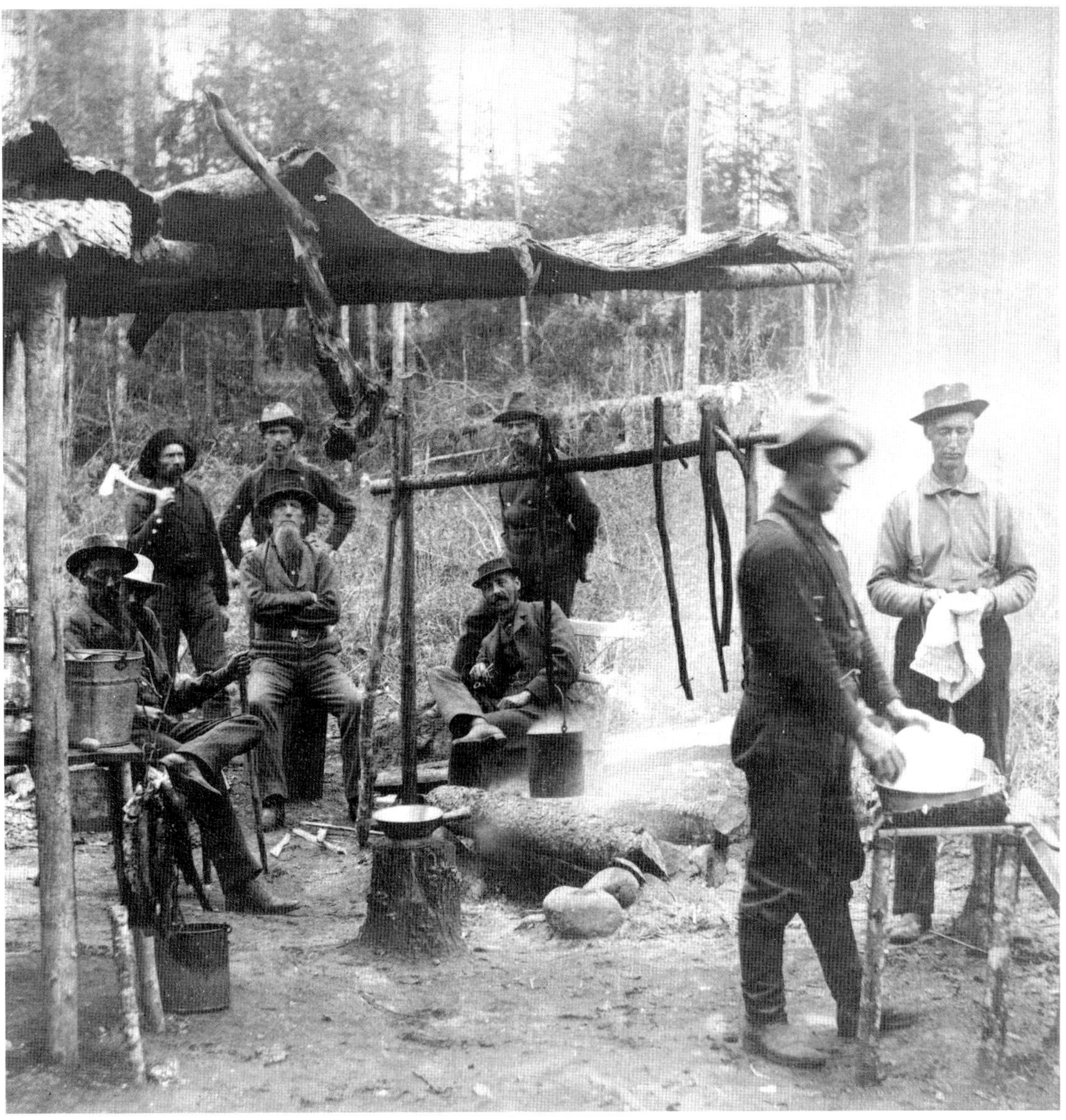

7. Kilburn Bros., *The Old Camp-Fire, Adirondacks*. One-half stereoview, 1882.

Great Camps

In the late nineteenth century, well-to-do summer visitors began to escape the fishbowl atmosphere of Lake George and other Adirondack resorts by purchasing land on which to build elaborate seasonal homes, or "great camps." These residences required visual validation, as did the urbane activities favored by their owners: golfing, tennis, boating excursions and races, memorable parties. Socially adept, big-city photographers were called upon to document these properties by their proud owners, with the expectation that resulting images would be published in magazines celebrating the possessions and accomplishments of their peers.

Conservation and Education

New York State government departments relied on photographers to record topography as well as to commemorate and publicize their activities over the years. **Verplanck Colvin,** superintendent of the Adirondack Survey from 1872, was among the first to recognize the importance of the camera in documenting landscape and landscape change. The New York State Forest Commission (renamed and reoriented a number of times) included photographs purchased from regional photographers as well as images taken by government employees in the lavish annual reports it published from the mid-1890s into the early years of the twentieth century. James S. Whipple, chief of the New York State Forest, Fish, and Game Commission between 1905 and 1910, often illustrated his speeches with lantern slides referencing regional projects in the one hundred public appearances he gave every year on behalf of forest propagation. Wealthy philanthropist, conservationist, and amateur photographer George D. Pratt, head of the New York State Conservation Commission from 1915 to 1921, oversaw the buildup of "the finest collection of conservation movies and still pictures in this country." Men associated at the local level with conservation efforts, among them forest rangers, recorded site conditions in their areas of operation, as did individuals committed to conservation, such as **Seneca Ray Stoddard**, who advocated on behalf of environmental protection.[24]

The New York State Department of Education's Division of Visual Instruction looked to the Adirondacks for photographs in specific subject areas when building its collection of more than twenty thousand unique lantern slides for loan to state schools between 1886 and 1939. So too, did Albert S. Bickmore, a founder and the first superintendent of the American Museum of Natural History, opened to the public in New York City in 1871. In 1884 Bickmore became the museum's curator of public instruction, in which role he amassed thousands of negatives in developing a series of illustrated lectures for teachers before 1903, among them existing and commissioned images from Adirondack photographers.

New Subjects of the Twentieth Century

In 1901 the Fonda, Johnstown and Gloversville Railroad added amusement facilities—theater, carousel, roller coaster, midway, and a miniature train—to Sacandaga Park, a onetime Methodist campground in the Fulton County village of Northville. Annual attendance at this summer cottage community and resort could reach ninety thousand during the heyday of what was called the "Coney Island of the North" prior to 1920, providing opportunities for a number of photographers.

Other Adirondack towns and villages with some resort appeal educated themselves in ways of capturing a piece of the tourist-industry pie with the aid of photography. Promoters of Lake Placid, Essex County, became particularly adept at doing so. The decision by Melvil Dewey, founder of the

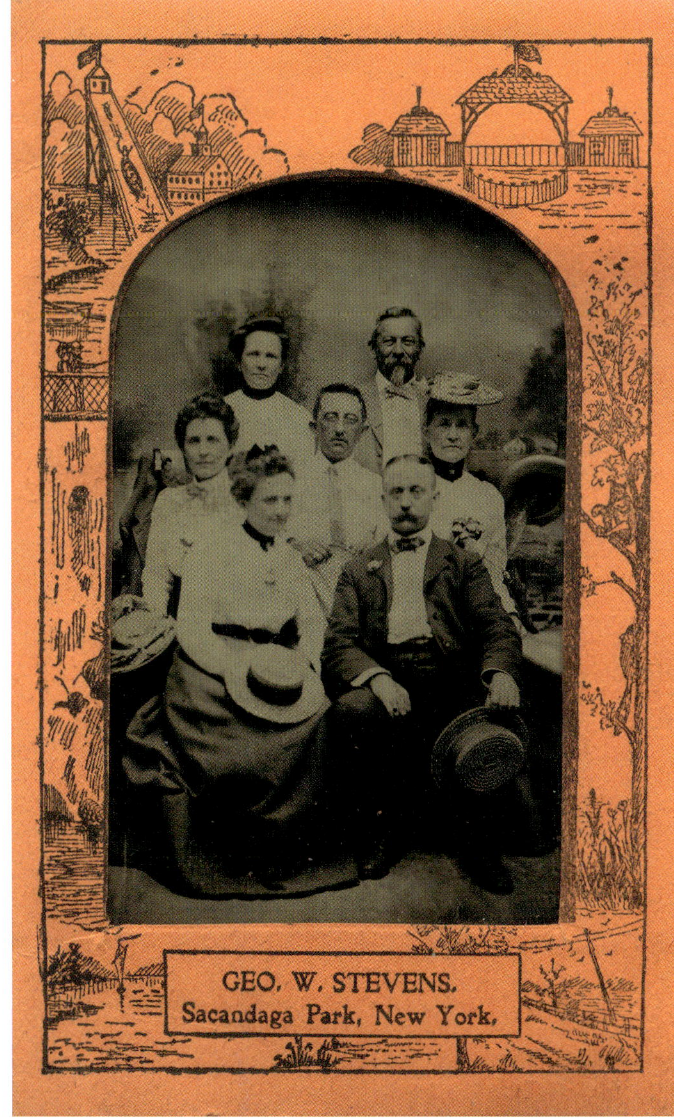

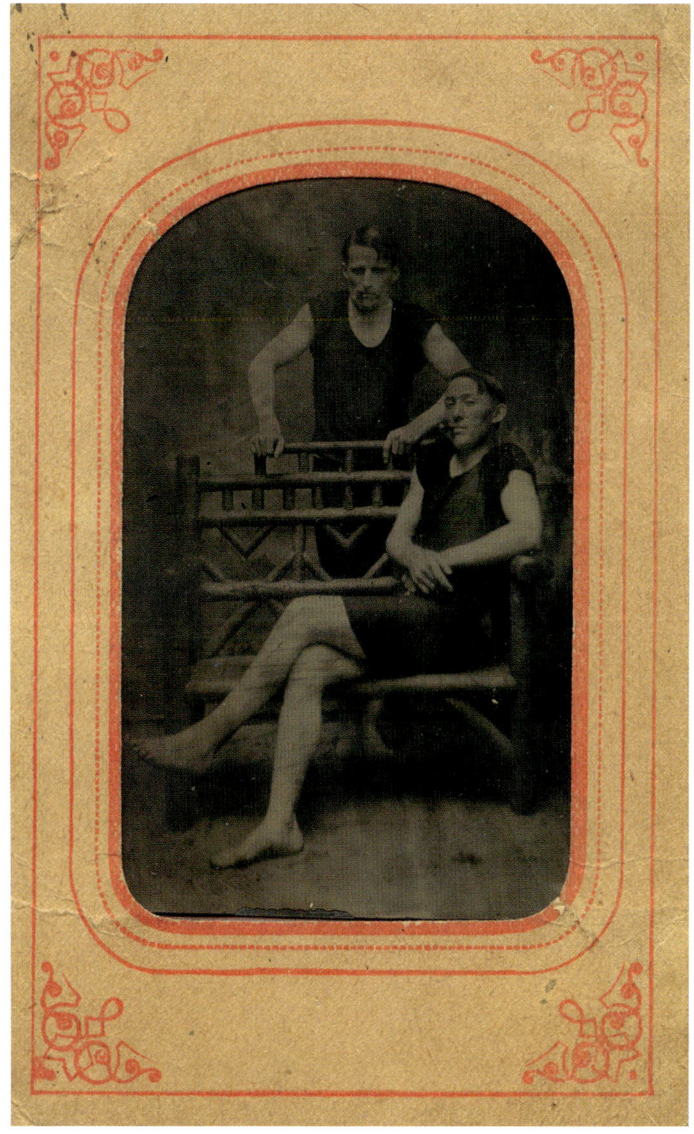

8. Tintype souvenirs from Sacandaga Park. Left: G. W. Stevens, 1900–1912. Right: Mann Bros., 1911–1912.

private Lake Placid Club, to keep the formerly summer-only club open in the winter of 1905–6, and to introduce winter sports to the community, enabled the village to claim the public relations title of pioneer American winter sports resort. It aggressively advertised this status over the following decades, thanks in part to the use of compelling images provided by a large stable of local photographers. Lake Placid's role in sponsoring national and international winter sporting events led to its selection in 1929 as the host of the Third Olympic Winter Games in 1932. Marketers of the village estimated in the winter of 1953–54 that its locally generated publicity reached an audience of more than twenty-three million people.[25]

The uniquely American phenomenon of sleepaway camping brought several million middle- and upper-class children from cities and suburbs to the Adirondacks for active, adult-supervised summer vacations. The earliest such institution, Camp Dudley, opened in 1891 on Lake Champlain in Westport, Essex County. At least one hundred more camps were founded over the next forty years. A few, usually with a religious focus, catered to entire families. The camps' presence in the region gave rise to a specialized field of photographic endeavor, as most of them recorded their activities in viewbooks to sustain campers' interest and market the camp product. Dude ranches, highlighting horseback-riding outings superintended by real cowboys from

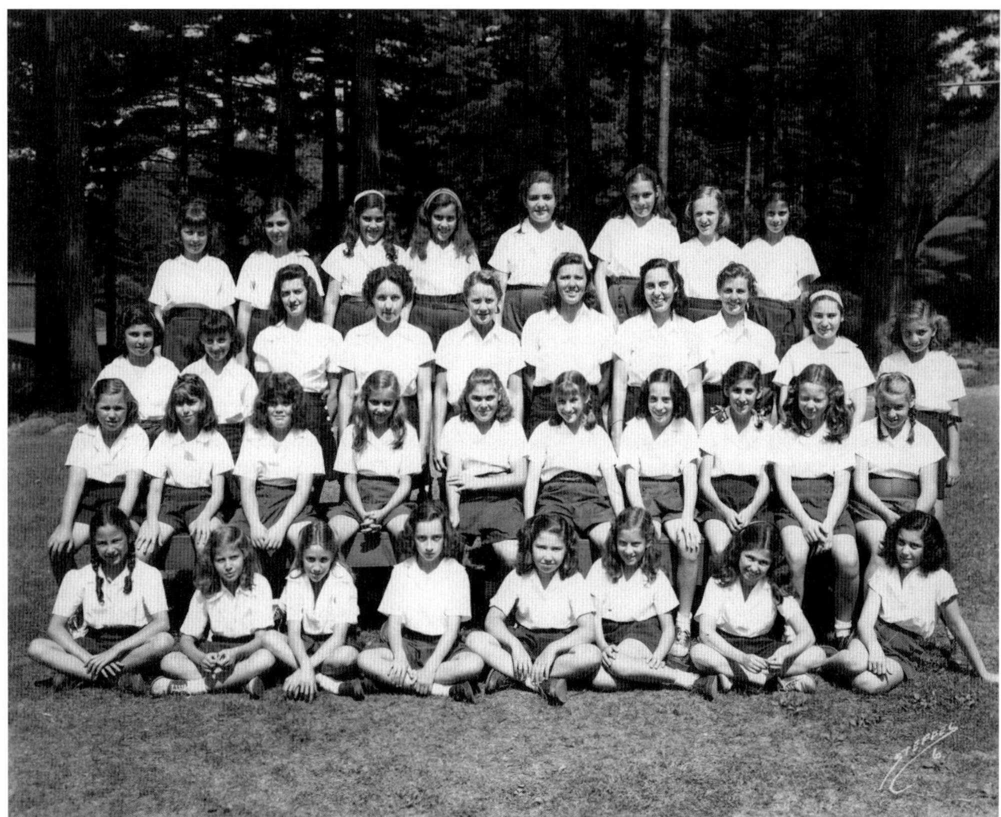

9. J. J. Steffel, Camp Red Wing campers, Schroon Lake, 1946–1948. Courtesy of Adirondack Experience.

the West, provided programmed camp activities for adults from the mid-1930s, primarily in Warren County.

Adirondack Photography after 1950

By the end of the nineteenth century, photography had become a multipurpose medium with applications in numerous commercial and noncommercial fields. Kodakers, however, continued to displace professional photographers as the primary recorders of people and events in out-of-the-way areas like the Adirondacks. The field evolved further in this direction over the course of the second half of the twentieth century.

There were fewer photographers making their living with a camera in the Adirondacks in 1950 than there had been in 1900. There are fewer today than there were in 1950. Local portrait studios have passed almost wholly into oblivion; regionally based professional developing and printing services have been replaced by unmanned machines in drugstore settings and by specialized facilities located in distant centers and found online. While commercial photography survives in the Adirondacks, providing comfortable livings for a few individuals, small-town, paying photographic enterprise is largely a part-time undertaking. This volume looks backward, celebrating the rich photographic world of the Adirondacks between 1850 and 1950 and the variety of photographers who peopled its sphere.

1. Davis, *Origins of American Photography*, 207; "Cottage near Hague, Lake George," *Gleason's Pictorial*, September 23, 1854; Hungerford, "Our Summer Migration," 570.

2. Gover, *The Positive Image*, 28–29; Johnston, "What a Woman Can Do with a Camera," 6; Rosenblum, *A History of Women Photographers*, 59; Denenberg, *Wallace Nutting and the Invention of Old America*, 201n56, 201n63.

3. Taft, *Photography and the American Scene*, quoting from the Editor's Table in the *Knickerbocker*, December 1839, 560.

4. Taft, *Photography and the American Scene*, 3, 14, 60; Stevens, "Fixed by a Sunbeam."

5. *Plattsburgh Republican*, February 24, 1842; *Essex County Republican*, May 23, 1846; Stevens, "Fixed by a Sunbeam"; Palmquist and Kailbourn, *Pioneer Photographers from the Mississippi to the Continental Divide*, 10.

6. *Plattsburgh Republican*, July 20, 1850; September 3, 1853; *Essex County Republican*, June 8, 1850; December 13, 1851.

7. Kasher, *America and the Tintype*, 19.

8. Davis, *Origins of American Photography*, 150; Crowley, *Seneca Ray Stoddard*, 14.

9. Darrah, *Cartes de Visite in Nineteenth Century Photography*, 5, 10.

10. Taft, *Photography and the American Scene*, 171, 175; Darrah, *World of Stereographs*, 70; Davis, *Origins of American Photography*, 170; *Lewis County Banner*, August 24, 1859.

11. Taft, *Photography and the American Scene*, 365, 367.

12. Keller, "'A Great Variety of New and Fine Designs,'" 1, 42, 48; *Plattsburgh Sentinel*, November 19, 1880; *Saratogian*, May 24, 1919.

13. Clark, *19th Century Card Photos KwikGuide*, 21, 43.

14. "Other Ways in Which Photography Is Indispensable to Trade," *Elizabethtown Post*, November 29, 1894; Pickands, "The Present Condition of Photography as a Business," 88.

15. Waggoner, *East of the Mississippi*, 207.

16. Vaule, *As We Were*, 52.

17. Bogdan and Weseloh, *Real Photo Postcard Guide*, 8–9; Sante, *Folk Photography*, 9.

18. Lacayo and Russell, *Eyewitness*, 34–35; Davis, *Origins of American Photography*, 176.

19. Museum of Modern Art, "The Exact Instant: Events and Faces," 4.

20. Perrottet, "Where Was the Birthplace of the American Vacation?"; Goodyear, "Constructing a National Landscape," viii–ix; *Malone Palladium*, January 13, 1898.

21. Horrell, *Seneca Ray Stoddard*, 108; Resser, "The Evolution of Ausable Chasm," 3–5; Bremer, *Homes of the New World*, 2:590.

22. *Plattsburgh Sentinel*, May 3, 1866; September 8, 1871; July 21, 1882; *Fitchburg (MA) Sentinel*, September 14, 1866; "Ausable Chasm," *New York Evening Post*, September 1, 1873; *Essex County Republican*, October 23, 1873; July 2, 1874; Porter, "History of the Town of AuSable"; S. R. Stoddard, *Catalogue of Photographs of New York Scenery*, 1877.

23. Lyden, *Railroad Vision*, 4, 7, 16, 47, 79.

24. Whipple, *Fifty Years of Conservation in New York State*, 176–77; "W. S. Carpenter Appointed," *Bennington (VT) Banner*, June 26, 1915; "Movies of the Adirondacks," *Rome Sentinel*, August 27, 1919.

25. "L. P. Publicity Has Readership of 23 Million," *Lake Placid News*, January 8, 1954; MacKenzie, *The Plains of Abraham*, 393–94.

Biographical Entries

ACOSTA, BERNARD MONGE (1884–1965)
Active Saranac Lake, Essex and Franklin Counties, 1932–1956

Bernard Acosta made his way from his native Costa Rica to New York City in 1918 and worked for five years as a photographer for Marceau Studios on Fifth Avenue before joining the Eastman Kodak Company in Rochester, New York. His job took him to South America and the West Indies as a technical representative and demonstrator of the firm's plates, papers, and film.

In 1931 Acosta moved to Saranac Lake after contracting tuberculosis, and in 1932 opened his first studio. A portrait specialist, he also produced color postcards, provided images documenting local events to regional newspapers, and took group and individual photographs for Saranac Lake's high school yearbooks and nearby summer camps. In 1940 he purchased **William L. Distin**'s Main Street studio and its thirty-year accumulation of negatives. Exhibiting his work from 1937, he had by late 1948 won thirty-nine blue ribbons and awards of merit at shows in the United States and abroad, and was designated a "master" of the profession by the Photographers' Association of America in 1951.[1]

Acosta was popular as a volunteer leader of Saranac Lake's amateur camera club and taught photography at the Study and Craft Guild, founded in 1936, and its successor, the Rehabilitation Guild, both established to provide education, job training, and enrichment to the local population of tuberculosis patients. He was active in professional organizations as well, serving in the early 1950s as vice president of the Professional Photographers' Society of New York State and in 1951 as chairman of its short-lived Adirondack Section.[2]

Acosta left Saranac Lake in early 1956. Midyear it was announced that June Myers, a thirty-five-year-old Saranac Lake woman who taught photographic oil coloring at the guild, was leaving her parents' home to become the seventy-two-year-old Acosta's bride. The couple settled in Sarasota, Florida, and married in 1959. Acosta's photo studio was listed in the Sarasota directory in 1959 and 1960. He died in Sarasota.[3]

1. *Adirondack Enterprise*, November 27, 1948; October 15, 1955; "Acosta Exhibition," *Guild News* (Saranac Lake, NY), July 1945; "Saranac Lake Resident Receives Photo Degree," *Plattsburgh Press Republican*, August 29, 1951.

2. *Lake Placid News*, March 23, 1951; *Lowville Journal and Republican*, May 31, 1951.

3. *Adirondack Enterprise*, August 13, 1956.

AGENS, ERNEST A. (1868–1933)
Active Western Adirondacks, 1907–1920

Ernest Agens was a jeweler by occupation. Born in Denmark, Lewis County, where his father was a dairy farmer, he passed the greater part of his life in Lowville. Agens was employed as a clerk for eight years after completing his schooling, six of them with the post office, before purchasing the Lowville jewelry business of W. J. Smith in 1898. In addition to diamonds and watches, he sold glasses, Edison phonographs, cameras, and photographic supplies. During the height of the postcard craze his shop carried his own real photograph postcards. Although the majority of his images were of Lowville, Agens also captured views around

Brantingham Lake, Lewis County, and in Webb, Hamilton and Herkimer Counties. He sold his store not long after suffering a "shock," or stroke, in 1928.[1]

1. *Lowville Journal and Republican*, January 18, 1923, reprising news of January 13, 1898; December 21, 1899; March 6, 1902; June 16, 1921; Obituary, *Lowville Journal and Republican*, November 16, 1933; *Watertown Daily Standard*, September 25, 1928.

ALLEN, ARTHUR NEWALL (1871–1909)
Active Saranac Lake, Essex and Franklin Counties, 1894–1909

Born in York, England, Arthur Allen was employed by the well-known London photographic studio of Elliott & Fry before immigrating to the United States in 1890 and entering the photographic studio of his brother, Charles H. Allen, in Davenport, Iowa. From there he relocated to Helena, Montana, "where he assumed charge of the Eitner Studio until the silver panic ruined trade in that part of the country." After returning to Davenport in 1893 to marry Iowa-born Frances, or Fannie, Staunton, he and his wife moved to New York City. There, as Allen told a Saranac Lake newsman in 1895, "he learned of the Adirondacks and determined to locate here." He worked briefly as an operator for Saranac Lake photographer **George W. Baldwin** before purchasing the **Charles J. Ferris** Studio in 1894 and setting himself up in Saranac Lake at the age of twenty-three. Allen advertised specialties in individual and group portraiture and buildings. As he announced in 1906, "If You want to see what kind of work I do go and look at my show cases. I have to WORK for my living and cannot seem to exist on fresh air." Among his photographs were night images of Saranac Lake's early winter carnivals.[1]

Tuberculosis, it transpired, had been Allen's reason for moving to Saranac Lake. In June 1909 he advertised his "paying studio" for sale in a photographic journal. Its owner, the item noted, "for reasons of declining health, must seek a change of climate. He is looking for a cash business at once.

A. N. ALLEN

Photographer

MAKES PORTRAITS OF PEOPLE THAT LOOK LIKE THE PEOPLE—AND HE DOES IT REASONABLE—

HE HAS NO AUTOMOBILE.

10. A. N. Allen, Advertisement, *Saranac Lake Directory*, 1908. Courtesy of Adirondack Research Room, Saranac Lake Free Library.

The business is good all the year round, has an excellent reputation, and presents a fine opportunity to the right person." Allen died four months later.[2]

Fannie Allen had worked alongside her husband in the studio. After losing their only child early in the couple's marriage, she took up photography and was listed as a photographer in the New York state census of 1905 and the 1910 *Saranac Lake Directory*. In 1911 "Mrs. A. N. Allen . . . formerly proprietress of the Allen Photographic Studio," wed Charles Phillips, onetime employee of Saranac Lake's Riverside Inn. The couple settled in Rochester.[3]

1. *Adirondack Enterprise*, unknown date, 1895; Talbot, "The Ice Carnival of Saranac"; "Trade Notes and News," *Snap-Shots* 21, no. 1 (January 1910): 39; *Plattsburgh Sentinel*, September 21, 1894; advertisement, 1906 *Adirondack Directory-Saranac Lake*, 34.

2. "A Paying Studio at a Bargain," *Photo-Era: The American Journal of Photography* 22, no. 6 (June 1909): 317.

3. *Malone Farmer*, October 11, 1911.

ALLETAG, ALBERT (1877–1973)
Active Wilmington, Essex County, 1905–1909

From Wertheim am Main, Germany, Albert Alletag arrived in the United States in 1897 as a twenty-year-old steerage passenger and spent his working

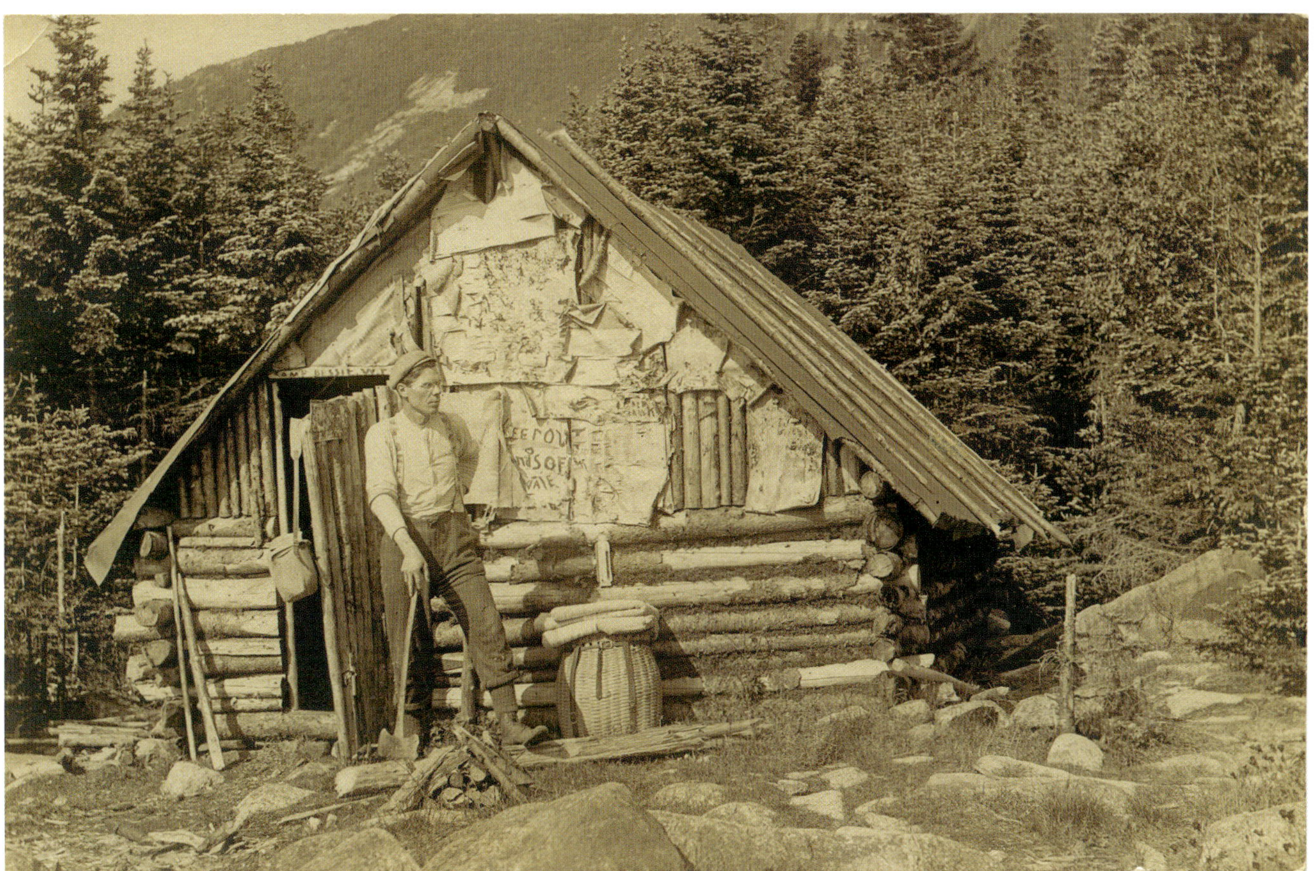

11. A. Alletag, Camp Welcome, Whiteface Mountain, A. J. Maynard, Prop. RPPC, 1905–1909.

life as butler to members of New York City's well-to-do, German-speaking, Jewish community. It is uncertain what circumstances led him to the Adirondacks, but between 1905 and 1909 he passed summers in Wilmington, Essex County, where he took photographs and marketed them to residents and visitors. "Mr. Alletag has some very fine pictures for sale of the M. E. Church at 50 cents each," the *Essex County Republican* announced in September 1909. "Each church member ought to have one whether they live in town or not." He also produced a few real photo postcards hand-stamped A. ALLETAG PHOTOS WILMINGTON N.Y. A 1917 issue of the *New York State Museum Bulletin* included a plate illustrating a river gorge near Wilmington credited to "A. Alletag, New York City."[1]

Alletag gave up photography in 1913, advertising his complete camera outfit for sale in a New York City paper at a sacrifice price "due to failing eyesight." He henceforth traveled extensively with his employer of more than twenty years, Alfred Heinsheimer, a partner in the banking firm of Kuhn, Loeb & Company, until Heinsheimer's death in 1929. During World War II Alletag worked for the War Department's Office of Censorship. He eventually lost his sight altogether and spent his final years in California. He died a ward of the state.[2]

1. *Plattsburgh Sentinel*, May 31, 1907; *Essex County Republican*, September 17, 1909; *New York State Museum Bulletin* 193 (January 1, 1917): plate 23.

2. *New York Evening Telegram*, February 2, 1913; "Alletag, Alfred," employee file, New York Foundation Records.

AMEDEN, ERNEST JOHNSON (1862–1940)
Active North River, Warren County, 1900–1935

Born in Hudson Falls, Washington County, Ernest Ameden was the son of a mill machine operator and, later, day laborer and carpenter/joiner. Identified in the 1880 US Census as an eighteen-year-old dental student living at home, he had spent childhood summers in this hamlet of Johnsburg, where his parents helped out in a general store owned by a relative before purchasing the business in the 1880s. Ameden joined his parents in the enterprise and was recorded in the New York state census of 1892 as a Johnsburg merchant (general). By 1900, however, he was a Chestertown, Warren County, carriage painter. Ameden returned to North River after his father's death that year, taking over the store management not long thereafter. He took up photography as well, setting up a darkroom and workspace on the first floor of the store and a modest portrait studio on the second. Becoming the hamlet's postmaster in 1901 (a position he held for thirty-nine years), Ameden began selling his own real photo postcards from a revolving rack next to the postal counter. He also wholesaled them to small business owners.[1]

Ameden documented the region's logging and garnet-mining industries, as well as skiing—a regional economic driver from the 1933 opening of the Gore Mountain Ski Club and the introduction in 1934 of weekend "ski trains" from New York City to neighboring North Creek. Many of his postcards bore no imprint but were recognizable from their rough handwritten captions and locational focus. Ameden appeared only once in census records as a photographer, in 1930. He was identified as a postmaster on his death certificate.[2]

1. Bogdan, *Exposing the Wilderness*, 136, 137, 145, 147, 154

2. Bogdan, 154, 157.

ANTHONY, E., AND H. T. AND COMPANY
Active throughout the Adirondacks, 1865–1874

Sons of New York City banker Jacob Anthony, Edward (1819–88) and Henry T. (1814–84) Anthony were partners in what became the leading nineteenth-century manufacturer and distributor of photographic supplies in the United States. The company was also one of the earliest and largest publishers of stereoviews in the world. Edward, an 1838 graduate of Columbia College and trained in science and civil engineering, was the first to enter the photographic field. Having taken lessons in the art of daguerreotypy from artist and inventor Samuel F. B. Morse in early 1840, he captured landscape images that year as part of a survey team that proved useful in settling an international border dispute along the Maine-Quebec border. In 1842 he opened a New York City daguerreian gallery, and in 1847 a separate shop for the sale of photographic supplies. He soon gave up daguerreotypy and expanded the business of furnishing materials to the trade and to amateurs. Henry, a civil engineer and banker, joined Edward in 1852.[1]

The Anthony Company began importing European stereographs in 1858 and building its own view inventory the following year. By 1873 the firm had a trade list numbering (with gaps) over eleven thousand titles as well as a comprehensive distribution network. Some views were commissioned, but most photos were by unattributed photographers. An 1860 advertisement for the Anthony American and Foreign Stereoscopic Emporium included an appeal to photographers: "First class Stereoscopic Negatives wanted. Send by mail a print unmounted, with price of Negative."[2]

There were no Adirondack images in Anthony's October 1862 *New Catalogue of Stereoscopes and Views*, but "Saratoga Springs and Lake George" were included in a December 1867 list of over four thousand subjects. Ninety-nine Lake George and vicinity views were eventually published by the company as well as forty-nine other Adirondack images: of Schroon, Blue Mountain and Raquette Lakes and John Brown's Tract in the Fulton Chain region. Some of these images were renumbered and recycled multiple times, usually in various sets: *Wanderings about Lake George*; *Wanderings about Lake Champlain*; *Gems of the Adirondacks*; *Stereoscopic Gems, American Scenery.* Views issued on cards with a 501 Broadway address were published before the company moved in 1869 to 591 Broadway. Anthony stopped producing new stereographs in 1874, although manufacturing continued until 1892.[3]

1. Hall, *America's Successful Men of Affairs*, s.v. "Edward Anthony"; Davis, *Origins of American Photography*, 171.

2. Marder, *Anthony, the Man, the Company, the Cameras*, 110.

3. Marder, 343–48; *New York Evening Express*, December 21, 1867; Treadwell, "The Stereoscopic Views Issued by the Anthony Company"; Darrah, *World of Stereographs*, 24.

ASHLEY, GEORGE T. (1881–1966)
Active Au Sable Forks, Clinton and Essex Counties, 1908–1915

George Ashley, born deaf and mute in Au Sable Forks, was one of nineteen children of a miner and, later, pulp maker. He was listed in the 1900 US Census as both an eighteen-year-old printer living with his parents and siblings in Au Sable Forks and a student in Malone, most likely at its unusual, state-supported boarding school then known as the Northern New York Institute for Deaf Mutes.

Ashley's career behind a camera was brief. He was employed from its 1908 founding by the *Adirondack Record*, a weekly newspaper in Au Sable Forks, for which he "ran advertisements" and worked as a photographer until his departure for Flint, Michigan, in 1915. He also marketed the occasional real photo postcard bearing the stamped imprint PHOTO BY G. T. ASHLEY, AU SABLE FORKS, N.Y. An Ashley view from Indian Face, a massive rock on Lower Ausable Pond in Keene, Essex County, served as the frontispiece for a *New York State Museum Bulletin* in 1920.[1]

Ashley worked in the factories of General Motors in Flint for over thirty years, at first with the Buick Motor Company, later with Chevrolet. His occupational listings in US censuses included "axle straightener" (1920), "gear cutter" (1930), and "clerk, auto manufacturing" (1940). The first president of the Flint Association of the Deaf, Ashley is buried in Durand, Michigan.[2]

1. *New York State Museum Bulletin*, January/February 1920, 229–30.

2. *Adirondack Record–Elizabethtown Post*, November 24, 1966.

ATHERTON, LEA ERWIN (1886–1987)
Active North Creek, Warren County, 1912–1914

Born in Battle Creek, Michigan, in the late 1890s Lea Atherton relocated with his parents and younger siblings to his mother's St. Lawrence County birthplace where his father was, according to the 1900 US Census, a Potsdam photographer. In 1912 young Atherton leased a photographic studio above a barber shop and jewelry store in the Johnsburg hamlet of North Creek. A portrait photographer, he supplemented his studio work with a summer tent operation in nearby Chestertown. In late 1914 he relocated his family and studio to Gouverneur, St. Lawrence County, and in the mid-1920s to Binghamton, Broome County, where he was recorded in the 1940 US Census as a "cameraman, photo studio." He died at the age of one hundred in Milpitas, Santa Clara County, California.[1]

1. *Warrensburgh News*, November 28, 1912; "Photograph Tent at Chestertown," June 19, 1913; *Watertown Times*, November 12, 1914.

AUSTIN, EARL CALHOUN (1896–1950)
Active Warrensburg, Warren County, 1933–1949

Earl Austin spent most of his life in Warrensburg; his father was a traveling salesman in the clothing line. His early adulthood was interrupted by World War I, into which he was drafted in September 1918 but got no farther afield than an artillery training camp in South Carolina before the conflict ended in November. Austin experimented with a number of occupations during the next fifteen years: town welfare officer; automobile, Mack and GMC truck salesman; and power-line laborer.

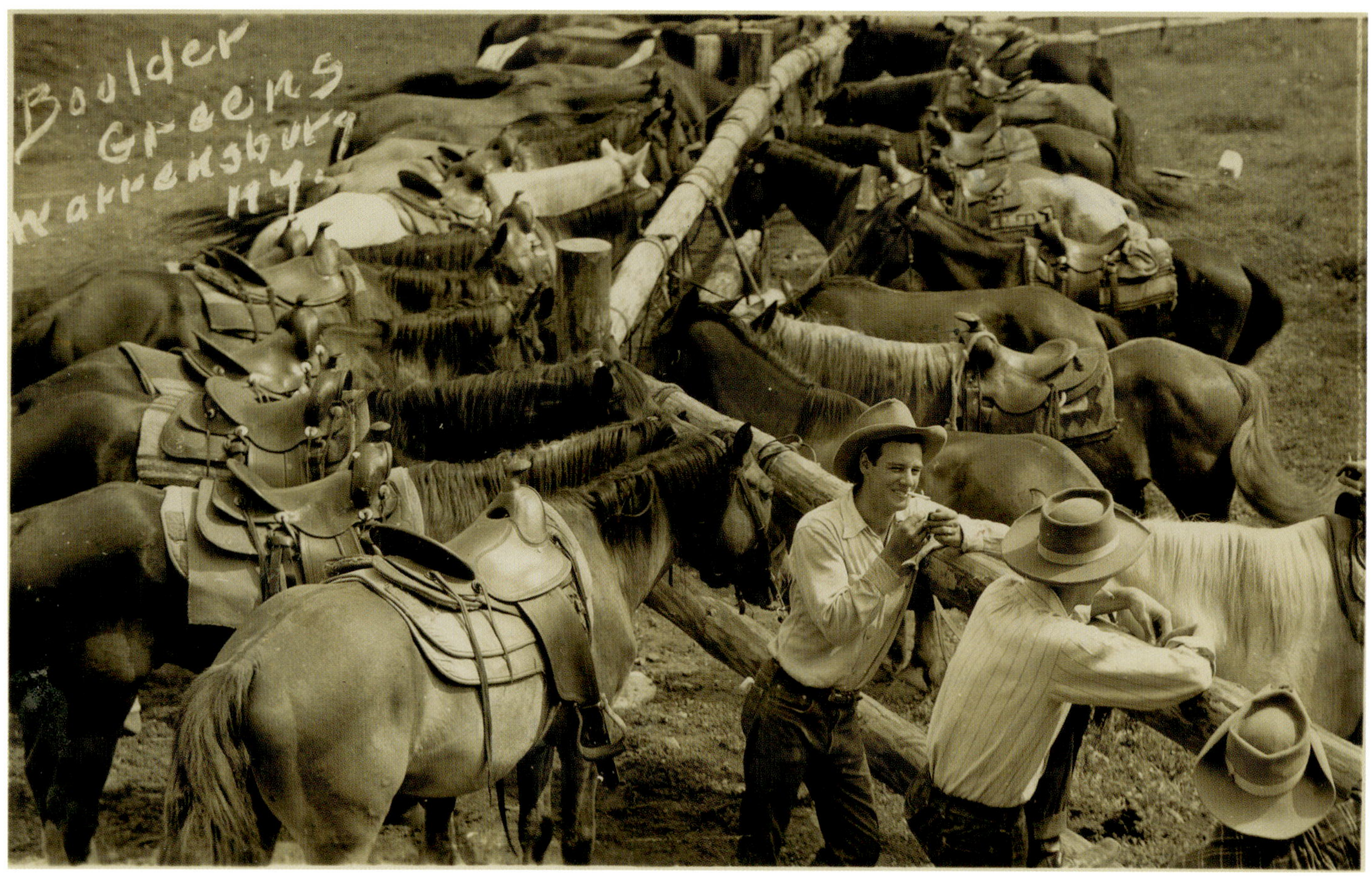

12. E. C. Austin, *Boulder Greens, Warrensburg, N.Y.* RPPC, 1937–1940s.

Austin made his first appearance in the photographic arena in 1929 as the "official photographer" for Warrensburg's American Legion post. In 1933 he began to advertise professional services as a photographer "Specializing in Babies and Small Children," and as a developer and printer of amateur work at his Old Homestead Studio. He took not only individual portraits but also site-based, large-format images of groups, among them guests and staff members at local ranch resorts. A platform attached to the top of Austin's car was designed to eliminate the need for stepladders in his work.[1]

A rare glimpse into shortages experienced by photographers during the immediate postwar period was alluded to in newspaper advertisements run by Austin in January and March 1945. The first announced the closure of his studio due to the absence of supplies; the second, on the studio's reopening, noted a limited supply of paper for printing, but "No Roll Films on Hand." Austin closed his studio in 1949 owing to ill health. He died in early 1950 "after a long illness."[2]

1. *Glens Falls Post-Star*, September 9, 1918; Warrensburgh Historical Society and Parisi, *Warrensburg*, 8–9; *Warrensburg News*, December 26, 1929, October 19, 1939; September 19, 1940; *North Creek Enterprise*, August 3, 1933.

2. *North Creek Enterprise*, January 3, 1945; March 21, 1945; October 5, 1949; February 22, 1950.

AVERILL, HENRY KETCHUM, JR. (1830–1918)
Active Northeastern Adirondacks, 1863–Early 1880s

Henry Averill, Jr. descended from distinguished Clinton County roots. His mother was a granddaughter of Zephaniah Platt, who in 1788 founded

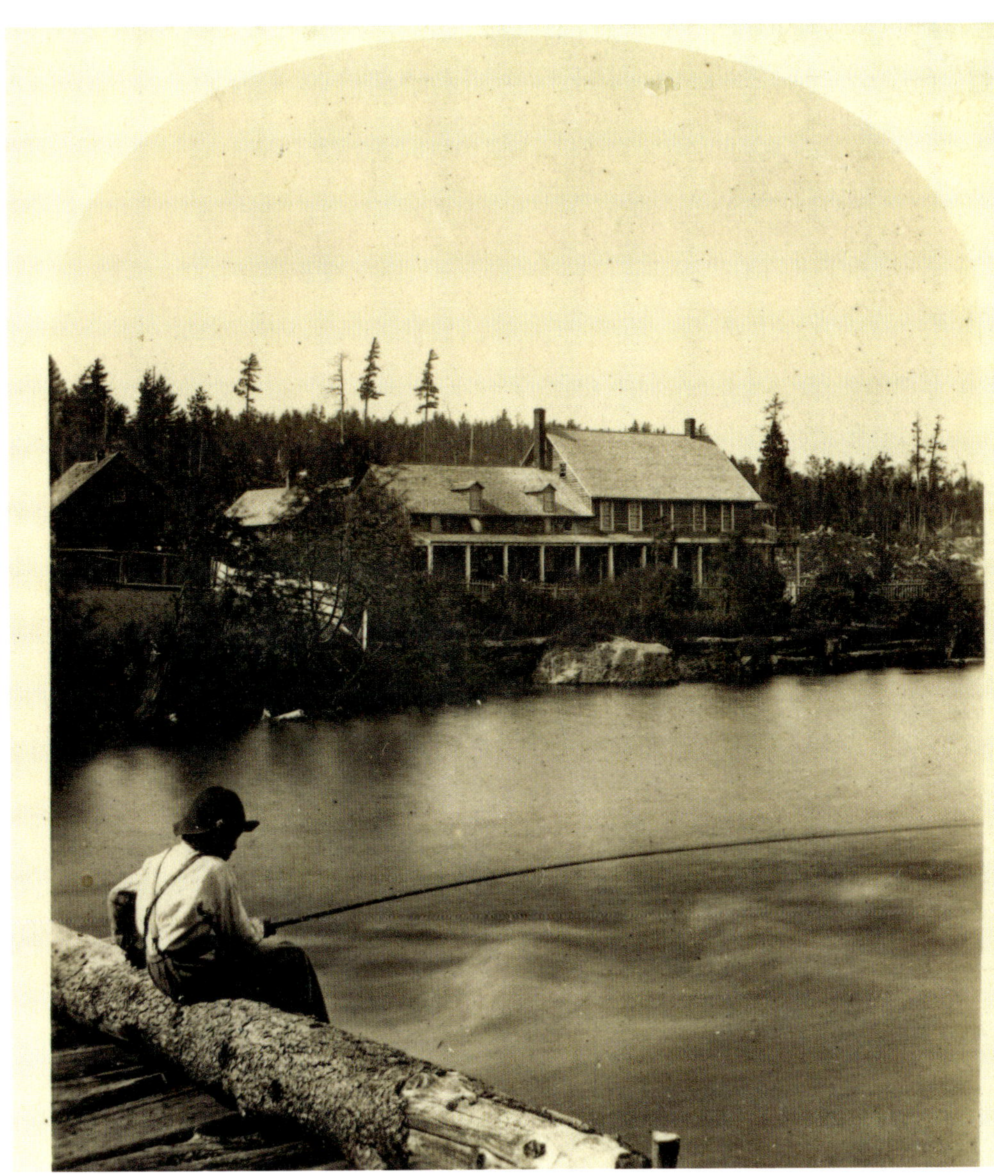

13. H. K. Averill Jr., *Bartlett's Hotel, Upper Saranac Lake*. One-half stereoview, late 1860s. Courtesy of Stereograph Collection, Boston Public Library.

the town of Plattsburgh. His father, H. K. Averill, Sr., born in the town of Peru and a Plattsburgh resident from 1800, was a member of the Clinton County Bar and long involved at the upper levels of the regional iron industry. After mastering surveying as an assistant engineer with the Plattsburgh and Montreal Railroad, Averill relocated to Iowa in 1851. He sited a 130-mile-long Iowa state road, served between circa 1852 and 1859 as surveyor for the state's Clayton and Winneshiek Counties, and was appointed a deputy US surveyor in 1853. By 1860 he had become a photographer in Decorah, Iowa.[1]

Returning to Plattsburgh in 1863, Averill practiced as a surveyor, while also purchasing the photographic gallery, negatives, and advertising logo of **Philemon Tenney Gates**. By the end of the year he was competing aggressively for the local portrait business with **James Jay Howard**. Simultaneous advertisements for the two galleries ran, often side by side, in the *Plattsburgh Sentinel* until both studios were destroyed in an August 1867 conflagration that consumed some seventy buildings in central Plattsburgh. Howard, whose "Photographic Saloon" was partially insured, re-established himself as a portrait photographer.

Averill, whose losses totaling $6,500 were uninsured, did not.[2]

Averill had been moving away from studio work in any event. In 1865 he published a set of twenty-two stereoscopic views of the "Chasm of the Au Sable," and in July 1867 announced an assortment of recent views of "the northern country," including Plattsburgh, Ausable Chasm, Ticonderoga, Paul Smiths, and the Saranac lakes. By late 1867 he was working from a home office as a "Surveyor and Draftsman" as well as a photographer of "Views of Buildings, Landscapes, Machinery, &c." He continued to take landscape photographs, particularly of rural scenery around Lakes Champlain and George. A September 1875 news article noting Averill's participation in a recent six-day "stroll" to Keene Flats and the High Peaks region of Essex County by nine members of Plattsburgh's Tahawus Club mentioned his thirty "choice" stereoscopic views that would be immediately offered for sale as the "Tahawus Club Series." Among them were images of the recently discovered and named Lake Tear of the Clouds, source of the Hudson River, as well as Mount Marcy from the summit of Mount Tahawus. These were, according to the photographer, "the first views ever attempted in that region."[3]

Averill became one of the most prominent surveyors in northern New York. Among his titles were topographical engineer of the Champlain Canal enlargement survey in 1870 and division engineer of **Verplanck Colvin**'s 1878 and several subsequent Adirondack topographical surveys. In 1877 he was awarded a patent for "improvements in attachments to parallel rulers." A geography of Clinton County for schoolchildren authored by Averill in 1879 identified him as a civil engineer, surveyor, notary public, patent solicitor, and draughtsman: able to provide "Coats of Arms, Monograms, Masonic Marks, Fine Lettering, and in short anything in the line of Draughting." An 1882–83 Plattsburgh directory advertisement noted other specialties: conveyancer, real estate agent, and landscape photographer. He relocated to Washington, DC, circa 1900 to be with his son, Frank, an engineer and partner in the busy architectural firm of Averill & Stone. He died at his daughter's home in East Hampton, New York.[4]

1. Palmquist and Kailbourn, *Pioneer Photographers*, 80; *Plattsburgh Sentinel*, April 1, 1881.

2. *Plattsburgh Republican*, October 29, 1864; *Plattsburgh Sentinel*, December 29, 1922, reprising news from August 21, 1867.

3. *Plattsburgh Sentinel*, July 11, 1867; November 22, 1867; November 13, 1868; "The Stroll of the Tahawus Club," *Plattsburgh Republican*, September 4, 1875.

4. Averill, *A New Geography and History of Clinton County*, inside front cover; *East Hampton Star*, April 5, 1918.

BACON, ASA G. (1839–1918)
Active Moriah, Essex County, 1864–1870

Born in Whitehall, Washington County, Asa Bacon was listed as the sixteen-year-old artist son of a Whitehall merchant in the New York state census of 1855. An army enlistee from Crown Point, Essex County, he served as a Civil War band musician with the Ninety-Sixth Infantry Regiment from late 1861 into mid-March 1862. Discharged to Ticonderoga, Essex County, Bacon was remembered more than fifty years later as the player of the first B-flat cornet in a popular twelve-man Ticonderoga cornet band that performed "at fairs, parades, picnics and political lectures . . . from Plattsburg to Whitehall."[1]

Bacon's Adirondack career was brief. He was identified as a Moriah artist in the New York state census of 1865 and a photograph artist in the 1870 US Census; his output included cartes de visite of people and buildings in the hamlets of Moriah Center and Port Henry. In late 1870 he moved his family to Minnesota, where he supported himself as a photographer and a farmer. He is buried in Brainerd, Crow Wing County.

1. "Ticonderoga's First Bands," *Ticonderoga Sentinel*, June 22, 1916.

BACON, CHARLES G. (1840–1913)
Active Northville, Fulton County, 1869–1879

Born in Peru, Massachusetts, Charles Bacon was the son of a carpenter. He grew up in Saratoga Springs, Saratoga County, learned the printing trade, and was at one time employed by the local newspaper, the *Saratogian*. After serving in the Civil War, he returned to Saratoga and was recorded in the New York state census of 1865 as a printer. By 1869 he relocated to Northville, a village in the town of Northampton; his entry in the 1869–70 Northampton directory read, "Photographer and general artist, dealer in picture frames, &c." In the 1880 US census he was again listed as a printer.[1]

Bacon left behind a quantity of carte de visite portraits. Appointed deputy sheriff for Northampton in the early 1880s, he became Northville's postmaster in December 1891, an office he held for eighteen years.[2]

1. *Saratogian Sentinel*, October 14, 1880; *Gloversville Leader*, January 27, 1900.
2. *Mohawk Valley Register*, unknown date, 1880–82; Frothingham, *History of Fulton County*, 463; *Saratogian*, December 30, 1913.

BACON, WILLIAM PENN (1848–1921)
Active Piseco Lake, Hamilton County, 1879–1885

Born in Ware, Massachusetts, William Bacon was the son of a barber. By 1870 he was a photographer in Oneida, Madison County. Leaving Oneida in search of an un- or underserved community in which to establish a photographic business, in December 1873 he settled in St. Johnsville, Montgomery County, a Mohawk River town some sixty miles to the east. The move was not a success. In January 1875 the following advertisement appeared in the *Philadelphia Photographer*: "For Sale. — A gallery, with north, top and side light; rent low; no opposition. Population 2500. Sold at a bargain. W. P. Bacon, St. Johnsville, N.Y."[1]

In late 1877 Bacon arrived in Rome, Oneida County, with his horse-drawn "photograph car," the *Bon Ton Gallery* (named for a popular-sized tintype). This was exchanged in the summer of 1879 for rooms with "a splendid skylight" above a hat store. "Bacon has come to stay," he advertised, "and he is making pictures of all kinds so cheap that the people will be glad that he came." In December 1883 Bacon displayed a "large and attractive" array of stereoscopic views, among them examples from his two known series: one of Rome and vicinity, and another, "Piseco Lake Views," of the Arietta hamlet just beginning to attract tourist interest. The series comprised twenty-seven scenes, many of them of rude huts and their tenants, who may have been visiting sportsmen.[2]

Bacon sold his Rome gallery in March 1885 and returned to Oneida, where he worked briefly as a photographer before operating a succession of stores offering "variety" and "fancy" goods. Selling out in 1895, he transferred to Syracuse and again took up photography. He was the proprietor of a photograph studio until shortly before his death.[3]

1. *Mohawk Valley Register* (Fort Plain, NY), December 12, 1873; *Philadelphia Photographer* 12, no. 133 (January 1875): 96.
2. *Rome Sentinel*, November 17, 1877; January 1, 1878; September 2, 1879; December 6, 1883.
3. *Syracuse Standard*, March 24, 1885; *Syracuse Herald*, March 3, 1895.

BALDWIN, CHARLES S. W. (DR.) (1850–1907)
Active Saranac Lake, Essex and Franklin Counties, 1892

Born into a farming family in Whiting, Vermont, Charles S. W. Baldwin spent much of the 1870s in Michigan, where he was recorded in 1877 as a dentist. Settled in New Jersey in 1884, he received a degree from the Baltimore College of Dentistry, conferred upon practicing dentists and requiring little or no coursework. He opened an office in New York City, became a regular contributor to dentistry journals, and invented Baldwin's Hydraulic Cement for tooth work.[1]

What led Dr. Baldwin to purchase the Saranac Lake photographic studio of **Charles Derby** in the spring of 1892—from which the "Dr. Baldwin, New York Art Studio" briefly produced large-format photos of local landscape subjects—is uncertain. He is known to have been a visiting dentist in Franklin County in 1890 and 1891, and was spotted vacationing in Lake Placid in 1891. Might he have given brief thought to settling in the region, or been a Saranac Lake tuberculosis patient indulging a hobby while curing in the village? He maintained a New York City dental practice in 1894.[2]

1. *Fifty-Sixth Annual Catalogue of the Baltimore College of Dental Surgery*, 24; *Southern Dental Journal* 11 (1892), advertisement following 366.

2. *Plattsburgh Sentinel*, April 29, 1892; *St. Regis Falls Adirondack News*, September 18, 1891; *Troy Daily Times*, August 20, 1991; "Baldwin Has Presence of Mind," *New York Herald*, March 1, 1894.

BALDWIN, GEORGE C. (?–?)

Active Ogdensburg, St. Lawrence County, 1878–1880; Chateaugay, Franklin County, 1880–1882; Malone, Franklin County, 1882–1889

Nothing is known about George C. Baldwin's birthplace or parentage; his name does not appear in any census records. It is possible, given the overlap in career trajectories, that he and **George M. Baldwin** were the same individual, but as no satisfactory explanation for the discrepancy in middle initials yet exists, readers will have to draw their own conclusions.

George C. Baldwin first appeared as the proprietor of a South Water Street photograph gallery in the Ogdensburg directory of 1879, at about which time he produced a few stereographs bearing the imprint G. C. BALDWIN'S PHOTOGRAPHIC AND GEM, from "Cor. Ford and Catherine Sts., Ogdensburg." Among them were several views of the Loon Lake Hotel in Franklin, Franklin County, where newspaper coverage reported him to have been "professionally engaged for most of the summer" of 1880—the resort's second season. He photographed John Brown's grave and residence in North Elba, Essex County, at the same time. In October 1880 he leased photographic rooms in Chateaugay, from which a number of views were published.[1]

By mid-1882 Baldwin was resident in Malone, and in July of that year was granted "the exclusive right of taking views" of Chateaugay Chasm, a county tourist attraction opened to the public earlier that month. He retained these rights for one or two years, issuing stereoviews and cabinet cards of the chasm before ceding the business to photographer A. B. Buell of Chateaugay. Another project from Baldwin's Malone years was a commissioned stereograph series titled "Adirondack Scenery reached by the Ogdensburgh & Lake Champlain Rail Road." A Main Street home and business listing in the 1889 Malone directory was the last known Adirondack reference to George C. Baldwin.[2]

1. *Ogdensburg Journal*, August 9, 1880; January 18, 1881; *Malone Palladium*, October 14, 1880.

2. *Plattsburgh Sentinel*, July 21, 1882.

BALDWIN, GEORGE M. (1843–1894)

Active Central and Western Adirondacks, 1869–1880 (See Preceding Entry)

George M. Baldwin was raised in Mooers Forks, Clinton County, from the age of four. Identified as a painter in the 1860 US Census, as was his father, he enlisted at the outbreak of the Civil War with the Sixteenth New York Infantry Regiment, serving for four months before being honorably discharged with a heart ailment. A member of his company later recalled that Baldwin spent the winter after his discharge taking "army pictures" in Alexandria, Virginia.[1]

Gravitating to Ogdensburg after the war, Baldwin married there in 1868. In 1869 he was listed in a Clinton County directory as a photographer in Chateaugay, Franklin County, although an 1881 application for a veteran's disability pension noted that since his army discharge he had been an Ogdensburg photographer. In 1891 he was reported to have been in an 1879 Ogdensburg partnership with **Frederick M. Crane** as Crane and Baldwin, which produced an Adirondack series of stereoviews. As a news article announced in August 1879, "Prepare yourselves for a treat, for Mr. Baldwin has just left for the above picturesque country, and upon his return, notice of which will be duly made, the people can procure a full line of views of the wild portion of the country. In the meantime Mr. Crane will attend to the business at the old stand No. 5 Water Street." The Crane and Baldwin partnership was dissolved, at Crane's instigation, in April 1880. Baldwin relocated to Malone, Franklin County, in 1883, where the Veteran's Schedule of the 1890 US Census listed him with disabilities: "Inflammatory rheumatism & pills." In January 1891, after a probable suicide attempt, Baldwin was adjudged insane and admitted to the new state asylum in Ogdensburg, where he died.[2]

1. US National Archives, Civil War Pension Files, "George M. Baldwin."

2. *St. Lawrence Republican and Ogdensburgh Weekly Journal*, January 28, 1891; "Adirondacks," *Ogdensburg Journal*, August 13, 1879; April 12, 1880.

BALDWIN, GEORGE W. (1849–1930)
Active Northeast and North Central Adirondacks, 1871–1904

Born in Jay, Essex County, to farming parents who migrated into the region from Vermont, George W. Baldwin grew up one of ten siblings on a farm in the adjoining town of Black Brook, Clinton County. In 1870 he was still living at home; his occupation was listed in that year's federal census as artist. After advertising a "just opened" photograph gallery in Elizabethtown for one month in May 1871, he removed to Port Henry, where he is thought to have worked for a local photographer. Baldwin, who "by his uniform kindness, courtesy, gentlemanly conduct and integrity of character" in Port Henry "won for himself a circle of friends who will not forget him," was in February 1872 rumored to be establishing a gallery there. Evidence that he briefly did so—in affiliation with his four-year-older brother, Daniel—are a few surviving cartes de visite bearing the imprint G. W. & D. A. BALDWIN'S GALLERY OF ART, PORT HENRY, N.Y.[1]

His October 1872 marriage to a resident of Au Sable Forks, Essex and Clinton Counties, led Baldwin and his brother to sell the Port Henry business to partners **Edgar A. Marvin** and **William H. Bigalow** in 1873. Baldwin relocated to Keeseville and opened a portrait studio, recommended to Keeseville visitors by **Seneca Ray Stoddard** in his 1874 guidebook. He also acted as sales agent for stereoviews and other images sold at the entrance lodge to Ausable Chasm, a geological site and tourist attraction on property that had historically been in his wife's family. An 1876 summer photographic tour included "Au Sable Forks, Jay, Wilmington, Keene, North Elba, Saranac Lake, Bloomingdale, Redford, Dannemora, etc."[2]

Baldwin began experimenting with stereography in late 1874 or early 1875. In the spring of 1876 he was commissioned by the Peru Steel and Iron Company of Clintonville to record its works in a series of stereoviews, possibly to complement the company's display at Philadelphia's Centennial International Exhibition. By 1879 he had on offer between four and five hundred views, some two hundred of which were of Ausable Chasm. He began taking views further afield in 1877 while continuing his portrait operation but ceased making stereographs around 1880.[3]

Baldwin was able to save his instruments but lost most of his negatives and stock in an August 1882 Keeseville fire. The conflagration, which destroyed fifty-nine buildings, propelled him to relocate his business later that year to Plattsburgh, where he maintained a gallery as "Baldwin, Artist," offering portraits and a selection of 8 x 10 inch landscape views of "Adirondack Scenery,"

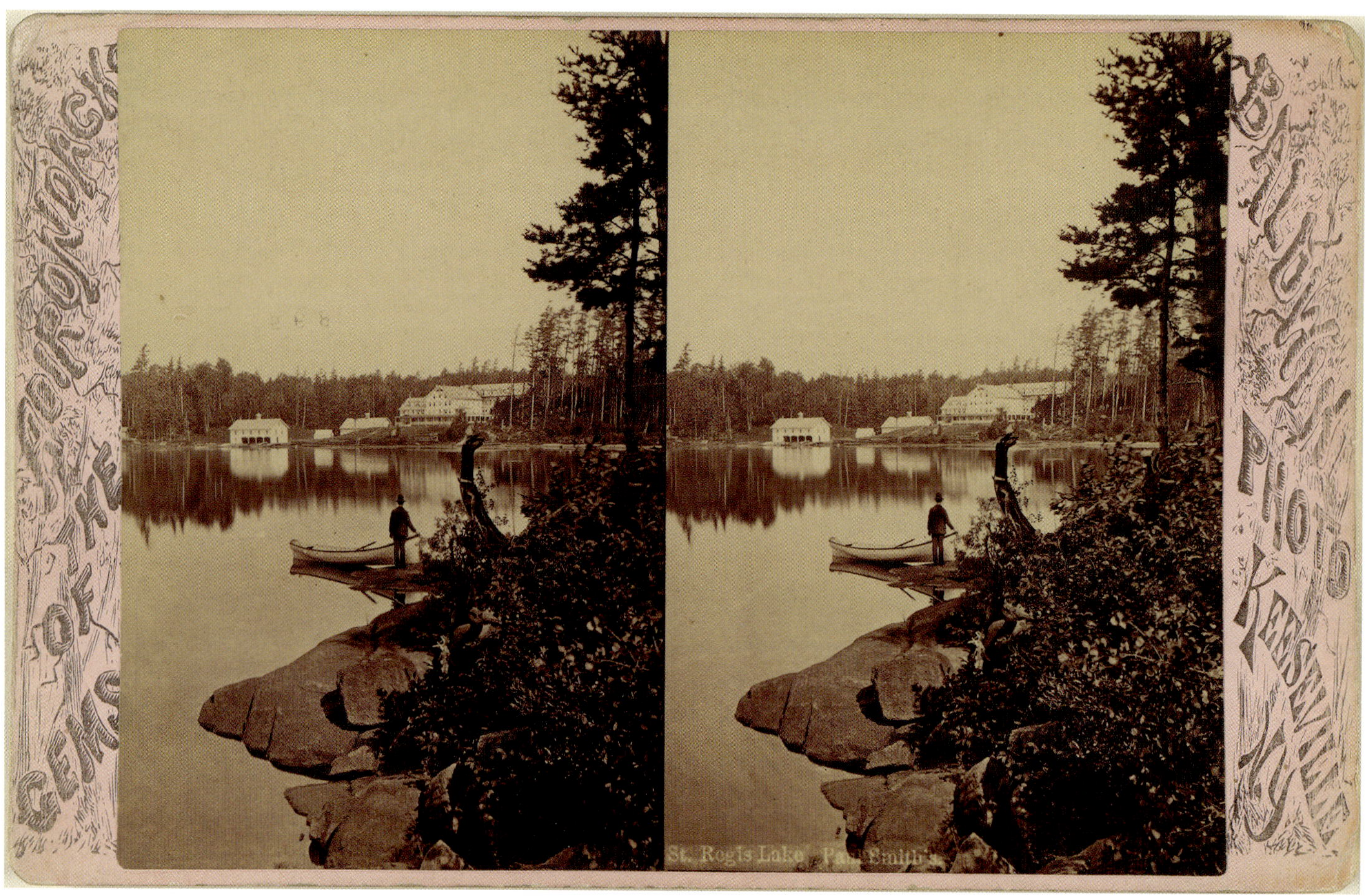

14. G. W. Baldwin, *St. Regis Lake, Paul Smith's*. Stereoview, 1875–1880. Digital image courtesy of the Getty's Open Content Program.

considered by many to be his finest work. In 1890 he sold the business to John W. Clay and moved to Saranac Lake, which was then becoming the center of a booming industry in the treatment of tuberculosis.[4]

Baldwin added a new dimension to his business life around 1892 in purchasing the sixty-room Lake Placid House in Lake Placid. He and his partner in this undertaking, Hilton L. French, sold the hotel in 1897 (although a mortgage foreclosure meant that the two men were tied up in litigation over the property until 1902). Employee **William L. Distin** acquired Baldwin's Saranac Lake studio around 1904 and Baldwin moved to Rutland, Vermont, where his ailing wife had relatives. There he purchased the business of photographer **Daniel Smith Brush,** formerly of Elizabethtown, who was returning to the Adirondacks after a stint in Rutland. The local business directory listed an address for Baldwin as a photographer through at least 1927. He died of injuries received after being struck by an automobile and is buried in Au Sable Forks.[5]

1. *Elizabethtown Post*, May 4, 1871; May 25, 1871; *Essex County Republican*, February 29, 1872. A number of Baldwin images were issued between 1876 and 1880 from a part-time, presumably seasonal, studio operation in Elizabethtown.

2. *Ter-Centenary of Lake Champlain*, 28; S. R. Stoddard, *Adirondacks: Illustrated* (1874 ed.), 203; *Plattsburgh Sentinel*, June 16, 1876; Bauer, "George W. Baldwin's 'Gems,'" 28.

3. Pollard, "Images of the 19th Century Adirondack Bloom Iron Industry," 4; Bauer, "Stereoviews of George W. Baldwin"; Bauer, "George W. Baldwin's 'Gems,'" 30.

4. *Plattsburgh Sentinel*, August 25(?), 1882; French, "History of the Adirondacks in 3-D"; *Plattsburgh Sentinel*, March 14, 1890; May 1, 1891.

5. MacKenzie, *Plains of Abraham*, 216, 219–20; Bauer, "George W. Baldwin's 'Gems,'" 32; *Elizabethtown Post*, July 4, 1904; *Rutland (VT) Herald*, December 11, 1930.

BARKER, B. BENTON (1866–POST-1937)
Active along the Shoreline of Lake Champlain, 1907–1915

New York State–born Benton Barker was a photographer in the largest studio in Havana, Cuba, prior to the 1898 Spanish-American War. Briefly a demonstrator for the Eastman Kodak Company, he settled not long after 1900 in Burlington, Vermont, where he marketed discounted portrait photographs to University of Vermont students. During the peak years of postcard mania Barker also published real photo views of towns and villages bordering the Vermont and New York shores of Lake Champlain. Leaving Burlington in 1918, and after brief stints in West Point, Virginia, and Orange, Massachusetts, in 1919 Barker became the proprietor of a studio in Northfield, Vermont, advertising "Fine Portraits and Local Views" to Norwich University students through 1930. His last-known business address was Huntington, Long Island.[1]

1. *Plainfield (NJ) Press*, September 19, 1898; *Greenfield (MA) Gazette and Courier*, March 15, 1919; *University [of Vermont] Cynic*, April 29, 1905; *Greenfield (MA) Gazette and Courier*, October 1919; "Artist's Wife Tells of Using Scotch Liniment for Relief of Pain," *Barre(VT) Times*, February 3, 1921; *[Norwich University] Reveille* (March 1922): 26; *Huntington Long-Islander*, January 26, 1934; *Brooklyn Eagle*, November 9, 1937.

BARNUM, ISAAC DELOS (1825–1873)
Active Lake George Region, 1867–1868

Deloss Barnum identified himself by a number of variants on his middle name during his career: D., Delos, DeLos, Deloss, De Loss, and Deblois. Born in Onondaga County, by 1856 he had taken up photography as a daguerreotype artist in Boston. Barnum was among the earliest American photographers to embrace the stereoscopic camera, noting in 1860 that the outdoor work he used it for paid "twice as well as" portraiture. He captured a few stereo images of Boston as early as 1857 before moving to New York City in 1861 or 1862 and documenting Central Park, Brooklyn's Green-Wood Cemetery, and Fort Lee, New Jersey. By

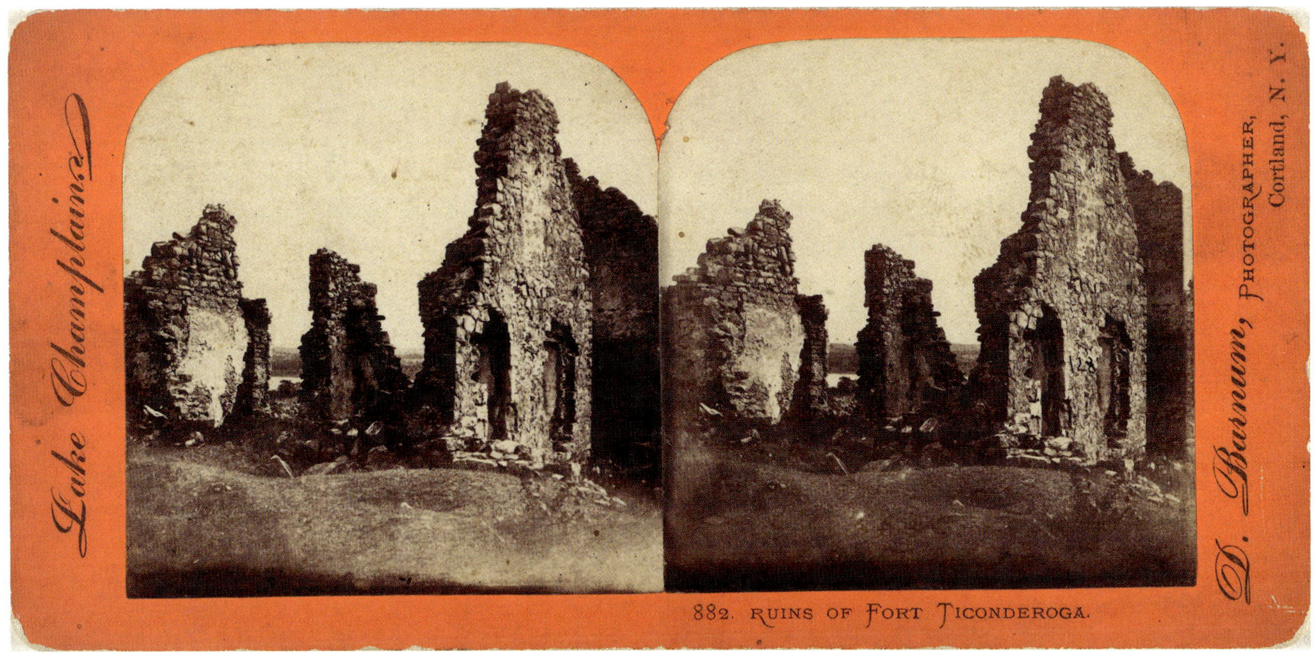

15. I. D. Barnum, *Ruins of Fort Ticonderoga*. Stereoview, 1868–1869. Digital image courtesy of the Getty's Open Content Program.

1865 he was in Solon, Cortland County, his wife's hometown, where he appeared in that year's New York state census as a farmer. In 1869, according to a Cortland County business directory, Barnum was a photographer in the town of Cortland. He is estimated to have produced more than two thousand stereoviews.[1]

Barnum briefly maintained a studio in the late 1860s in Saratoga Springs, Saratoga County, as "Deloss Barnum, Photograph Artist." In 1868 he sent "a number of fine views taken at Lake George and vicinity, including Cauldwell [*sic*], Bolton, the Steamer Min-ne-ha-ha and others" to *Humphrey's Journal of Photography*. Barnum died "after a short illness" at the age of forty-eight in Cortland.[2]

1. Darrah, *World of Stereographs*, 23, 25; "Out-Door Photography," 57.

2. *Humphrey's Journal* 20, no. 15 (December 1, 1868): 233; *Cortland County Standard and Journal*, October 7, 1873.

BARRETT, CHARLES F. (1859–1925)
Active Chestertown, Warren County, Early-1880s–1893

Born in Chestertown, Charles Barrett was a farm worker on his parents' farm before taking up portrait photography in his hometown. He departed for Hampton, Iowa, in 1893, where, according to an obituary, "for twenty-five years he was one of the leading photographers of that place." In failing health, he returned to upstate New York in 1917 to farm in Verona, Oneida County.[1]

1. Obituary, *Warrensburgh News*, November 19, 1925; *Rome Sentinel*, November 10, 1925.

BAYLE, FRANCIS (1894–1982)
Active High Peaks and Lake George Regions, 1915–1970

In 1902 Francis Bayle relocated with his family from Worchester, Massachusetts, to Glens Falls, Warren County, where his father was president of the Glens Falls Portland Cement Company. Bayle later joined the company, working at first as a draftsman and later as plant engineer. A skilled camera hobbyist, he chronicled the Adirondack landscape, particularly from the vantage point of a lover and enthusiastic hiker of the region's High Peaks. From 1928 to 1932 he edited *High Spots*, the magazine of the Adirondack Mountain Club and the occasional publisher of his images and camera hints. In his later years Bayle presented variations on a slide show, *Adirondacks—Past and Present*, featuring his early black-and-white images as well as more recent Kodak color slides. The Chapman Historical Museum in Glens Falls has mounted two exhibits of Bayle's photographs: in 1974 and 1980.[1]

1. Bayle, *An Adirondack Portfolio*, v, vi, 290; Mellon, "The Eyes of Francis Bayle," 8.

BEACH, HENRY M. (1863–1943)
Active throughout the Adirondacks, Principally in Its Central and Western Sections, 1906–Early 1920s

Henry Beach was born in Watson, Lewis County, a town partially inside the Adirondack Park, where his father was a farmer, lumberman, and descendant of a family with deep regional roots. Leaving school at sixteen, he appeared in the 1880 US Census as a "hawker." Beach entered the world of photography by a side door in 1881, advertising "oilgraph" portraits he produced in Watson: enlarged, hand-colored copies of photographic prints, tintypes, and daguerreotypes. Beach "copies pictures cheaper than anybody in this section," announced one ad, "and better than the best."[1]

It was not long before Beach took up the camera himself. Newspapers in Jefferson and St. Lawrence Counties reported in 1885 and 1886 that "H. M. Beach, landscape artist, of Lowville," had been "taking some very fine photographic views" in the vicinities of Adams and Hammond, "including groups" (often of families standing in front of

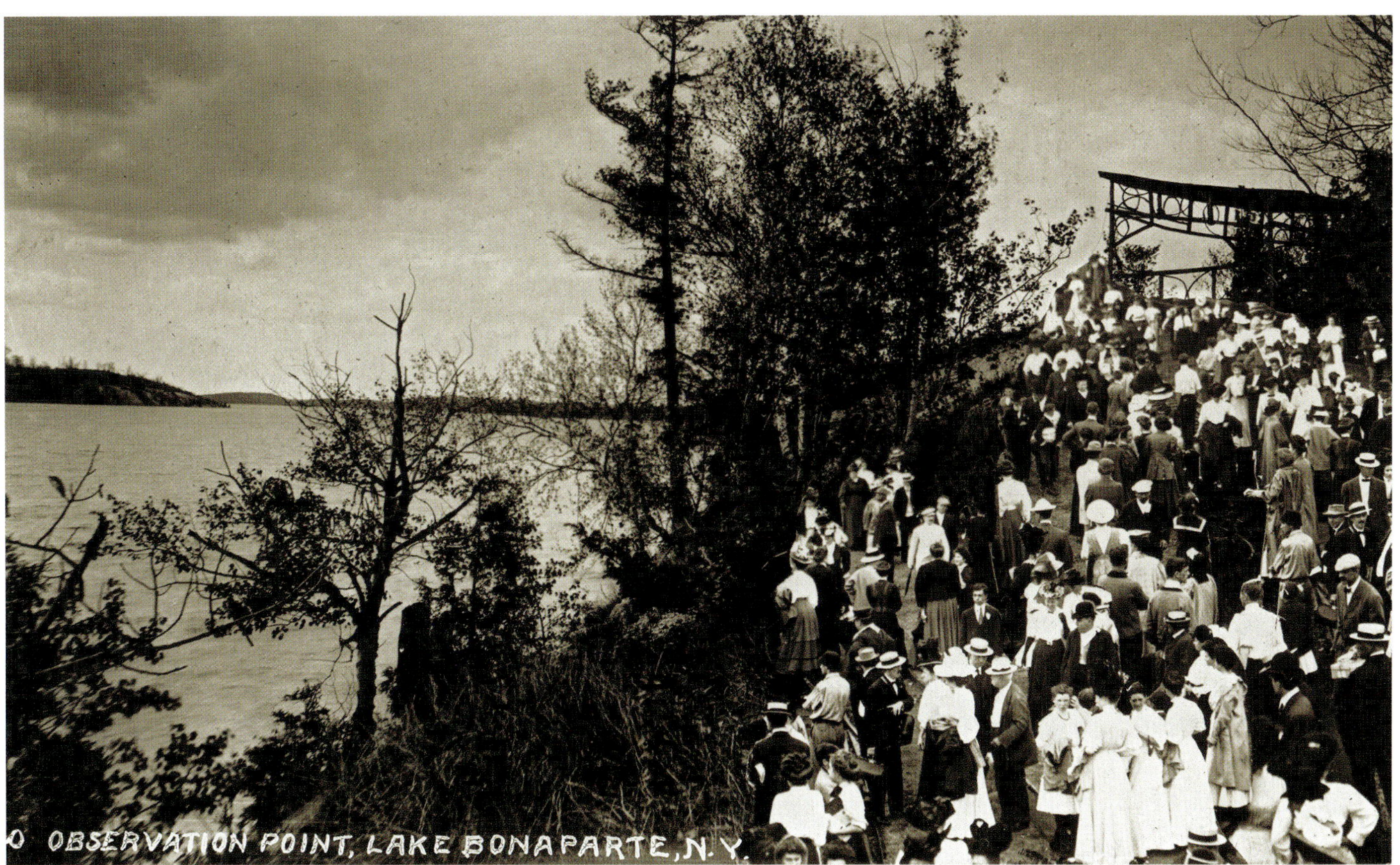

16. H. M. Beach, *Observation Point, Lake Bonaparte*. RPPC, 1906–1916. Composite image with fabricated crowd.

their homes). The mainstay of Beach's work from the 1880s into the early 1900s, however, was studio portraits. He advertised "photo jewelry" and "your photo on a button" in 1901 and "new style Photos at $1 dozen" in mid-1903. When a change in building ownership led to the loss of his Lowville business lease in October 1903, Beach relocated briefly to Carthage, Jefferson County. He and his family were identified as living in both Lowville and Carthage in the New York state census of 1905.[2]

By mid-1906 Beach had moved to Remsen, Oneida County, a village on the southwestern edge of the Adirondack Park. The next ten years would be his most productive, as he expanded the real photo postcard business he had begun shortly before postal regulations changed in 1907 to allow appropriation of the entire face of a postcard for an image. He also produced cards at a few cents each for amateur photographers.[3]

Beach was the Adirondacks' most important postcard photographer in the years of the craze for real photo postcards, documenting the region in thousands of photographs. While producing some images of grand hotels and private camps of the moneyed class, his favorite subjects were rural communities and small-town life, industrial sites, logging operations, and modest resorts. His work, noted Robert Bogdan, who took up Beach in two books (one a monograph on the photographer), was unusual in its "down-to-earth directness." Beach, he added, "related straightforwardly to local subjects, spontaneously producing innovative elements in his compositions." He generated a number of panoramic photographs as well as many composite postcards. The latter might focus on one small town or advertise his own or others' business operations with multiple photo images, fancy lettering, drawings, and often, images of artificial flowers.

Another specialty was the "freak" or "exaggeration" postcard, an outlandish montage of cutout photo images against the background of a named location illustrating a catch of seemingly gigantic fish or trolley cars and people crowding the main street of a country town. A traveling photographer in the 1910 US Census, Beach relied on the sale of postcard views in bulk to retailers as his largest income source. Two of his three sons (Henry Jr., or Harry, and Wellington, born in 1889 and 1893, respectively) worked with their father at one time or another. Style and technical quality remained consistent in postcards produced under Beach's name.[4]

Beach had his share of legal difficulties in the mid-teens. As "a commercial traveler living in Remsen," he was declared a "voluntary bankrupt" in 1914, owing $612 and having "no assets except a second hand Buick automobile which he says is worth about $50 and some copyrights of no value." In January 1915 Beach was appointed treasurer of the Alaska Film Company and expected to "take an active part in producing" silent movies at a camp in Saranac Lake outfitted with sledges and sled dogs. Three months later Beach sued the company's president, William F. Cooper, for breach of contract in withdrawing the job offer. He nevertheless experimented with motion pictures on his own: the H. M. Beach Motion Picture Production Company produced a film documenting the Lewis County Fair in 1916.[5]

Beach relocated abruptly to Fort Plain, Montgomery County, in 1916, where he and son Harry operated two outlets: Beach's Studio, specializing in portraits, and Beach's Art Shop and Amateur Supplies. The photographer's regional reputation was spotlighted in July 1917 news accounts relating to the tragic death of his only daughter in an automobile accident, with one article referring to him as "a famous Adirondack photographer, having taken thousands of views of scenes, animals, and places in the North Woods." Beach and his wife spent several months later that year and into 1918 in South Carolina, where Wellington was undergoing military training and Beach took panoramic photographs of his army training camp. These, and several photographs of the 1911 flood in Austin, Pennsylvania, were among his few out-of-New-York-State images.[6]

In mid-1920 Beach opened a portrait studio in Canajoharie, some three miles from Fort Plain. In November 1921 he announced that he was "retiring from portrait photography" and returning to his "old home" in Lewis County. Harry, he added, would continue "the amateur finish and kodak work at the studio." This arrangement ended a year later, with Beach declaring that "my son has made a bunch of money here and gone to Colorado." The Canajoharie operation was sold in 1923. Beach continued to produce and reproduce a few postcard images from Watson (identified on their backs as from Glenfield, his postal delivery address), but his name appeared primarily from the early 1920s in classified newspaper advertisements for his "Big Bronze" turkeys and turkey eggs.[7] Beach is buried in a family plot at Beaches Bridge Cemetery in Watson.

1. *Lowville Times*, January 6, 1881. This meaning of the word *oilgraph* was suggested by Mark Osterman, Photographic Process Historian at the George Eastman Museum, in an email to the author, February 7, 2018.

2. *Jefferson County Journal*, July 23, 1885; *Hammond Advertiser*, May 13, 1886; *Lowville Journal and Republican*, December 12, 1901; March 5, 1903; September 3, 1903; *Lewis County Democrat*, October 7, 1903.

3. Bogdan, *Adirondack Vernacular*, 19, 21.

4. Bogdan, *Exposing the Wilderness*, 63–64; Bogdan, *Adirondack Vernacular*, 22, notes 10 and 34.

5. "Auto His Only Asset," *Lowville Journal and Republican and Lowville Times*, September 3, 1914; *Boonville Herald*, January 14, 1915; "Moving Picture Men at Odds in Saranac Lake," *Essex County Republican*, April 16, 1915; *Lowville Journal and Republican*, September 28, 1916.

6. "Young Woman Killed When Auto Overturns," *Gloversville Herald*, July 19, 1917; *Fort Plain Standard*, December 20, 1917; Bogdan, *Adirondack Vernacular*, 25.

7. *Fort Plain Standard*, July 29, 1920; *Canajoharie Courier*, November 9, 1921; June 6, 1923; *Amsterdam Recorder*, November 10, 1921; *Utica Observer-Dispatch*, October 15, 1922; *Lowville Journal and Republican and Lowville Times*, April 17, 1924; Bogdan, *Adirondack Vernacular*, 27, 32.

BEAMAN, ELIAS OLCOTT (1837–1876)
Active Essex, Hamilton, and Warren Counties, 1873

Elias Beaman is celebrated as the photographer during the first eight months (May 1871–February 1872) of Major John Wesley Powell's second exploration and survey of the Colorado River under the auspices of the Smithsonian Institution. Little is known of his childhood, except that he was the eighth of nine children born to grocer and hotelier Elias Beaman and Sarah Stark in Chateaugay, Clinton County, and passed several early childhood years in Ohio, where the couple's last child was born in 1840 and the parents died in 1840 and 1841. Fellow members of the Powell expedition remembered Beaman as from New York City, where he may have learned his photographic skills.[1]

The stereograph publishing and photographic supply concern of **E. and T. H. Anthony** recommended Beaman to Powell for the arduous Colorado River trip. He produced some 350 stereoviews during the expedition and, experienced in handling watercraft, took the helm of one of the three boats that carried the party downriver. He left the survey following increasing friction with its leader, and has been recorded in expedition histories as a "temperamental and recalcitrant" participant

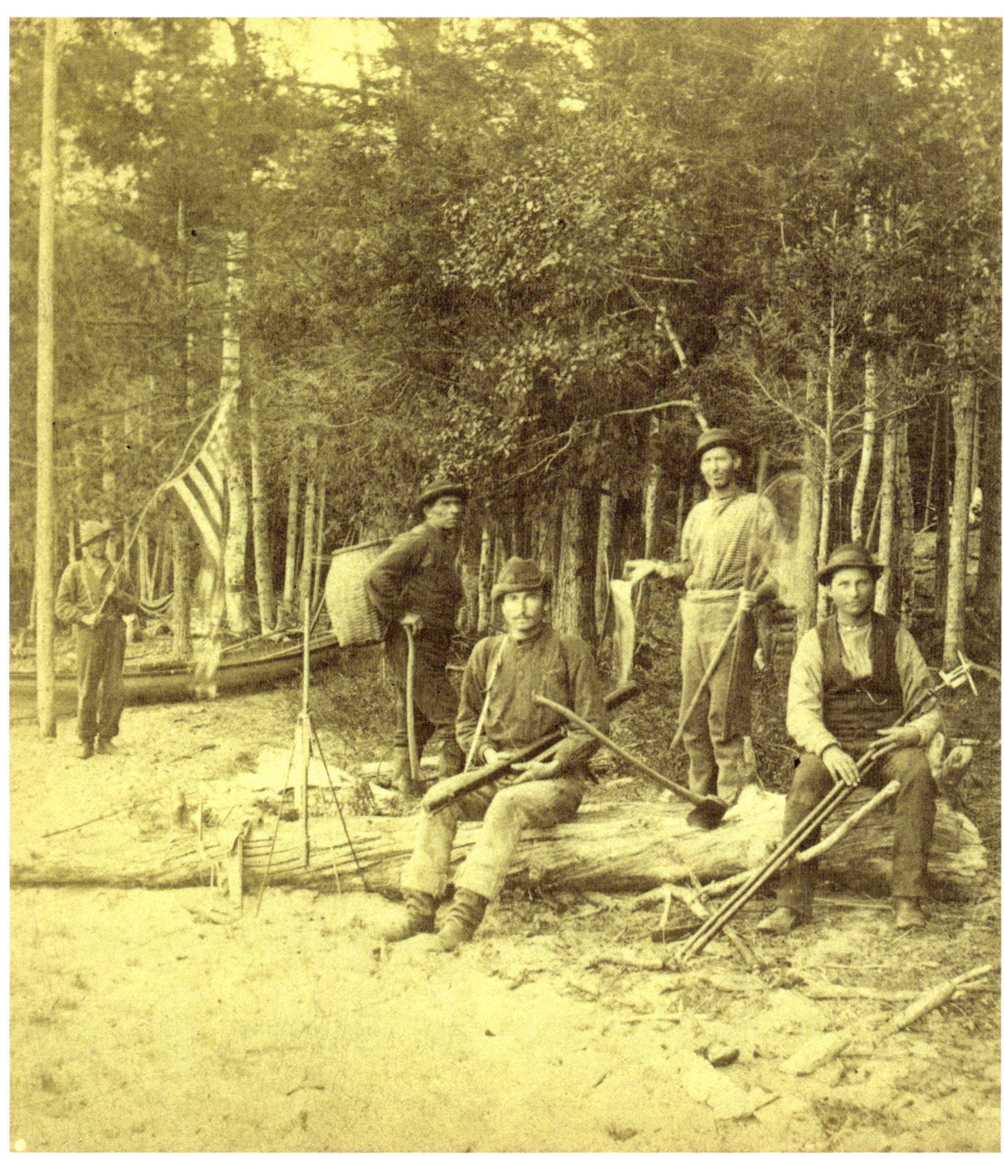

17. E. O. Beaman, V. Colvin's Adirondack Survey, at Holland's Sand Beach, Blue Mountain Lake. One-half stereoview, 1873. Courtesy of Adirondack Experience.

who "balked at taking orders and frequently argued with Powell over plans and procedures." He later quarreled with Powell over the ownership of rights to his images, many of which were intentionally recaptioned, redated, and recredited by Powell to Beaman's photographic successors. Some attributed Beaman views were published by the Anthony firm and others after his return to the East. Wood engravings from his work illustrated Beaman's detailed account of his western adventures in *Appletons' Journal* between April 18 and May 30, 1874, an account that effectively upstaged Powell in getting the expedition story before the public. The quality of Beaman's writing in this seven-part chronicle and his numerous literary allusions suggest more than a rudimentary education.[2]

Beaman appears to have struggled in the years after his return from the West. Despite their estrangement, in 1873 and 1874 he offered to make stereograph copies for Powell of his expedition output and to act as his "visual aids assistant" when Powell gave lectures. He later proposed to sell Powell negatives of images he had made of Native Americans in Colorado and Arizona after leaving the Powell party. Neither offer was accepted. In 1873 Beaman was in the Adirondacks (his presence was reported in Schroon Lake in early October) generating a set of sixty-five stereoviews labeled SCENES ON THE UPPER HUDSON AND THE ADIRONDACK MOUNTAINS. Views took in Lakes Luzerne, George, and Schroon, Warren and Essex Counties; the High Peaks; and Indian, Raquette, and Blue Mountain Lakes, Hamilton County. (Two Beaman images were used as the basis for wood engravings in **Verplanck Colvin**'s report on the 1873 work of his Adirondack Survey.) As *Anthony's Photographic Bulletin* observed of Beaman's Adirondack images: "All who have a weakness for a 'life in the woods' but can't get away, may have their longings gratified to some extent by providing themselves with his truthful counterfeits." In 1874 Beaman toured a popular magic lantern lecture series on Yellowstone, which led to an invitation to participate in Philadelphia's 1876 Centennial Exhibition. Beaman died suddenly that year in Camden, New Jersey, of "congestion of the brain."[3]

1. Wooden, *Beaman and Clark Genealogy*, 70.

2. Terrell, *Man Who Rediscovered America*, 128; Worster, *River Running West*, 220, 237; Jeremy Rowe Vintage Photography, https://www.vintagephoto.com/reference/stereolists/702beamanlist.htm.

3. Worster, *River Running West*, 594n8; *Essex County Republican*, October 2, 1873; Treadwell and Darrah, *Photographers of the United States*, 56; *Anthony's Photographic Bulletin* 4, no. 11 (November 1873): 336; Jeremy Rowe Vintage Photography.

BEER BROTHERS: SIGISMUND (1819–1895) AND LOUIS (DATES UNKNOWN)

Active Lake George and Champlain Regions, 1861–1865

Immigrants from Frankfurt, Germany, Sigismund and Louis Beer were, according to Trow's 1862–63 *New York City Directory*, in the business of "photographs" as Beer Brothers at 35 Wall Street. Information on the verso of a stereoview from this period identifies "Beer Bros." as "publishers of stereoscopic photographs & cards de visite." Despite a primary focus on New York City, the brothers offered a series of twenty-eight views of Lake George and vicinity subjects.

The partnership dissolved in 1863, when Sigismund Beer took over the business. (Louis Beer was listed in Trow's 1865–66 directory as an artist, but had no subsequent known connection to photography.) The name Beer & Company was used briefly in a transitional period before S. Beer of 564 Broadway began issuing views under his name in 1864, the year in which he published a diminished but not identical selection of stereoviews of Lakes George and Champlain. He listed his offerings as "all kinds of Stereoscopic and other Photographs . . . Parlors, buildings, interiors, monuments, machinery, engines, sculpture work, coaches and horses, . . . celebrated instantaneous street views."[1]

Trow's 1865–66 directory gave Beer's business address as 481 Broadway. In 1867, located at 142-1/2 Broadway, he won a bronze medal at the Paris Exposition for "stereographic proofs"; in 1868–69 he was a "photographer and inventor of seasoning wood" at 390 Broadway. This directory listing was Beer's last as a photographer. His primary interest in the following years would be in promoting his product for preserving or "Beerizing" wood to make it "undecayable," stronger, and more attractive.[2]

1. *Instantaneous* became a favored early adjective to reference shortened exposure times.

2. Morford, *Paris in '67*, 233; *Scientific American*, December 31, 1881, 431.

BETTS, JAMES TILLISON (1868–1944)

Active Conklingville, Saratoga County, 1888–1892; Warrensburg, Warren County, 1892–1893; Corinth, Saratoga County, 1893–1904 and 1911–1915; Gloversville, Fulton County, 1905–1909

James Betts was born into a Providence, Saratoga County, farming family. The seventh of nine children, by 1880 he was a twelve-year-old farm laborer in Edinburg. After learning how to take pictures from a book (*Wilson's Quarter Century in Photography*, published in 1887), Betts became a portrait photographer, at first in the Day, Saratoga County, hamlet of Conklingville, and then in nearby Warrensburg. He captured a series of images of Warrensburg's Whitby & Company Woolen Mill for the 1893 World's Columbian Exposition in Chicago.[1]

In 1893 Betts sold his Warrensburg business to **Alonzo L. Mix** and transferred to Corinth, where he operated a studio for more than ten years. In late 1904 he partnered briefly with Saratoga photographer H. J. Epler as Epler & Betts before relocating to Gloversville in 1905. Although recorded in the 1910 US Census as a photographer, Betts spent some of his time in Gloversville traveling "in the interest of the glove business." In 1909 he took a job in the plant of the General Electric Company in Schenectady, Schenectady County.[2]

Betts repurchased his Corinth studio in 1911, but took another career detour in 1916–17 as Saratoga County undersheriff and jailer at the county jail in Ballston Spa. In 1918 Betts moved to Albany, Albany County, where he maintained a studio specializing in children's portraits for nearly twenty years.[3]

1. Hastings, "From the Sheep to the Man," 1, 3; email from John L. Scherer, Betts's great-grandson, to the author, December 23, 2016.

2. *Saratogian*, October 27, 1904; May 13, 1908; *Ballston Spa Journal*, December 20, 1915; December 30, 1918.

3. *Saratogian*, September 6, 1911; November 17, 1939; "Corinth Man Named as Saratoga Jail Keeper," *Knickerbocker Press*, January 2, 1916.

BIERSTADT, CHARLES (1819–1903)

Active Warren and Hamilton Counties, 1883

Older brother of **Edward Bierstadt**, Charles was Edward's photographic partner in New Bedford, Massachusetts, through 1867. The following year he relocated to Niagara Falls, Niagara County, where he made a reputation as a stereographic specialist. He won a high honor, the Philadelphia Medal of Merit, at the 1876 Centennial International Exhibition in Philadelphia with a display of his collection of six hundred stereoviews. An extensive traveler in the United States and abroad, Bierstadt made one documented trip to the Adirondack interior, checking into the Prospect House on Hamilton County's Blue Mountain Lake in June 1883 in the company of William West Durant, cousin of the hotel owner. During that visit he stopped at the Adirondack Club (later the Tahawus Club) in the town of Newcomb, Essex County, writing next to his name in the remarks column of the club register: "Photographer, after fine weather." Among the small number of Bierstadt images taken in the region were views of Stony Creek, Warren County, and Long Lake, Hamilton County.[1]

1. DiLaura, "Niagara Falls," 19; Verner, "Edward Bierstadt's Adirondack Artotypes," 10; *Prospect House Hotel Register*.

BIERSTADT, EDWARD (1824–1906)
Active Hamilton, Warren, and Essex Counties, 1884–1888

Born in Solingen, Prussia, Edward Bierstadt grew up in the whaling port of New Bedford, Massachusetts, after his family immigrated to the United States in 1831. His father was a cooper, and Edward the middle of five children. Brother Albert, a painter in oils and "a distinguished artist," experimented with stereoview photography on an 1859 trip to the West. Upon returning east he handed his negatives over to brothers Edward and Charles, who had opened the Bierstadt Brothers Photographic Gallery in New Bedford after the family wood-turning shop was lost to fire in early 1859. In 1860 they issued a catalog listing their own stereographs of New Bedford and New Hampshire's White Mountains as well as fifty-two of Albert's western views.[1]

Charles and Edward went their separate ways in 1867. Edward moved his family to the New York City area, where his primary interest became photographic reproduction. Acquiring the American rights to a German photomechanical "collotype" process that produced photographic images with delicate tonal gradations, he launched the Photo Plate Printing Company in 1870—the first collotype printing establishment in the United States. In 1878, in short-term partnership with Gilbert Harroun as Harroun & Bierstadt, Bierstadt began producing "artotypes," or "gray, softened, slightly veiled pictures," by an improved process based on the original collotype patent. Bierstadt's name was associated with artotypes for the rest of his working life.[2]

While Bierstadt's post-1867 output was not large, he continued to wield a camera. He took 12 x 24 inch views of Central Park with a specially commissioned panoramic camera around 1880, and extensively documented the 1880–81 arrival and installation of the obelisk known as Cleopatra's Needle in Central Park. His portrait of President James A. Garfield was used as the basis for a postage stamp issued several months after Garfield was assassinated in 1881.[3]

Bierstadt spent three months in the Indian Lake, Hamilton County, hamlet of Blue Mountain Lake in 1884, checking into the Prospect House, a luxurious hotel opened the previous year, on July 10. It is thought that the hotel's builder/owner, Frederick Durant, or his uncle Thomas C. Durant (a large central Adirondack landowner and the builder of the Adirondack Railroad that made the hotel accessible) commissioned Bierstadt to take promotional photographs of the hotel and the region. Artotype images generated from more than two hundred Bierstadt views, some from his 1884 visit and others taken somewhat later, appeared in a number of formats over the ensuing decade, among them as bound books in various editions (some assembled for private collectors) and individual prints sold at the Prospect House office and packaged in special Bierstadt boxes. In 1889 *Anthony's Photographic Bulletin* acknowledged the receipt of a Bierstadt compilation, *The Adirondacks: Artotype Views in the North Woods*, and described the volume's forty-nine photographs as "admirably selected, beautifully reproduced and artistically bound in a little portfolio. To those who wander in the New York wilderness in summer, these will prove a charming set of souvenirs." A number of Bierstadt's Adirondack views were produced around 1900 in Germany as printed postcards.[4]

1. Campbell, "Albert Bierstadt and the White Mountains," 14–15; Sandweiss, *Print the Legend*, 136–40.

2. Adler, *Early Days in the Adirondacks*, 147.

3. "Panoramic Views by Harroun and Bierstadt," 216–17.

4. Stickler, *The Adirondacks as a Health Resort*, 169–70; *Prospect House Hotel Register*; Verner, "Edward Bierstadt's Adirondack Artotypes," 7, 11; Bierstadt, *The Adirondacks*; "Views Caught with the Drop Shutter," 576.

BIGALOW, WILLIAM H. (1848–1929)
Active Port Henry, Essex County, 1873–1929

A lifelong resident of Moriah, of which Port Henry is a hamlet, William Bigalow was born into a farming family in Mineville, another hamlet of the town. In 1873, in partnership with **Edgar A. Marvin**, he purchased the business of **George W. Baldwin** and his brother and opened a portrait gallery, Marvin & Bigalow, in Port Henry. Marvin resigned from the partnership after the studio was destroyed by fire the following year; Bigalow continued the business as a sole proprietor.[1]

Bigalow closed his studio for up to four months each summer during his early working years and became an itinerant photographer, pitching a tent in other Essex County population centers and into Warren County for one or more weeks at a time: "Under the big elm" or in "Butler's Meadow" in Schroon Lake (1896, 1899); on the "Court House grounds" in Elizabethtown (1900); on the "Spread Eagle Lawn" in Keene Valley (1901). He served as Port Henry's tax collector for several years.[2]

1. *Ter-Centenary of Lake Champlain*, 28; Smith, *History of Essex County*, 589.

2. *Plattsburgh Sentinel*, July 21, 1882; *Essex County Republican*, August 6, 1896; *Glens Falls Times*, July 28, 1899; *Elizabethtown Post*, July 5, 1900; August 8, 1901; *Ticonderoga Sentinel*, March 7, 1929.

BIGELOW, WILLIAM A. (1831–1901) AND BIGELOW STUDIO

Bigelow Active Plattsburgh, Clinton County, 1869–1901; Bigelow Studio Active 1901–1935

Born in Worcester, Massachusetts, William Bigelow passed his young adulthood in Haverhill, Massachusetts, and Thompsonville, Connecticut, before landing in the Adirondacks in the late 1860s as assistant to photographer **Elbert M. Johnson** of Crown Point, Essex County. In 1868 he removed to Plattsburgh, and the following January launched a "gallery of art" in partnership with a Mr. Vaughn. In May it was reported that Vaughn had retired, and that henceforth the gallery would be under Bigelow's exclusive proprietorship. In 1872 Bigelow improved his competitive position in marrying Kate Lansing, daughter of Wendell Lansing, the founder in 1839 of Keeseville's *Essex County Republican* and from 1864 the owner of both the *Republican* and the *Plattsburgh Sentinel*. In 1889 Bigelow took over the apparatus, negatives, and space formerly occupied by photographer **James Jay Howard**.[1]

Bigelow was primarily but not exclusively a portrait photographer, advertising in 1884 that he took "Instantaneous Photographs of Children Sure Every Time." An 1894 promotional incentive read, "For a few days only, I will give free of charge, to any man or woman over seventy years of age, one cabinet photo, if they will come and sit for the negative. It will be our best work." Occasional portable studios were set up elsewhere, as in the towns of Mooers and Champlain, north of Plattsburgh.[2]

After Bigelow's death in 1901, what had generally been identified as Bigelow's Photograph Gallery or Bigelow's Studio became the Bigelow Studio. Primarily a family affair, its first proprietor was Bigelow's widow, Kate (1849–1921), whose occupation was listed as photographer in the New York state census of 1905 and who continued to be listed as the firm's owner through 1920. The Bigelows's son, W. Lansing Bigelow (1885–1969), worked in the studio as a photographer by 1904; one of three Bigelow daughters, Mabel (b. 1882), was employed in 1905 as a studio clerk and in 1913 as a retoucher. A July 1916 advertisement announced that the Bigelow Studio was "making post cards and other pictures at night" and that Mrs. K. Bigelow Davis, as Kate Bigelow became after a remarriage, had taken a studio at Plattsburgh's Cliff Haven, the 450-acre Plattsburgh site of a Catholic summer school (sort of a Catholic Chautauqua). There she would "make a specialty of class portraiture and pictures of important events as well as be available to photograph groups at the nearby Hotel Champlain." The Bigelow Studio closed in the mid-1930s, and in late 1935 Lansing Bigelow advertised from his Plattsburgh home that he specialized in home portrait photographs "with new equipment and new styles of work." The following year he returned to what he still referred to as the Bigelow Studio as an employee of Mrs. Frederick S.

Laing, who had taken over the business the year before and was running it as the Laing Studio, offering portraits, yarn, and an assortment of art-craft materials.[3]

1. "Photographers: W. A. Bigelow," *Plattsburgh Press*, December 31, 1897; October 24, 1931; *Plattsburgh Press Republican*, January 3, 1966; *Plattsburgh Sentinel*, January 15, 1869; May 28, 1869; June 28, 1872; December 13, 1889; February 14, 1890.

2. *Essex County Republican*, December 18, 1884; *Plattsburgh Sentinel*, May 23, 1873; March 14, 1890; August 26, 1892; February 2, 1894; June 7, 1897.

3. *Plattsburgh Press*, April 7, 1909; July 3, 1916; December 6, 1935; "Laing Studio Opens at 66 Margaret St.," April 9, 1936.

BISHOP, BAINBRIDGE (1837–1905)
Active New Russia, Essex County, Late 1860s

Bainbridge Bishop was a farmer in New Russia, where his grandfather Elijah Bishop had settled from Vermont in 1793 and constructed a sawmill and gristmill. The second youngest of eight children, Bishop was a self-taught painter, and among his several sisters were painters, poets, and a botanist, leading poet and journalist William Cullen Bryant to characterize the Bishops as the "American Brontë Family." Claiming to be "neither musician nor mechanic," Bishop patented an "improvement in violins" in 1868, and "attachments for key-board musical instruments" in 1877 with which he built three "color-organs" combining colored lights on a screen with live music in keeping with his theory of "painting music."[1]

An amateur photographer, Bishop produced an unusual stereoview series of delicate, snowy landscapes taken around New Russia in the 1860s. Titled *Winter in the Adirondacks*, the hand-numbered sequence included more than fifty landscape images.

1. George Levi Brown, *Pleasant Valley*, 31, 37; "Unveiling Bishop Memorial Tablet," *Au Sable Forks Record Post*, September 12, 1929; Bishop, *A Souvenir of the Color Organ*.

BIXBY, MARQUIS JESSE (1835–1894)
Credited with Views of Ausable Chasm, Clinton and Essex Counties, 1870s

Born in Shalersville, Ohio, and raised in Mount Holly, Vermont, Marquis Bixby served in the Civil War in 1862–63 and took up photography upon his return to the state (a skill he may have learned from other Bixby family members who had careers in the field). In 1869 or 1870 Bixby purchased the Burlington photographic gallery of the recently deceased **Guy B. Davis**, renaming it the City Photograph Gallery. His specialty was portraiture. It is likely that the few stereographs he offered, including a number of views of Ausable Chasm, were acquired in his purchase of Davis's business. In 1877 Bixby built a boat livery and modest seasonal hotel for the accommodation of sportsmen on Lake Bomoseen in Castleton. He was recorded on his death certificate as a hotelkeeper.[1]

1. Treadwell and Darrah, *Photographers of the United States*, 75; H. P. Smith and Rann, *History of Rutland County, Vermont*, 932.

BOURKE-WHITE, MARGARET (1904–1971)
Adirondack Projects, 1933, 1939

Margaret Bourke-White achieved many firsts in her well-documented career. She was the first western photographer allowed into the Soviet Union, the first woman accredited as a photojournalist by the US Army, a pioneer employee of *Fortune* and *Life* magazines who took the photographs for the lead or "keynote" stories in the first issues of both. By her 1940s account, she photographed "almost every famous person in the world." Within the scheme of her overall output, Bourke-White's association with the Adirondacks was minimal, but nevertheless fits her for inclusion in this compendium.[1]

Eleven of Bourke-White's Adirondack images were taken for Kenneth Durant, a son of the owner of Camp Cedars, built in 1880 on the shore of Forked Lake, Hamilton County. She

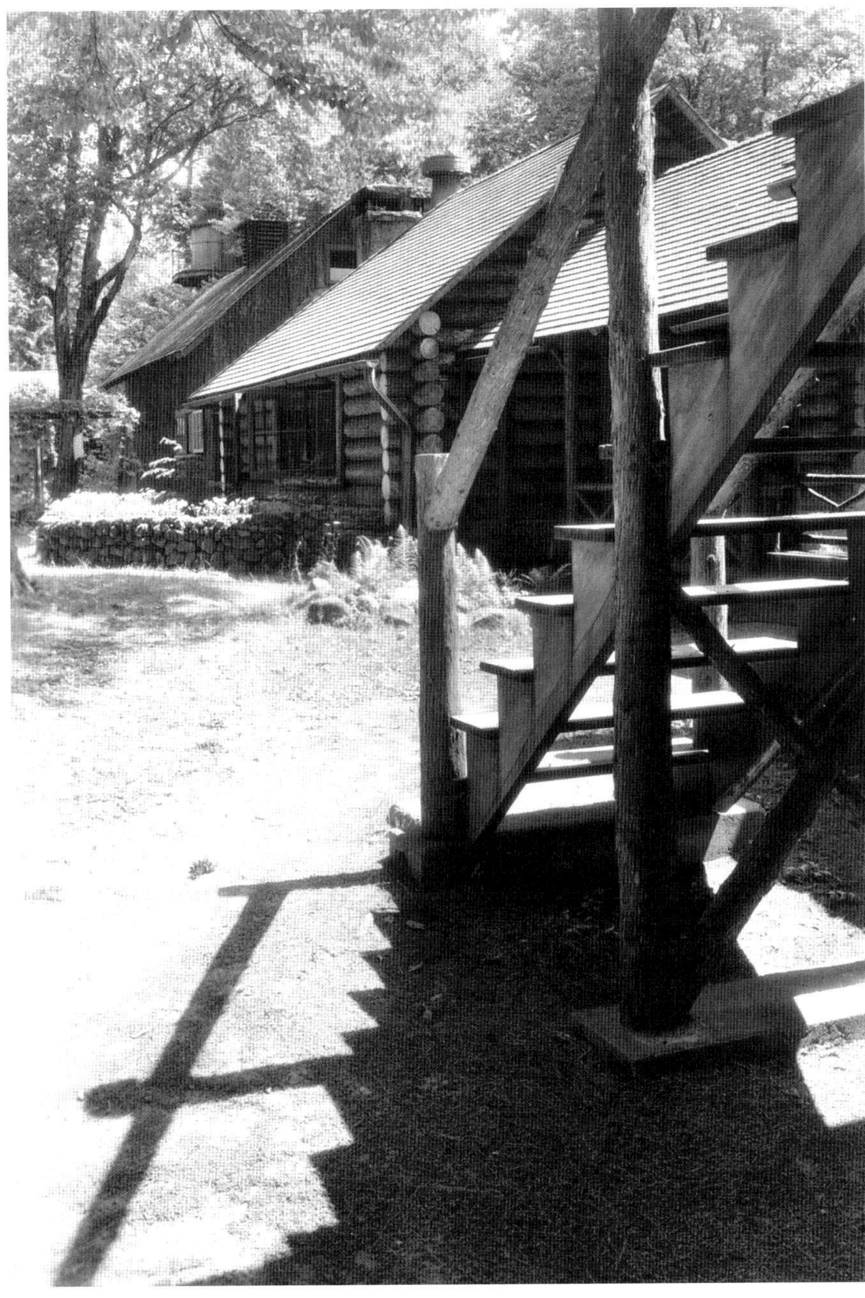

18. M. Bourke-White, Camp Cedars, Forked Lake, July 4, 1933. Courtesy of Adirondack Experience.

and Durant were friends, knowing one another through their shared interest in Russia. (Durant was head of the US bureau of the Soviet news agency TASS; Bourke-White wrote a first-person account of her experience in the USSR, *Eyes on Russia*, published in 1931.) While her work was well-known by 1933, Bourke-White was not so far removed from her early post-college days spent photographing the estates of the landed gentry in Cleveland, Ohio, that she refused Durant's request to visually document his family's summer retreat. The two visited Forked Lake on July 4 of that year. Bourke-White gave the negatives from their Camp Cedars outing to Durant and, in 1958, a set of signed prints and their image copyright to the recently founded Adirondack Museum in Blue Mountain Lake.[2]

"The Hudson River," an essay with photographs by Bourke-White, appeared in a 1939 issue of *Life* and included aerial views of Manhattan and images from "deep in the stormy Adirondacks," including portraits of three roughhewn Essex County Adirondackers: a "singer of old Valley songs," a "teller of tall stories about the bygone lumbering days," and "Teddy Roosevelt's guide in the North Woods on the day news was received there of President McKinley's assassination."[3]

1. Bourke-White, *Portrait of Myself*, 70, 206.

2. Letter, Margaret Bourke-White to Kenneth Durant, May 27, 1960, Bourke-White file, Adirondack Experience Library, Blue Mountain Lake.

3. "The Hudson River," 57–65.

BOWDISH, ROBERT FREDERICK (1833–1908)
Active Hamilton and Herkimer Counties, 1860–1870

Born in Carthage, Jefferson County, Robert Bowdish was working alongside his father, a Boonville, Oneida County, farmer at the time of the 1850 US census. By 1855 he was a carpenter; by 1860 a Boonville photographer. An early 1867 advertisement for his Bowdish Gallery in nearby Turin, Lewis County, proffered studio portraits and "mammoth size" (12 x 17 inch) views of Turin and other Lewis County communities, along with "many other beautiful landscapes" and "a fine assortment of Frames, Cases, Lockets, and Albums."[1]

Bowdish photographed a number of sites around Blue Mountain Lake and the Fulton Chain of Lakes from 1865, including early scenes of sportsmen and their guides. Heading west circa 1870, he took pictures in and near Columbus, Ohio, and later in Illinois; a portrait from this period bears the imprint FROM BOWDISH'S TRAVELING GALLERY. Bowdish returned to New York State by mid-1884 and settled for several years in Rochester, Monroe County, where an early partnership with photographer G. R. Hoagland as Bowdish & Hoagland marketed itself as "Landscape and Commercial Photographers" with "apparatus being arranged especially for traveling." The pair focused on "Out-of-Door Photography, Residences, Manufactories, Machinery, Livestock, etc." and offered "the largest photographs ever made in the State." By 1889 Bowdish was again working alone. Circa 1890 he relocated to the New York City area.[2]

1. *Lewis County Democrat*, April 24, 1867.

2. "Rochester Photographic Association," 88; advertisement, *Rochester Directory* (for year beginning July 1, 1884), 736; *Rochester Democrat and Chronicle*, April 14, 1889; "Death of Fred Bowdish," *Boonville Herald*, August 6, 1908.

BOWERS, SERENO ALONZO (1847–1911)
Active Essex County, Mid-1870s

Sereno Bowers, a New York State native, made regional news in early 1871 when it was reported that as "operator of Van Alstine's Photographic rooms" in Watertown, Jefferson County, he was "creating considerable excitement" by taking "spirit pictures." In doing so, he was following in the fashionable footsteps of photographer William Mumler, who claimed that departed ancestors could, upon a portrait sitter's request, imprint their ghostly images on photographs, a claim for which Mumler was tried for fraud in 1869 but acquitted.[1]

After a short stint as an operator for the Fredricks celebrity portrait studio in New York City, Bowers relocated to Burlington, Vermont, in 1872. He briefly associated with "portrait painter Mills" in the former studio of **Adin F. Styles** before affiliating in portrait work with renowned engraver James H. Hills (1814–98) at the same location. In mid-1875 Bowers was reported to be "taking views of the quarries, works, and the residences" of Willsboro, Essex County, for the firm. Hills & Bowers published under their name a large selection of stereoviews previously taken by others, including Bowers's studio predecessor, Styles, in series labeled *American Scenery*, *Vermont Scenery*, *New England Scenery*, and *Florida*. The partners' Vermont Gallery of Art was taken over by photographer E. O. Wormell in September 1876. Bowers stayed on in Burlington, selling stereoviews under his own name before relocating to Concord, New Hampshire, circa 1889. By 1909 he was president of the Technical Photo Company in Manhattan.[2]

1. *Watertown (VT) Times*, February 23, 1871.
2. *Middlebury (VT) Register*, November 26, 1872; *Burlington (VT) Weekly Free Press*, September 15, 1876; *Essex County Republican*, June 17, 1875; Treadwell and Darrah, *Photographers of the United States*, 90, 354.

BOWMAN, ISAAC ELLSWORTH (1861–1941)
Active Northville, Fulton County, 1885–1900, 1927–1930

Isaac Bowman was born and grew up on his family's farm in Northampton (of which Northville is a part); his occupation in the 1880 US Census was recorded as "works on farm." Sometime in the early 1880s he went west to Michigan, where he "learned the business" of photography before returning to his hometown. Identified as an engineer at the time of his 1883 marriage, Bowman took over the photographic rooms of former Northville photographer **Thaddeus E. Hewitt** in 1885. His work included individual and group portraits and landscapes. Still listed in the 1900 US Census as a photographer, Bowman purchased a one-half interest that year in a Northville drugstore, henceforth named Kested & Bowman, and gave up his previous occupation. He appears to have sold his negatives at this time, as some unpeopled scenes of Sacandaga Park taken by him were published by others as postcards in the early years of the twentieth century. Bowman, who served three terms as village president, remained a druggist until his retirement in 1927, when he entered into a brief photographic partnership, Bowman & Greenfield, with Charles F. Greenfield, who relocated to Northville from Edinburg, Saratoga County, in 1928. Greenfield died in early 1930.[1]

1. Greene, *History of the Mohawk Valley* 3: 125–26; *Fulton County Republican*, July 1, 1885; *Gloversville Herald*, April 21, 1927; "Well Known Resident Dies," February 8, 1930.

BRADY, MATHEW B. (1822–1896)
One of the Most Celebrated Figures in American Photographic History, Brady Took no Adirondack Pictures but Grew Up in the Region, Affording Sufficient Grounds for at Least a Mention Here

Almost nothing is known about Matthew Brady's early years. He was circumspect about his past, answering in response to a reporter's query in 1891 only that "I go back to near 1823–'24; that my birthplace was Warren County, N.Y., in the woods about Lake George, and that my father was an Irishman." (Some contemporary historians believe that Brady was born in Ireland, a fact he chose to conceal in the face of anti-Irish sentiment.) He grew up in Johnsburg, a rural Warren County community that provided livings in farming, logging, mining, and leather tanning for its 1820 population of 727.[1]

In the mid-1830s Brady relocated to Saratoga, Saratoga County, from there to Albany, Albany County, and by 1839–40 to New York City, where he studied daguerreotypy with artist and inventor Samuel F. B. Morse. He opened a daguerreotype gallery in New York in 1844, and "Brady of Broadway" became synonymous with fashionable portraiture. He and his staff photographed many celebrities, among them the young Prince of Wales on his 1860 visit to the United States and Abraham Lincoln in an image that would later embellish both the Lincoln penny and the five-dollar bill. Brady is best known for the thousands of Civil War images taken by his studio of battlefield action and camp life. Reporting on an exhibit, *The Dead of Antietam*, mounted in 1862 in Brady's New York studio, a *New York Times* journalist wrote, "Mr. Brady has done something to bring home to us the terrible reality and earnestness of war. If he has not brought bodies and laid them in our door-yards and along the streets, he has done something very like it." Brady's circumstances declined after the war. Alcoholic, bankrupt, and lonely after the death of his wife in 1887, he died in the charity ward of New York City's Presbyterian Hospital. He is buried in the Congressional Cemetery in Washington.[2]

1. Townsend, "Still Taking Pictures"; Paul Post, "Missing Historical Marker."

2. "Brady's Photographs; Pictures of the Dead at Antietam," *New York Times*, October 20, 1862.

BROWN, HOBART J. (1846–1918)
Active Essex, Essex County, 1867–1873

Born in Underhill, Vermont, Hobart Brown appeared in the 1860 US Census as a fourteen-year-old carpenter living in the residence of a local manufacturer. He served in the Civil War with the Eighth Vermont Infantry. By the late 1860s Brown was a portrait specialist in Essex; an early carte de visite imprint read H. J. Brown, Photographer, and Ambrotypist. Brown returned to Vermont around 1873 and moved to Newport, New Hampshire, circa 1878, where he produced stereoviews of "everything of interest in the vicinity of Newport, Lake Sunapee, and Unitoga Springs." By the mid-1890s he was in the city of Laconia. Local directories listed Brown at first as a photographer, but by 1901 as in the business of "second-hand furniture" and "auction."

BROWNELL, WILLIAM WALLACE (1847–1935)
Active Lake Placid, Essex County, 1894–1905

W. Wallace Brownell was born in Chesterfield, Clinton County, to immigrants from Vermont. His

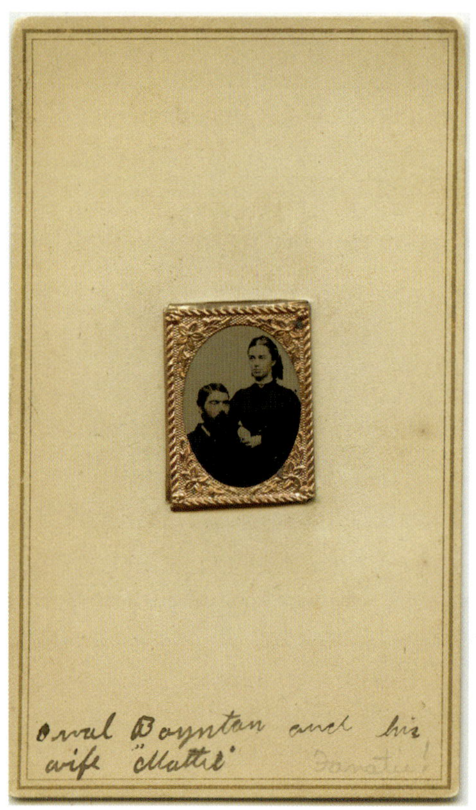

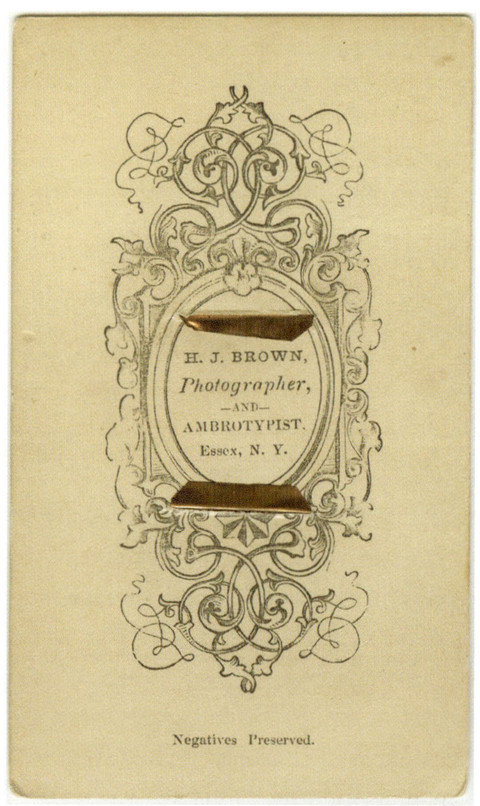

19. H. J. Brown, gem tintype, 3/4 x 1 inch, mounted on carte de visite, 1867–1873.

father was a house painter. How Brownell spent his early manhood is unclear, but by 1892 he was a mechanic in Lake Placid. A photograph dated September 1894 places him in a Lake Placid photographic partnership with a Mr. Fry, about whom nothing is known. (Fry was not a Lake Placid resident at the time of the New York state census of 1892 and may have had no more than a financial interest in the undertaking.) In July 1897 the *Plattsburgh Press* reported that Brownell had "moved his photographic gallery on to the lot belonging to Newell & Co., and has purchased the camp and tent which were occupied by Chas. Wood last summer. This gives him a large roomy gallery." He became a sole proprietor not long thereafter. The studio was seasonal; Brownell was noted in the 1900 US Census as having been unemployed for eight months during the previous year.[1]

In 1901 Brownell took on an associate, **Henry J. Kaiser**, who became his partner a year later and

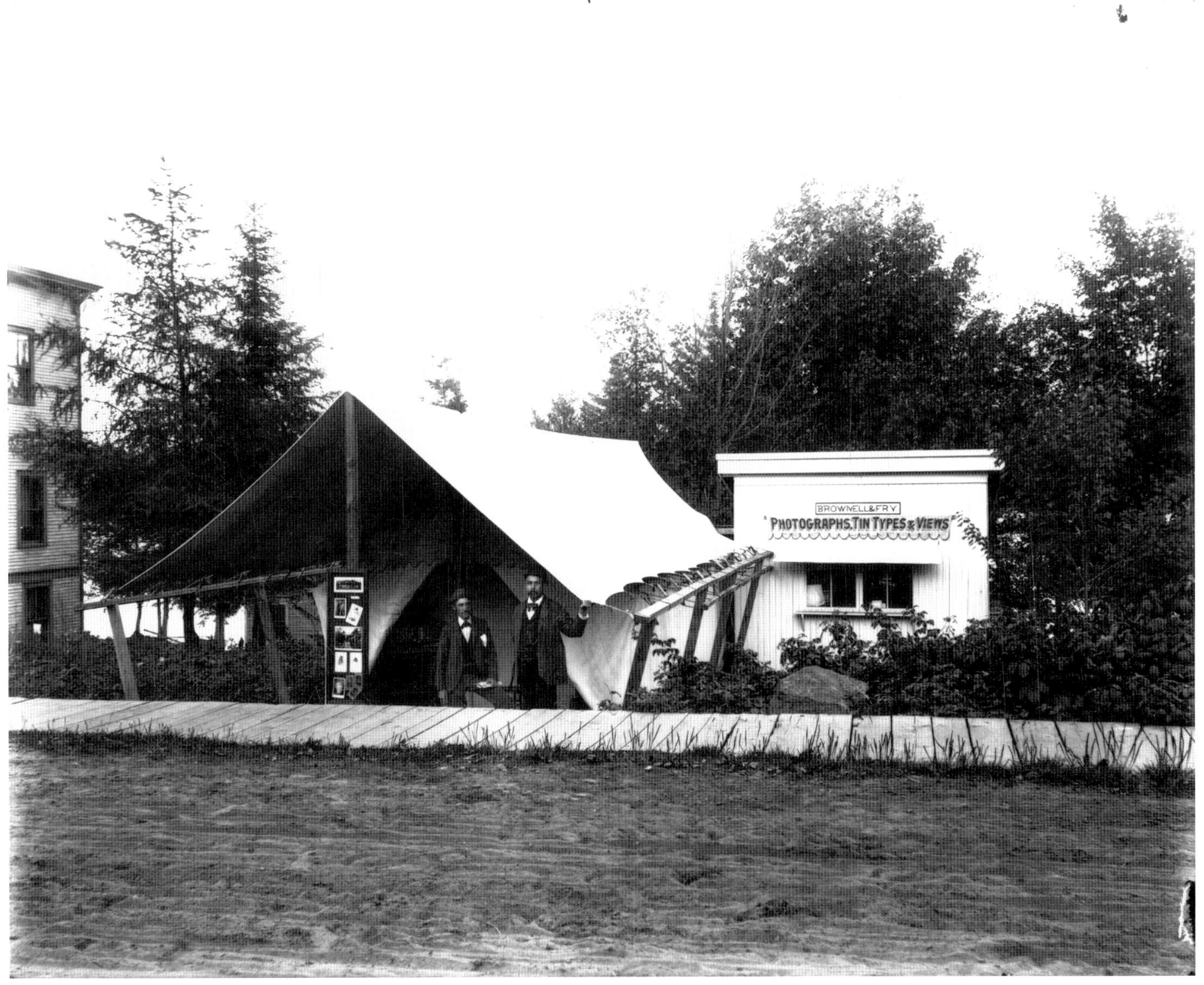

20. W. W. Brownell, Main Street, Lake Placid, premises of Brownell and Fry, 1897. Courtesy of Special Collections, Feinberg Library, SUNY College at Plattsburgh.

bought the business in late 1903. The New York state census of 1905 recorded Brownell as a Lake Placid photographer, but by 1910 he and his family had relocated to Oakland, California. There, according to census records and local directories, his occupations included house carpenter, clerk for the Pacific Gas and Electric Company, and mechanic during more than twenty-five years of residence.[2]

1. Adirondack Experience online database, image no. P000198; *Plattsburgh Press*, July 3, 1897; "Find Collection of Old Town Photo Plates of '90s," *Lake Placid News*, May 13, 1938.

2. *Elizabethtown Post*, October 15, 1903; October 22, 1903.

BRUSH, DANIEL SMITH (1863–1938)
Active Elizabethtown, Essex County, 1888–Late 1890s; Plattsburgh, Clinton County, 1912–1925

Except for a brief period during his childhood when his father tried farming in Macon, Missouri, Daniel (Dan) Brush grew up where he was born, in Elizabethtown. From 1882 through 1885, when he graduated from high school, he spent his summers as an apprentice to Crown Point photographer **Elbert M. Johnson**. (Brush "now has his tent pitched at Long Lake," it was announced in August 1884.) After teaching at a country school during the 1885–86 school year in the town of Lewis, in the fall of 1886 Brush enrolled at Madison (later Colgate) University in Hamilton, New York. He spent the summer of 1887 in Chestertown, Warren County, with photographer **J. F. Holley**, and left university in the spring of 1888 to set himself up as a photographer in his hometown. "Although Mr. Brush is still a young man he is, nevertheless well prepared to do the work he has undertaken," the *Elizabethtown Post* reported in May. "He was "brought up among us and we feel an interest in him. We point with pride to his record as a citizen and wish him success in his business." Brush's specialties were portraits and "inside and outside views to order." He also offered copying, enlarging, and frames.[1]

By early 1889 Brush had erected a building to serve as a photographic gallery on his father's farm outside of Elizabethtown, but much of his business through the mid-1890s derived from summer tenting tours in Essex County: to Essex, Keene, Keene Valley, Lewis, Ticonderoga, Wadhams Mills, Westport. He also ventured into Hamilton County and across Lake Champlain to Vermont, where he transported his equipment to the State Fair in Burlington for a week in September 1888. During winters, he was often elsewhere: in 1892 he worked for several months in the studio of Charles F. Tupper in Binghamton, Broome County, and in 1893 began to "aid" Rutland, Vermont, photographer George H. Emery, with whom he continued until about 1899. Brush still called Elizabethtown home during these years, and photographs taken from his Elizabethtown base bore his imprint. The death in 1895 of his twenty-three-year-old wife, Alice Sabattis (daughter of Long Lake, Hamilton County, Native American guide Mitchel Sabattis), two years after their marriage from tuberculosis left Brush with an eleven-month-old son who would be his only child. He remarried in Rutland in 1896.[2]

By 1900 Brush had settled in Vermont and opened a Rutland studio. He sold this in 1904 to Adirondack photographer **George W. Baldwin** and moved back across Lake Champlain to Plattsburgh, where he was employed in the studio of **George T. Woodward** before purchasing the business in 1912. He sometimes augmented his income with a satellite undertaking at Plattsburgh's Cliff Haven summer school. Brush retired circa 1925. He is buried beside his first wife in Elizabethtown.[3]

1. *Elizabethtown Post*, August 9, 1884; December 8, 1887; May 3, 1888; April 19, 1894; September 6, 1900.

2. *Elizabethtown Post*, January 17, 1889; April 6, 1893; April 19, 1894; "Daniel S. Brush Dies Suddenly; Photographer," *Plattsburgh Republican*, November 23, 1938.

3. *Elizabethtown Post*, July 4, 1904; May 9, 1912.

BUTTOLPH, SEYMOUR ERASTUS (1819–1901)
Active Malone, Franklin County, 1854–1865

Seymour Buttolph's father was a Connecticut migrant who became a Potsdam, St. Lawrence County, millwright and proprietor of the town's first hotel. Born in Potsdam, the younger Buttolph took to the road in the early 1850s in a "travelling daguerreotype car," working a territory from Potsdam to Brockton, Chautauqua County. In 1854 he convinced maternal cousin Eugene K. Hough to "oblige" him by accepting his wheeled vehicle in exchange for Hough's daguerreotype studio in Malone, which he named Buttolph's National Gallery.[1]

During the Civil War Buttolph formed a partnership, Buttolph & Fay, with Malone ambrotypist **Christopher R. Fay**. The two men shadowed the Army of the Potomac, taking portraits of soldiers to be sent home to their families and friends. In 1865 Buttolph sold the National Gallery to Fay and William H. Barney before taking up farming.[2]

1. Stiles, *History of Ancient Wethersfield, Connecticut*, 196; Dilley, *Biographical and Portrait Cyclopedia of Chautauqua County*, 228; *Malone Palladium*, February 9, 1865.

2. *Malone Palladium*, May 11, 1865; "Seymour E. Buttolph," March 7, 1901.

CARPENTER, JAMES H. (1832–1904)
Active Warrensburg, Warren County, and Lake George Region, Mid-1860s–1871

Vermont-born James Carpenter worked as a carpenter and builder as a young man, and, for one year, had charge of a steamboat on Lake Michigan. He appeared as a Saratoga, Saratoga County, merchant in the New York state census of 1865 and a Warrensburg "photographist" in an 1870 state business directory. At some point during the mid-1860s he partnered with novice photographer **Seneca Ray Stoddard** to produce a small group of Lake George stereoviews bearing the imprint CARPENTER & STODDARD.[1]

Carpenter sold his Warrensburg photography business to **James Fuller** around 1871. In 1872 he acquired the Caldwell House in Caldwell, renaming it Carpenter's Hotel (also referred to as Carpenter House). He sometimes ran the hotel himself, sometimes leased it to others, and owned it at his death. Carpenter held the Caldwell offices of town clerk and assessor; the Lake George Fire Company was originally named the James H. Carpenter Hose Company.[2]

1. Smith, *History of Warren County*, 655.

2. *Warrensburgh News*, January 22, 1925; French, "History of the Adirondacks in 3-D"; Smith, *History of Warren County*, 569, 655; *Journal of the Senate of the State of New York* (1903): 85; "Hotel Man Dead," *Glens Falls Times*, June 2, 1904; *Warrensburg–Lake George News*, July 21, 1977.

CARPENTER, WARWICK S. (1881–1966)
Active throughout the Adirondacks, 1907–1921

Born in Hoosick Falls, Rensselaer County, Warwick Carpenter was a writer, a publicist, and an accomplished outdoor photographer. A non-graduating member of Columbia University's class of 1904, he became a journalist, and by 1907 was both the manager of the National Publications Bureau of New York and writing and editing for *Industrial Magazine*. Settling by 1910 outside of Bennington, Vermont, Carpenter began to contribute articles illustrated with his own photographs (often of the Adirondacks) to magazines devoted to open-air pastimes and the sporting life, such as *Outing* and *Field and Stream*. He also served, from January 1910 through April 1911, as managing editor of the National Tuberculosis Association's *Journal of Outdoor Life*, first published from Saranac Lake, Essex and Franklin Counties. In May 1911 Carpenter accepted a position as head of the Publicity Bureau in the office of Vermont's secretary of state, with responsibility for luring "dwellers in the crowded communities of other States" to visit, even locate permanently in, Vermont. He authored two books: *Winter Camping* (1913) and *The*

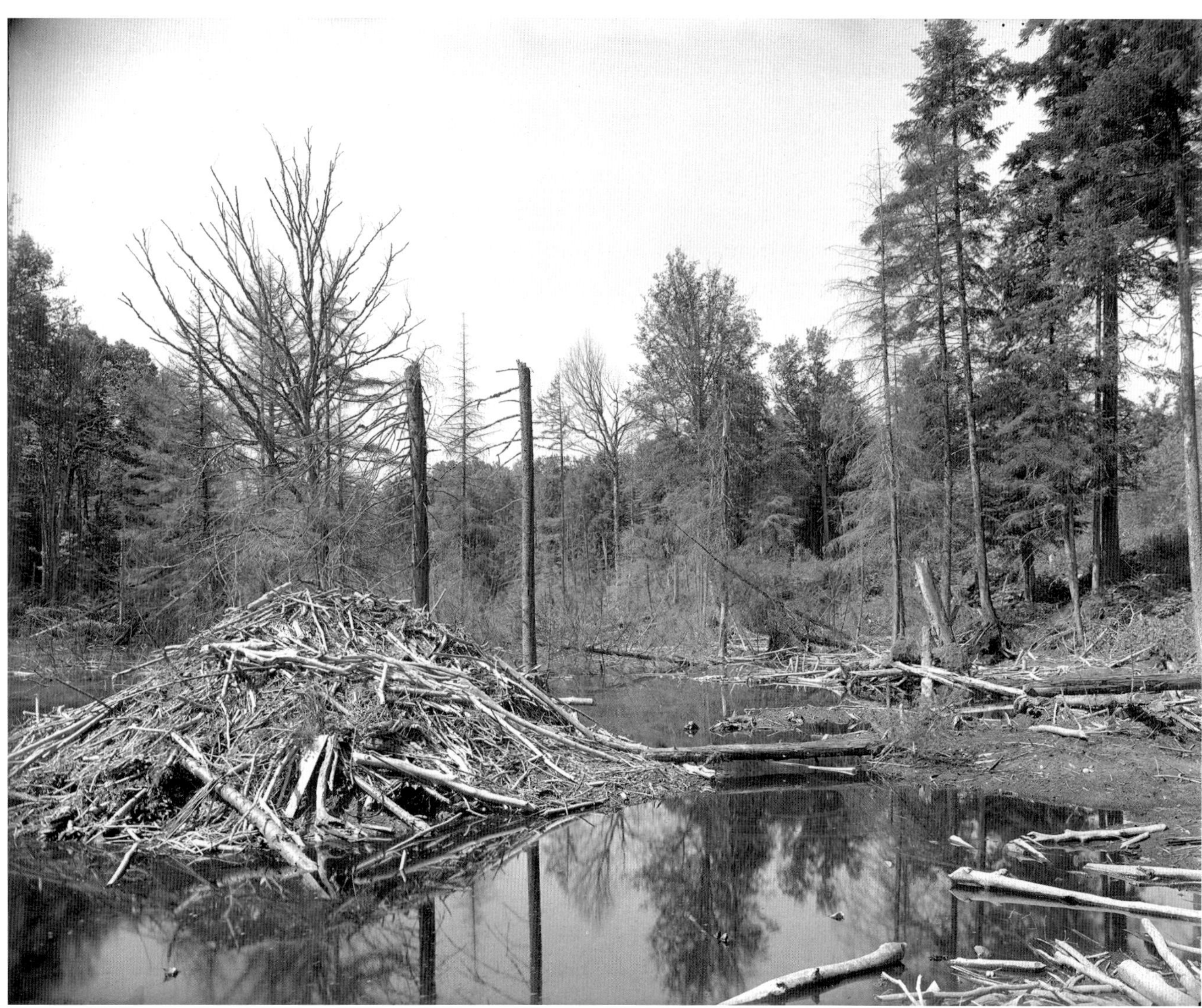

21. W. S. Carpenter, beaver dam on Indian Brook, Fourth Lake, Webb, Herkimer County, 1919. Courtesy of New York State Archives and New York State Conservation Department.

Summer Paradise in History (1914). In the final of four articles on photography he wrote in 1914–15 for *Outing* magazine, Carpenter made use of his own Adirondack images to demonstrate ways in which to improve photographic quality during the printing process.[1]

As a Vermont resident, Carpenter was active in conservation efforts. This background led to his appointment in 1915 as secretary of the New York State Conservation Commission under George D. Pratt, who was looking for "a man who could properly make public the aims and objects of the department." Carpenter made many films and still photographs for the department during his tenure. His employment with the commission ended in 1921, when his relentless exposure of what he thought to be sweetheart deals enabling illegal New York lumber-cutting led to his firing by Commissioner Pratt and Pratt's forced resignation shortly thereafter.[2]

Carpenter moved his family to California in 1922, where he became a business economist and analyst. Settling in Santa Barbara, he undertook marketing studies for a variety of business categories, from hotels to funeral services; was director of marketing in the West for *Sales Management* magazine; and in 1950 was honored for his "leadership in marketing" by the Southern California chapter of the American Marketing Association. Semi-retired after 1960, Carpenter died in Santa Barbara.[3]

1. *Industrial Magazine* 7 (1907); *Bennington (VT) Banner*, May 4, 1907; "The Publicity Campaign," *Burlington (VT) Weekly Free Press*, May 18, 1911; Carpenter, "The Fine Art of Printing."

2. "Vermont Should Conserve Own Water Power," *Bennington (VT) Banner*, January 13, 1913; "W. S. Carpenter Appointed," June 26, 1915; Ellen Apperson Brown, "ADK's Dramatic Beginning," 30.

3. "Warwick S. Carpenter," *Bennington (VT) Banner*, May 9, 1966.

CARTER, GEORGE. W. (1848–1928)
Active Western Adirondacks, 1866

George Carter was born in Seneca Falls, Seneca County. His father was a stonemason. Growing up in Lowville, Lewis County, he studied photography as a student of Lowville photographer **Elisha M. Van Aken**, who, impressed by his work, sent several of his stereoviews "of wild and lovely scenery around and about Lowville" to the *Philadelphia Photographer* for review in early 1867. These would have been from Carter's only known stereograph series, *"No. 4" Scenery: John Brown's Tract*, of the upper Beaver River valley in northern Herkimer County.[1]

Primarily a portrait photographer, Carter relocated briefly to Utica, Oneida County, around 1871, but returned to Lowville some four years later and purchased the Van Aken Gallery. He maintained his studio in the same second-story quarters above a store for more than fifty years.[2]

1. *Philadelphia Photographer* 4, no. 38 (February 1867): 64.

2. "Fiftieth Wedding Anniversary," *Lowville Journal and Republican and Lowville Times*, November 30, 1922; "George W. Carter," August 9, 1928.

CHANDLER, WILLIAM D. (1853–1941)
Active Loon Lake, Franklin County, 1880s

William Chandler was recorded in the 1880 US Census as a St. Albans, Vermont, photographer. An entry for him in an 1889 volume on Vermont noted that, in addition to his "portraits and views of all points of interest about St. Albans," Chandler had "a large number of negatives of Adirondack, Green Mountain, and White Mountain scenery." His only known Adirondack photographs were of summer life as he captured it at the seasonal Loon Lake Hotel during its heyday in the mid-1880s.[1]

According to the 1930 US Census, Chandler was still following the occupation of photography in his St. Albans studio at the age of seventy-eight.

1. *Vermont: Its Resources and Industries*, 133.

CHEESMAN, WILLIAM F. (1871–1931); EARLY SPELLING "CHEESEMAN"
Active Au Sable Forks, Clinton and Essex Counties, 1894–1902; Lake Placid, Essex County, 1899–1910

William Cheesman, born in Chazy, Clinton County, relocated to Au Sable Forks and opened a photograph gallery in 1894. An image from this period lists his occupation as "view artist." He remained in Au Sable Forks until 1902, but around 1896 began to spend summers working in the busy summer resort community of Lake Placid: perhaps at first for another photographer. By 1899 he was in his own Lake Placid studio. In 1901 the entrepreneur commissioned the construction of the substantial "Cheesman block" on Lake Placid's Main Street, housing ground-floor shops and apartments above. Moving his family to Lake Placid, Cheesman operated a shop in one of its retail spaces. As an advertisement for the business in the 1902–3 Adirondack directory read: "Photographer, Adirondack Views, Portraiture, Finest Finish. Souvenir Art Store. Kodaks and Cameras, Amateur Supplies,

Finishing in 24 Hours." Real photo postcards were attributed to "Cheesman's Kodak Dept."[1]

Photography became subsidiary to Cheesman's other interests as a Lake Placid businessman, real estate owner, and booster. Listed in the 1910 and 1920 US Censuses successively as "retail merchant, stationery," and "merchant, art shop," Cheesman retired in the mid-1920s and began to winter in Orlando, Florida.

1. *Plattsburgh Sentinel*, December 21, 1894; January 24, 1902; "Ausable Forks News," *Plattsburgh Press*, June 12, 1899; *Ticonderoga Sentinel*, October 1, 1896; May 23, 1901; *Lake Placid News*, June 6, 1924; August 16, 1940.

CHURCH, ARTEMUS MAYNARD (1852–1934)
Active Fulton Chain of Lakes, Hamilton and Herkimer Counties, 1880s–1910

Artemus (Artie) Church, born in Morristown, St. Lawrence County, was the son of another Artemus M. Church, a carpenter. A Lyonsdale, Lewis County, laborer at the time of the New York state census of 1875, in 1879 he built the first camp on Seventh Lake in Inlet, Hamilton County.[1]

A resident from 1884 of Boonville, Lewis County, for thirty-five years Church was a taxidermist during the winter months and a wilderness guide from spring through fall. He was employed by the same hunting and fishing parties year after year, guiding one client for thirty consecutive years. He took up photography to complement his guiding activities, and "his duffel seldom failed to include a huge box-like apparatus and tripod with a goodly supply of 5 x 8 plates." As one reporter noted, "His pictures of wild animals, no doubt helped develop his technique as a taxidermist." Church mounted and sold his prints, among them an 1891 *Adirondack Views* series, from the satellite taxidermy lab and photography shop he maintained in Old Forge, Herkimer County, into the 1920s. He also issued the occasional pre-1907 photo postcard. An "able writer," cartographer, and secretary and treasurer of the Brown's Tract Guides' Association for twelve consecutive years, Church was affectionately remembered for his "insistent and intelligent advocacy of conservation and good sportsmanship in relation to the Adirondacks."[2]

1. Grady, *The Adirondacks*, 263.

2. "Adirondack Guide, Taxidermist, Dies," *Utica Press*, January 8, 1934; "Artemus M. Church," *Rome Daily Sentinel*, January 8, 1934; Grady, *The Adirondacks*, 263.

CHURCH, DWIGHT P. (1891–1974)
Active Western Adirondacks from 1910; throughout the Adirondacks, 1930–1970

Nicknamed "Dippy" (a name derived from his initials, D. P., and perhaps his eccentricity), Dwight Church spent his working life in the town of Canton, St. Lawrence County, not far from the farm on which he grew up. He dropped out of high school at seventeen and, self-taught as a photographer, began a career behind a camera. Scouring the countryside on a motorcycle, he sold the results of his early picture-taking efforts to the owners of the farms and businesses he photographed—a working model he would follow for some fifty years.[1]

In 1929 Church qualified for a pilot's license. From then on, he "zoomed from one end of this section to the other, like a bird, taking 'shots' of every conceivable spot which was picturesque." He logged over two thousand hours and seventy-five thousand miles in the air in pursuit of what he called "skyviews" of the Adirondacks and St. Lawrence Valley, shooting photographs through a hole cut in the floor of his plane, a porthole next to the fuselage, or an open door.[2]

Most of Church's business was in real photo postcards. Besides "skyviews," his primary subjects were unpeopled ground-level town- and landscapes and individual buildings. At first he called his business the Photo Park Company or the "$5.00 Bill" Photo Company, but shortened the name in the late 1920s to the $5-Photo-Co. Later cards were printed on glossy white stock showing

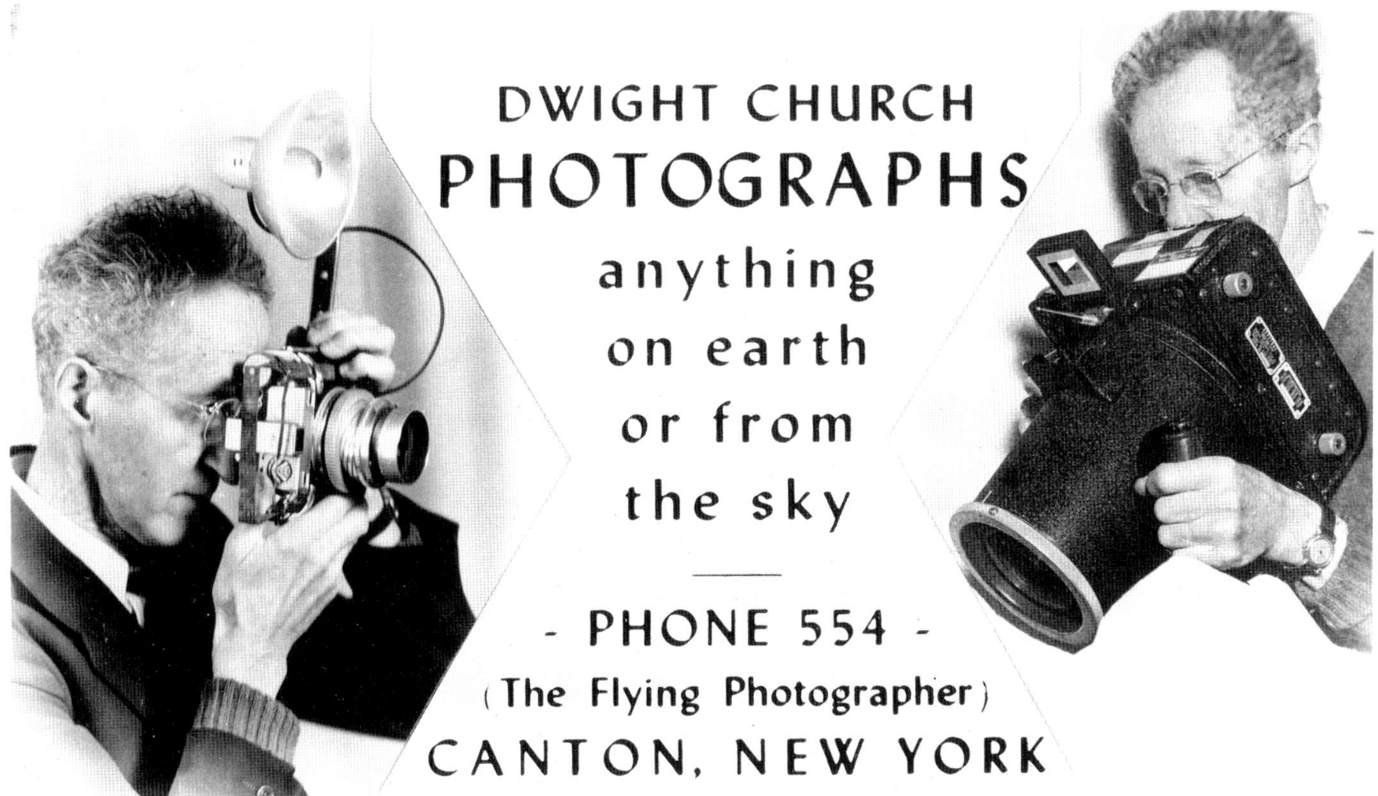

22. D. P. Church, advertising postcard, 1930–1940. Courtesy of the St. Lawrence Historical Association.

deep contrast, with subjects identified by typed titles printed on celluloid and taped to negatives to show as white on finished stock. Church was an early mail-order film processor for amateurs and maintained a traditional portraiture operation for at least twenty-five years. A 1937 journal advertisement made a "special suggestion" to would-be portrait patrons in the truncated spelling of which he was fond: "If u have not had a good photograph of yourself for five years let us make several negatives and proofs now while u r alive. U need not place any order, but in the case of death friends and relatives can have pictures finished off. Scarcely a day goes by that someone does not bring in a faded print or very old photograph of someone who has died and want us to copy and enlarge it."[3]

Church advertised a charter flying service as a sideline, offering local as well as long-distance flights: to California, New Orleans, New York City for the 1939 World's Fair. According to Clarence Petty, aviator and ardent conservationist, Church "had a frontier mentality. He was an individualist, self-reliant, kind of a do-it-yourselfer. He wanted to do things his own way. He wasn't willing to abide by too many regulations." By World War II, Church's real photo views were the most commonly found postcards on store racks throughout much of the Adirondack region. He left behind more than thirteen thousand images—an impressive pictorial record of northern New York at mid-twentieth century.[4]

1. Bailey, "Dwight Church," 5, 8; Burdick, "A Wing and a Prayer," 55.

2. Burdick, "A Wing and a Prayer," 55.

3. Bailey, "Dwight Church," 11–12, 20, 22, 26; *Canton Commercial Advertiser*, November 30, 1937.

4. Bailey, "Dwight Church," 35–36; Burdick, "A Wing and a Prayer," 55, 56.

CLEVELAND, GROVER JESSE (1887–1975)
Active Lake Placid, Essex County, 1924–1959

One of hundreds of children named in honor of the American president during his two terms of office, Grover Cleveland was born in Oneida, Madison County, the son of a carpenter. At the age of seventeen he began work as a photographer at the Varney-Gordon Photo Company in Syracuse and held a variety of jobs over the next thirteen years: with Eastman Kodak, Remington Typewriter, the Syracuse Portrait Company, Western Electric, Bell Telephone, and Smith Typewriter. He also worked as a news photographer for the *Syracuse Post-Standard* and a freelance photographer for two other newspapers. In the summer of 1910 Cleveland was a photographer in the Webb, Herkimer County, hamlet of Big Moose.[1]

A bout with tuberculosis led to Cleveland's spending several months from November 1915 as a patient at the Ray Brook State Hospital, located between Lake Placid and Saranac Lake, Essex and Franklin Counties. Following a brief visit home, he relocated to Lake Placid in June 1916 to work in the Main Street photography studio of **Irving Lynn Stedman**. Cleveland was one of Essex County's first draftees after the United States entered World War I, and served overseas with the 302nd Field Artillery. Discharged in 1919, he returned to Lake Placid to work for former Stedman employee **George T. Rabineau** before going into business for himself in 1924. Cleveland and his family occupied the same Main Street apartment overlooking Mirror Lake for fifty-five years.[2]

Primarily a landscape photographer, Cleveland made a specialty of postcard views. A photo-printing machine enabled him to control light so as to produce prominent cloud effects in his finished work, and he printed titles on his own printing press. Related income streams included photographing newsworthy local events, among them the 1932 Winter Olympics, and work as a "master photo finisher." Lake Placid's importance as a resort town and its Olympic prominence gave Cleveland the opportunity to photograph a number of visiting and resident dignitaries over the years: Presidents Calvin Coolidge and Franklin Roosevelt, ice skater Sonja Henie, actor Efrem Zimbalist Jr., and singer Kate Smith. Cleveland retired in 1959.[3]

1. Unpublished Cleveland biography in office of North Elba/Lake Placid historian; "Yesteryears," *Lake Placid News*, January 29, 1976.

2. Unpublished biography; *Au Sable Forks–Adirondack Record*, July 27, 1917; Obituary, *Adirondack Enterprise*, December 23, 1975; Flynn, "North Country at Work"; "Yesteryears," *Lake Placid News*, January 29, 1976.

3. Unpublished biography; *Lake Placid News*, May 18, 1928; "Yesteryears," *Lake Placid News*, January 29, 1976.

COLVIN, VERPLANCK (1847–1920)
Documented with a Camera the Topographical Surveys He Conducted for New York State, Early 1880s–1899

Born in Albany, Albany County, to comfortably well-to-do parents, Verplanck Colvin took up the study of law at Colvin & Bingham, his father's law office, at the age of seventeen. But his interests, he discovered, did not lie in the law. In 1869 he wrote an article for a popular national magazine about an outing in the Helderberg Mountains south of Albany that indicated not only an easy literary style but also wide knowledge of natural and scientific subjects. The piece was illustrated with wood engravings from his own delicate pencil and India ink drawings: of scenery, fossils, a hibernating bat.[1]

In 1871 Colvin left his father's law office. Having originated a plan for an Adirondack park in an 1870 report to the regents of the University of New York, he pursued the idea of undertaking an accurate topographic and geological survey of the Adirondack region. Possessing a moderate independent income, Colvin was prepared to launch the survey at his own expense, but on the advice of others approached the state legislature for assistance. He was successful in his petition. In 1872 Colvin was appointed to the position of superintendent of

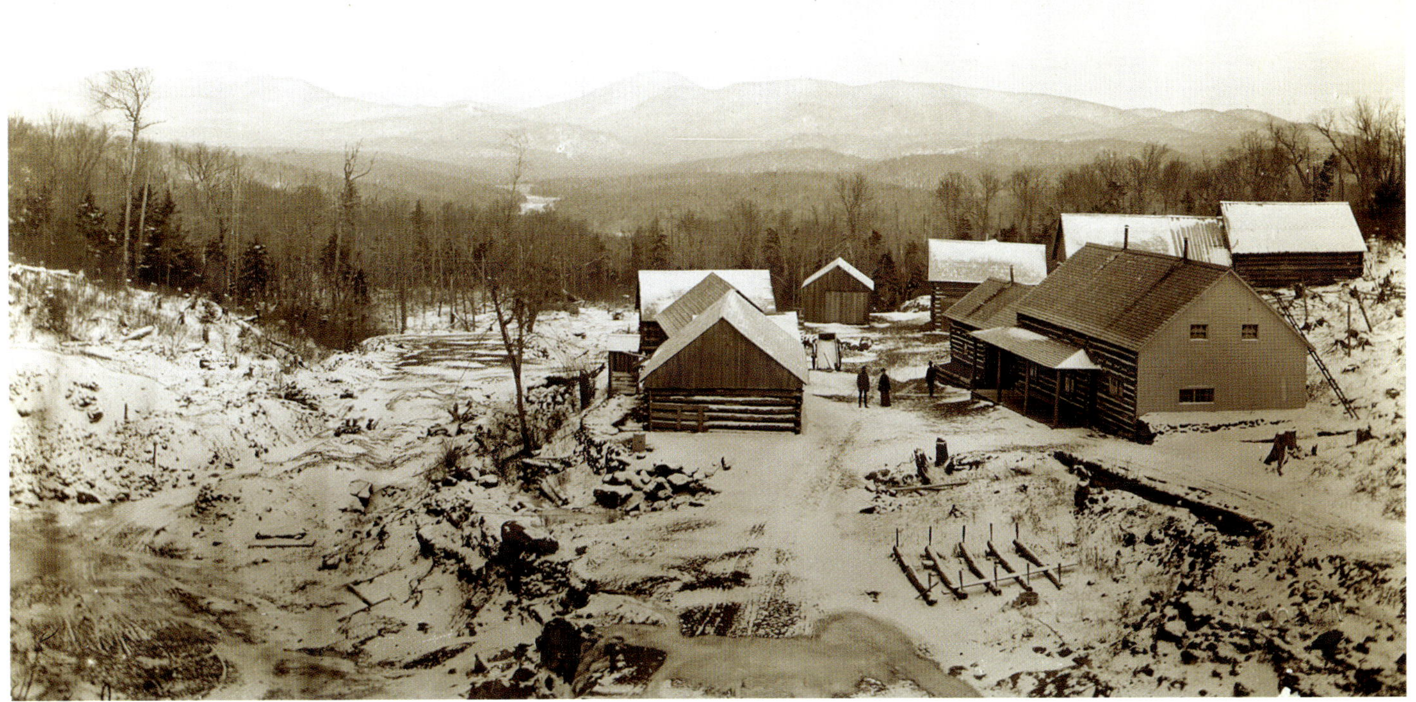

23. V. Colvin, Barton Garnet Mine buildings, Puffer Mountain, Bullhead Mountain, and Sabael Range, 1895. Courtesy of Adirondack Experience.

what was to be called the Adirondack Survey and provided with a first-year appropriation to "aid in the completion of a survey of the Adirondack wilderness of New York, and a map thereof . . ." The job was one that would consume him, despite shifting politics and sometimes with minimal legislative support, for twenty-eight years. Colvin was the first person to accurately ascertain the height of Mount Marcy, the highest mountain in New York State, and to determine the exact position and elevation of the pond source of the Hudson River, which he named Lake Tear of the Clouds.[2]

The written reports of survey progress, prepared for the state legislature at irregular intervals, are considered a uniquely valuable contribution to Adirondack history. Colvin authored and produced the reports himself, enlivening early accounts with his drawings—considered by him "so important for reference" in serving as "a check and explanation in the transfer of the topography from the preliminary to the secondary reconnaissance maps." In his report on the survey work of 1873, Colvin included two wood engravings based on photographs. The original images, by **Elias Olcott Beaman**, an accomplished photographer working in the Adirondacks that summer, were taken on the summit of Blue Mountain, Hamilton County. It is evident that Colvin was unfamiliar with the medium of photography but recognized its potential as a working tool. "The value of good photographs of mountain ranges, etc., in a topographical survey, cannot be over-estimated," wrote the young superintendent in referencing one image, "and I would suggest that, in all further topographical surveys by the State, provision be made for the employment of a skillful operator, one who, like the gentleman referred to [Beaman], has the skill and courage to climb to the top of a lofty spruce tree, and take an 'instantaneous' photograph, with aid of one hand, while hanging to the tree with the other." Had such a record keeper been on hand during the survey's first season, he added, it would have relieved him "of a vast amount of labor" in sketching survey activity. Colvin appreciated photography's power to capture detail, noting of the wood engraving from one Beaman image that it "fails to show the intricate mass of limbs and tree trunks, of felled timber, which, in the photograph, and on the mountain, give an appearance of its having been swept by cannon—a storm of shot and shell . . ."[3]

In 1878, having that year received an unusually generous financial allocation from the state legislature, the survey team included a photographic division headed by **Seneca Ray Stoddard**. More than two hundred photographs were taken to Colvin's explicit directives, among them 360-degree panoramic view compilations from mountaintops and other key locations as "checks upon the work of the topographers in the different parties." The camera used "was provided with compass, and with bubbles for levelling it. Each negative contains an angle of thirty degrees of arc, so that twelve plates afford a circle at any given station."[4]

Colvin began to experiment with photography himself, noting in 1883 that he carried a camera with him on the job "for the purpose of securing views to illustrate the character of the region surveyed." His images appeared often in subsequent reports. Some captured long-distance views and highlighted the mountains serving as backdrop. Others featured survey crews at work and at rest. Occasionally Colvin provided written details to augment report images. Of a photograph titled *Camp in the Snow* in the narrative of the 1895 survey, Colvin reported: The site "was most picturesque . . . The ruins of the old lumber shanty, against which they had reared the fly of their tents as a protection against the storm, the rude out-door camp, with a stone fire-place, where the campfire blazed and roared regardless of the snow, made a wild, picturesque camp scene, which the men, well-accustomed to outdoor life, thoroughly enjoyed. Partaking of a few morsels, I secured a photograph of the camp and, saying goodbye, set out . . ."[5]

Colvin pursued his Adirondack Survey—and the State Land Survey (of which he became superintendent in 1883)—until 1900, when Governor Theodore Roosevelt abolished his position. At the age of fifty-three he found himself at loose ends. In the following years he endured bouts of depression, and in the winter of 1916–17 suffered a concussion as the result of falling on ice from which he never recovered. Diagnosed as a "lunatic" in early 1919, Colvin spent more than a year as a mental patient in the Marshall Infirmary, Troy, before his death the following year. Colvin is warmly remembered in the Adirondacks thanks to his longtime passion for the region and its environment as well as his effective advocacy for its preservation.[6]

1. Webb, *Footsteps through the Adirondacks*, 5–6, 14, 11, 18; Colvin, "The Helderbergs," 652–67.

2. Webb, *Footsteps through the Adirondacks*, 33, 34–35; Leonard, *Who's Who In New York City and State*, s.v. "Colvin, Verplanck," 314.

3. New York State, *Report on the Topographical Survey . . . for the Year 1873*, plates 8 and 9 (opposite pages 45 and 46), 169.

4. New York State, *Seventh Annual Report on the Progress of the Topographical Survey . . . to the Year 1879*, 40, 60–61, 353.

5. New York State, *Report on the Adirondack and State Land Surveys to the Year 1884*, 14; New York State, *Report of the Superintendent of the State Land Survey*, 1896, plate 27, 133.

6. Webb, *Footsteps through the Adirondacks*, 147, 149, 157, 159.

COMMO, LEO A. (1898–1968)
Active Saranac Lake, Essex and Franklin Counties, 1919–1968

Born in Saranac Lake, Leo Commo grew up in the village, save for the few years surrounding 1905 when his plumber father moved the family to Plattsburgh, Clinton County. After briefly serving in the US Navy at the close of World War I, he returned to Saranac Lake and opened a photographic studio in partnership with local baker's son Bernard Carlin as the C. C. Shop or C. C. Studio (Carlin & Commo). Carlin returned to the family bakery business by 1930; Commo retained the studio and its name. He specialized in portraits, especially of children, and was known for his First Communion group photographs. The studio published the occasional postcard and at various periods made keys and sold musical instruments. A brother, Medore, briefly ran a Plattsburgh branch of the studio in the mid-1920s. Commo's second wife, Roma, and son-in-law, Michael Harrigan, carried on the business for a short time after his death.[1]

Commo's most widely circulated image was a portrait of Noah Rondeau, an eccentric who spent thirty-three years living in the isolated Adirondack wilderness at Cold River Flow, some twelve miles south of Saranac Lake. Rondeau turned his social reclusion into a commercial asset, traveling for several years from 1947 on to New York and other big-city sportsmen's shows with Adirondack exhibitors. Replicas of his crude cabin were generally on display, and he sold copies of the Commo photograph autographed by the "Adirondack Hermit."[2]

1. *Adirondack Enterprise*, April 17, 1968; Finn, "Behind the Lens"; Photographers' File, Adirondack Research Room, Saranac Lake Free Library; *Adirondack Record–Elizabethtown Post*, April 22, 1937.

2. *Adirondack Enterprise*, August 25, 1967.

CONE, LELAND DEFOREST (1867–1956)
Active Ticonderoga, Essex County, 1902–1911

DeForest Cone grew up in the farming community of Peru, Massachusetts, not far from the New York State border. Between 1885 and the late 1890s he worked at a variety of paper companies around nearby Springfield before pursuing a course of study at the Illinois College of Photography in 1899, one of the first schools of its kind in the country. In September 1902 he opened a portrait studio in Ticonderoga. The "artist photographer" announced a year later that he had on his "books a total of over 1400 negatives made, proving that my earnest application and careful methods are not un-appreciated." By 1908 Cone was advertising "over 150 styles to choose from."[1]

Cone demonstrated a marketing flair unusual in the brotherhood of small-town Adirondack photographers. Others might use the same wording in their newspaper advertisements for years, but his ads were often changed and often refreshing, featuring short, catchy, bold-print captions and unpredictable texts. The headline "I'll Be There Mary Dear" signified that patrons had debated the merits of other studios and chosen his; "Here's A Hummer" promoted a new card mount.[2]

As official photographer for the Ticonderoga Historical Society, organized in 1897, Cone created an "artistic pictorial souvenir" of the town in 1909. In 1910 and 1911 he occasionally leased the Crown Point, Essex County, studio of **Elbert M. Johnson** for portrait sessions. He quit Ticonderoga in late 1911 and in January 1912 took possession of a studio in Bennington, Vermont, where he became "one of the town's well known photographers." Giving up this studio circa 1926, Cone located briefly in Glens Falls, Warren County, and was recorded over the next several years as working for both the Obenaus Studio in Schenectady and the Troy Studio of Photography in Troy. By 1937, Cone was retired.[3]

1. *Ticonderoga Sentinel*, September 4, 1902; August 20, 1903; October 15, 1903; November 18, 1908.

2. *Ticonderoga Sentinel*, March 26, 1903; June 25, 1903.

3. *Ticonderoga Sentinel*, July 16, 1908; May 26, 1910; May 4, 1911; advertisement, *Travel Magazine*, October 1909, 494; *Bennington (VT) Evening Banner*, December 2, 1911; "L. DeForest Cone Dies at Age 88," *Bennington (VT) Evening Banner*, February 7, 1956.

CONKEY, GEORGE W. (1837–1910)
Active Glens Falls, Warren County, and Lake George Region, 1861–1895

Born in New York City, George Conkey received his photographic training from two city-based daguerreian artists: Silas A. Holmes and Charles D.

Fredricks. In 1859–60 he conducted a New York gallery in partnership with James M. Arnout as Conkey & Arnout before his marriage in 1860 to a girl from Albany, Albany County. Conkey relocated to Glens Falls the following year, opening rooms across from the post office and becoming Warren County's first photographer. He occasionally formed partnerships with other photographers: Crandell & Conkey with Isaac Crandell (1865–66); Conkey & Orr with **Alexander Orr Jr.** (late 1860s); Conkey & Hultz (1879–80); Conkey & Hibbard (1892–94). He operated in Fort Edward for several years before his retirement.[1]

Conkey identified his studio specialties as "babies, children and old people"; photographer and guidebook author **Seneca Ray Stoddard** referred to him in 1888 as "one of the best portrait-photographers in northern New York." He also advertised "stereoscopic and other views made to order" and captured many fine landscapes and group portraits in the Lake George region. In July 1882 Conkey announced that he was chartering a steamer and devoting "his time during the month of August to taking views of camping groups and all kinds of photographs at different points on the lake." In 1888 he maintained a "summer studio" on Fourteen Mile Island, a Lake George island owned by the Delaware and Hudson Railroad and fitted up for the accommodation of excursion parties with refreshment rooms, a bandstand, dancing pavilion, and swings. He berthed his own steam yacht, *Camera*, on Lake George for several years from 1890.[2]

Conkey's Adirondack stereographs included series devoted to two Lake George hotels (the Sagamore and Marion House) as well as several with broader content: *Scenes on Lake George*, *Stereoscopic Gems from Lake George*, and *Gems from Lake George and the Hudson*.

1. H. P. Smith, *History of Warren County*, 656, 658; Photographers' File, Chapman Historical Museum, Glens Falls, New York; *Glens Falls Morning Star*, October 9, 1896.

2. *Glens Falls Times*, July 28, 1882; October 30, 1886; *Warrensburgh News*, May 1, 1890; April 21, 1910; S. R. Stoddard, *Lake George (Illustrated)*, 77; Adler, *Early Days in the Adirondacks*, 59.

CONLEY, WILLIAM A. (1859–1954)
Active St. Regis Falls, Franklin County, 1891–Early 1930s

William Conley was born in Columbia County; in the New York state census of 1875 he was recorded as living with his mother and stepfather on a farm in Burke, Franklin County. He became a St. Regis Falls photographer in 1891. "He is rather young and inexperienced," observed a local journalist, "but gives promise of making things lively for his only competitor in town." He would be the village's primary photographer for the next forty years.[1]

Conley's principal business was portraiture, in conjunction with which he made near-annual tenting tours in late August and September from 1891 through at least 1909 to county fairs in northeastern New York: Lowville, Lewis County; Gouverneur, St. Lawrence County; Malone, Franklin County. "He confines himself to tintypes on these trips which usually are quite remunerating ventures," it was reported. Conley undertook a few nonportrait commissions, among them the capture of "a picture of ten nice deer," and was noted by a journalist in February 1902 as having taken "some fine pictures of the snow banks and business places in different sections of the village. How cool and refreshing they will look next July." Conley's wife, Ada Belle Van Zandt, was the proprietress of a millinery establishment.[2]

1. *St. Regis Falls Adirondack News*, May 9, 1891.

2. *St. Regis Falls Adirondack News*, August 29, 1896; November 10, 1899; February 22, 1902; August 27, 1904; August 28, 1909.

COONROD, ARTHUR EMERY (1874–1961)
Active Elizabethtown, Essex County, 1901–1905

Born in Elizabethtown, Arthur Coonrod trained locally as a civil engineer, becoming a licensed land

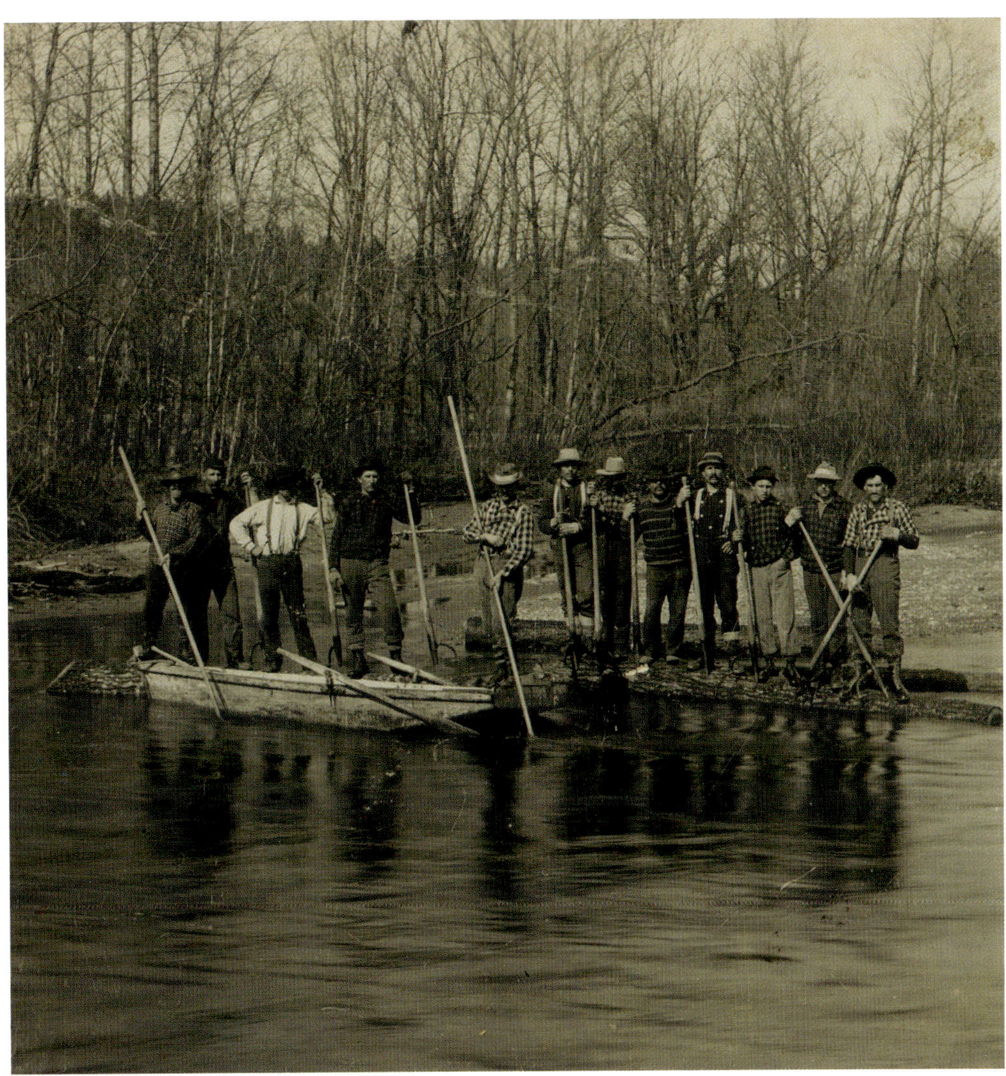

24. A. E. Coonrod, Frank Peterson's drive on the Boquet River. One-half stereoview, 1903.

surveyor. He used his amateur photographic skills in the execution of his occupation, and for a few years marketed photographs—inspired to do so, perhaps, by the enthusiastic response to his 1901 offer to "furnish copies to those desiring them" of his image of a full lumber wagon from which a wood engraving was created for use in the *Elizabethtown Post*. From 1902 through 1904 Coonrod systematically placed newspaper advertisements for his "Adirondack views, as well as photographs of all kinds," with "special attention given to Landscapes, Views and Interiors." In 1912 Coonrod became the superintendent of Calvin Pardee's private Hale Brook Park in Lewis, Essex County, a position he held for twenty-five years.[1]

1. *Elizabethtown Post*, April 30, 1896; "Frank Colby's Big Load of Spruce Logs," March 7, 1901; January 15, 1903; Obituary, *Adirondack Record–Elizabethtown Post*, January 19, 1961; Obituary, *Valley News*, January 20, 1961.

COPELAND, GEORGE TROWBRIDGE (1843–1916)
Active Fulton County, 1870s

Photography was an occupational sideline for George Copeland. A native of Edinburg, Saratoga County, he spent his early working years in his father's carriage shop and was identified as a seventeen-year-old Edinburg carriage maker in 1860, a wheelwright on his 1863 Civil War draft registration, a mechanic in 1865, and a cabinetmaker in 1870. Copeland moved his family to Brattleboro, Vermont, in 1873, where he spent a decade working for the Estey Organ Company. During these years he summered regularly at Canada Lake in Caroga, Fulton County, where he maintained a summer photographic studio and recorded resort life. He also photographed and sold several short stereoview series: *Canada Lake and Vicinity*, *Northville Camp-Ground*, *Gloversville*.[1]

Copeland returned from Vermont to the Adirondack region in 1883, settling in Gloversville. Directory and census records from 1888 forward list him as the proprietor of a repair shop, a mechanic, and a cabinetmaker. Sidelines now included selling wood and corn popping. In 1885 he received a patent for a long-legged corn popper and was awarded the corn-popping concession for the 1895 Gloversville County Fair.[2]

1. McMartin, *Caroga*, 57–63; "George Trowbridge Copeland," *Gloversville Herald*, October 21, 1916.

2. "George Trowbridge Copeland," *Gloversville Herald*, October 21, 1916; *Gloversville Leader*, August 14, 1895.

COWAN, WILLIAM MICHAEL ANGELO (1865–1952); ALTERNATIVE SPELLING "COWEN"

Active Willsboro, Essex County, 1896–1897; Ticonderoga, Essex County, 1898–1905; Chestertown and Warrensburg, Warren County, 1905–1911; Essex, Essex County, 1935–1948; Westport, Essex County, 1948–1950

William Cowan was an unusually peripatetic photographer during his nearly sixty-five years in the business. Born in Monckton, Vermont, he moved at the age of five with his family to Essex, where his father was a marble worker and headstone salesman. He apprenticed with Port Henry photographer **Elbert M. Johnson** before establishing a photographic studio in Vergennes, Vermont, in 1893. In 1896 he returned to Essex County and opened an "art store" and photographic "gallery" in Willsboro, where, a journalist noted, Cowan had "the honor of being the first artist ever settling . . . We hope he will do well." Cowan left Willsboro less than a year later, briefly returned to Vermont, and then established himself in 1898 as successor to retiring photographer **Lavius H. Fillmore** in Ticonderoga, Essex County.[1]

Cowan promoted himself as specializing in "View Work, out-door groups, etc. Fine interior views of your home." According to one early advertisement: "I make a specialty of taking Babies photographs, am never cross to little folks. Look pleasant please." He toured with a tent during the summers, primarily around Essex and Warren Counties. Despite clever advertising and innovations (adding a line of "photo jewelry" to his retail mix), Cowan struggled in Ticonderoga. "I need money and urgently request all owing me or having photos or crayons uncalled for to attend to the matter at once," cautioned one 1901 advertisement. He threatened to "sell out and establish [him] self in business elsewhere" in 1902, and did so in 1905, relocating to Warren County. There Cowan opened studios, and may have lived in, both Chestertown and Warrensburg, for both communities later claimed him as a former resident.[2]

In 1911 Cowan moved again, this time to Hudson Falls, Washington County. In 1912 he returned to Warren County, opening a studio in Glens Falls, where, according to the local newspaper, "a good business is predicted for this hustling picture man." He operated there for a year only, and by 1916 had returned to Hudson Falls. He was back in Glens Falls as proprietor of the Cowan Studio between approximately 1921 and 1930, then moved to Troy, Rensselaer County, and ran a photographic business out of his home. In 1935 Cowan began to spend long summers in Essex, where he operated the "summer" Cowan Studio for some thirteen years before transferring it to the Grange Hall in nearby Westport in 1948.[3]

1. *Essex County Republican*, October 15, 1896; September 9, 1897; "Beauty of Life Seen after 61 Yrs. of Photography," *Lake Placid News*, August 2, 1946; *Ticonderoga Sentinel*, October 6, 1898; May 10, 1900.

2. *Ticonderoga Sentinel*, September 1, 1898; September 22, 1898. September 13, 1900; February 21, 1901; September 18, 1902; April 9, 1903; May 4, 1939; May 8, 1902; *Warrensburgh News*, September 21, 1905; April 21, 1910; January 16, 1919.

3. *Ticonderoga Sentinel*, September 7, 1911; *Glens Falls Post-Star*, February 19, 1912; "Dean of New York State Photographers," *Essex County Republican*, July 26, 1946.

CRANE, EDWIN N. (1865–1928)
Active Tupper Lake, Franklin County, 1896–1908

Edwin Crane acquired his photographic knowledge from older brother **Frederick M. Crane**, an Ogdensburg, St. Lawrence County, photographer. The Ogdensburg directory for 1882 documented seventeen-year-old Edwin and twenty-seven-year-old Fred as boarding together; the occupation of both was given as "photographer." The brothers continued to share an Ogdensburg studio into the mid-1890s. Sometime in 1896, or shortly thereafter, Crane relocated to Tupper Lake, a logging community then experiencing rapid growth as a junction point for two railway lines. Billing himself as a "portrait and landscape photographer," he was on hand in July 1899 to record the aftermath of a conflagration that purportedly destroyed 169 Tupper Lake buildings.[1]

In May 1908 Crane was reported to be leaving Tupper Lake "in a few days for Pennsylvania where he will be in business during the summer. He expects to make his home in Texas winters. Mr. Crane understands his business thoroughly, and will undoubtedly be a success wherever he goes." Whether Crane made it to Texas or not is unknown, but he disappeared from northern New York records until 1920, when he was documented in the US Census as single, following no occupation, and living in Ogdensburg with a sister. The 1925 Ogdensburg directory identified Crane as a commercial traveler.[2]

1. *Tupper Lake Herald*, November 24, 1899.

2. *Tupper Lake Herald*, May 8, 1908.

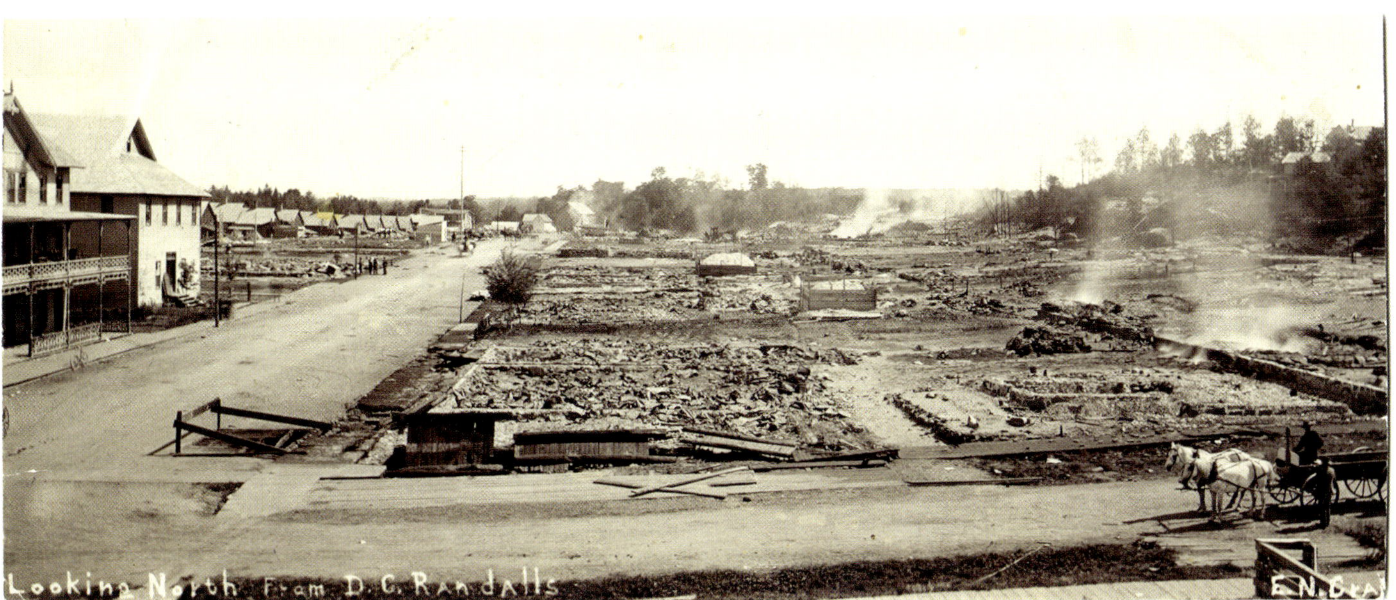

25. E. N. Crane, *Looking North from D. C. Randalls* after Tupper Lake fire, 1899. Courtesy of Goff-Nelson Memorial Library Archive, Tupper Lake.

CRANE, FREDERICK M. (1855–1934)
Partnered **George M.** *or* **George C. Baldwin** *in Ogdensburg, St. Lawrence County, 1879–1880*

Frederick Crane was born in Ogdensburg, a son of cabinetmaker William Crane. Although a portrait photographer, his was the lead name in Crane & Baldwin: a short-lived partnership responsible for a number of North Country stereoviews in a sequence titled *Adirondack Scenery*, some of it subtitled *Raquette River and Tupper Lake Series.* In April 1880 Crane gave notice that the partnership had been dissolved. He spent most of the next quarter century as an Ogdensburg photographer. A younger brother, **Edwin N. Crane,** was a pioneer photographer in Tupper Lake, Franklin County.[1]

1. Curtis, *Our County and Its People*, part 3, "Personal Sketches," 110; *Ogdensburg Journal*, August 13, 1879; April 12, 1880.

CUNNINGHAM, ARTHUR J. (1895–1976)
Active Primarily in Hamilton, Herkimer, and St. Lawrence Counties, Mid-1930s–Mid-1950s

The "energetic, enterprising and progressive" Arthur Cunningham was a native of Utica, Oneida County. The son of a butcher, he began finishing photos for amateurs in his basement at the age of seventeen. After serving for a year as a photographer in France during World War I, Cunningham expanded his film-developing enterprise while experimenting with motion picture filming of industrial and news subjects (including footage picked up by Pathé News of Great Britain for its internationally known newsreels). Cunningham Studios, incorporated in 1925, focused solely on photo finishing after 1932. It serviced some two hundred dealers in central and northern New York at its peak and processed as many as sixteen thousand prints a day. Cunningham sold the company in the mid-1950s. It went bankrupt in 1970.[1]

Awarded a number of patents during his career, Cunningham developed an internationally recognized training program for the photo-finishing industry. He also maintained a hobbyist interest in photography, serving as president of the Utica Camera Club; his photographs were exhibited at Utica's Munson Williams Proctor Institute in 1940, and he authored a book on photography: *How to Take Better Pictures with Your Camera* (1975). Cunningham, owner of a second home from 1923 into the 1960s in Raquette Lake, Hamilton County, took many photographs of Adirondack landscapes, buildings, and winter sporting venues for real photo postcards—a sideline that fit comfortably into the Cunningham Studio's distribution system.[2]

1. Greene, *History of the Mohawk Valley* 3:77–78; "Arthur J. Cunningham, Popular Kiwanian," *Utica Observer*, November 10, 1920; "Industrial Movies Taken by Uticans," September 4, 1920; "Cunningham Studios Commercial Work Is Transferred to Firm," *Utica Observer-Dispatch*, February 27, 1932; Pflane, "People Worth Knowing"; "Arthur J. Cunningham, 80, Ex-Photo Finisher," *Utica Press*, November 18, 1970; "Arthur J. Cunningham, 80; Active in Photo Field," *Utica Observer-Dispatch*, May 4, 1976.
2. "'Pinocchio' Exhibit Set," *Utica Observer-Dispatch*, December 1, 1940; "Arthur J. Cunningham, 80; Active in Photo Field," *Utica Observer-Dispatch*, May 4, 1976.

DANDURAND, BURNELL FREDERICK (1888–1926)
Active Ticonderoga, Essex County, 1911–1926

Born in Shoreham, Vermont, Burnell Dandurand was raised in Crown Point and, later, Ticonderoga, where his father was a house painter and decorator. A Ticonderoga carpenter in the 1910 US Census, he became a photographer not long thereafter and was remembered years later for the strips of "ping-pong" photographs (five postage-stamp-size portraits in different poses) he offered every spring "for 2 bits a copy. And what school kid didn't have his picture taken!" Primarily a portrait photographer, Dandurand was also responsible for the images in a 1926 Ticonderoga Chamber of Commerce promotional booklet printed in a run of one hundred thousand and distributed throughout the country.[1]

Dandurand died of a stroke at the age of thirty-eight. He was, according to an obituary, "held in high esteem and respect" by the community, and "considered the leading photographer of the town" during his tenure. The Dandurand Studio advertised under his wife's proprietorship into 1928, claiming "sixteen years' experience back of our guarantee to satisfy you." It is not known who was behind the camera during its final years.[2]

1. *Ticonderoga Sentinel*, April 16, 1914; January 7, 1926; September 4, 1947.

2. *Ticonderoga Sentinel*, July 15, 1926; February 23, 1928.

DAVIS, GUY B. (1837–1869)
Active Ausable Chasm,
Clinton and Essex Counties, 1865–1868

A native of Hinesburgh, Vermont, Guy Davis relocated to Burlington in 1858 and worked as a shoe-store clerk before studying photography with **Adin French Styles** in 1860. Developing a close relationship with his mentor, he joined Styles in a brief partnership along with Styles's younger brother, Adoniram, as Styles, Davis & Styles (1860–61), moving in 1860 to Montpelier to take charge of the business's local operation. Davis operated a gallery on his own in Montpelier after the termination of the partnership and did occasional work for Styles before returning to Burlington in 1865 and acquiring the "photographic rooms," picture stock, and apparatus of the late Charles Miller. A recorder of Vermont views, Davis advertised "Residences, Scenery, &c., all sizes, taken at short notice." He was one of the many photographers to offer stereographs of Ausable Chasm.[1]

Davis died of tuberculosis at the age of thirty-two. "A young man of integrity and character, with excellent business habits," according to his obituary, "he was a favorite among his numerous acquaintances and friends, here and elsewhere. Though never prominent before the public, yet he was one of those good, substantial citizens, whose place it is not always easy to fill." Plattsburgh photographer **Henry K. Averill Jr.** purchased a number of his images shortly before or after his death; several stereoviews survive in which Davis's name has been crossed out and Averill's substituted. Others may have passed to photographer **Marquis Jesse Bixby** when he acquired Davis's Burlington studio in 1869 or 1870.[2]

1. Advertisement, *Burlington (VT) City Directory*, 1865; *(Montpelier) Vermont Watchman and State Journal*, May 5, 1865; *Rutland Weekly Herald*, March 18, 1869, copying undated *Burlington (VT) Free Press* obituary.

2. *Rutland Weekly Herald*, March 18, 1869; Treadwell and Darrah, *Photographers of the United States of America*, 31.

DEAN, RICHARD K. (1913–2008)
Active Primarily in Adirondack
Resort Areas, 1947–2002

Born in Brooklyn, Richard (Dick) Dean relocated with his family to Glens Falls, Warren County, when he was five years old; his father operated a drugstore in nearby Warrensburg. Dean studied photography at the Rochester Institute of Technology, graduating in 1935. From 1936 to 1947 he worked for Rochester's Defender Company as a film tester and color printer, heading the company's Sensitometry Department for government tests during World War II. At the same time, he provided instruction in color photography at Rochester Institute's Evening School. More interested in the pictorial than the technical aspects of photography, Dean returned to Glens Falls and opened Dean's Distinctive Photography in 1947. A newspaper advertisement from 1948 read: "Resort Photography—Specializing in Direct Color—Groups—Scenics—Promotional—Developing and Printing—Amateur Color Film—For the Trade." By 1950 Dean was promoting "Aerial" and "Candid Wedding" photographs, "Lake George Scenic Views in Stock," and "Natural Color Post Cards Made to Order."[1]

Dean photographed the Adirondacks for more than fifty years. Thousands of his images appeared as color photo postcards, accounting in 2001 for 75 percent of what was by then a family business,

Dean Color Photo. Output between 1949 and 2001 was estimated at twenty-five million cards, including wide sales as exclusive postcard franchisee for the 1980 Olympic Winter Games, held in Lake Placid. Other products included custom brochures, calendars, note cards, placemats, large-format color prints, even computer mousepads. Dean's work won numerous awards from the International Post Card Distributors Association.[2]

In the course of his long career, Dean documented not only the scenic beauty of the Adirondacks but also regional history: now-disappeared Warren County dude ranches and resorts as well as "what some scholars," noted the *New York Times*, "call roadside culture, the study of the sometimes goofy accouterments of post-World War II America, when the cars were big, the roads went everywhere and some cheese shops were built in the shape of cheese wedges." Dean's businesses ended with his death, although descendants maintain his archive and make images available upon request.[3]

1. *Plattsburgh Press-Republican*, November 15, 1973; *Lake George Mirror*, August 27, 1948; July 21, 1950; Obituary, *Glens Falls Post-Star*, February 13, 2008; Crane, "The Dean of Photography," 10–12, 15–16.

2. Marvel, "Dick Dean"; DeDe, "He's the 'Dean' of GF Photographers."

3. Glaberson, "50 Years of Wishing You Were Here."

DEGRAFF, ESTHER H. (1877–1954)
Active Old Forge, Herkimer County, 1909–1911

Born Esther H. Collins outside of Binghamton, Broome County, Esther DeGraff appeared as a Binghamton stenographer in the 1900 US Census. In April 1909 she married New York City–born violinist Mynderse DeGraff, a recent widower. She accompanied him that summer to Old Forge, where he and his first wife, a pianist, had spent several summers through 1908 as hotel musicians after their marriage in 1900, and where Mynderse operated a souvenir shop.[1]

Esther, who never identified as a photographer, took scenic views as E. H. DeGraff for mechanical reproduction as black-and-white postcards offered for sale in her husband's shop. Winter months in 1910–11 and 1913–14 were passed in Saranac Lake, where she gave ballroom dancing lessons. Mynderse provided violin accompaniment for his wife's lessons, offered tuition in violin, and played in a band. The DeGraffs disappeared from Old

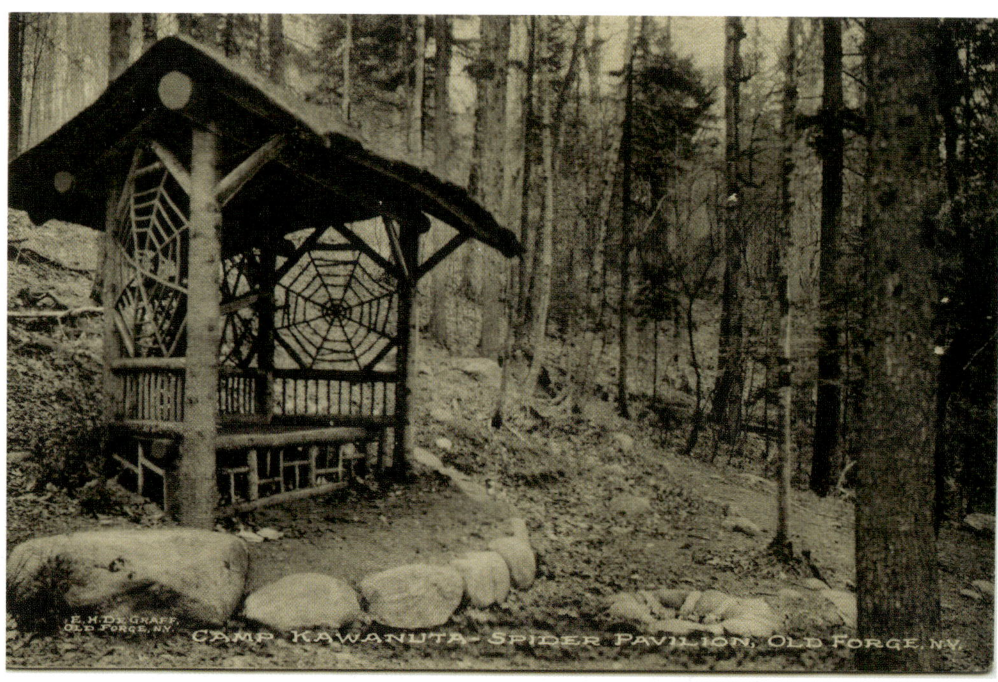

26. E. H. DeGraff, *Camp Kawanuta—Spider Pavilion, Old Forge, N.Y.* Postcard, 1909–1911.

Forge seasonal reports after 1911. They settled in Binghamton in 1914, where Mynderse operated a violin school with branches in Elmira, Scranton, and Cortland in which Esther became an instructor of violin, banjo, and guitar. She took over the school after her husband's death in 1934.[2]

1. "Mrs. M. E. DeGraff," *Utica Press*, August 5, 1908; *Utica Herald-Dispatch*, June 11, 1909.

2. *Utica Herald-Dispatch*, June 30, 1911; *Tupper Lake Herald*, February 3, 1911; *Lake Placid News*, February 5, 1914; January 30, 1914; "M. E. DeGraff Succumbs in Hospital," *Binghamton Press*, October 15, 1934.

DERBY, CHARLES (1848–1910)
Active Morrisonville, Clinton County, and Paul Smiths, Franklin County, 1889–1900

Charles Derby's background is uncertain beyond the fact that he was born in New York State. The birth certificate of his second child, filed in 1876 in Prescott, Ontario, listed him as a photographer. The 1881 Canadian Census listed him as a "marchand" (shopkeeper or salesman) in the Prescott community of Hawkesbury. In 1889 Derby was a photographer in VanKleek Hill, Champlain, Ontario.[1]

In 1889 Derby purchased land in the Plattsburgh, Clinton County, hamlet of Morrisonville, where he operated as a photographer through the turn of the twentieth century. He built a gallery on the site of the old Morrisonville schoolhouse and very briefly owned a studio in Saranac Lake, which he sold to Dr. **Charles S. W. Baldwin** of New York City in 1892. Derby's bread-and-butter business was portraiture, and he spent much of the year traveling to Clinton County villages and hamlets—Au Sable Forks, Champlain, Chazy, Dannemora, Ellenburgh Depot, Lyon Mountain, Peasleeville, Mooers Forks, St. Regis Falls, Standish—where he set up tents for a week or two at a time to capture the images of residents. "Now girls look your prettiest, but for goodness sake don't grin," ran the newspaper text announcing a Derby visit to Dannemora in 1896.[2]

The highlight of Derby's photographic career was his annual "summer campaigns" to the Franklin County resort of Paul Smiths during the 1890s to take pictures of its activities, seasonal residents, and transient guests. (Some prints identified this as his business location.) He produced a series of views of Plattsburgh's Saranac River Pulp and Paper Company and photographs of logging operations, including winter and early spring images of record-breaking sledloads of logs. Derby made several real estate investments in Morrisonville, purchasing two parcels for an apple tree orchard of five hundred trees and becoming part owner of a woodlot. Despite his industry, Derby's businesses did not prosper. His real estate holdings were foreclosed in 1900 and no reference was made thereafter to his photographic work. Enumerated as a merchant with a general store in Luzerne, now Lake Luzerne, Warren County, in the 1910 US Census, Derby died not long after the census was completed.[3]

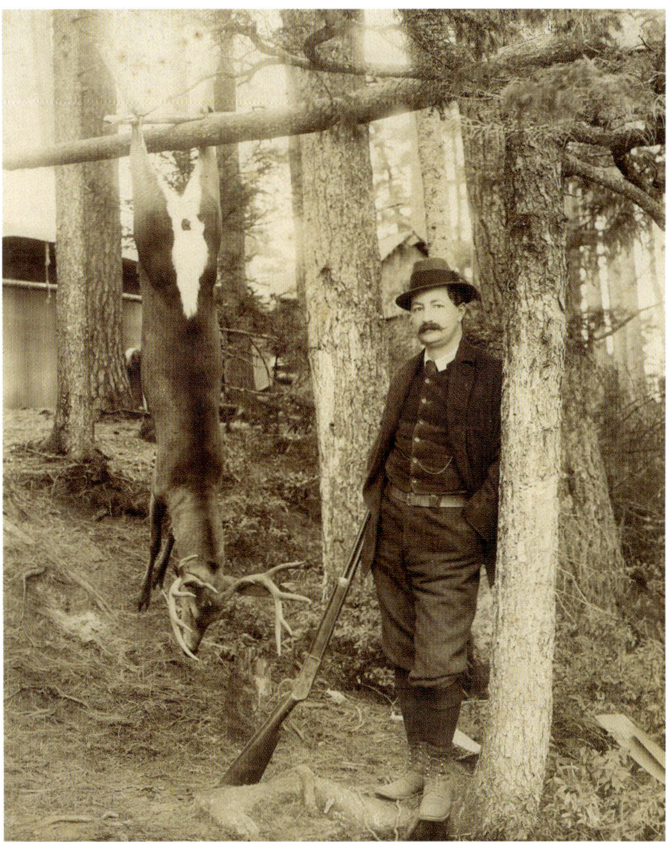

27. C. Derby, portrait of Henry Martin, 1890–1900. Image courtesy of Joan Weill Adirondack Library Archives, Paul Smith's College.

1. Gagel, *Directory of Photographers*, 337.

2. *Plattsburgh Sentinel*, January 29, 1892; April 29, 1892; May 6, 1892; December 9, 1892; November 24, 1893; June 7, 1895; *Plattsburgh Press*, May 25, 1895; July 3, 1896.

3. *Plattsburgh Sentinel*, May 6, 1892; February 9, 1894; March 23, 1894; June 1, 1894; June 2, 1900; *Plattsburgh Press*, May 25, 1895.

DETROIT PUBLISHING COMPANY (1897–1932)
Active throughout the Adirondacks, 1900–1906

A large postcard publishing firm with a network of staff photographers, the company was a pioneer in the creation of colored postcards from hand-colored negatives. In all, it produced some sixteen thousand views, surpassing all other postcard publishers of its day in geographic coverage and technological proficiency. The Adirondack region, particularly its resort areas, was well represented in its output and accounted for at least three hundred images.

Originally a subsidiary of the Detroit Photographic Company, by 1904 the firm was listed in the Detroit city directory as the Detroit Publishing Company. An early objective was the acquisition of a stock of images for postcards, and in late 1897 the company brought on board Adirondack-born photographer **William Henry Jackson** as a part-owner and director. With him came an estimated twenty thousand glass-plate negatives. Jackson traveled the country during his early years with Detroit, including northeastern New York State, reshooting outdated views and taking additional photographs for the company's use. At least two other Detroit photographers, **Lycurgus Glover** and **Henry Peabody,** worked on the company's behalf in the Adirondacks.[1]

Landscape represented the Detroit Publishing Company's largest category of images, and conventional broad views dominated its Adirondack oeuvre. Generic images on a smaller scale also appealed to its market: *An Adirondack Hand Cart Carry, An Adirondack Mountain Stream, Fishing in the Adirondacks.* The company's most prolific years were 1902 through 1910, with 1904 representing perhaps its peak in output. The delicate coloring system it used became expensive, time-consuming, and difficult to produce competitively against innovations in cheaper half-tone processes. Sales decreased with the advent of World War I, and a general business recession in 1920–22 badly impacted the company. In 1924 the firm went into receivership. Although it continued to publish a few contract issues—for railroads, hotel and restaurant chains—during the next several years, its debts mounted and the company was liquidated in 1932.[2]

1. Miller and Miller, *Picture Postcards*, 146, 149, 150; Hales, *William Henry Jackson*, 261, 265.

2. Hales, *William Henry Jackson*, 265, 266, 269; Miller and Miller, *Picture Postcards*, 152.

DEWEY, GUY CLARK (1866–1947)
Active Duane, Malone, and Other Franklin County Locales, 1890–1900

Born in Moira, Franklin County, Guy Dewey was an "enthusiastic amateur photographer." He "devoted considerable time" to his hobby in the late 1890s, skillfully documenting weekend and longer holiday trips in central and northern Franklin County: to Lake Clear, Goldsmith, Meacham Lake, Lake Titus, Indian Lake, Mountain View. His work has been reproduced numerous times without attribution, although a number of images were credited to him by name in the 2008 publication, *Adirondack Lifestyles Volume 1*.[1]

Dewey appears to have given up photography not long after his 1900 purchase of an interest in C. H. Breed's drugstore, in which he had been a pharmacist since the 1880s. Dewey and partner Wallace W. Smith bought out Breed in 1906, renaming the business Dewey & Smith.[2]

1. "A Photographic Curiosity," *Franklin Gazette*, February 26, 1897; *Adirondack Lifestyles Vol. 1*, iii.

2. *Malone Farmer*, February 7, 1900; February 8, 1906.

DISTIN, WILLIAM LANGMEAD (1864–1930)
Active Saranac Lake, Essex and Franklin Counties, 1904–1930

Born in Barrie, Ontario, William Distin spent his early life in Montreal and was listed as a machinist in the 1881 Canadian Census. By 1892 he and his family were settled in Plattsburgh, Clinton County, where he was employed as a decorator and japanner for the Williams Manufacturing Company, a Montreal-based maker of sewing machines. Distin moved to Saranac Lake in 1898 to work for photographer **George W. Baldwin**, purchasing the studio circa 1904. He briefly retained the business's previous name: Baldwin Art Studio.[1]

Having studied painting in his youth, Distin continued to pursue art as an avocation, providing eight pen-and-ink sketches for Saranac Lake–based Alfred J. Donaldson's short compendium of poetry, *Songs of My Violin* (1901). His sister Ella worked in his studio for some thirty years between 1900 and 1920 as an artist and photographer. Distin's eldest child, William G. Distin, became a well-known Saranac Lake architect. The Distin Studio continued to operate for ten years after its founder's death (1931 and 1932 telephone directories listed its proprietor as Victor Campbell) before it was purchased in 1940 by **Bernard Monge Acosta.**[2]

1. *Plattsburgh Press*, August 18, 1896; *Outdoor Life* 1, no. 1 (February 1904): 123; "William L. Distin Dies at Home Here after Long Illness," *Adirondack Enterprise*, July 25, 1930.
2. Donaldson, *Songs of My Violin*, passim.

DIXON, GEORGE W. (1849–1937)
Active Tupper Lake, Franklin County, 1890–1896

Born in England, George Dixon lived on both sides of the Canadian border after immigrating to North America in 1868. The first child from his marriage to a French Canadian was born in Beauharnois, Quebec, in 1878; six other children were born from 1880 in northeastern New York State.

Dixon advertised himself as a Tupper Lake photographer in a circa 1890 pamphlet promoting the Northern Adirondack Rail Road, noting: "I make a specialty of Sporting camp views, and scenes of all kinds. Will go to camps when desired. I also keep a line of confectionery &c." A newspaper ad running for four months between August and November 1895 reiterated his specialty in scenes and "sporting camp views." As Dixon did not always include identifying information on his printed images, his work remains generally unknown.[1]

Dixon's brass band, and later, his family band, were in demand during the years of his Tupper Lake residence. "This is a family of natural musicians," it was reported in 1895. "Five members of the family compose the band, the youngest player not being over eight years old. They furnish us excellent music on all popular occasions and at frequent intervals . . . Mr. Dixon also does excellent photographic work." By 1900 the family was living in Malone, where Dixon appeared in that year's US Census as a photographer. Local directories gave

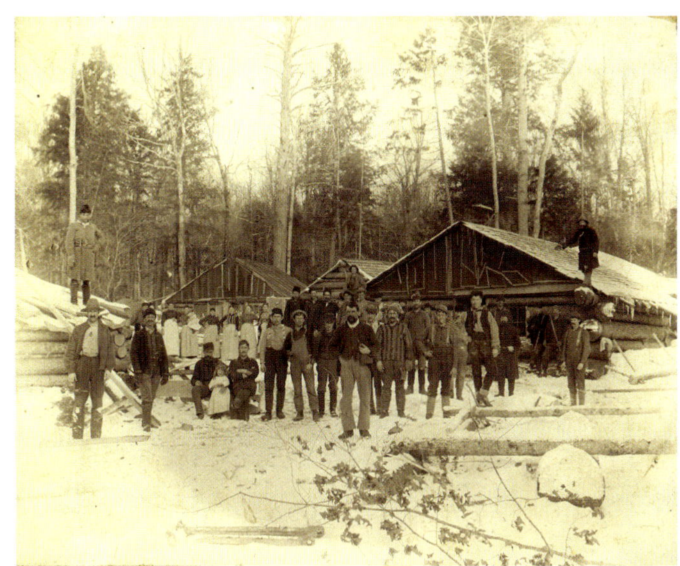

28. G. W. Dixon, lumber camp, 1890–1895. Courtesy of Goff-Nelson Memorial Library Archive, Tupper Lake.

an East Main Street business address for Dixon between 1903 and 1905; by 1910 he was a carpenter in a carpentry shop.[2]

1. Advertisement, *Northern Adirondack Guide*, 40; *St. Regis Falls Adirondack News*, August 10, 1895; August 24, 1895.

2. *St. Regis Falls Adirondack News*, August 24, 1895.

DODGE, FRANKLIN OSCAR (1882–1959)
Active Stratford, Fulton County, 1910–1917

Franklin (Frank) Dodge was born in Fairfield, Herkimer County. A farm laborer in 1900, Dodge attended college for two years before graduating in 1904 from the Ilion Teachers Training Class, a one-year program to prepare high school graduates to teach in the state's public schools. He taught briefly in Norway, Herkimer County, and by 1910 was a teacher in the Stratford district school.[1]

Dodge's photographic work paralleled his Stratford teaching career. He sold his images as prints and real photo postcards—primarily landscapes and village scenes from around Stratford, the adjoining town of Salisbury, and into Hamilton County. Some are identifiable only by the presence of locational information, generally in black type, on their faces.

Dodge left teaching, and photography, in 1917. Subsequent years were spent in Stratford and Salisbury as a sawmill bookkeeper, a lumber surveyor, and a carpenter. Following in his father's footsteps, Dodge served for twelve years as Salisbury town supervisor.[2]

1. *Utica Herald-Dispatch*, September 9, 1903; September 4, 1912.

2. "Republican Nominees for Supervisors," *Little Falls Journal and Courier*, October 23, 1923; *Gloversville and Johnstown Herald*, September 4, 1935; "Frank Dodge Dies at 77 in Salisbury," *Utica Press*, September 14, 1959.

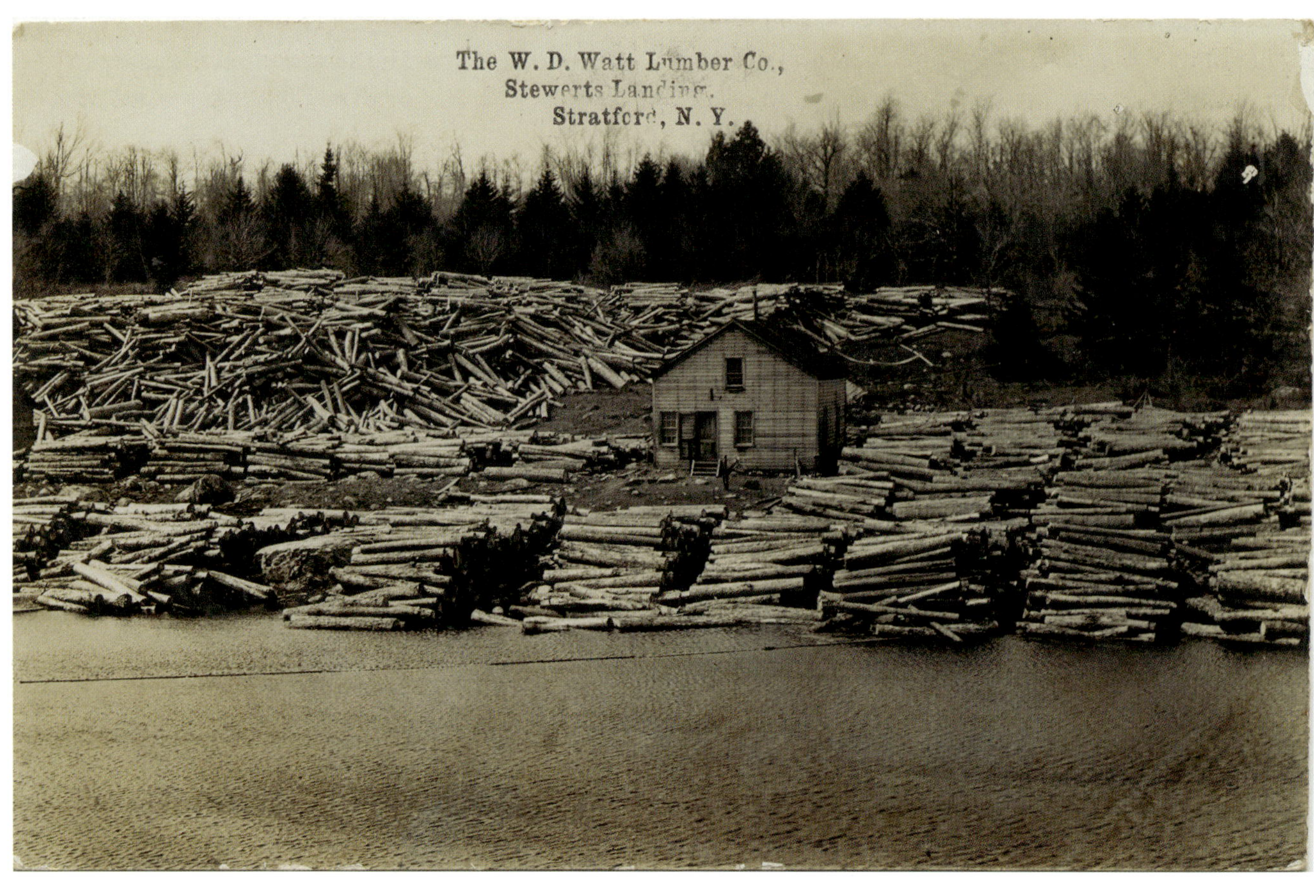

29. F. O. Dodge, *The W. D. Watt Lumber Co., Stewerts Landing, Stratford, N.Y.* RPPC, 1910–1917.

DOUGLAS, EVAN CAMPBELL (1889–1971)
Active Saranac Lake, Essex and Franklin Counties, 1915–1922

Evan Douglas was born in Lakeland, Ontario. His Canadian-Scots father, Campbell Mellis Douglas, a retired British army surgeon-major and lieutenant colonel, moved his family from Canada to Britain in 1894, and Douglas grew up in England and Scotland before immigrating alone to the United States in 1908 as an agriculturalist. In 1913 he landed in Saranac Lake with an advanced case of tuberculosis. While convalescing in a privately run cure cottage Douglas took advantage of his enforced leisure to learn photography in a sanitarium occupational training program. He was still in Saranac Lake in 1920, when his occupation was recorded in the US Census as "TB patient."[1]

By 1923 Douglas relocated to Prescott, Arizona, where he appeared in the town directory that year as a professional in "hand colored photography." His specialties, according to a March 1924 listing of new members of the International Photographic Association, were "Adirondack mountain landscape, Northern Arizona landscape; for general—animal or child studies." Douglas remained in Prescott as a photographer and photofinisher through at least 1936, the year in which he became a naturalized American citizen. By 1940 he was living in Albuquerque, New Mexico, the proprietor of the Douglas Photo Shop.[2]

1. "Campbell Mellis Douglas," *Canadian Encyclopedia*; tuberculosis registration card for E. C. Douglas, Saranac Lake, on file in the Adirondack Research Room, Saranac Lake Free Library.

2. *Camera Craft* 31, no. 3 (March 1924): 156.

DUNLOP, JOSEPH K. (1857–1935)
Active Northville, Fulton County, Late 1880s–Early 1930s; Corinth, Saratoga County, 1918–1925

The son of a Scots painter, according to the 1870 US Census, Joseph Dunlop grew up in Brooklyn. By 1880 he was living in the household of an older sister and working as an "artist in drawing." (In 1892 he would state that he had formerly been "employed for some time as a crayon artist for the government.") It is unknown what lured Dunlop to upstate New York, but he was a Gloversville resident by the time of his marriage in 1886. Listed in the 1888 Gloversville directory as a photographer working from his residence, Dunlop purchased a cottage on the Midway in Northville's Sacandaga Park from which he operated a barbershop and photo studio in the summer of 1891. His cottage was one of only nine to survive a devastating 1898 park fire.[1]

A brief photographic 1889–91 partnership with G. B. Hamlin preceded Dunlop's opening of his own Gloversville studio. By 1902 only a post office box listing appeared for him in the Gloversville directory. Short-term photographic stints followed in Mechanicville and Schuylerville, Saratoga County, and Greenwich, Washington County, after which Dunlop disappeared from local view for more than ten years. In 1919 he settled in Corinth, where he "conducted the local studio" until relocating in 1925 to Ballston Spa.[2]

Despite his wanderings, Dunlop continued to spend summers in Sacandaga Park. His well-appointed photographic operation there offered outdoor portraits and a studio outfitted with twenty-five-foot-wide backdrops: of forested Adirondack scenery, cornstalks, even the rear vestibule platform of an observation car on the San Francisco Limited passenger train. "Little pictures" of sitters in a series of poses were popular, and Dunlop kept a wide collection of headgear on hand to enable subjects to experiment with a variety of personae. His wife, Emma, ran a seasonal souvenir shop from the family living room selling knickknacks and postcards, some of them published under her name from her husband's hand-colored negatives. Although Dunlop focused his later years on photographing students and school groups, he could still be found taking pictures during the last summer of his life in what remained of Sacandaga Park after its dismantling in connection with a flood control system for the Hudson River.[3]

1. *Gloversville Leader*, July 13, 1891, September 5, 1892; *Schuylerville Standard*, May 5, 1886.

2. *Gloversville Leader*, December 3, 1891; September 28, 1894; *Mechanicville Saturday Mercury*, May 31, 1902; *Saratogian*, March 18, 1903; March 11, 1925.

3. Kostroff, *Life in Sacandaga Park*, 11, 15, 70; *Saratogian*, November 11, 1919.

EASTERN ILLUSTRATING AND PUBLISHING COMPANY (1909–1980s)

Active throughout the Adirondacks, 1914–Early 1950s

Eastern Illustrating and Publishing was founded in Belfast, Maine, by Harold Cassens (1876–1948) in 1909. His intention was to offer real photo postcard views of towns and villages on what he called the "Transcontinental Trail" from "Maine to California." While this goal was never realized, Eastern's photographers captured more than fifty thousand black-and-white postcard images. Among them were approximately eleven thousand views of New York State, of which a good portion were of the Adirondacks. Company cameras recorded bird's-eye views and details of small towns and rural areas not documented by others for postcards: roadside inns, tourist homes, campgrounds, grocery stores, filling stations (prime Eastern postcard clients), industrial sites, and children's summer camps. Occasional images were purchased from outside photographers.[1]

No more than four photographers worked for Eastern at any one time. They took to the road in June after repeat orders for existing postcards from old customers had been processed. Although salaried, they also relied on commissions. Some developed reputations as card salesmen first and photographers second—it was "joked that it was much easier to make a good photographer out of a salesman than a salesman out of a good photographer." They learned about local landmarks from townspeople and stayed at the same hostelries and campgrounds as the tourists who appeared in their pictures. Because the pace of change in many localities was slow, some images had long shelf lives. Views showing later model automobiles and clothing styles generally represented new territories. Fred W. Cassens (1874–1942), Harold Cassens's brother, was the company's photographer and salesman in upstate New York during the 1920s and 1930s.[2]

Eastern's factory work—from developing and captioning negatives to printing and shipping cards—was carried out in Belfast, primarily during the summer months; many of the company's dozen or more employees were members of Harold Cassens's extended family. During its peak years, the

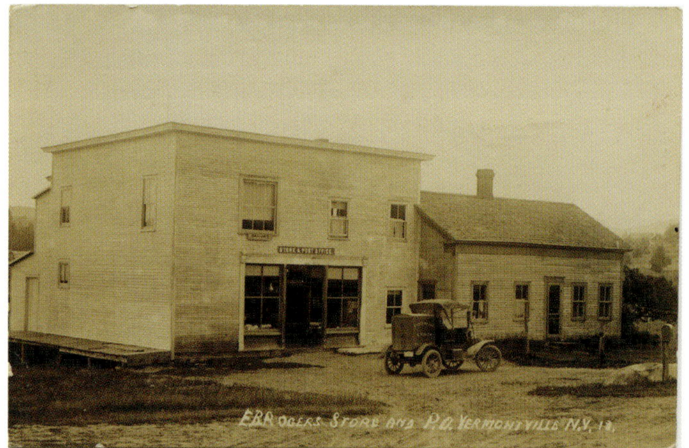

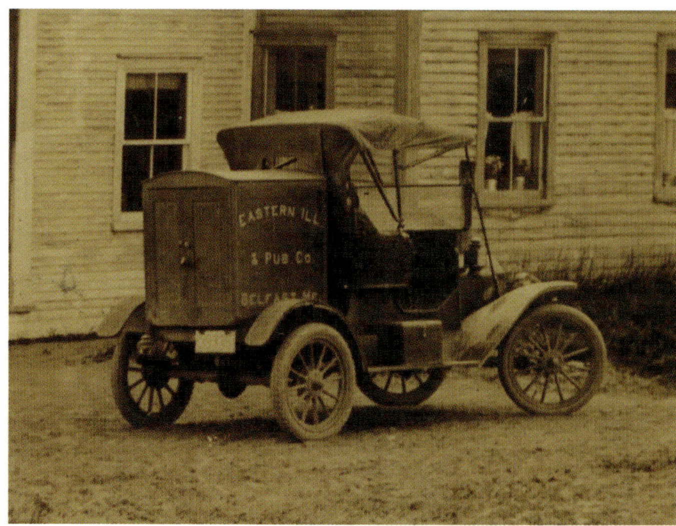

30 (a and b). Eastern Illustrating and Publishing Co., *E. B. Rogers Store and P.O., Vermontville, N.Y.*, with inset showing Eastern Illustrating company car. RPPC, 1914–1925.

1920s, the company published a million postcards a year. Cards were not always identified with the company name, particularly in busy summers when the business was called upon to quickly fill orders and printed cardstock was low. Most, however, are recognizable from their labeling style: hand-printed on the negative in neat capital letters, showing as white on card faces, and stating the subject's name, location, and a number or number/letter code. (New cards from circa 1940 and later had machine-printed labels, but, again, were not always identified.) Eastern's pace of activity flagged with the passing of the postcard craze, and Cassens sold the enterprise in 1947, a year before his death. The company changed hands several times before closing for good in the 1980s.[3]

1. Harding, *Roadside New England*, 5; Bogdan, *Exposing the Wilderness*, 214; email from Kevin Johnson, photo archivist, Penobscot Marine Museum, to the author, December 11, 2017.

2. Harding, *Roadside New England*, 6, 7, 8; Bogdan, *Exposing the Wilderness*, 207–8.

3. Harding, *Roadside New England*, 6, 7; Kevin Johnson email, December 11, 2017.

EBY, HAROLD MORRISON (1892–1967)
Active Saranac Lake, Essex and Franklin Counties, 1943–1967

Harold Eby was raised in Huntingdon, Pennsylvania, and attended the University of Pennsylvania's Wharton School of Finance but did not graduate. He became a photographer, at first an unsuccessful one, filing for bankruptcy from his Huntingdon studio in 1921. Relocating to Buffalo, New York, he worked for Juanita Ball, a prominent Pennsylvania-born society photographer and proprietor of the Juanita Ball Studio. In 1927, a year after the death of his first wife, Ely married Ball and joined her in running her studio.[1]

In 1943 Ball's tuberculosis diagnosis took the couple to Saranac Lake, where Eby was henceforth the only photographer in the family. He became the official photographer for the Whiteface Inn in Lake Placid, Essex County, and the Saranac Inn in Santa Clara, Franklin County. In 1945 he was named publicity agent for the Saranac Lake Bobsled Club. In 1961 it was estimated that "about 99 percent of the bride and groom pictures" in the Saranac Lake newspaper were Eby's work. He frequently took senior class portraits and group photographs for *Canaras*, the Saranac Lake High School yearbook. Eby was eulogized by Lake Placid photographer **David W. Jones** after his sudden death from a heart attack as "a peach of a guy, and a wonderful friend."[2]

1. Slattery, "Personalities"; *Bulletin of Photography* 29, no. 748 (December 7, 1921): 729; *Buffalo Courier-Express*, February 9, 1933; July 26, 1967; *Dunkirk Observer*, November 2, 1934; "Harold Eby," *Huntingdon and Mount Union (PA) News*, July 22, 1967.

2. *Tupper Lake Free Press and Tupper Lake Herald*, May 6, 1943; *Lake Placid News*, November 12, 1943; *Essex County Republican*, December 7, 1945; *Adirondack Enterprise*, October 25, 1952; July 6, 1961; July 20, 1967.

FAY, CHRISTOPHER R. (1838–1916)
Active Malone, Franklin County, 1857–1873, 1876–1912

Christopher (Christie) Fay migrated with his parents to Canada from County Antrim, Ireland, before he was two years old, and spent his boyhood just south of the Canadian border in Fort Covington, Franklin County. He trained in his father's occupation as a boot- and shoemaker, but was drawn to art, particularly portraiture, for which he obtained painting supplies at a carriage paint shop. By 1857 Fay relocated to Malone, where in 1862 he was identified as an ambrotypist. Through much of the Civil War, Fay associated with Malone photographer **Seymour Erastus Buttolph,** proprietor of Buttolph's National Gallery, in following Union army regiments to photograph soldiers who wished to send likenesses home to their families. ("The soldiers are very good customers," it was reported, "as long as their money holds out.")[1]

Fay and William H. Barney took over Buttolph's National Gallery in 1865, renaming the business

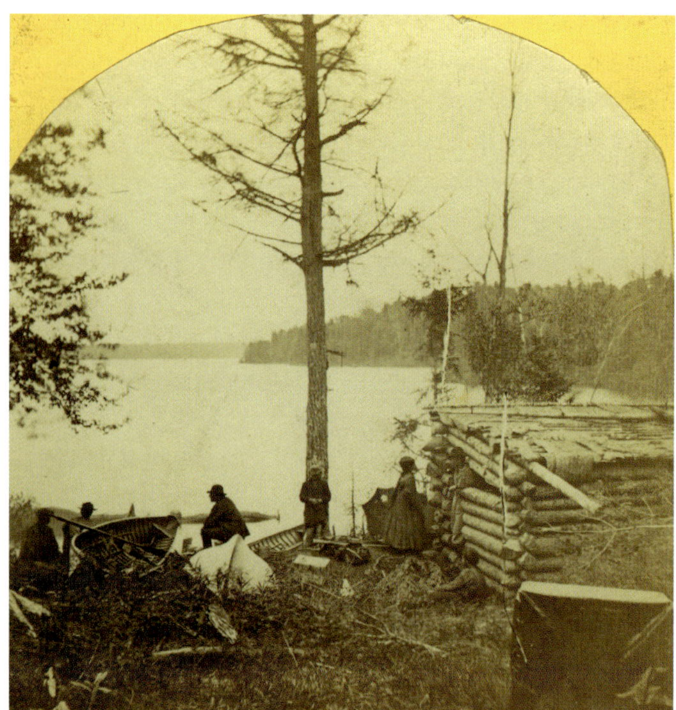

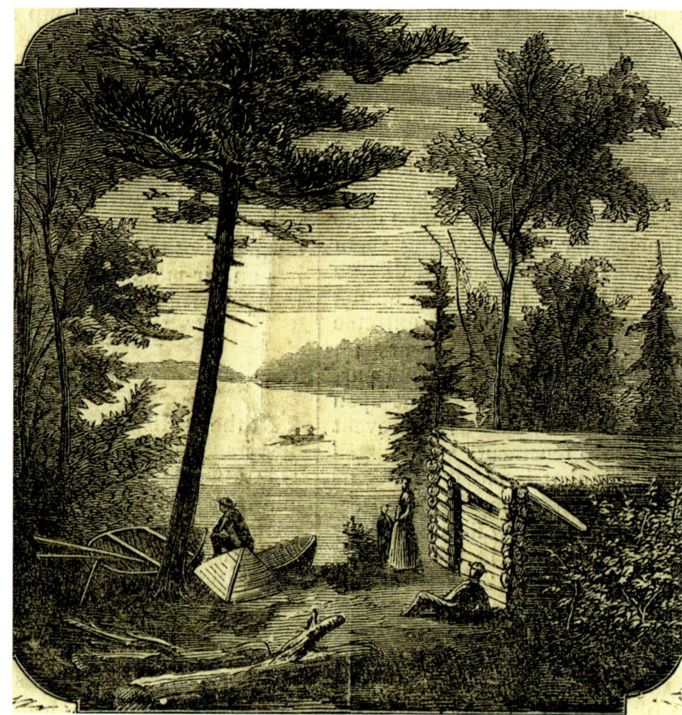

31. C. R. Fay, Left: *Big Clear Pond*, Franklin County. One-half stereoview, 1867. Right: Wood engraving from image, *Harper's Weekly*, August 31, 1867. Both images courtesy of Adirondack Experience.

Fay & Barney's National Gallery. The partnership dissolved in early 1867. Fay maintained brief partnerships with other portrait photographers: George Farmer from mid-1867 and **Charles H. Ferris** in 1868. He produced stereoviews for two series during early summer fishing outings of the Black Fly Club of Malone, of which he was a member. The first, published in 1867 by Fay & Farmer and popular for twenty years, included forty-two *Adirondack Views*, most of them from around Franklin County's Meacham, St. Regis, and Saranac Lakes. Nine wood engravings based on images from the series appeared in an August 1867 issue of *Harper's Weekly*. As the journal *Philadelphia Photographer* commented of the "nicely taken" views, they showed "what an advantage a photographer has over any one else, of making a *pleasure* trip *profitable*." The second series, *Views in the Adirondacks, or the Hunting Grounds of New York*, published by Fay & Ferris, captured scenes taken during the club's 1868 excursion to Hamilton County.[2]

Fay contributed not only photographs for engravings but also descriptions of Malone and the northern Adirondack lakes to the first edition of Edwin R. Wallace's *Descriptive Guide to the Adirondacks*, appended to Perry Smith's 1872 *Modern Babes in the Wood*. Wallace acknowledged Fay's contributions in subsequent editions of his guide, published as an independent volume through 1899.[3]

Fay went on the road again in 1873, taking portrait photographs in upstate New York from a mobile gallery he shared with St. Lawrence County photographer brothers George P. and Ralph W. Huested. He appeared as a merchant living in his parents' Fort Covington household in the New York state census of 1875, but by 1877 was back in Malone in another photographic partnership, this one with Martin C. Goodell, which lasted until early 1880. Fay and Ferris briefly rejoined forces in 1882.[4]

Except for a brief 1895–96 partnership as C. R. Fay & Son, Fay spent the rest of his career as a solo portrait photographer; his crayon portraits were said to be "of the best, and brought him much outside business." In the roughly forty years during which he worked in Malone, noted his obituary, he "probably photographed more people in this county than any other man who ever lived in it . . . picturing people when they were children, after they had grown up, and after them their children." Fay continued to do crayon portraits at home after retirement and to retouch negatives for other Malone photographers until shortly before his death. His negatives eventually passed into the ownership of Malone photographer **Eli Robideau,** who bought his studio from a successor.[5]

1. Seaver, *Historical Sketches of Franklin County*, 733; Davis, *Origins of American Photography*, 187; letter from Fay's grandson George H. Fay to William Verner, curator, Adirondack Museum, August 30, 1964, in "Fay," Photographers' File, Adirondack Experience.

2. "The Adirondack Mountains," *Harper's Weekly*, August 31, 1867, 548; *Malone Palladium*, February 13, 1868; *Philadelphia Photographer* 5, no. 49 (January 1868): unpaged "Specialties" section following p. 34; notes of unidentified interviewer's conversations with Fay on October 10, 11, and 12, 1910, "Fay," Photographers' File, Adirondack Experience.

3. H. P. Smith, *Babes in the Wood*, 298–300, 304–17.

4. "G. P. Huested Dead," *Oswego Palladium*, May 20, 1922; "George P. Huested," *Sandy Creek News*, May 18, 1922.

5. Seaver, *Historical Sketches of Franklin County*, 733; *Malone Farmer*, July 26, 1916.

FELL, WILLIAM J. (1832–1902)
Active Broadalbin, Mayfield, Northville, Fulton County; Wells, Hamilton County, 1891–1893

Born in Canada, William Fell was an artist in Iroquois Village, Dundas, Ontario, in 1871. By the early 1880s he was a portrait photographer in Sandy Creek, Oswego County. He relocated circa 1890 to Fultonville, Montgomery County, from which he worked for three years as an itinerant photographer, setting up his portable gallery on available ground for several weeks or months at a stretch. In July 1891 he was in Broadalbin, in early December 1891 in Mayfield, in April 1892 in Wells, and in October 1892 in Northville, positioning himself on the "corner of First and Bridge streets." Fell was back in Broadalbin in July 1893, locating on the Rawson lot next to the new town hall, where, it was remarked, his temporary "building" looked "just the same as it used to except an addition has been built on." Fell left Broadalbin for Galway, Saratoga County, in November 1893 and was not seen again in the Adirondacks. He returned to Sandy Creek for the remainder of the decade and may have operated a photograph gallery there. In 1900 he moved to Fort Ann, Washington County, where his son, Albert, was a photographer.[1]

1. *Gloversville Leader*, July 24, 1891; November 27, 1891; July 12, 1893; October 20, 1893; *Johnstown Republican*, April 28, 1892; *Saratogian*, October 13, 1892.

FELT, THOMAS C. (1808–1870)
Active Elizabethtown, Essex County, 1855–1870

Thomas Felt's father, Aaron, was an early settler of Wadhams Mills, a hamlet of Westport, Essex County, and built the community's first grist mill before the family relocated to nearby Elizabethtown. Thomas Felt opened Elizabethtown's first "daguerreotype establishment" in a small Maple Street building that in 1861 was moved as a prank by Civil War recruits into the Boquet River. "Felt said his shop being down there might 'make talk' and he wished the 'boys' would move it back"—which they did. Felt was listed as a "photographist" in a New York State business directory for 1870, the year in which he died.[1]

1. George Levi Brown, *Pleasant Valley*, 111, 393.

FERRIS, CHARLES H. (1828–1891)
Active Malone, Franklin County, 1861–1887

Charles H. Ferris was noted at his death as "one of the pioneer photographers of New York, whose work thirty years ago was in almost every home in Franklin County." A farmhand in Lawrence, St. Lawrence County, according to the 1850 US Census, he was living in Malone by the early 1860s and specializing in portrait photography. An 1862–63 directory for Franklin and Clinton Counties advertised Ferris's "Ambrotypes, Melaneotypes, Photographs, Carte D'Visites [*sic*], and Standing Card Pictures taken in any weather and at reasonable prices." Partnerships with **Christopher Fay** in 1868 and again in 1882 identified him with that artist in the production of stereoviews, although it is probable that all the stereo images on which his name appeared during the affiliation were Fay's work. Ferris built the Ferris block on Malone's East Main Street around 1881, partially as a gallery and studio. In 1887 he leased his studio to **Charles J. Ferris** (unknown relationship), who had worked for him during the previous year at what was then called the Elm City Studio, and retired from photography.[1]

1. *Franklin Gazette* (Fort Covington, NY), January 1, 1892; August 5, 1887; *Malone Palladium*, February 13, 1868.

FERRIS, CHARLES JOHNSON (1864–1940)
Active Malone, Franklin County, 1887–1889; Plattsburgh, Clinton County, 1889–1892; Saranac Lake, Essex and Franklin Counties, 1892–1894

Charles J. Ferris briefly tried his luck as a photographer in three upstate communities. Born into a farming family in Canada, he was raised in Westville, Franklin County, and in 1886 went to work for Malone portrait photographer **Charles H. Ferris** (unknown relationship). He took over Ferris's Elm City Studio the following year and advertised a specialty in portrait "enlargements, finished in crayon, pastel and water colors."[1]

In 1889 Ferris "sold his entire photographic business and outfit, including the Elm City Studio and subsidiary galleries in Malone, Moira, Dickinson Center, and St. Regis Falls to Messrs Stone & Wilcox of Canton" and relocated briefly to Plattsburgh, where his occupation was given as photographer in the 1891 city directory. He moved on to Saranac Lake in 1891 or 1892. A few photographs survive from this phase of his career, primarily of buildings and patient life at the Trudeau sanitarium. In late 1894 Ferris sold the business to **Arthur Newall Allen**. After stints in Springfield and Westfield, Massachusetts, and Greenwich, Connecticut, (where in 1900 he was a bicycle dealer), Ferris eventually removed to California. He appeared from 1908 in San Diego County directories and, later, in Brawley, Imperial County, census records as a carpenter, builder, rancher, and farmer.[2]

1. *Franklin Gazette* (Fort Covington, NY), August 5, 1887; *Malone Palladium*, September 8, 1887; June 28, 1888.
2. *St. Regis Falls Adirondack News*, December 7, 1889; *Plattsburgh Sentinel*, September 21, 1894; *Malone Palladium*, November 22, 1894; December 17, 1896; March 4, 1897; August 3, 1899; "Mrs. Ferris, 80, Dies in California," *Malone Telegram*, May 26, 1946.

FILLMORE, LAVIUS HARTSHORN (1836–1905)
Active Lake George Region, 1872–1898

Distantly related to President Millard Fillmore, Lavius Fillmore was born in New Haven, Vermont. By 1872 he was in Whitehall, Washington County, where he identified himself on an early stereograph as a "Landscape Photographer." A view series from these years was titled *Gems from Lake George*. In late 1877 Fillmore moved to Ticonderoga, Essex County. Reported to be "an expert in making faces," Fillmore associated briefly with photographer **Amos S. Nickerson** before opening his own studio in 1878; in 1894 his workspace in the new Brust block was described as the "largest and best furnished rooms in town." One 1896 advertisement ran, "Should you want a first-class photo of your house, horse or baby, call on Fillmore; Lake George and Ticonderoga views on hand." Summers were given over to "campaigns" to the resort communities along the western shore of Lake George. Fillmore and his wife spent the high season at a modest lake cottage on state-owned Uncas Island from circa 1890 until New York reclaimed possession of its Lake George islands in 1899.[1]

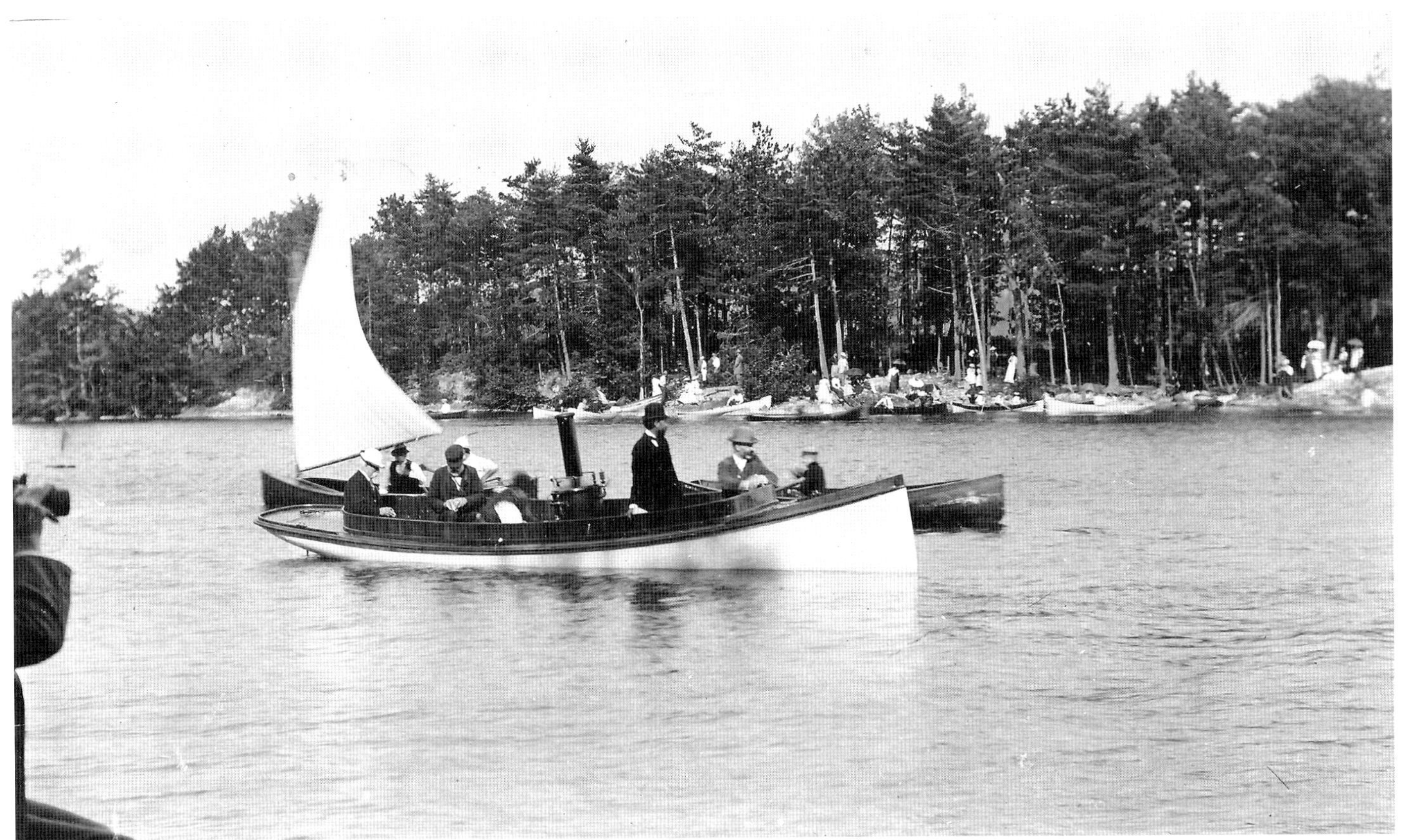

32. L. H. Fillmore, *Steam Launch, Hague Regatta*, Lake George, 1887–1898. Courtesy of Sally DeLarm Rypkema, Hague town historian.

In late 1897 Fillmore and **Frank H. Grimes** were responsible for photographic images used as the basis for engravings in a "handsome pamphlet" produced for the Ticonderoga Historical Society. In 1898 Fillmore sold his studio to photographer **William M. A. Cowan** and retired to Whitehall.[2]

1. *Ticonderoga Sentinel*, November 30, 1877; November 1, 1878; March 7, 1879; May 17, 1894; November 14, 1895; February 6, 1896; *Glens Falls Times*, December 10, 1898.

2. *Ticonderoga Sentinel*, October 1, 1896; *Plattsburgh Press*, March 2, 1898.

FLANDERS, MARTIN POST (1840–1915)
Active Au Sable Forks, Clinton and Essex Counties, Early 1870s

Born into a farming family in North Jay, Essex County, Martin Flanders was listed in various federal and New York state census records as day laborer (1860), farmer (1865), and carpenter and joiner (1870). By early 1874 he was the overseer of the new separator at the J. & J. Rogers Iron Works in Au Sable Forks. His stint as a photographer either preceded or paralleled this period of employment and is evidenced only by the existence of a few cartes de visite bearing his imprint. In 1877 Flanders's eldest daughter married George A. Stevens, proprietor of the fashionable Stevens House hotel in Lake Placid, and Flanders and wife moved to Lake Placid to live next door to the growing Stevens family. His designated occupation in later US and state censuses was mechanic (1892), day laborer (1900), and "own income" (1910).[1]

1. *Essex County Republican*, February 19, 1874; "Lake Placid Loses Aged Citizen," *Elizabethtown Post*, February 11, 1915.

FOOTE, NORMAN STEWART (1883–1964)
Active Primarily in Essex County, with Excursions into Hamilton and Warren Counties, 1908–1930

Born in Cornwall, Vermont, the son of a sheep breeder, Norman Foote was enumerated in the 1900 US Census as a seventeen-year-old Cornwall farm laborer. He lived thereafter in Middlebury, St. Albans, and Rutland. Foote's early occupational interests were in fire insurance and real estate—a 1905 advertisement from Middlebury announced, "I Have 300 Farms to Sell." He energetically promoted summer properties (posting numerous advertisements in Adirondack newspapers), and cooperated with other agents to create a sales catalog of seasonal homes. Foote's second career was as a surveyor for real estate projects, among them the acquisition of land for Adirondack water power development and the development of property belonging to the Port Henry, Essex County, Light and Power Company.[1]

Albums of Foote landscape images, most of them taken in conjunction with his role as surveyor but some as an enthusiastic amateur, are held by the Adirondack Experience.

1. *Middlebury Register*, March 10, 1905; "Meeting of Vermont Real Estate Men, February 24, 1905; *Plattsburgh Press-Republican*, November 2, 1964.

FULLER, JAMES (1819–1876)
Active Warrensburg, Warren County, 1870–1876

A lifelong resident of Warren County, James Fuller was identified in the New York state census of 1855 and the 1860 US Census as a dry goods merchant and storekeeper, at first in Stony Creek and then in Warrensburg. In 1870 he purchased a Warrensburg general store, the upper rooms of which were at the time rented to **James H. Carpenter** for use as a photographic studio. Fuller acquired Carpenter's "paraphernalia" and negatives not long after taking over the building and, "as a side line, took pictures of customers and a few of the [town's] more important buildings."[1]

1. *Warrensburgh News*, January 25, 1925, quoting letter from Fuller's daughter, Nelly Fuller Hubbell.

FYNMORE, JAMES FRANCIS (1912–1983)
Active Central Adirondacks, 1945–Late 1960s

Born in Syracuse, Onondaga County, the son of a motorcycle dealer, James (Jim) Fynmore was by the early 1940s the manager of a chain grocery store in Boonville, Oneida County. A camera hobbyist, Fynmore began at that time to develop his photographic interest into a career sideline. An early 1946 newspaper advertisement for "Commercial

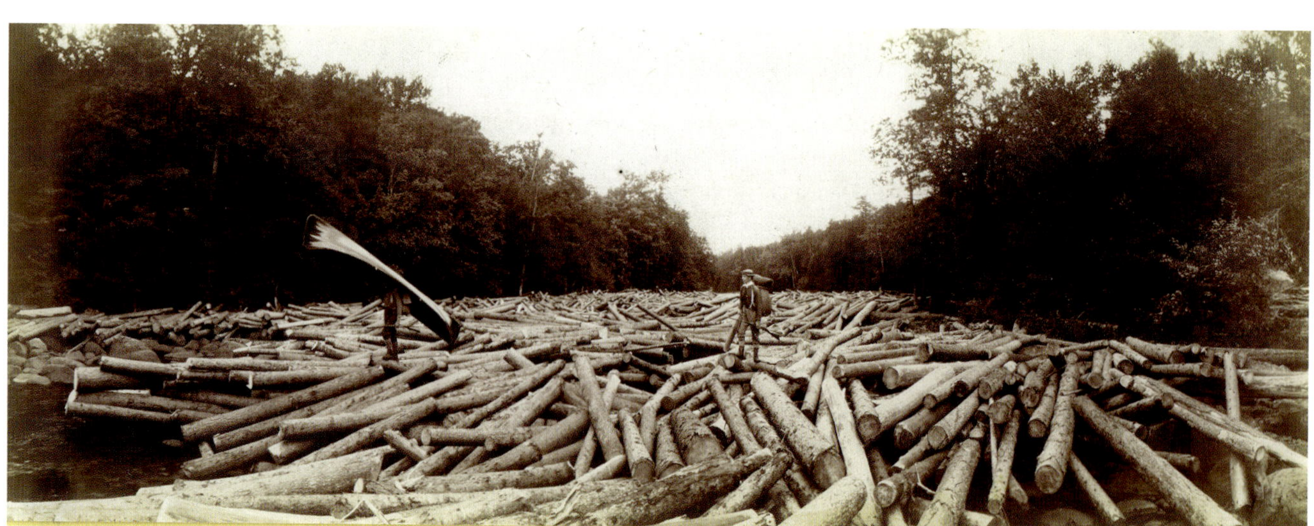

33. N. S. Foote, crossing log jam on Upper Hudson River near Newcomb, 1914–1930. Courtesy of Adirondack Experience.

and Portrait Photography," with "Baby Pictures a Specialty," listed only Fynmore's phone number and the hours he was available for appointments: "Any evening and Thursday afternoon." His grocery store employment was terminated shortly thereafter.[1]

By 1948 Fynmore was staff photographer of the *Boonville Herald*. In 1949 he opened the Fynmore Studio (alternately, Fynmore Studios) in Boonville, where it became a local tradition for wedding parties to stop at the studio on their way to post-ceremony receptions after driving around town "with decorated cars and honking horns." Photography for schools and Adirondack children's summer camps became business staples, as did custom framing.[2]

In 1954 Fynmore collaborated with author Ron Ryder on *Black Cotton Stockings*, a book of text and photographs focused on early days in Boonville. In 1955 he published his own book of 133 regional photographs, *The Central Adirondacks: A Picture Story*. Some of his images, including aerial views, were reproduced as postcards.

Fynmore largely gave up photography by 1970 to develop specialties in cleaning and restoring oil paintings, making and repairing frames, and lecturing on framing techniques. His son, Edward P. Fynmore (1938–2021), joined the business in 1964.[3]

1. *Boonville Herald*, March 14, 1946; email from Denise Fynmore, Fynmore's daughter, to the author, December 12, 2016.

2. *Boonville Herald*, January 29, 1948; Denise Fynmore email, December 12, 2016.

3. *Rome Sentinel*, October 2, 1962; Denise Fynmore email, December 12, 2016; Edward P. Fynmore obituary, May 2021, https://www.millsfuneralhomes.com/obituary/edward-p-fynmore.

GALUSHA, RAE (1898–1973)
Active North Creek, Warren County, 1921–1941

The son of a North Creek farm laborer, Rae Galusha's early work experience included "electric work" as a laborer at General Electric in Schenectady, Schenectady County, in 1920, and night watchman in a North Creek bolt and handle mill in 1921. He opened his Adirondack Studio in late 1921 with local advertisements for Christmas portraits and joined the International Photographic Association in 1924.[1]

Galusha recorded the people and landscape in and about his hometown, a hamlet of Johnsburg, chronicling the annual log drive on the Upper Hudson River and class groups at nearby schools. He was active in the mid- to late 1930s as the publicity chairman of Gore Mountain, the local ski resort; was an early photographer-writer for the short-lived *Empire State Ski News*; and reported on Gore Mountain ski conditions for regional newspapers. He was popular at Gore Mountain as a square dance caller. Galusha and his wife left North Creek in the summer of 1941 and settled in Schenectady, where Galusha worked as a maintenance man with General Electric for twenty years.[2]

1. *Warrensburgh News*, March 10, 1921; November 10, 1921; *Camera Craft*, February 1924, 103.

2. "Adirondack Museum Collection Includes Skiing Information," *Niagara Falls Gazette*, December 31, 1967; *Schenectady Gazette*, March 3, 1939; February 24, 1973; *New York Sun*, January 24, 1940.

GATES, GEORGE F. (1835–1904)
Active Clinton, Franklin, and Essex Counties, Late 1860s–Mid-1870s

Born into a farming family in Broome County, George Gates grew up in the Finger Lakes region of central New York and by 1855 was a miller in Spencer, Tioga County. In 1864 Gates and a brother established Gates Brothers, a photographic studio and wholesale stereoview operation in Watkins (Watkins Glen from 1926), Schuyler County. Publishing on his own as G. F. Gates, Gates was responsible for hundreds of stereographs of Watkins's two scenic gorges, Watkins and Havana Glens, as well as views of Niagara Falls; Mauch Chunk, Pennsylvania; Saratoga, Saratoga County; and the northeastern Adirondacks, particularly Ausable Chasm.[1]

In 1878 Gates relocated to Syracuse, Onondaga County, where his view list was reported to offer "thousands of negatives of the most beautiful and wonderful scenery in the country," most of them the work of others. In 1883 Gates moved to Chicago. He was a resident of South Haven, Michigan, at his death.[2]

1. *Yates County Chronicle*, January 4, 1866.

2. *Syracuse Sunday Times*, March 3, 1878; "Photographers' Association of America: Milwaukee Convention," *Photographic Times and American Photographer* 13, no. 152 (August 1883): 432.

GATES, PHILEMON TENNEY (1831–1892)
Active Plattsburgh, Clinton County, 1850–1863

Philemon Gates was one of the first photographers to advertise himself as permanently established in the Adirondack region. Frequent newspaper announcements placed between 1850 and 1862 kept the North Country well apprised of his specialties and, concomitantly, of new developments in photography.

Born in New Hampshire and the son of a physician, the teenaged "Prof. T. P. Gates, Daguerrean," promised in his first advertisement for the Sky-Light Photographic Palace of Art in Plattsburgh to "aim at the highest perfection possible" and noted his areas of expertise as "perfect likenesses taken of children WHEN AWAKE" and "miniatures of sick and deceased persons, at his rooms or elsewhere." By late 1858 "piano fortes" were also among gallery offerings. In 1859 he hyped his new "DOUBLE CAMERA" for taking two pictures "at the SAME INSTANT!" as well as a "MAMMOTH CAMERA (the only one that will be found out of the LARGE CITIES) which executes Life-Sized Portraits!"[1]

Listed as a Plattsburgh photographer in the 1860 US Census, Gates was described as "a robust man . . . of fine personal appearance." He married Susan Abigail Fouquet, a descendant of the locally influential Platt and Mooers families, shortly before selling his gallery to **Henry Ketchum Averill Jr** in 1863. A patent taken out in 1866 for a "reversible wristband" gave a hint as to his subsequent career direction: an 1867–68 northern New York business directory identified him as Plattsburgh "patentee of Gate's Roofed Carriage Boot." By 1870 Gates was a "manufacturer" living in Chazy, Clinton County.[2]

Gates relocated his family to the New York City area in the early 1870s. Working as a "broker," he continued to register inventions and take out patents: for Acheson's Hair Generator, a dye and "restorer" (1876); a sectional extension ladder (1884); an improved washboard (1885); a fruit and vegetable parer (1886); a method of applying ferrules to handles (1892). At the time of his death, from a heart attack suffered in his Manhattan office, Gates was president of the O.K. Cutlery Company and the Emery-Gates Sectional Ladder Company.[3]

1. *Plattsburgh Republican*, July 13, 1850; April 26, 1856; October 2, 1858; October 23, 1858; May 19, 1859.

2. *Plattsburgh Sentinel*, April 22, 1892.

3. *New York Times*, April 16, 1892.

GATES, WILLIS D. (1860–1926)
Active Lake George Region, 1881–1882

A son of **George F. Gates**, Willis Gates was a Watkins photographer from 1881. His W. D. Gates and Company dedicated itself to "the business of scenic and mercantile photography," taking photographs and filling orders to copy negatives "of nearly all the principal watering places and points of interest in this country and also many of foreign countries," probably for his father. The company dissolved in 1882. Gates appeared as a paperhanger in the 1900 US Census, and a "merchant, paper" in the New York state census of 1925.[1]

1. *Watkins Democrat*, October 5, 1881; October 18, 1882.

GIBBON, CHARLES (1878–1959)
Active Inlet, Hamilton County, 1907–1918

Born in Marcellus, Onondaga County, and raised in Whitesboro, Oneida County, Charles Gibbon was recorded as a photographer in the 1895 directory for nearby Utica. He was for more than twenty years nominally associated with two elder photographer brothers: J. Herbert and George E. Gibbon of Utica and Clinton. Gibbon spent the winter season of 1904 in Daytona, Florida, managing a recently opened photographic studio for former Whitesboro resident and Lake Placid photographer **Henry J. Kaiser**. From 1907 through 1918 he operated a photography and souvenir business from his seasonal camp on the channel between Fourth and Fifth Lakes in Inlet, Hamilton County. By 1919 Gibbon was listed in the Utica directory as a paperhanger, a livelihood he pursued until his retirement in 1953.[1]

1. *Utica Observer-Dispatch*, October 5, 1942; *Utica Herald-Dispatch*, December 28, 1903; "Charles Gibbon," *Utica Press*, August 18, 1959.

GILLIES, JOHN WALLACE (1883–1927)
Active Central Adirondacks, Early 1920s

John Gillies was well-known as an architectural photographer, popular with architects for his ability to record their buildings as they would wish to have them seen. He grew up outside of New York City, where his father was a builder. A 1905 graduate of Columbia University, he became a New York City civil engineer. Photography was a hobby before becoming Gillies's profession around 1912. Of his specialty, he wrote in 1920: "My job is to put architectural things on paper, and the camera is the easiest way to do it so I use photography." His photographic interests were not, however, strictly limited to architecture. In 1920 Gillies advertised "Portraits of Personalities by Photography," and in 1923 published what he called an "immature dissertation upon photography," *Principles of Pictorial Photography*. The book examined photographs by other photographers, analyzed and critiqued his own, and became a minor classic of photographic literature. He also wrote regular how-to articles for popular photographic journals.[1]

Gillies's contribution to Adirondack photography was circumscribed but influential. He was the photographer for a 1923 journal article on Kamp Kill Kare, a great camp in the Raquette Lake region designed by the well-known architectural office of John Russell Pope. At about the same time he took sixty-eight photographs used in architect Augustus D. Shepard's popular *Camps in the Adirondacks*, published in 1931 and based on Shepard's work at the Adirondack League Club in Old Forge, Herkimer County. His name as credited in this volume was John Wallace Gillies, Inc., the *Inc.* having perhaps been added to facilitate the marketing of Gillies's images after the photographer's early death from pneumonia. Gillies is buried in Green-Wood Cemetery, Brooklyn.[2]

1. "John W. Gillies Dead," *New York Times*, February 1, 1927; "Fifth of The Tribune's Series of Camera Artists," *New York Tribune*, May 2, 1920; *New York Post*, February 18, 1920; Gillies, *Principles of Pictorial Photography*, 10.
2. "Kamp Kill Kare: The Adirondack Lodge of Francis P. Garvan, Esq."; Shepard, *Camps in the Adirondacks*, passim.

GJERSVIK, TORLEIF (1920–1971)
Active Keeseville, Clinton and Essex Counties, 1950–1951; Plattsburgh, Clinton County, 1952–1953

Many Norwegian merchant seamen employed on oceanic vessels when Germany invaded Norway in April 1940 chose not to return to their occupied country. Twenty-year-old Torleif Gjersvik was among them. He shipped along the west coast of Canada and the United States for more than a year before arriving in New York City via Cartagena, Columbia, in April 1942. Having contracted tuberculosis during his long confinement in close ship quarters, he, as well as some five hundred other Norwegian seamen, "cured" in and around the village of Saranac Lake, Essex and Franklin Counties, in the early 1940s. Gjersvik spent much of this period as a patient at the Stony Wold Sanatorium, some fifteen miles northeast of Saranac Lake.

Gjersvik learned photographic skills in a program providing education, job training, and enrichment to tuberculosis patients. After marrying a Stony Wold nurse, he stayed on in the United States. The couple lived at first in Buffalo and then with members of her family in Keeseville. They spent nearly two years, from 1947 until 1949, in Bergen, Norway, before returning to Keeseville. Gjersvik worked as a dockmaster for the Lake Champlain Transportation Company at Port Kent and took pictures: in September 1950 an "outstanding" image of the destruction by fire of Keeseville's Hotel Ausable Chasm made the front page of the *Essex County Republican*. By December Gjersvik was promoting his home-based Torleif Studio. "No finer or more appreciated gift than a portrait, especially with your home in the background," suggested one advertisement. He relocated his business to Plattsburgh in 1952, moving it to "a larger and more suitable location" in February 1953. The studio closed abruptly three months later, marking the end of Gjersvik's photographic career in the Adirondacks.[1]

Gjersvik became a registered biological photographer, supervisor of the audiovisual department of the Children's Medical Department at the University of Tennessee Medical Units in Memphis, and a contributor to professional journals. After his early death he was buried in Tysnes, Hordaland, Norway.[2]

1. *Essex County Republican*, July 22, 1949; September 29, 1950; December 1, 1950; *Plattsburgh Press-Republican*, May 10, 1952; February 5, 1953; May 18, 1953.

2. *Memphis Commercial Appeal*, December 6, 1971; Gibson, *Biological Photographic Association, Its Half Century*, 52, 134.

GLOVER, LYCURGUS SOLON (1858–1935)
Active Essex and Franklin Counties; Old Forge, Herkimer County, 1901–1903

Lycurgus Glover grew up in a farming family in Logan County, Illinois. He spent much of the decade of the 1890s in and around San Diego, California, where his occupations included liquor dealer, clerk, and bookkeeper. By 1900 he was a photographer in Detroit, where he worked for what became the **Detroit Publishing Company** for some twenty-five years. Twelve company negatives credited to Glover of landscapes and hotels in Keene Valley and around the Saranac and St. Regis Lakes and the Fulton Chain were copyrighted in 1903 and 1904. By 1930 Glover was retired and living in Los Angeles, California.[1]

1. Detroit Photographic Company "Negative Registers," 107.

GOCKELER, EDWARD L. (1899–1964)
Active Essex and Franklin Counties, 1932–1964

Born in Washington, DC, the son of a hardware clerk, Edward Gockeler grew up in New Rochelle, Westchester County. After graduating from high school in 1917 he went to work in the office of the Committee of Information in wartime Washington, lasting at the job less than four months before contracting tuberculosis. After struggling with the disease for several years, Gockeler relocated to Saranac Lake in 1921. He was confined to bed for eighteen months after his arrival.[1]

Gockeler stayed on in the village, only partially regaining his health. He mastered photography in an occupational/recreational therapy class, and began entering his images in amateur competitions—the earliest of them sponsored in 1932 by the photographic magazine *Camera Craft*. One Gockeler image, a farm scene, took first place in 1939 in a competition sponsored by the *New York Herald Tribune* and was displayed in an exhibition at New York City's Radio City Music Hall. Other examples of his work were acquired by newspapers. A trio of Gockeler images illustrated a 1938 article published in central New York State newspapers about the recently opened Whiteface Veterans' Memorial Highway near Lake Placid.[2]

Circa 1939 Gockeler began working as a photographer for the Saranac Laboratory, a facility devoted to research in tuberculosis. For the next twenty-five years he recorded the progress and results of lab work and took the occasional faculty portrait. He continued a hobby interest in color landscape photography, selling bucolic images for use on brochures, greeting cards, and calendars. Several of his photographs appeared as magazine covers in the 1950s: for *Woman's Day*; *This Week*, a nationally syndicated Sunday magazine; and *Vermont Life*. Gockeler died of a heart attack on a rural Vermont roadside while loading equipment into his automobile after a photographic outing.[3]

1. Gallos, *Cure Cottages of Saranac Lake*, 74; Senate Committee on Claims, *Report to Accompany H. R. 419 for the Relief of Edward L. Gockeler*, 75th Cong., 1st sess., 1937, S. Rep. 507, 3.

2. *Camera Craft* 39 (1932): 83; *Lake Placid News*, October 27, 1939; "Top of World on Adirondack Peak Attracts Many Tourists in New York," *Skaneateles Press*, May 20, 1938.

3. *Adirondack Enterprise*, September 29, 1955; June 1, 1964; Gallos, *Cure Cottages*, 74.

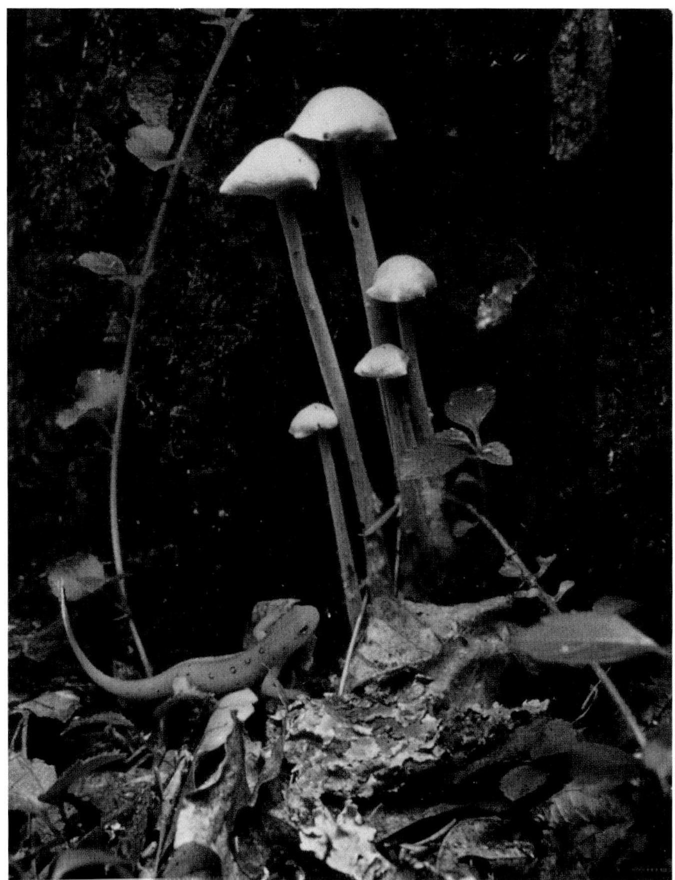

34. S. H. Gottscho, *Adirondack Forest: "Still Life,"* 1942–1943. Courtesy of Gottscho-Schleisner Collection, Library of Congress, Prints and Photographs Division, LC-USZC2-4237.

GOTTSCHO, SAMUEL H. (1875–1971)
Active Schroon Lake Region, Essex and Warren Counties, 1910–1950s

Born in Brooklyn, Samuel Gottscho achieved a national photographic reputation. He was best known for his iconic images of New York City, the "quintessential modern metropolis," from the mid-1920s through the 1930s. His work has been celebrated by the Museum of the City of New York in three dedicated exhibitions mounted between 1934 and 2005.[1]

Gottscho followed his father's occupation as a traveling salesman for twenty-five years, with specialties in laces, embroideries, and fabrics. He was also a camera hobbyist, purchasing his first camera in 1896. After selling a few amateur images, Gottscho made the decision in 1925, at the age of fifty, to turn his hobby into a career. His architecture, estate, garden, and flower photographs appeared in such magazines as *American Architect*, *House and Garden*, *Colliers*, *Town and Country*, and *Woman's Day*.[2]

Based in Jamaica, Queens, Gottscho indulged in a long summer love affair with the Adirondacks. Although he "still worked very hard all year" as a photographer, he wrote in 1951, "the great objective, as always, was the summer vacation which was spent year after year near a beautiful Adirondack lake." His favored lake was Schroon. The Library of Congress's extensive Gottscho-Schleisner Collection holds images from the region by and of Gottscho from 1910, the year he married. "We continued to spend our summers in the lovely Adirondack mountain section," added Gottscho, "but when [1942] gas-rationing made us walk instead of ride, my picture-taking was confined to a narrow radius from the hotel. To this I owe my first interest in wildflowers as a subject for my camera, for I began to take color pictures of the flowers on the roadside and along the fences though I had no knowledge as to what species were shown in my pictures." Gottscho became more than familiar with the subject, writing occasional columns on wildflowers for the *New York Times* through the mid-1960s, speaking on "Adirondack flowers" at the Brooklyn Botanic Garden and elsewhere, and authoring and illustrating a 1951 wildflower guide. One of Gottscho's Schroon Lake images was reproduced in an unusual format: as a fabric design called *Big Sky*. Available in four colorways (summer, autumn, sunset, and twilight), it was issued by Covington Fabrics in 1952. Gottscho gave up his annual Adirondack vacations sometime in the 1950s, but remained active as a photographer until shortly before his death at the age of ninety-five.[3]

1. Albrecht, *Mythic City*, 26.

2. Gottscho, *Wildflowers*, 9; Albrecht, *Mythic City*, 26–27; "Samuel Gottscho, Photographer, Dies," *New York Times*, January 29, 1971.

3. Gottscho, *Wildflowers*, 9–10; Haley, "Here and There."

GRIMES, FRANK H. (1859–1941)
Active Ticonderoga, Essex County, 1896–1898; 1918–Late 1920s

A peripatetic photographer and florist, Frank Grimes was born in Whitehall, Washington County, and moved with his parents to Rutland, Vermont, in 1863. His father was a laborer. A twenty-one-year-old Rutland house painter in 1880, Grimes was first listed as a photographer in the 1889–92 Rutland city directory. An 1891 compendium of Vermont businesses profiled Grimes as having purchased a photographic gallery the previous year in nearby Brandon after "having been engaged in the same line of business in Rutland for two years." The volume described Grimes as a "first-class photographer for every variety of pictures" with "a widespread reputation both in commercial and social circles."[1]

In 1896 Grimes relocated briefly to Ticonderoga, Essex County; his "cycloramic" photograph for the Ticonderoga Historical Society of Ticonderoga's famous battlefield, made from four images, appeared in 1898 in the journal *Spirit of '76*, and he was one of two photographers whose images were used as the basis for engravings in a "handsome pamphlet" produced for the society.[2]

Grimes returned to Vermont in early 1898 (although he was spotted in Ticonderoga in 1907 "taking pictures to be used on souvenir post cards"). A Rutland farmer in the 1910 US Census, he threw in his lot shortly thereafter with his son, a Rutland florist, with whom he returned to Ticonderoga in 1911. Father and son established the Grimes Floral Company. Grimes Sr. also took on the oversight of a branch photographic studio opened that year by **Burnell F. Dandurand** in Whitehall. By late 1918 he was advertising himself again as a "first-class photographer in all its branches" in Ticonderoga, where the Grimes Studio and Grimes Floral Company coexisted for a number of years. By 1930, Grimes was retired and working as a Rutland gardener.[3]

1. *Industries and Wealth of the Principal Points in Vermont*, 85.

2. *Ticonderoga Sentinel*, June 4, 1896; January 27, 1898; February 17, 1898; March 10, 1898; Grimes's "cycloramic" photograph appears without attribution in *Spirit of '76* (January 1898): 142–43.

3. *Ticonderoga Sentinel*, July 4, 1907; November 2, 1911; December 11, 1913; January 1, 1914; January 4, 1917; December 19, 1929.

GROVER, LYMAN PAUL (1898–1987)
Active Ticonderoga, Essex County, 1925–1927 and 1930–1931

Paul Grover was one of few Adirondack-based photographers to attend a professional school of photography. Born in Moriah, Essex County, after 1910 his family relocated to Ticonderoga, where he was remembered years later as having built as a high school student the first wireless radio in town. His initial job as a telephone worker was interrupted by World War I, during which he served a brief, late stint in the army. After the war Grover enlisted in the navy as a radio electrician and saw something of the world.[1]

In 1924, Grover, along with fellow Ticonderoga resident **Mason Charles Smith**, enrolled at the Illinois College of Photography in Effingham, Illinois. Upon his return to Ticonderoga, he partnered with Charles King Jr. in a photographic enterprise, Grover & King. As a December 1926 advertisement read, "The gift some loved one is wishing you'd surprise them with Christmas morning. Your portrait." The affiliation, which also offered real photo postcards, lasted little more than a year; Grover appears to have been its sole photographer. He subsequently worked as a railroad detective and graduated from the New York State Police School before taking a job in early 1930 with the US Customs Service at the border crossing in Rouses Point, Clinton County. He returned to Ticonderoga in December 1930, announcing that he would be taking up "his old trade of photography." Rather than equip a studio, he added, he planned to take photographs in the homes of his patrons "at no extra charge." Grover ran one newspaper advertisement and placed one fire-related image on the front page of the local paper before returning by May 1931 to his former job at Rouses Point. He remained with the Customs Service until retiring in 1963.[2]

1. *Ticonderoga Sentinel*, August 15, 1940.
2. *Ticonderoga Sentinel*, January 8, 1925; December 16, 1926; December 4, 1930; May 14, 1931; *Plattsburgh Republican*, March 21, 1925; *Plattsburgh Press-Republican*, December 12, 1987.

GUILD, JONATHAN FRANCES (1871–1940)
Active Westport, Essex County, 1890s

Jonathan Guild was recorded as a Dedham, Massachusetts, photographer in local directories from 1893. His specialties, according to an 1896 advertisement, included "portraits, outside views & groups." He is known in the Adirondacks for his slender 7 x 9 inch souvenir viewbook, *Westport on Lake George*, containing ten photographs of the village.[1]

1. Steele and Polito, *A Directory of Massachusetts Photographers*, 222.

HAND, GEORGE A. (1866–1946)
Active Lake Placid, Essex County, 1906–1916

Born in Potsdam, St. Lawrence County, George Hand was, according to the 1880 US Census, working in a Potsdam photographer's shop at the age of fourteen. He made his first appearance in the village of Lake Placid in 1905, establishing a summer studio at the Hotel Ruisseaumont as a photo watercolorist. In June 1906 he was designated as the general manager of Kaiser Photographic Services, an enterprise of departing Lake Placid resident **Henry J. Kaiser.**[1]

Hand spent the summers between 1906 and 1916 overseeing the Lake Placid Kaiser summer operation and briefly supervised the Kaiser shops in Florida. He appeared in the 1910 US Census as a Palm Beach landscape artist; in the New York state census of 1915 as a Lake Placid photographer. He ran advertisements for the Kaiser Photographic Shop through 1915 (that year promoting "Portraits, Amateur finishing, Exteriors and Interiors"), and was active in the Lake Placid community as a singer and founding member of the board of trustees of the Adirondack Temple, a planned but unexecuted meeting hall for musical, educational, religious, and other programs. After his five-year-old son drowned in Lake Placid's Mirror Lake in the summer of 1916, Hand leased the former Kaiser shop and studio to **George T. Rabineau** and left the village. In 1924 he moved his family from Florida to California. The 1930 US Census recorded him as an art instructor in Pasadena. He died in San Bernardino.[2]

1. *Potsdam Herald-Recorder*, August 4, 1905; *Potsdam Courier-Freeman* quoting *Troy Record*, June 13, 1906.

2. *Ticonderoga Sentinel*, April 20, 1916; *Lake Placid News*, July 23, 1915; July 14, 1916; "Drove from One Ocean to Another," August 29, 1924; *Plattsburgh Sentinel*, November 24, 1916.

HARRIS, DAVID (1850–1914)
Active Raquette Lake Region, Hamilton County, 1904–1908

Immigrants from Pembrokeshire, Wales, the Harris family settled in Utica, Oneida County, in 1861. By the age of fifteen, David Harris was a live-in attendant at Utica's New York State Lunatic Asylum. In 1871 he appeared as a photographer in the Utica directory, and in 1876 began a twelve-year association with Utica photographer G. W. Gurley, at first as an operator and from about 1881 in partnership as Gurley & Harris. In 1888 he partnered with "practical photographer" Lewis H. Greene in Harris & Greene, a busy portrait studio until its closure in 1904. Harris worked briefly for his own account during the next several years, during which he took a number of photographs at Alfred Gwynne Vanderbilt's Camp Sagamore. In 1910, 1912, and 1913 Utica directories Harris's occupation was listed as "porter."[1]

1. *Clinton Courier*, January 11, 1882; *Utica Press*, November 27, 1888; *Utica Herald-Dispatch*, June 7, 1904.

HART, HAROLD J. (1908–1993)
Active Keeseville, Clinton and Essex Counties, 1949–1950; Plattsburgh, Clinton County, 1954–1974

A native of Peru, Clinton County, Harold "Hobby" Hart was a salesman for the American Agricultural Chemical Company in Carteret, New Jersey, before becoming a soldier in 1942. During his three-and-a-half years in the armed services he was attached to the Seventh Photo Technical Squadron, trained to provide photographic intelligence for air and ground forces in the China-Burma-India Theater of World War II. Putting his photographic skills to use after the war, he opened the Hart Photographic Studio in Keeseville in the late 1940s, offering "chauffeur prints, candid wedding pictures, FHA and beer license prints." He closed his studio in June 1950 to work briefly for Elizabethtown photographer **Carl F. Huttig**, and after at least one subsequent job as an operator, joined forces in 1954 with Plattsburgh photographer Richard D. Hagar in the Hagar-Hart Studio. Hart retired in 1974.[1]

1. *Plattsburgh Press-Republican*, June 28, 1943; April 29, 1974; October 6, 1993; *Essex County Republican*, April 21, 1950; June 23, 1950.

HASTINGS, PHILIP ROSS (1925–1987)
Active around Rail Lines and Depots in Essex, Franklin, and St. Lawrence Counties, 1949–1950

Philip Hastings represented a subspecies of amateur photographer: train hobbyist, or railfan, who recorded the last days of steam rail in North America. His work featured prominently from the 1950s in *Trains* and other railroading magazines and he authored a number of books on rail subjects.

A native of Bradford, Vermont, Hastings photographed trains at work in the Adirondack region while a student at the University of Vermont's School of Medicine. He was a leader in moving train photographers away from the so-called smoking wedge shot (a three-quarter view focused on the locomotive of an approaching train) to a style that took in a broader, more people-oriented view of the railroading environment, and experimented with unusual camera angles, panoramic shots, and dusk and night views.[1]

Certified as a psychiatrist in 1959, Hastings moved his family to Iowa, where he established a practice. Later photographic interests included diesel-powered trains and the twilight years of Iowa's electric interurban lines. In 1985 Hastings received the annual Photography Award from the Railroad and Locomotive Historical Society for a lifetime of outstanding achievement. After his death, his family donated his massive archive, including some

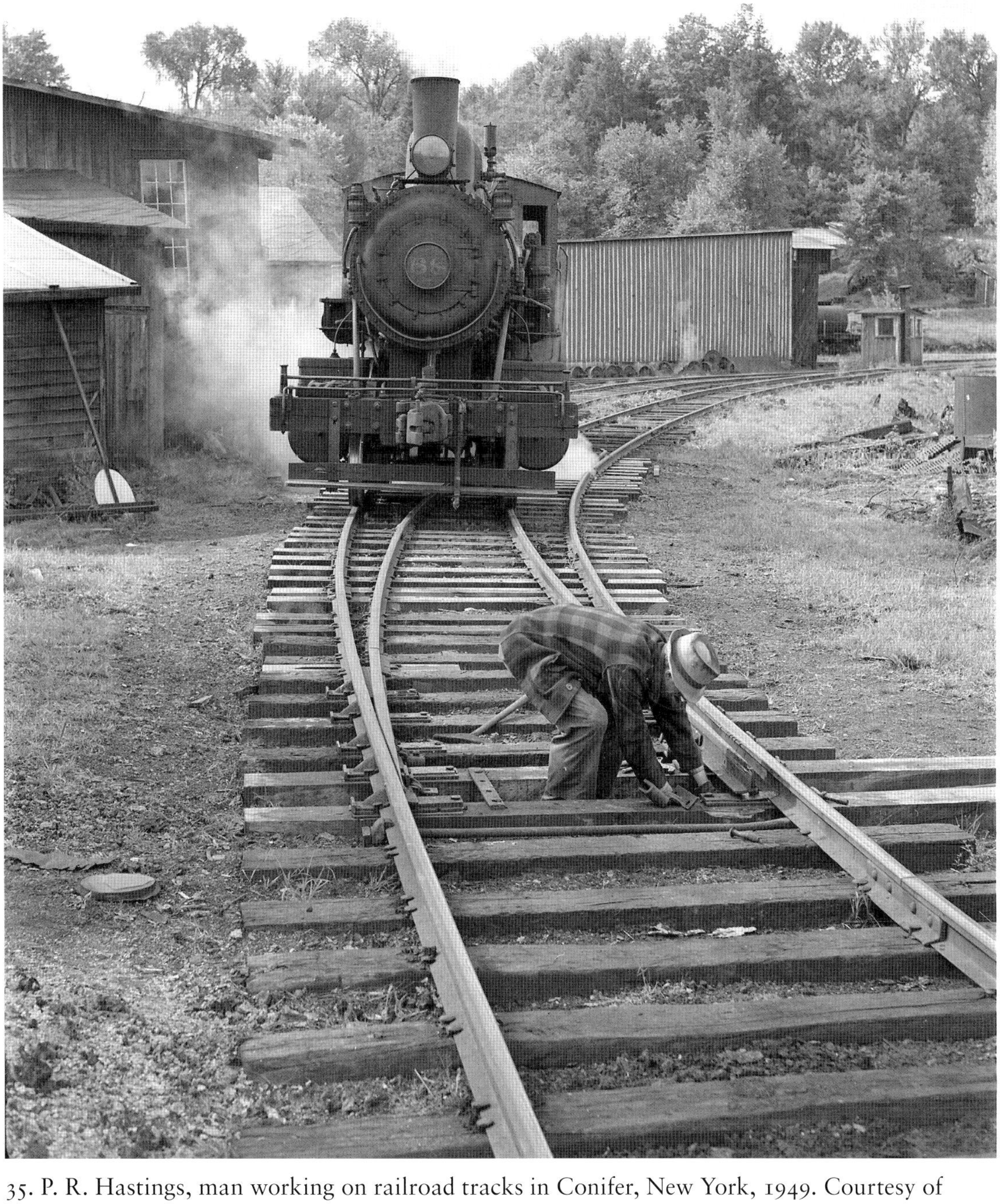

35. P. R. Hastings, man working on railroad tracks in Conifer, New York, 1949. Courtesy of California State Railroad Museum Library and Archives.

forty-six thousand black-and-white negatives and thirty-two thousand color slides, to the California State Railroad Museum in Sacramento.[2]

1. California State Railroad Museum, "Beyond Shades of Gray," 1; Nicola Smith, "Bradford, Vt. Celebrates a Native Who Photographed Railroads."

2. California State Railroad Museum, "Beyond Shades of Gray," 1; Smith, "Bradford, Vt."

HEWITT, THADDEUS E. (1824–1891)
Active Northville, Fulton County, 1870–1882

Born in Saratoga County, Thaddeus Hewitt was a daguerreotypist in Amsterdam, Montgomery County, by 1858. After partnering with his brother-in-law George Searles in Amsterdam's Hewitt & Searles in the late 1860s, he relocated to Northville as a portrait photographer. He may subsequently have spent some years in Wells, Hamilton County, or operated a satellite gallery there; by 1883 he had returned to Amsterdam. Hewitt's last years were spent in Edinburg, Saratoga County.[1]

1. *Troy Daily Times*, June 4, 1891; J. M. B., "From My Note Book—No. 16, Amsterdam Thirty-Four Years Ago," *Amsterdam Daily Democrat*, February 15, 1894.

HIBBARD, CHARLES P. (1848–AFTER 1920)
Active Ausable Chasm, Clinton and Essex Counties, 1888–1890

Charles Hibbard's parents, of Newbury, Vermont, went west after their marriage in 1842, and Hibbard was born in Wisconsin. His father left for California during the Gold Rush, met with success in mining, and started home, never to be heard from again. His wife returned with her children to her father's farm in Lyman, New Hampshire, where Hibbard appeared as a photographer in the 1870 US Census and a printer in 1880. In 1885 he moved to Burlington, Vermont, from which he photographed Ausable Chasm, his only Adirondack subject. Returning to New Hampshire in late 1890, Hibbard settled in the town of Lisbon and specialized in landscape photography before relocating by 1910 to Tehama County, California. He was enumerated in the 1910 and 1920 US Censuses as a farmer who "works out."[1]

1. Wells, *History of Newbury, Vermont*, 455; Child, *Gazetteer of Orange County, Vermont*, 285.

HINCKLEY, HARVEY H. (1864–1914)
Active Westport, Essex County, 1894–1897

Born on the North Elba farm previously owned by abolitionist John Brown, Harvey Hinckley's Essex County roots went back two generations. But Hinckley had seen something of the world by the time he landed in Westport in the mid-1890s as a photographer, including Minneapolis, where he tried his hand at real estate, and California, where the second of his three children was born in 1893.[1]

Hinckley's specialty was portrait photography. But in September 1897, shortly after the death of his six-year-old daughter, the photographer announced his intention of leaving Westport after a residence of only two years. He left the field of commercial photography at the same time. A Storm Lake, Iowa, merchant in 1900, by 1903 Hinckley was in Joplin, Missouri, as president of the Adirondack Lead and Zinc Company. He, his wife, and three residents of Malone, Franklin County, were five of the seven stockholders in the company (which contributed more than thirty thousand dollars in royalties to the town of Joplin's coffers in its first four years). By 1910 he was again in Minneapolis as a real estate agent. An Essex County obituary recalled Hinckley as "a man of fine qualities. His courteous manner and winning ways, and cordial companionship made him many friends wherever he went." He is buried in Westport's Hillside Cemetery beside his wife and daughter.[2]

1. *Essex County Republican*, February 29, 1896.

2. *Essex County Republican*, September 16, 1897; August 14, 1914; *Malone Palladium*, July 30, 1903; *Mining Reporter* (Denver, CO), August 8, 1907), 133; *Elizabethtown Post*, August 20, 1914.

HODGES, FREDERICK ATHERTON (1888–1958)
Active Central and Southern Adirondacks, 1910–1955

Frederick Hodges was born in Rome, Oneida County, where his father, Frederick B. Hodges, was well-known as a photographer, camera historian, writer, and botanist who identified several previously undiscovered plants. In 1897 the family began to spend summer vacations on the Fulton Chain of Lakes in Hamilton and Herkimer Counties, and young Fred fell in love with the Adirondack region. A 1905 news article detailed a weeklong, 185-mile canoe trip recently completed by the sixteen-year-old boy and a school friend, a follow-up to his 150-mile canoe excursion of the previous summer.[1]

After finishing his education in Rome's public schools and Colgate Preparatory School in Hamilton, Madison County, Hodges took up photography. He trained with a series of photographers in New York, Boston, and Chicago, but rarely missed his summer vacations in the Adirondacks. In 1913 he made an attempt to establish himself as a Rome portrait photographer, then worked again as an operator for other photographers in Boston and Rome before opening his own studio in New Hartford, Oneida County, circa 1923. In 1931 he relocated permanently to Utica.[2]

A taciturn man, Hodges "good-naturedly endured" his career as a studio photographer and was good at it: a portrait of an Adirondack guide was exhibited at the Albright Gallery in Buffalo in 1926. But landscape photography was his first love, and Hodges eventually generated more than eight thousand landscape images as well as twenty-three reels of sixteen-millimeter film. "He thinks the Adirondacks are the most beautiful mountains anywhere," reported a journalist. "He's never even bothered to take pictures of any others." The market for his photographs was seasonal and barely remunerative, but Hodges persevered. He displayed and sold enlarged, mounted, hand-colored views

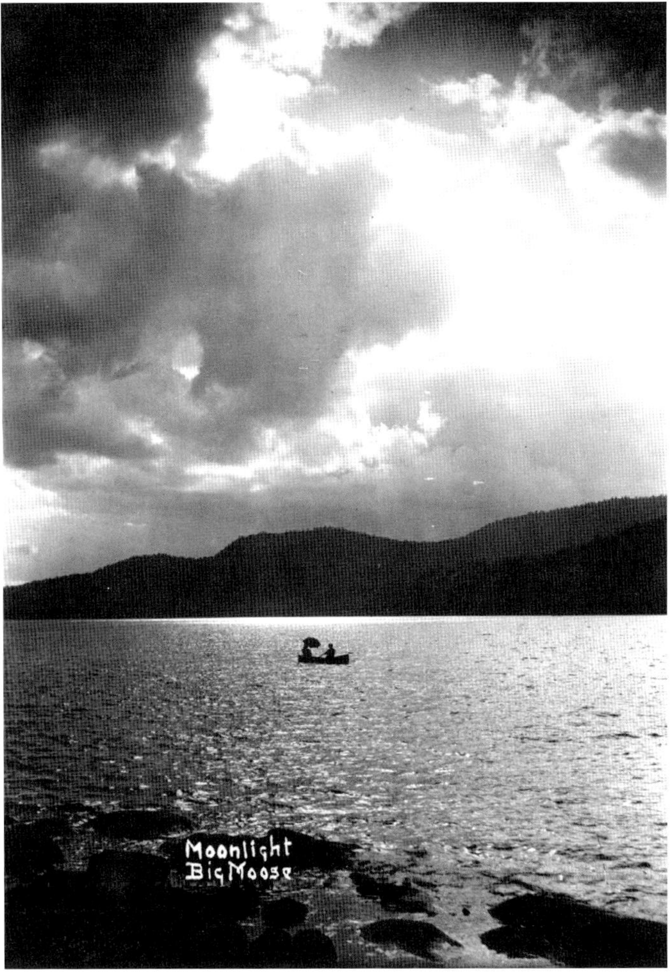

36. F. A. Hodges, *Moonlight, Big Moose*, 1924. Courtesy of Adirondack Experience.

through hotels; narrated presentations of his films; and made the occasional sale of individual images to postcard publishers. His "moonlight pictures" sold best, according to Hodges, although they were "always faked . . . taken in broad daylight with the camera facing the sun." Images of white birch trees ranked second in popularity, and Adirondack trails third.[3]

Hodges's affinity for the Adirondack region and his skill as an outdoorsman garnered him the nickname "Adirondack Hodges." From the early 1940s his center of summer operations was the Indian Lake, Hamilton County, hamlet of Blue Mountain Lake, where the Hedges, a local resort, gave him permission to erect a camp and granted lifetime tenancy. During the last summers of his life Hodges worked at the recently opened Adirondack Museum in Blue Mountain Lake where, as he modestly noted in his 1955 letter of application, his "many years in the Woods and knowledge of Adirondack customs and ways" might make him of some use. He died suddenly of a heart attack at the museum.[4]

1. DeSormo, *Heydays of the Adirondacks*, 163–65 (DeSormo was Hodges's son-in-law); "A North Woods Canoe Trip," *Rome Sentinel*, July 31, 1905.

2. *Rome Sentinel*, November 26, 1913; Obituary, *Utica Observer Dispatch*, August 16, 1958.

3. DeSormo, *Heydays of the Adirondacks*, 163, 165; *Buffalo Courier*, January 24, 1926; Beetle, "Press Parade."

4. DeSormo, *Heydays of the Adirondacks*, 165; Frederick A. Hodges to Robert Bruce Inverarity, director, Adirondack Museum, September 12, 1955; Hodges file, Adirondack Experience Library.

HOLLEY, JAMES FRANK (1853–1942)
Active Warren and Hamilton Counties, Late 1870s–1902

Frank Holley, a lifelong resident of Warren County, was born in Bolton. By 1870 he was living on a Horicon farm with his parents and the youngest four of his seven siblings. Enumerated as a photographer in the 1880 US Census, Holley worked from the Horicon hamlet of Adirondack on the shores of Schroon Lake before relocating in the mid-1880s to the village of Chestertown, some seven miles away.

Holley operated a portrait gallery during the winter months, but when warm weather arrived he took to the road. Favorite destinations included Blue Mountain and Raquette Lakes, Hamilton County, both of which were represented in his series of albumen prints labeled *Adirondack Views*. Summer assistant photographers also moved about from the late 1880s and tented in resort communities to take photos "in the interest of J. F. Holley" that carried his imprint.[1]

Holley pursued a number of commercial opportunities besides photography. He acquired a Chestertown livery in 1886 and opened a Chestertown

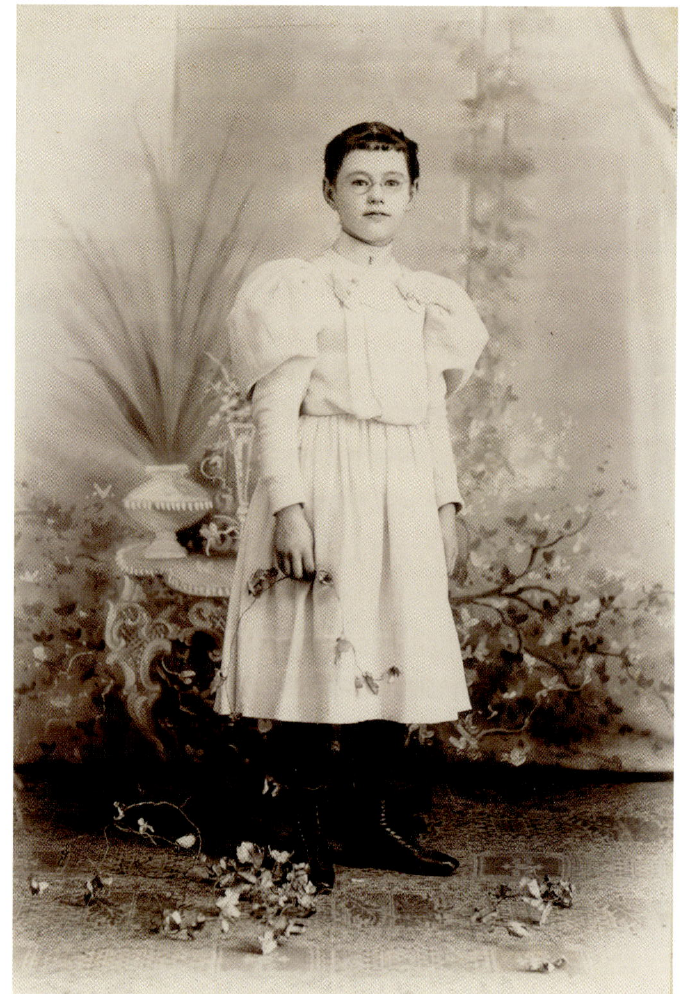

37. J. F. Holley, portrait, 1890s.

toy and notion store in 1896. In 1900 he was a general merchant. He tried his hand at dentistry, clock repair, and, as a "commercial traveler," represented an assortment of products over the years: musical instruments (primarily organs and pianos), bicycles, candy, groceries, and cigars. Moving his family in 1902 to Glens Falls, Holley left the photography field, advertising the availability that year of "two photographic Tents and full outfits. On good summer routes. Will sell cheap." Holley appeared in the 1910 US Census as a Glens Falls store proprietor and continued to agent for other businesses. During Holley's 1911 visit to the Rising House, a Chestertown hotel, it was reported that "his smiles help to sell pianos up here and he places a goodly number of them every year."[2]

1. *Elizabethtown Post*, May 3, 1888; May 20, 1897.

2. *Glens Falls Times*, November 19, 1886; *Warrensburgh News*, February 28, 1895; March 26, 1896; November 19, 1896; December 3, 1896; April 15, 1897; April 1, 1909; June 22, 1911; *Ticonderoga Sentinel*, June 29, 1893; *Glens Falls Star*, March 24, 1902; *Photographic Times-Bulletin* 34, no. 6 (June 1902): 288.

HOUGHTON, GEORGE HARPER (1826–1870)

Active Franklin County, 1864

George Houghton qualifies as an Adirondack photographer on the basis of a single image—notable as the first-known photograph of both Bartlett's Hotel, a celebrated inn established in 1854 on a major canoe route through the Adirondacks, and a specialized watercraft, the Adirondack guideboat.

Born in Putney, Vermont, Houghton operated a photograph gallery in Brattleboro from early 1860. He attained a wide reputation with 1861–63 photographs of Vermont soldiers at the front during the Civil War. His 1864 Adirondack photograph appears to have been taken during a pleasure trip to the Adirondack interior. No other images from the expedition have been identified.[1]

1. *Vermont Phoenix*, May 12, 1860.

HOWARD, JAMES JAY (1835–1892)

Active Plattsburgh, Clinton County, 1862–1889

Born in Hampton, Connecticut, James Howard arrived in Plattsburgh, Clinton County, in 1862, taking over the studio of H. P. Dow and advertising on July 2, 1864, that Howard & Co. was "prepared to take any number of pictures any day—even the Fourth of July." An early motto was "Small Profits and Ready Sale." Losing his first studio to fire in 1867, Howard opened a second later that year with "new instruments, fixtures, and other necessaries of the latest styles."[1]

While Howard's specialty was portraiture, his gallery also offered in its early days "photographic views of all the places of interest on Lake Champlain, Lake George, Chazy and Saranac Lakes;

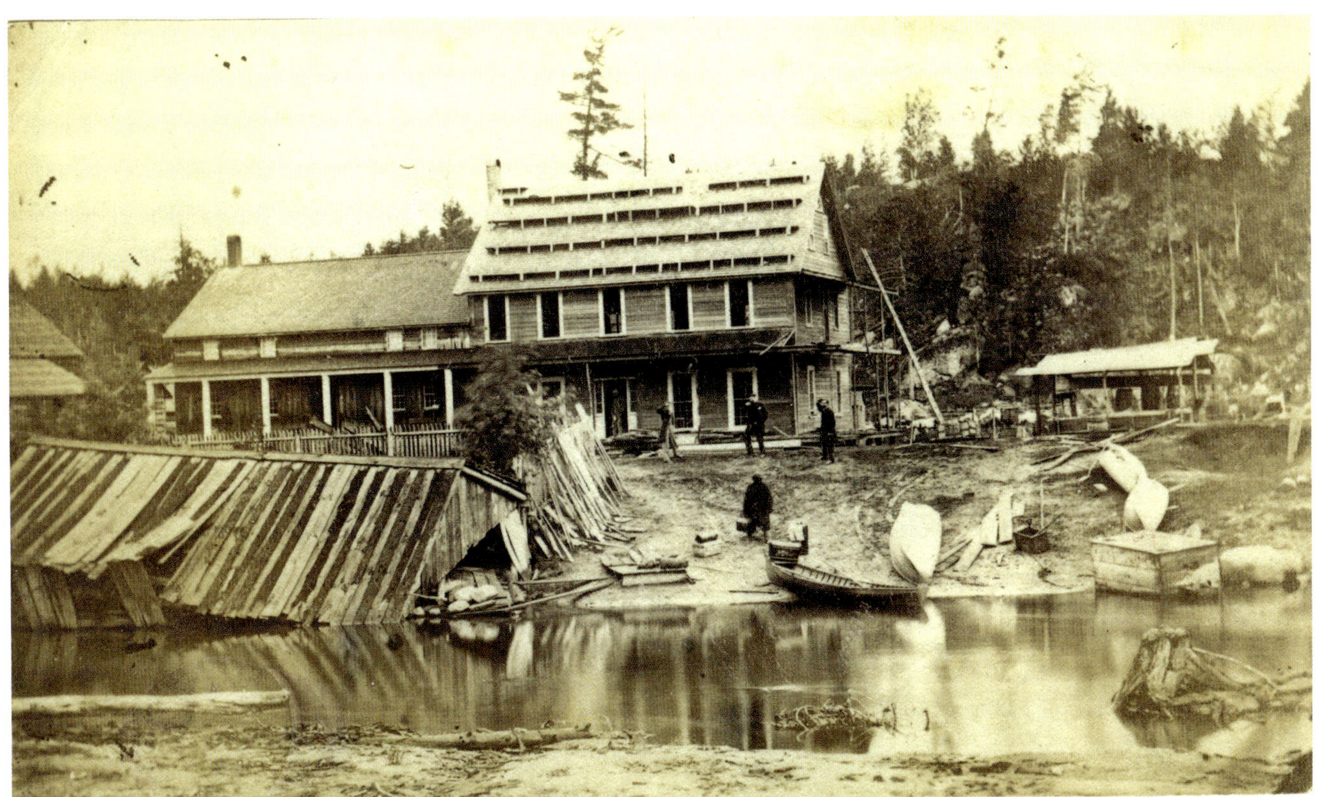

38. G. H. Houghton, Bartlett's, Upper Saranac Lake, 1864. Courtesy of Adirondack Experience.

also of Smith's at the St. Regis Lake." Howard may have acted as marketing agent for these views rather than photographer. He enjoyed the occasional leave of absence from his studio, as suggested in his 1880 announcement that, having spent the past three years "among the leading galleries east and west, we are able to produce far superior work than ever before." The gallery had short-term satellite galleries: in LaColle, Quebec, in 1864; in Burlington, Vermont, in 1886–87.[2]

In 1889 Howard sold his studio to photographer **William A. Bigelow**. He died three years later in New York City. As a local obituary read, Howard "was a long time resident of Plattsburgh and a well-known photographer who loved his art, and had one of the most popular photograph galleries in Northern New York."[3]

1. *Plattsburgh Sentinel*, June 23, 1864; November 22, 1867; January 14, 1870; July 20, 1926; *Plattsburgh Republican*, June 27, 1863; July 2, 1864; September 16, 1865.

2. Winslow Cossoul Watson, *Descriptive and Historical Guide to the Valley of Lake Champlain and the Adirondacks*, xxiii; *Plattsburgh Republican*, December 3, 1864; April 3, 1880; unpaged advertisement in 1886–87 Plattsburgh directory.

3. *Plattsburgh Sentinel*, December 13, 1889; February 26, 1892.

HOWARD, LEROY (1891–1944)
Active Westport, Essex County, 1915–1940

But for the winter of 1919–20, which he and his family passed in Florida, LeRoy Howard seldom ventured far from his Westport birthplace. The son of a farmer, he became an assistant US postmaster not long after graduating from high school. In 1915 he purchased the Westport photographic shop of Arthur N. Marshall (opened in 1902 and providing Kodak supplies, developing and finishing services, and clock, watch, and jewelry repair). Howard served as Westport's "experienced and successful photographer" for some twenty-five years while continuing, on occasion, to fill the role of assistant or substitute mail carrier.[1]

1. *Ticonderoga Sentinel*, December 10, 1914; August 19, 1915; November 20, 1919; *Essex County Republican*, May 21, 1920; *Elizabethtown Post*, June 5, 1902; *Adirondack Record–Elizabethtown Post*, November 23, 1944.

HUDSON, HENRIETTA (1862–1942), MARRIED NAME HENRIETTA BILLWILLER
Active Bolton Landing, Warren County, 1916–1930s

Not only was Henrietta Hudson a woman photographer, but she was a wealthy one, leaving behind at her death an estate valued at nearly two million dollars. Born in Hudson City (now Jersey City), New Jersey, to German carpenter John A. Stienhauser and Austrian Victoriene Schilling, her maternal background was aristocratic. A great-grandmother had been first lady-in-waiting to the Empress Elizabeth of Austria; her grandfather Ernst Schilling was the head of an esteemed Viennese medical center and politician before fleeing to New York City after the failure of the 1848–49 Austrian revolution.[1]

In 1883 Henrietta Stienhauser married Charles Billwiller, from the embroidery center city of St. Gallen, Switzerland, who flourished in New York as an importer of St. Gallen's luxury product. After settling their family in Brooklyn, the Billwillers bought a summer home in the mid-1890s on 110 lakeside acres in the fashionable Bolton hamlet of Bolton Landing. Henrietta was active as a Brooklyn clubwoman, particularly on behalf of women's suffrage and women's education. The Billwillers separated during the first decade of the twentieth century, but never divorced. Henrietta adopted the professional name "Hudson" from the town of her birth.

Hudson began experimenting with color photography in 1913. She burst upon New York City's photographic scene in October 1916 with the display of an image at an American Institute of Graphic Arts exhibition of a "fragile soap bubble in all its iridescent beauty." (The photograph was printed in her Bolton studio.) Although modestly claiming in 1917 that she was "but an amateur in photography and gathered her knowledge from the magazines," a journalist noted it as evident that Hudson had "brought to her reading . . . a wonderful perception and appreciation of color, combined with incredible patience and a lot of hard experimental work." Hudson's mastery of direct color printing was a major accomplishment in the young field of color photography, and she was elected to membership in both the AIGA and the Royal Photographic Society of London. "As an ardent student of personal efficiency," she announced that she would "project" her photographic hobby "into the commercial," and would "make the usual professional charge for such work as she may be called upon to do for individuals, the proceeds of her labors in this field being devoted to charity." She wrote for a 1920 book, *Careers for Women*, that she considered the most interesting branch of photography to be color research, "as it gives the chance of seeking and perhaps finding a perfect process for movies in color, or a way of photographically printing in color on paper." Spending more time at her Bolton home in the 1920s, Hudson continued her commitment to photography and photographic professionalism. Several of her images of Lake George appeared in the resort newspaper *Lake George Mirror*. In 1921 she advertised a "projection slide department" at her Bolton-based Hudetta Laboratories ("Henrietta Hudson, Technical Director"), and in 1930 that, as a photographer, she "interprets practically gardens and estates." A newspaper review of a 2008 exhibition in Glens Falls, Warren County, of historical photographs of the gardens of the town's wealthy Pruyn sisters singled Hudson's photographs out as the "most artistic" in the show.[2]

"Henrietta Hudson Billwiller" contributed landscape views and text to a 1929 publication about Lake George in support of a Bolton Episcopal Church building project. She taught photography at a Bolton Girl Scout camp, and in 1930 became a year-round Bolton resident. Her occupation was noted in the US Census that year as "photographic research, independent." At the time of her death Hudson was a consultant for the Eastman Kodak Company and for Agfa Ansco, a firm producing photographic films, papers, and cameras. She is buried in Green-Wood Cemetery, Brooklyn.[3]

1. *Glens Falls Post-Star*, November 13, 1942; "Henrietta Hudson, Color-art Pioneer," *New York Times*, April 4, 1942.

2. "Direct Color Photography at Lake George," *Lake George Mirror*, July 3, 1915; August 13, 1921; April 27, 1925; July 12, 1930; *Photographic Journal of America* 54, no. 1 (January 1917): 29; "An Appreciation of the Color Work of Henrietta Hudson," *Photo Miniature* 14, no. 158 (February 1917): 98; Hudson, "The Direct Color Printer," 61; Bjornland, "Rare Photos Reveal the Private Gardens of the Pruyn Family."

3. *Lake George Mirror*, April 25, 1925; August 31, 1929; *Memorial Gift Book: Lake George and Vicinity*; *New York Times*, April 4, 1942.

HUESTED, HERBERT R. (1874–1943)
Active Conifer, St. Lawrence County, 1920s

Herbert Huested, along with his father, an uncle, and a cousin, constituted a northern New York State photographic dynasty during the late nineteenth and first decades of the twentieth century. Herbert Huested, taken up here, was born in Chase Mills, St. Lawrence County. He grew up in Mannsville and Adams, Jefferson County, and Sandy Creek, Oswego County, where his father, George P., and uncle Ralph W. operated photographic galleries and a number of part-time satellites from the 1870s—sometimes in partnership and sometimes alone. In 1903 Herbert opened a studio with his father in Watertown, Jefferson County, and bought out his father's interest several years later to become the sole proprietor of the popular business until his retirement in 1942.[1]

Huested specialized in portrait work but also undertook the occasional commercial commission. One of these was the documentation of the Adirondack operations of the Emporium Lumber Company, one of the largest hardwood operations on the East Coast before the Great Depression. A photograph album in the collection of the Adirondack Experience, bearing the seal H. R. HUESTED,

WATERTOWN, includes twenty-nine images of the Emporium-dominated hamlet of Conifer, the Grasse River Railroad that serviced the Emporium venture, and the exterior and interior of the company's sawmill on the shore of Cranberry Lake.

1. "George P. Huested, Sandy Creek, Dies," *Sandy Creek News*, May 18, 1922; "Herbert Huested Dies in Hospital," *Sandy Creek News*, January 19, 1944.

HUTTIG, CARL F. (1891–1950) (ALSO KNOWN AS CHARLES HUETTIG AND CARLOS HUETTIG) AND EMILY D. HUTTIG (1891–1966)

Active Elizabethtown, Essex County, 1935–1963

Carl Huttig was the principal photographer in Elizabethtown, Essex County, from 1935 until his death. Born in Cologne, Germany, he and his wife from 1913, Emily, of Neustadt, Germany, landed in Laredo, Texas, in 1922 from Tampico, Mexico, where he had owned or worked in a photographic studio. His 1923 American naturalization papers gave his occupation as photographer. Huttig came to know Elizabethtown in the late 1920s as valet/butler to Edward Lee Campe, a wealthy New York City manufacturer of men's clothing and the owner of an Elizabethtown summer residence, Camp Ledgewood.[1]

In 1935 Huttig purchased the Red Cedar Cabin camp property and gas station in the Elizabethtown hamlet of New Russia, running it with his wife as Carl's Place (later the Cobble Mountain Inn and Motel). The operation included a restaurant noted for its excellent cuisine. He built a photographic workshop, Carl's Studio, on the property, and began to manage the photographic business of the Underwood Studio for the widow of its recently deceased owner—Elizabethtown's long-ensconced photographer **Clarence Underwood**. Huttig continued the Underwood business under its original name after Mrs. Underwood's 1937 death and relocated it to a former Methodist church building in 1947, the year in which he sold his New Russia establishment. The Underwood Studio was primarily a seasonal business specializing in portrait photography.[2]

Emily Huttig took over the studio after her husband's 1950 death. She, too, kept its original name and advertised as Mrs. Charles F. Huttig of Underwood Studio. She offered "Modern Portrait and Commercial Photography, Developing and Printing," and specialized in "Wedding Portraits, Candid and Formal" as well as high-school graduation photos. She was reported in 1962 as "devoted to her work," which she "has carried on with only occasional help. Hours of work are not counted at Underwood Studio."[3]

1. *Adirondack Record–Elizabethtown Post*, October 3, 1929; *Elizabethtown Valley News*, March 8, 1962.
2. *Adirondack Record–Elizabethtown Post*, August 8, 1935; December 5, 1935; November 5, 1942.
3. *Adirondack Record–Elizabethtown Post*, April 12, 1951; "Mrs. Huttig's Photographs Are Record of Town History," *Elizabethtown Valley News*, March 8, 1962; "Mrs. Emily D. Huttig," September 6, 1966.

IRISH, GEORGE S. (1847–1920)

Active Lake George Region, Late 1860s–Early 1890s

George Irish was born into a farming family in Caldwell (later Lake George), Warren County. He was listed as a "photographist" with a post office address in the incorporated Queensbury village of Glens Falls in an 1870 New York State business directory. Still resident in Caldwell in the later 1870s, he maintained a Glens Falls studio, producing cartes de visite of people and scenes around Caldwell and Glens Falls as well as landscape stereoviews bearing the imprint G. S. or GEO. S. IRISH, GLEN'S FALLS.

Celebrated photographer **Alfred Stieglitz** (b. 1864), whose family spent summers at hotels in the Lake George region during the 1870s, remembered being photographed by "tintyper" Irish, who was so decidedly cross-eyed that when he pointed to a tree and said, "look here" and "don't move," it seemed he was talking about a different tree from the one toward which he pointed. But I was a good boy, very serious, and never laughed nor moved during an exposure.

Pictures were taken of me with a bow and arrow, with a straw hat, and without a straw hat. I invariably accompanied Mr. Irish into his darkroom. I still see him developing his tintypes and drying them over an alcohol flame. He would take a fine camel's hair brush and dip it into some rouge with which he touched up the cheeks. . . .

Mr. Irish and I became friends.[1]

Irish appeared in the New York state census of 1892 as a photographer. By 1900 he was the proprietor of a Caldwell "souvenir" or "variety" store.

1. Norman, *Alfred Stieglitz*, 21.

ISAAC, ABRAHAM (1903–1996)
Active Lake Placid, Essex County, 1947–1949

Born in New Jersey, the son of a scrap iron executive, Abraham Isaac was an Elizabeth, New Jersey, stationer and printer in 1930. By the early 1940s he was a commercial photographer. He operated Olympic Photo in Lake Placid for two years, specializing in wedding photography. An April 1948 advertisement targeting June brides-to-be promised "a complete record" of the event, including a photographic wedding book. Isaac's most memorable Lake Placid professional achievement was a photograph of a speedboat belonging to **Henry J. Kaiser** that was shown on Albany's WGRB television channel in 1949. Not long thereafter Isaac returned to New Jersey, opened a photography shop in Elizabeth, and became a staff photographer for the *Elizabeth Daily Journal*.[1]

1. *Lake Placid News*, April 9, 1948; June 3, 1949; December 2, 1949.

JACKSON, WILLIAM HENRY (1843–1942)
Active Essex, Franklin, Hamilton, and Warren Counties, 1890, 1900

William Henry Jackson is considered one of the best landscape photographers of the early American West. Adirondack-born in Keeseville, Clinton and Essex Counties, he was the first of George and Harriet Jackson's eight children. His father was a native Adirondacker as well, born in 1820 on a farm near Keeseville and a Keeseville blacksmith and carriage-building shop proprietor at the time of his son's birth. His mother was a watercolorist.

After two or three early years in Georgia and one in Plattsburgh, Clinton County, young Jackson was raised on a farm in nearby Peru until the age of eight, when the family moved to Petersburg, Virginia, and on to Philadelphia as his father sought economic opportunities before settling in Troy, Rensselaer County, in 1853. Leaving school after the eighth grade, in 1858 Jackson was taken on by Troy photographer C. C. Schoonmaker as a part-time retoucher and painter of portrait backgrounds. This job was followed two years later by a full-time position with Rutland, Vermont, photographer Frank Mowrey as a studio artist (with a year out to serve in the Civil War with the Twelfth Vermont Volunteers, primarily as a landscape sketcher). In 1864 he went to work for Burlington photographer **Adin French Styles.** There, according to a newspaper report, Jackson "finished" upwards of three hundred photographs in 1865 in oil, watercolor, and India ink. Mortification over the breakup of an informal engagement led him to leave Styles's studio "without notice" in April 1866.[1]

Heading west, Jackson spent a year as a bullwhacker, or driver of ox teams transporting freight between Nebraska and Montana. A brief stint as a colorist for an Omaha photographer followed. While recognizing that his "business lay properly with the pallet and the brush," Jackson allowed that he "could not resist the temptation to dabble among the chemicals," and opened an Omaha

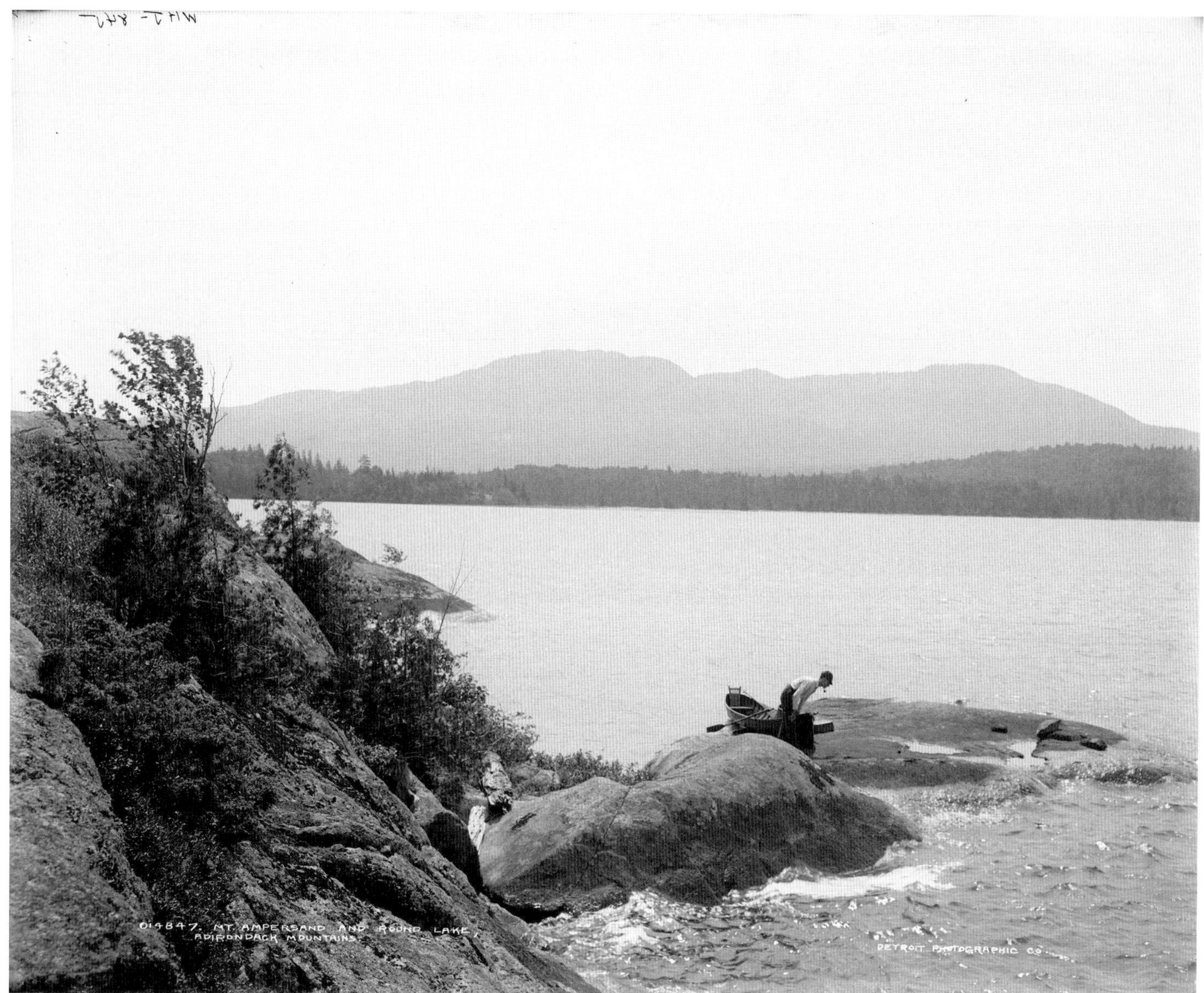

39. W. H. Jackson, *Mt. Ampersand and Round Lake, Adirondack Mountains*, 1900. Courtesy of Library of Congress Prints and Photographs Division, LC-D4-14847.

studio in 1868 with his brother Edward, who joined him from Troy. On the basis of work produced during an 1869 assignment to record scenery along the routes of the Union Pacific Railroad, Jackson was invited to join annual government-supported geological surveys in the West under the direction of Ferdinand Hayden between 1870 and 1878. His majestic, large-format (20 x 24 inch) photographs of the Yellowstone region played a role in the creation by Congress of the Yellowstone National Park in 1872. In 1879 Jackson relocated to the booming city of Denver, Colorado. In 1890 he began traveling the East Coast for railroad companies, copyrighting a number of Adirondack images that year while exploring all branches of the New York Central Railroad. He achieved the occasional panoramic effect by producing single prints from aligned glass-plate negatives. Crittenden & Cowles, a stationery and photographic supply store in Glens Falls, Warren County, displayed a mammoth Jackson photograph exploiting this technique in its shop window in 1893: a 2 x 7 foot image taken down Lake George from the front lawn of the Fort William Henry Hotel, "with coloring admirably executed."[2]

In 1893 Jackson photographed the World's Columbian Exposition in Chicago and in 1894–96 took more than nine hundred photographs as a member of the World's Transportation Commission, endowed by Marshall Field of Chicago to study individual transportation methods around the globe. During his long absence from the United States, his western work was repackaged by various corporations and publishers without acknowledging Jackson's authorship. His Denver studio fell on economic hard times, partly in reaction to the Panic of 1893, partly as a result of the availability of better image production for magazines, and partly as a result of amateur photographers taking up his landscape specialty. Jackson found himself in severe financial difficulty upon his return. Coming to a fire-sale arrangement in 1897 with the Detroit Photographic Company, later the **Detroit Publishing Company**, he agreed to join the firm as a partner at what he later called "a comfortable salary." As part of the arrangement Jackson transferred to the company the ownership of some twenty thousand negatives.[3]

In 1898 Jackson went back on the road, his assignment to procure for the company the photographs deemed necessary to satisfy an apparently insatiable demand for scenic landscape images. In 1900, at the close of a summer taking pictures in eastern Canada and the Thousand Islands, he made "a quick trip through the Adirondacks." Some ninety Adirondack views from that visit—of Loon and the St. Regis Lakes, the Lake Placid–Saranac Lake–Cascade Lake region, and south to Long, Blue Mountain, and Raquette Lakes—were copyrighted, colored, and mass produced as postcards. The summer of 1902 was Jackson's last behind a camera. He took on the "indoor" job of plant manager for Detroit (a welcome change and "as good as retirement," according to Jackson), and stayed with the company until it effectively closed down in 1924. He resided thereafter primarily in Washington, DC, and New York City, a "publicly recognized and revered figure" and "a sort of benign living figurehead for the rising tide of Western nostalgia and interest." In 1934, and again in 1939 (at the age of ninety-six), Jackson returned to the Keeseville vicinity for his only visits since 1864. He spoke at a local camera club meeting in 1939, and "derived much satisfaction" from identifying the site of the Peru farm on which he had spent his early years. He is buried in Arlington National Cemetery, Virginia.[4]

1. Jackson, *Time Exposure*, 3, 5–7, 11, 16, 25–26, 34, 73–76, 83; "William H. Jackson," *Wilson's Photographic Magazine*, 228; *Burlington (VT) Free Press*, December 29, 1865; *Rutland Weekly Herald*, April 26, 1866.

2. Elmo Scott Watson, "Back-Tracking an Old Trail"; Newhall and Edkins, *William H. Jackson*, 135–36; Jackson, "Field Work," 91; "William H. Jackson—Landscape Photographer," 230; *Glens Falls Star*, May 10, 1893.

3. Jackson, *Time Exposure*, 323; Hales, *William Henry Jackson*, 40, 67–70, 200–203, 213, 259–61.

4. Jackson, *Time Exposure*, 325–26, 330, 332, 338–39; Hales, *William Henry Jackson*, 264, 293; Detroit Photographic Company "Negative Registers," 97–98; "Country's Most Noted Photographer Speaks at Camera Club Meet," *Plattsburgh Press*, October 10, 1939.

JOHNSON, ELBERT M. (1844–1910)
Active Westport, Essex County, 1869–1870; Essex, 1870–1873; Crown Point, 1873–1909

Elbert Johnson, born in Addison County, Vermont, was raised from early childhood on a farm in the Westport hamlet of Wadhams Mills. During the Civil War he served for ten months with Company E of the Second New York Harris Light Cavalry, Custer's Division. Returning to the North and looking about for a means of supporting himself, he pursued a course at Eastman Business College in Poughkeepsie and spent several months working as a hotel clerk in Iowa before returning to his parents' Adirondack home. Johnson was recorded as a Westport "photographist" in an 1870 New York State business directory. He spent nearly three years as a photographer in the town of Essex before opening a studio in late 1873 in Crown Point, some thirty miles to the south, a location that would henceforth serve as Johnson's working base. He was, announced a regional newspaper, "prepared to take all kinds of pictures hereafter, and as 'life-like and bland' as in any city."[1]

Portrait photography was Johnson's bread and butter. As a journalist noted in 1886, the artist had a "rare talent" for "making pretty pictures . . . It is very generally remarked that his pictures have a cheerful expression—no long drawn out seven days 'sackcloth and ashes,' but *seven days Sun-shine*." Johnson closed his studio every summer for two or three months and followed a fluctuating Essex County circuit for stays of one or two weeks. Newspapers provided explicit information as to where his "snowy canopy tent" might be found: "On the slope of the hill, near the road, in Mrs. Amanda Sheldon's orchard" (Willsboro, 1874); "in Major Douglass's meadow. Corner Church and South Main Street" (Port Henry, 1884). In later years Johnson eased up on his summer schedule, announcing in August 1897, for example, that "owing to the rainy season," he "has delayed going out tenting until he has concluded to wait until next year."[2]

Johnson was a talented landscape photographer as well as a portraitist. (Among his more dramatic images was a series of stereoviews recording the setting and equipment of the Crown Point Iron Company.) He trained a number of young men as apprentices, wording an 1891 "help wanted" advertisement as follows: "To a young man of ability and fair education this is a good opportunity to start in a paying business. Apply at once."[3]

Popular and active in the community, Johnson died of heart disease and was buried beside the first of his two wives in Crown Point.

1. *Essex County Republican*, January 5, 1871; December 18, 1873.

2. *Essex County Republican*, September 24, 1874; *Elizabethtown Post*, July 22, 1886; *Ticonderoga Sentinel and Ticonderogian*, June 20, 1884; *Ticonderoga Sentinel*, August 26, 1897.

3. *Ticonderoga Sentinel*, May 21, 1891.

JONES, DAVID WILLIAM (1919–1968)
Active Lake Placid, Essex County, 1947–1968

Born in Camden, Maine, David Jones relocated with his parents and eight siblings to Lake Placid circa 1928, where his father became the superintendent of grounds at the village's Grand View Hotel. A 1938 graduate of Lake Placid High School, he spent four years in the army during World War II. Jones was first mentioned as a Lake Placid photographer in 1947, when the Village Board granted him permission to take aerial photographs of points of interest over Lake Placid while flying at an altitude lower than normally permitted. He became the longtime proprietor of Adirondack Photo Service, a shop first located at 338 Main Street and from 1949 at 111 Main Street in a building he purchased in 1953. He recorded local sporting and other events; his action photograph of a bobsled team negotiating a difficult turn at Lake Placid's bobsled run won a blue ribbon in an annual contest held by the Professional Photographers Society of New York in 1948. He also published a few photo postcards, took some portraits, and sold the occasional image to the *Lake Placid News*. Jones's business emphasis, however, was on servicing the needs of amateur photographers, with his shop generally processing between 100 and 150 rolls of film a day. In 1959 he purchased the studio and negatives of retiring photographer **Eugene H. Pierson**. Jones's business was sold shortly after his death in an automobile accident.[1]

1. *Lake Placid News*, March 18, 1938; March 5, 1943; July 25, 1947; April 30, 1948; November 25, 1949; April 19, 1957; December 11, 1959.

KAISER, HENRY J. (1882–1967)
Active Lake Placid, Essex County, 1901–1906

A titan of American industry in the mid-twentieth century, Henry Kaiser spent several early years as a photographer and photofinisher in Lake Placid. The fourth child and only son of German immigrants, a shoemaker and a practical nurse, Kaiser

AT THE KODAK PLACE!
EVERYTHING FOR THE KODAKER
KAISER PHOTOGRAPHIC STORES
LAKE PLACID, N. Y. DAYTON, FLA.
and PALM BEACH, FLA.
Amateur Finishing in 24 Hours. Mail Orders Given Immediate Attention. Prices on Application.
Interior, Exterior, Group and Flash-Light Photography.
Out Door Portraiture a Specialty.
GEO. A. HAND, General Manager

40. H. J. Kaiser, advertisement for Kaiser Stores, *Plattsburgh Courier and Freeman*, June 27, 1906. Courtesy of New York State Library.

was born in Sprout Brook, Montgomery County, and passed his childhood in Whitesboro, Oneida County. Eager to get started on life, he left school at the age of thirteen and went to work, at first as a cash boy and then a drapery salesman in a Utica dry goods store. A subsequent stint as a traveling and inside salesman for a dealer in photographic supplies facilitated Kaiser's education in the art and science of photography. To supplement his meager income, he took pictures.[1]

Kaiser visited Lake Placid on a 1901 sales trip, was taken with the village, and made an irresistible offer to local photographer **William Wallace Brownell**. He would work in Brownell's Main Street studio and photo finishing shop for nothing—until he doubled his business, at which point he was to be rewarded with 50 percent of Brownell's profits. The offer was accepted. It wasn't long before Kaiser tripled Brownell's trade, and a new sign, BROWNELL & KAISER, went up outside the premises they now shared. Brownell, after working with Kaiser for two years, sold the business to him in October 1903.[2]

The outgoing Kaiser, billing himself as "the Man with a Smile," prospered in Lake Placid. As he admitted in later years, his principal interest was not in picture-taking. "I couldn't do what people wanted in portrait photography," he is quoted as saying. "They all wanted to look like actors or actresses, not like themselves, so I went to landscape photography. I took a photo of a landscape—all natural—and it didn't sell at all. Then I took another—everything fake—and it sold wonderfully, so I decided to get out of that, too." Kaiser's business grew through marketing photo supplies and finishing services to amateurs; no attributed Lake Placid photographs have yet been discovered.[3]

Kaiser grew restless in what was primarily a summer resort, its streets quiet for seven months of every year. On the advice of a local businessman he began spending winters in Florida, and in 1904 opened a photo shop in Daytona Beach (overseen during its first season by photographer **Charles Gibbon**). Before long he owned two more Florida outlets. Kaiser might have gone on in this way indefinitely, shuttling between his summer and winter enterprises, but his life changed when Bess Fosburgh, a young woman from Boston, walked into his Lake Placid shop in the spring of 1906. Within weeks the two were engaged. His fiancée's father, a Virginia lumberman, disapproved of Kaiser's itinerant lifestyle and laid out three conditions for obtaining his approval for their marriage: that he abandon the resort milieu and establish himself in a stable business, that he hold down a job paying at least $125 a month, and that he have a home ready for his bride before their wedding. Kaiser fulfilled all three conditions within a year, heading to Idaho and then to Spokane, Washington, where he became a top traveling salesman for a wholesale hardware business. The couple married in Boston in April 1907 and honeymooned in Lake Placid.[4]

Before leaving for the West, Kaiser took his first step into big business with the June 1906 incorporation of the Kaiser Photographic Stores. Capitalized at ten thousand dollars, the new entity took over Kaiser's Lake Placid and Florida photo shops. Its initial board of directors comprised Kaiser (without title), a president/treasurer, a vice president, and a secretary. **George A. Hand**, installed by Kaiser as general manager of the operation, later referred to the business as a "photo finishing plant with side lines."[5]

In 1909 Kaiser began working for Washington gravel and cement dealers, and in 1914 founded a road-paving company that grew to become a prime contractor in, among other projects, construction of the Hoover and Grand Coulee Dams. As the head of Kaiser Shipyards, builder of Liberty ships during World War II, he became known as the "father of modern American shipbuilding." Other enterprises included Kaiser Aluminum and Kaiser Steel, two unsuccessful automobile companies (Kaiser-Frazer and Kaiser Motors), and Kaiser Permanente, a prepaid healthcare plan for Kaiser workers and their families. The Henry J. Kaiser Family Foundation, with over $550 million in assets, now focuses primarily on health, media, and education.[6]

Kaiser spent most of his adult life in Oakland, California, and returned only once to the Adirondack village he had left behind. A lover of fast boats since his Lake Placid ownership of a skiff with a one-horsepower engine, he chose the village as the site for 1949 speed trials of two custom-made watercraft with which he hoped, but failed, to beat the existing motorboat speed record. He still took the occasional picture. In 1951, shortly after the death of his first wife, Kaiser married for a second time. The glamorous studio portrait of the bride accompanying the official press announcement of the upcoming marriage had been taken the day before by Kaiser.[7]

1. MacKenzie, "Henry Kaiser's Road"; Heiner, *Henry J. Kaiser*, 7–15; "From Dam Builder to World Planner," *Rochester Times-Union*, February 3, 1945.

2. MacKenzie, "Henry Kaiser's Road"; *Elizabethtown Post*, October 15, 1903.

3. *Lake Placid News*, July 23, 1915; August 28, 1942; Heiner, *Henry J. Kaiser*, 16.

4. MacKenzie, "Henry Kaiser's Road"; *Utica Herald-Dispatch*, December 28, 1903.

5. *Potsdam Courier-Freeman* quoting *Troy Record*, June 6, 1906; *Lake Placid News*, Aug 28, 1942.

6. Heiner, *Henry J. Kaiser*, 17–20.

7. MacKenzie, "Henry Kaiser's Road"; Steve Gifford, untitled typescript about Kaiser accompanying letter from Dean Stansfield to Mary MacKenzie, North Elba/Lake Placid Historian, February 21, 2001, North Elba/Lake Placid historian's office.

KELLOGG, ELMER E. (1862–1916)
Active Hamilton County, 1900–1915

Elmer Kellogg was born into a farming family in Port Leyden, Lewis County, not far to the west of the Adirondacks. As a young man he worked for several years at the Remington Typewriter Company factory in Ilion, Herkimer County, before opening an Ilion photographic studio. In 1906 he returned to Port Leyden, at first operating a photographic portrait studio and then a general store while also selling goods from a wagon.[1]

"Following a severe illness," Kellogg "was ordered by his Doctor to spend the Summers in the North Woods away from the city heat." He did so, passing a good part of every summer from 1900 on with his wife and daughter in Blue Mountain Lake. The Kelloggs lived at first in a tent pitched on the hamlet's main street. Later, they occupied a small camp cabin that Kellogg, because he was kept so busy as a photographer, christened Camp-Seldom-Out. He took pictures for families staying at hotels and camps around Blue Mountain Lake; furnished them with film and finishing services; and sold mounted landscape photographs, including winter scenes of the region, and real photo postcards. "The genial photographer," it was reported in the summer of 1913, "is a capable artist and is more than busy." Kellogg died at the age of fifty-four of Bright's disease, now referred to as acute nephritis.[2]

1. Mrs. William S. Bass, neé Erma Kellogg, to Craig Gilborn, July 17, 1972, Photographers' File, Adirondack Experience; *Lowville Journal and Republican*, November 1, 1906.

2. Bass to Gilborn, July 17, 1972; *Utica Daily Press*, August 12, 1913.

KELLY, HUGH A. (1862–1951)
Active Tupper Lake, Franklin County, 1914–1948

Hugh Kelly's photographic base was Tupper Lake Junction, or Faust, as downtown Tupper Lake was called during the forty years prior to 1959. At the

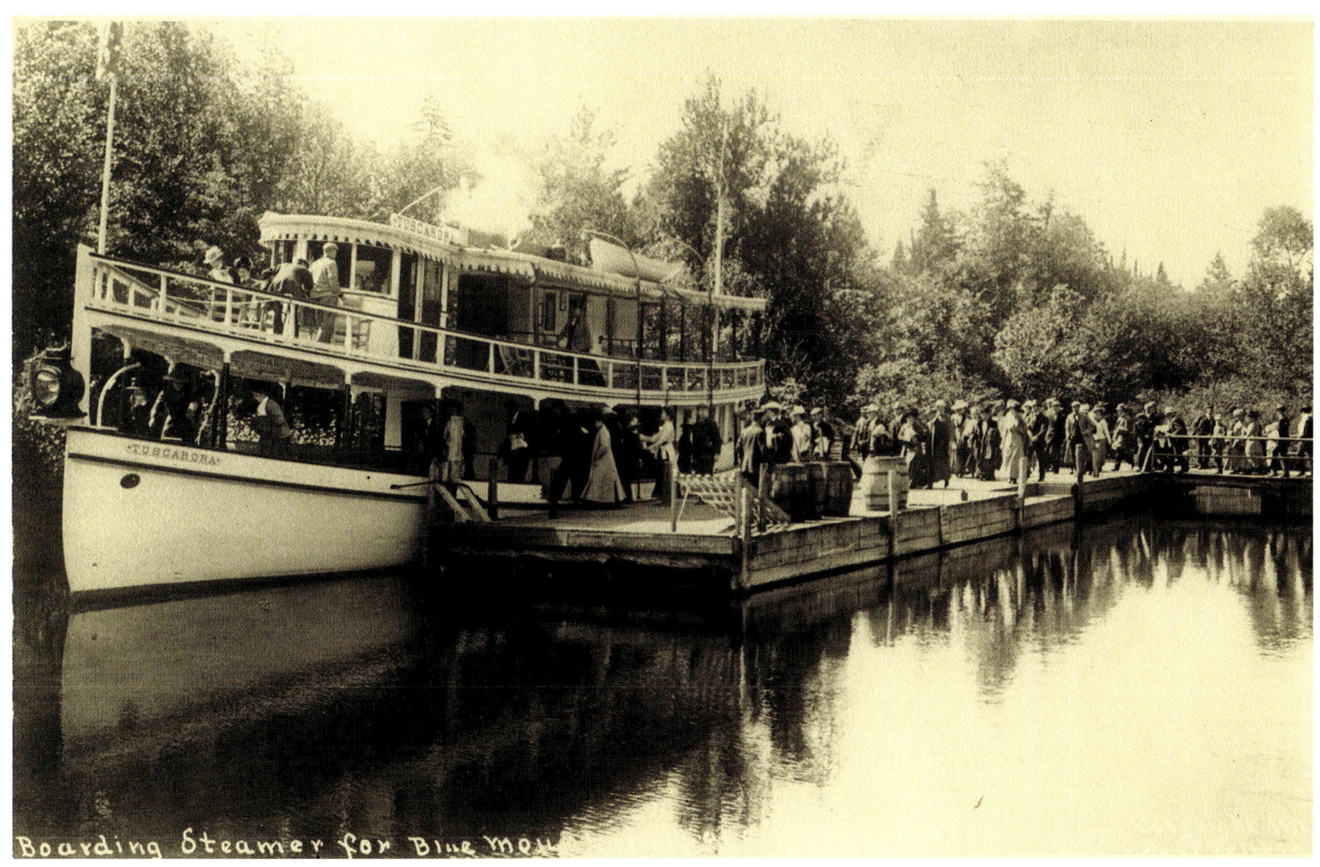

41. E. E. Kellogg, *Boarding Steamer for Blue Mountain Lake*. RPPC, 1911. Courtesy of Adirondack Experience.

intersection of two railway lines and a mile and a half from uptown Tupper Lake, this community maintained a distinctly separate personality from the larger village of which it was a part.

Born in Owego, Tioga County, Kelly grew up in Pennsylvania and began teaching at a Meshoppen, Pennsylvania, country school at the age of eighteen. He left after five terms to pursue a commercial course at Keystone Academy in nearby Factoryville, and for more than thirty years handled records and bookkeeping for lumber companies in Pennsylvania, New England, and northern New York. Taking up photography shortly after arriving in Tupper Lake as a lumber company employee in 1912, Kelly developed his hobby into a paying sideline and then a full-time occupation—making "outside work a specialty" and taking hundreds of photographs of logging crews and construction gangs. From foreign-born loggers' practice of sending pictures home, boasted Kelly in 1945, he believed that his photos had "found their way into practically every country in the world," although his generally unsigned work is little known in Tupper Lake.[1]

Kelly also captured images of hunting and fishing parties and their big fish, deer, and other game specimens, "taking them out of the 'fish story' class for proud sportsmen throughout this area." A dedicated fisherman himself, Kelly received in 1950, at the age of eighty-seven, a patent for a fish gaff to hold a fish securely while removing it from a fishing line.[2]

1. *Tupper Lake Free Press and Tupper Lake Herald*, June 20, 1940; May 10, 1945; May 9, 1946.

2. *Tupper Lake Free Press and Tupper Lake Herald*, May 9, 1946; "An Old Friend Passes On," *Tupper Lake Free Press and Tupper Lake Herald*, March 1, 1951.

KIBBE, WILLIAM H. (1846–1910)
Active Johnstown, Fulton County, 1871–1910

Primarily a portrait photographer, William Kibbe was long popular as a recorder of the faces of southern Adirondack residents. Born in Johnstown and a skilled painter in oils and watercolor, he worked as a decorator in a paint shop before spending four years with the renowned engraver Vistus Balch, then based in Utica, Oneida County. In 1869 Kibbe entered the employ of a local Johnstown photographer; in 1871 he opened his own Main Street studio. When the building in which his business was housed was destroyed by fire in 1881, Kibbe erected another at the same location, known as the Kibbe Block, where he maintained a third-floor studio for nearly thirty years. He advertised a specialty in baby pictures, but his output included images of sitters of all ages as well as genre scenes. Kibbe contributed to photographic journals and exhibited occasionally at the Fulton County Fair.[1]

1. "Photographers Old and New: W. H. Kibbe," *Wilson's Photographic Magazine* 30, no. 440 (August 1893): 373–74; Obituary, *Wilson's Photographic Magazine* 47, no. 640 (April 1910): 192; *Johnstown Daily Republican*, Special Edition, October 1891.

KILBURN BROTHERS: BENJAMIN WEST (1827–1909) AND EDWARD (1830–1884)
Active Ausable Chasm and Ticonderoga, Clinton and Essex Counties, 1871, Early 1880s

Sons of Josiah Kilburn, an iron founder who produced Franklin stoves in Littleton, New Hampshire, Benjamin and Edward Kilburn apprenticed in the foundry business and joined their father's flourishing firm before serving brief stints in the Civil War. In 1865 the brothers began marketing stereographs of New Hampshire's White Mountains and Franconia Notch from a portrait studio launched by Edward. Having successfully manufactured and sold some twenty-five thousand views by 1867, they opened a Littleton factory that year. The business grew rapidly. By 1869 their plant, including production, sales, and studio facilities, was one of the largest of its kind in the country. Benjamin was the primary photographer, while Edward looked after the enterprise's manufacturing side. Edward resigned in 1875; Benjamin changed the company name to B. W. Kilburn & Company, although standard-sized stereoview mounts continued to be identified as from "Kilburn Brothers" until 1890. He gradually extended the firm's national and international coverage after 1877 by hiring more photographers and purchasing and pirating the work of others.[1]

Kilburn Brothers published a northern New York series in 1871, including images of Fort Ticonderoga and Ausable Chasm. A sequence of at least seven stereographs showcasing a group of male *Adirondack* campers appeared in the early 1880s from earlier negatives by Baltimore photographer William Moody Chase (1817–1901). Extravagant new titles for individual images in the series—*A Home in the Woods for Me*, *The Bear Story by the Camp-Fire*—hewed to a favorite Benjamin Kilburn marketing ploy from this period when he was said to have laughingly stated, "It is the titles to my pictures which make them sell." Outlasting its major competitors, the Kilburn firm reached its peak of production in 1905, when it generated some five million images. By the time it closed, a year after Benjamin's death, its catalog included over seventeen thousand unique stereoviews. The bulk of these were taken over by the Keystone View Company.[2]

1. Southall, "Kilburn Brothers," 5, 6, 25, 26, 29, 38, 54, 99; Treadwell, "A Perspective: Comments on Kilburn," 3.

2. Compare Moody's *Deer Hunters' Camp, Adirondacks*, with Kilburn Brothers's *A Home in the Woods for Me, Adirondacks*, both from New York Public Library's Robert N. Dennis Collection of Stereoscopic Views; Southall, "Kilburn Brothers," 49, 77.

KIRK, FRANK ARTHUR (1870–1948)
Active Keeseville, Clinton and Essex Counties, 1892–1903, 1925–1948; Malone, Franklin County, 1903–1908

Frank Kirk's career as a photographer spanned nearly sixty years, most of them spent in or near the Adirondacks. Born in Peru, Clinton County, he was the son of a laborer. He trained as a photographer under **George F. Marvin**, whose Keeseville studio he bought in 1892. Kirk's advertisement in S. R. Stoddard's 1893 *Adirondacks: Illustrated* repeated much of the language of Marvin's from the previous year: "Adirondack and Au Sable Chasm views [most likely acquired as part of the Marvin purchase]; Portraits in all the popular styles and sizes; All Field Work, Views and Interiors promptly executed." Kirk, as had Marvin, included his summer tour schedule in his advertisement, which was to take him south that year to Keene, Keene Valley, and Lake Placid. "A good many people" in Au Sable Forks, it was reported in September 1893, were "anxiously awaiting the coming of Kirk and Company, photographers."[1]

Kirk transferred his business by mid-1903 to Malone, Franklin County. In 1908 he moved to Burlington, Vermont; in 1910 to Leominster, Massachusetts; and in 1923 back to Burlington before returning to Keeseville for good in 1925. Portraiture was his specialty ("his ability with the posing and photographing of children being of high quality"). Kirk operated out of his home until days before his death more than twenty years later.[2]

1. *Elizabethtown Post*, November 24, 1892; S. R. Stoddard, *Adirondacks: Illustrated* (1893 ed.), 269; *Plattsburgh Sentinel*, September 1, 1893.

2. *Malone Farmer*, August 5, 1903; *Malone Palladium*, November 19, 1908; *Essex County Republican*, October 30, 1925; May 15, 1936; November 26, 1948.

KOLLECKER, WILLIAM F. (1879–1962)
Active Saranac Lake, Essex and Franklin Counties, 1905–1940s

William (Bill) Kollecker grew up in the northern reaches of Little Germany, today part of Manhattan's East Village and once its most heavily populated neighborhood. His father was a naturalized German tailor; his mother died five days after her son's birth. Contracting tuberculosis while a teenaged messenger boy for a Wall Street brokerage house, Kollecker was sent to Saranac Lake to cure through the sponsorship of Grace Church, one of the wealthiest Episcopalian parishes in New York City and the parent organization of an outreach chapel that provided assistance to residents of the

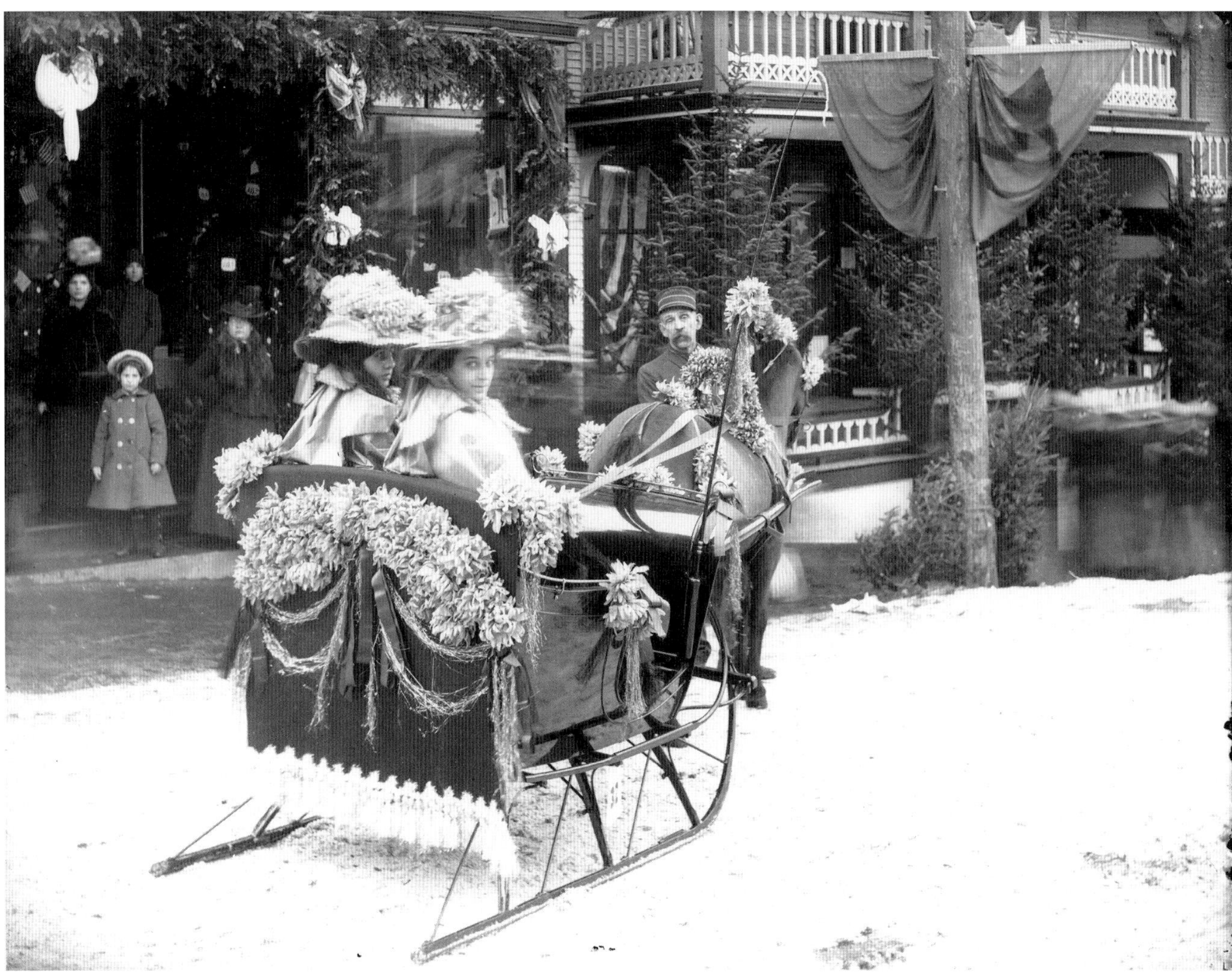

42. W. F. Kollecker, Fowler's Livery parade entry, Winter Carnival, 1905–1910. Courtesy of Adirondack Research Room, Saranac Lake Free Library.

Kollecker family's immediate neighborhood. (Kollecker later expressed himself as indebted to the Reverend George H. Bottome, the chapel's vicar, for the opportunity to cure in Saranac Lake.) He arrived in the village in January 1896, was settled into a cure cottage, and began to recover his health. In late 1897 or early 1898 he transferred to Fletcher's Farm, a sanatorium facility six miles north of Saranac Lake where he worked for room and board; he spent the summer of 1898 as a bellhop at the nearby Loon Lake House. It was at about this time that he began to take pictures.[1]

By 1901 Kollecker was living in nearby Lake Placid and employed in the local branch of A. Fortune's Saranac Lake furniture store. Photographer **William F. Cheesman** hired him as a summer assistant in 1903 and kept him on when the season ended. The two men developed a close, lifetime friendship. By 1905 Kollecker had absorbed enough photographic knowledge to go out on his own, and, with a $200 loan from Cheesman, leased a photography studio above a lakeside boathouse in Saranac Lake recently vacated by **Frederick W. Rice.** Within a year Kollecker set himself up in downtown Saranac Lake, at first in a small shop at 71 Main Street and, from around 1910, in spacious quarters next door at 73 Main Street. He remained there for the rest of his life, overseeing his ground floor business while living in a bachelor apartment above.[2]

Kollecker did not, like most village photographers, rely on portraiture as the bedrock of his operation. He took as his subject Saranac Lake: its local citizenry and visiting guests, activities, and buildings. He and the part-time operators he employed (among them **Winchester MacDowell** and **Edward T. Start**) photographed community events from baseball games to winter carnivals, often focusing the camera on bleachers filled with identifiable folk who might want to purchase their own images. Real photo postcards were a business mainstay, as was serving amateurs. Photographs and Kodak apparatus dominated the carefully tended picture window fronting the store, considered by Kollecker to be his primary advertising venue.[3]

In the 1920s Kollecker began experimenting with silent movies and recorded many incidents of village life on color film. He made a brief venture into real estate, purchasing a Main Street business building in 1921 in partnership with Cheesman that they sold in 1925. In the mid-1920s he began spending part of most winters in Florida.[4]

By the early 1940s Kollecker was pursuing photography "just for fun" and devoting an increasing amount of his shop space to souvenirs. A quiet man who never went in for town boosterism in a big way, he remained a popular village figure until his death. After a service at St. Luke's Episcopal Church in Saranac Lake, Kollecker was buried in the Cheesman plot in North Elba Cemetery. Cheesman's son Clyde was one of his pallbearers.[5]

1. Bogdan, *Exposing the Wilderness*, 95–97; Kollecker diary, William F. Kollecker and Hannah Clark Collection, Adirondack Experience Library; *Journal of the One Hundred and Fifteenth Convention of the Diocese of New York*, 157. 80; *Plattsburgh Sentinel*, October 7, 1898.

2. Bogdan, *Exposing the Wilderness*, 101–2, 105.

3. Bogdan, *Exposing the Wilderness*, 102; "Selling Power of Pictures," 6–7.

4. *Lake Placid News*, October 7, 1921; *Plattsburgh Sentinel*, May 8, 1925; *Chateaugay and Franklin County Democrat*, July 2, 1926.

5. *Adirondack Enterprise*, August 27, 1962; February 14, 1962; Bogdan, *Exposing the Wilderness*, 131.

LABARRE, ISAAC D. (1834–1903)
Active Adirondack Shoreline of Lakes Champlain and George, 1863–1871

Born in Hartford, Washington County, Isaac LaBarre spent his early adult years as "a sailor and steamboat captain" on Lake Champlain and the Hudson River. Settled in Whitehall, Washington County, he was assessed for taxes to support the Union war cause as a photographer in 1863. He produced portraits, but landscape was his primary subject. In early 1871, lured by an Ohio speculator's newspaper advertisement "setting forth in rather glowing colors the desirable features of 'free homes—free lands' along the line of the Union Pacific Railroad," LaBarre went west with the Soldiers' Free Homestead Colony to take up land under the Homestead Act in Gibbon, Nebraska. LaBarre became a merchant, initially from a boxcar set on a railroad siding, and then from "the first store building in Gibbon" and "the first painted store in Buffalo County." He was also a farmer and the town's first postmaster (there is a LaBarre Street in downtown Gibbon).[1]

1. *Biographical Souvenir of the Counties of Buffalo, Kearney and Phelps, Nebraska*, 232–35; Bassett, *Buffalo County, Nebraska and Its People*, 76; typescript of undated newspaper obituary in the collection of the Buffalo County Historical Society.

LENNON, FREDERICK P. (1900–1975)
Active Tupper Lake, Franklin County, 1924–1938

Born in Ireland, Frederick (Fred) Lennon was raised in England until, at the age of eleven, he arrived without family in Canada—one of some one hundred thousand "home children" to do so between 1869 and 1932 through Britain's assisted juvenile emigration program. He entered the United States in 1920 via Massena, and by 1925 was a Tupper Lake photographer. His output included high school yearbook and group photos, including images of loggers and employees at the Oval Wood

Dish Factory. Naturalized in 1937, Lennon was by 1942 employed as an assistant at the Veterans' Administration's Tupper Lake Sunmount Hospital for veterans with tuberculosis. In 1942–43 Lennon served a seven-month stint as an army aerial and ground photographer in the West Indies and Africa before returning to Tupper Lake but not, apparently, to photography.[1]

1. *Malone Evening Telegram*, August 15, 1925; *Tupper Lake Free Press and Tupper Lake Herald*, May 6, 1943; "Fred Lennon Dies at Moongate Nursing Home, Canton," *Tupper Lake Free Press and Tupper Lake Herald*, November 12, 1975.

LOCKE, HARRIS LEON (1878–1931)
Active Wanakena, Cranberry Lake, and Star Lake, St. Lawrence County, 1903–1911

Harris (Harry) Locke, born in Owego, Tioga County, spent his early adult years as a West Carthage, Jefferson County, millworker. By 1903 he was living in the Fine, St. Lawrence County, hamlet of Wanakena, founded the previous year by the Rich Lumber Company, where he reportedly "ha[d] employment." There he took up landscape and group photography; Locke was recorded in the New York state census of 1905 as a Fine photographer. By early 1907 he had relocated to Harrisville, a village some thirty miles to the west in the town of Diana, Lewis County, and established a rudimentary portrait studio while continuing the business in real photo postcards he had begun in Wanakena. As a journalist covering Fine noted in December 1907, "Mr. Locke, of Harrisville, was in town Friday taking photos of the houses."[1]

Locke's postcards bore imprints from both Wanakena and Harrisville, although many cards were unattributed. Some are identifiable only from their crudely printed, capital-letter titling; others from signature typeface titles in semitransparent, upper-case, white block lettering. Photography provided an inadequate living for Locke. In 1910 he lost a $205.80 financial judgment by default in

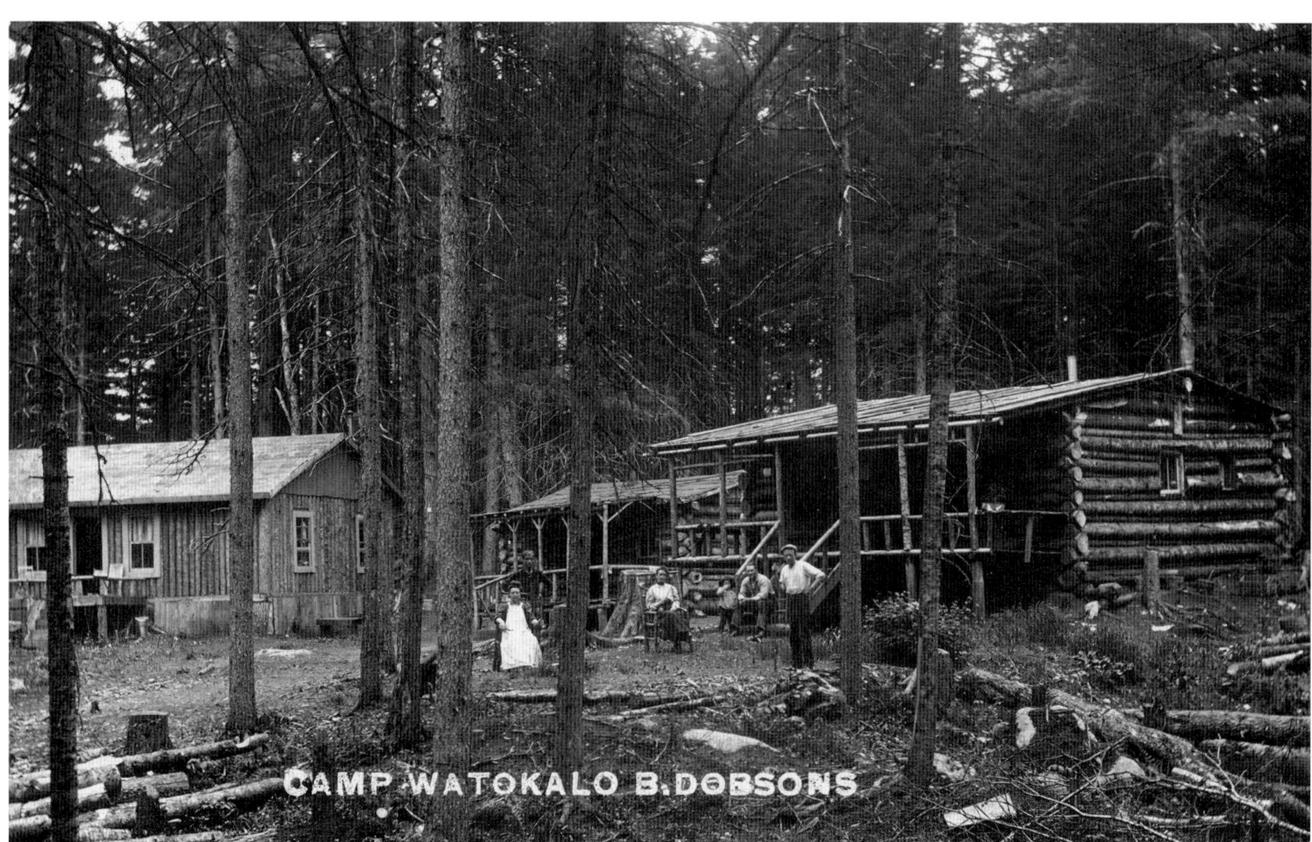

43. H. L. Locke, *Camp Watokalo*, Wanakena. RPPC, 1903–1911. Courtesy of Mark Friden, Clifton Town Historian.

Watertown, the Jefferson County seat, for "photographic supplies." He sold a few negatives to **Henry M. Beach** and others and moved his family to Syracuse, Onondaga County, becoming a chauffeur for the Chicago Quick Repair Company. He eventually owned his own Syracuse trucking business, in 1927 advertising a specialty "in the sale of sand, gravel, crushed stone and cinders." By 1930 he was a general trucker.[2]

1. *Watertown Times*, July 20, 1903; *St. Lawrence Republican*, January 30, 1907; *Ogdensburg Journal*, December 11, 1907.

2. *Watertown Re-union*, December 24, 1910; *Syracuse Herald*, September 15, 1911; *Syracuse Journal*, November 7, 1927.

LYON, HARRY WESTON (1886–1945)
Active Au Sable Forks, Clinton and Essex Counties, 1917–1935

Born in Au Sable Forks, Harry Lyon appeared as an eighteen-year-old laborer in the New York state census of 1905. In 1909 he went on the stage as a performer in a dramatic stock company, Whiteside-Strauss, which played opera houses in New England and northern New York. His own stock company, the Loker-Lyon Players, formed in late 1916, failed the following year. Many references were later made to Lyon's "years of experience on the professional stage" in news articles.[1]

By mid-1917 Lyon had established himself as the resident photographer in Au Sable Forks. He took pictures of local groups and events and advertised Lyon Studio specialties as "amateur" finishing: "Printing, developing and enlarging." His place of business was twice destroyed by fire—once in 1921 and again in 1925—but the photographer persevered into the mid-1930s. Lyon was identified in the 1940 US Census as a paper finisher at the local J. & J. Rogers paper mill.[2]

1. *Adirondack Record*, June 18, 1909; "Loker-Lyon Players Satisfy Big House," *Adirondack Record*, December 8, 1916; *Adirondack Record–Elizabethtown Post*, April 24, 1924; *Plattsburgh Republican*, May 12, 1930.

2. *Adirondack Record*, October 5, 1917; May 31, 1918; *Essex County Republican*, May 27, 1921; *Adirondack Record–Elizabethtown Post*, May 14, 1925.

MACDOWELL, WINCHESTER H. (1882–1956)
Active Old Forge, Herkimer County, 1908–1913

"Wynn" or Mac MacDowell was born in Brooklyn, the son of a civil engineer. After the early death of his mother he lived with relatives in New Jersey, followed by a number of years in the Adirondacks, where his occupation was recorded as woodsman upon his enlistment in the US Army in 1904.

Stationed at Brooklyn's Fort Hamilton, MacDowell enrolled in a six-month General Art Evening Program in commercial art at Pratt Institute in September 1907. The following April he purchased his discharge from the army and relocated to the Webb hamlet of Old Forge, hometown of Clara Brown, his wife from 1906, where for several years he maintained a photographic business as Winchester MacDowell Studio. In 1913 MacDowell moved his family to Saranac Lake, Essex and Franklin Counties. He appeared as a photographer in the New York state census of 1915; his September 1918 draft registration listed his employer as **William F. Kollecker**. Federal and state census records for 1920, 1925, and 1930 enumerated MacDowell as a sign painter.

MacDowell created murals as well as signs, lettered shop windows in gold leaf, and designed letterheads and advertisements for local businessmen. In the early 1930s he developed an unusual specialty: painting designs on ice for ice shows, at first for Lake Placid ice carnivals mounted by son-in-law Gustave Lussi, a skating coach. He toured with the Ice Follies as a prop decorator and scenic artist in 1937 and 1938 and provided ice decor for the film *Ice Follies of 1939*.[1]

1. Email from Lisle Henderson, registrar, Pratt Institute, to the author, April 13, 2018; *Utica Herald-Dispatch*, April 9, 1909; "W. H. MacDowell Dies; Cremation in Troy," *Adirondack Enterprise*, December 29, 1956.

MAGINLEY, CHARLES H. (1852–1905); LATER SPELLING "MCGINLEY"
Active Horicon, Warren County, 1870–1871; Moriah, Essex County, 1871–1875

Born in Kingston, Ulster County, to Irish parents Charles and Ellen Magenly, Charles Maginley grew up in the Horicon hamlet of Adirondack and worked on the family farm and in the woods before taking up commercial photography. He at first identified himself as Schroon Lake-based, referring to Horicon's location on the Schroon lakeshore, before opening a studio in late 1871 over Woodruff's Furniture Store in Moriah Center. His local production was scant, but included both portraits and stereoviews. In 1875 Maginley moved to Forestville, Michigan, where, it was reported, he "has erected a fine gallery for the purpose of taking the faces of the Western people." A price list included the option "pictures taken in exchange for all kinds of salable produce."[1]

Maginley studied law privately and was admitted to the State Bar of Michigan in 1878. He became "one of the best-known criminal lawyers in Michigan," acting as "counsel and attorney in some of the largest murder and other criminal cases of the State." In 1888 he moved to Minden City and represented Sanilac and Huron Counties in the Michigan Senate in 1893–94 (where he was a vocal minority proponent of women's suffrage). In 1896 he made a nominating speech for William Jennings Bryan at the National Silver Party Convention in St. Louis. Later settling in Detroit, Maginley was the lead name in at least two prestigious law partnerships. He died in the Adirondacks, succumbing to pneumonia near Paul Smith's St. Regis Lake resort where he, his wife, and daughter were vacationing.[2]

1. *Essex County Republican*, November 23, 1871; September 9, 1875; "Western Correspondence," *Ticonderoga Sentinel*, November 19, 1875; Michigan Historical Commission, *Michigan Biographies*, 2:55. Tinder, *Directory of Early Michigan Photographers*.

2. Michigan Historical Commission, *Michigan Biographies*, 2:55; "Van Wyck for Vice-President," *Detroit Free Press*, December 3, 1899; "Charles H. McGinley," *New York Times*, July 13, 1905.

MANDEVILLE, WILLIAM GARRETT, JR. (1864–1947)
Active Western Adirondacks, 1905–1920

William (Bill) Mandeville was born in Norwich, Chenango County, where his father, a onetime hatmaker, associated with his wife in running the florist shop and gardening business she founded. Their son learned the basics of his future occupation as an assistant to Norwich portrait photographer Alston E. Hotchkiss, and moved to Lowville in 1886 to work in the gallery of **George W. Carter**. After a brief return to Chenango County in 1887, where he operated a studio in Oxford, Mandeville purchased the Lowville studio of **Frank E. Slocum** in late 1888. He remained a Lowville photographer for nearly sixty years.[1]

Mandeville was primarily a portrait photographer, but produced a substantial number of high-quality real photo postcards of Lowville and its neighborhood from the early days of the 1905–20 postcard craze. Adirondack images were mostly taken in the vicinity of Fenton House in Number Four, Watson, a hotel on the shore of Beaver Lake catering to wealthy hunters and urban families seeking summer relaxation. Mandeville never owned an automobile, seldom ventured far from home, and did not court the tourist trade. He retired in 1946 and died on his eighty-third birthday the following year.[2]

1. Bogdan, *Exposing the Wilderness*, 25–26; *Utica Morning Herald*, December 8, 1888.

2. Bogdan, *Exposing the Wilderness*, 49–50; "William Mandeville, Photographer, Succumbs on 83rd Birthday," *Lowville Leader*, July 3, 1947.

MANN BROTHERS (DATES UNKNOWN)
Active Northville, Fulton County, 1911–1912

The Mann Brothers gallery was a one- or two-season wonder in Sacandaga Park, Northville. During its run, however, the name was prominently displayed. At least one mechanically printed postcard depicted the gallery; another showed a banner bearing the Mann name strung across the Midway.

The brothers did not advertise outside the park; tintypes occasionally come onto the vintage resale market labeled MANN BROS. PHOTO GALLERY, SACANDAGA PARK, N.Y. The operation was also active at Electric Park in Kinderhook, Columbia County, popular between its opening in 1901 and the outbreak of World War I.

MANN, JAMES W. (1871–1940)
Active Warren and Clinton Counties, 1914–1923

Photography was an occasional sideline for James Mann, born the son of a carpenter in Medford, Massachusetts. A Medford woodturner in 1900, by 1903 he had relocated to Glens Falls, Warren County, where he became a window trimmer for B. B. Fowler's department store. He did well at Fowler's, winning first prize in 1906 against 216 competitors in the annual contest sponsored by the *Merchants Record and Show Window* for "the most attractive designs in window dressing." Mann remained with the store through at least 1930, advancing to buyer and department manager.[1]

Mann's "attractive display of hand-colored photos" received compliments at the 1921 Industrial Exposition of Warren and Washington Counties at the Glens Falls Armory. In 1922 and 1923 Mann sold hand-painted, mounted, landscape photographs of local scenery and "Christmas novelties" from his sister's home in Plattsburgh. He also produced the occasional real photo postcard.[2]

1. *Glens Falls Morning Star*, November 14, 1903; *Warrensburgh News*, December 13, 1906.

2. *Glens Falls Post Star*, September 16, 1921; *Plattsburgh Daily Press*, December 6, 1922; *Plattsburgh Daily Republican*, November 23, 1923.

MARR, THOMAS EDGAR (1849–1910)
Active Long Lake, Hamilton County, 1901

Thomas Marr photographed the homes and home lives of the rich and famous in the Northeast. His work appeared widely in magazines, and those who employed him knew that his reputation burnished their own social status.

Born to English parents in Digby, Nova Scotia, Marr immigrated to the United States in 1864, settled by 1871 in Boston, and became a naturalized citizen in 1894. Appearing in Boston directories as a portrait and landscape painter from the late 1880s, he established his photographic niche by 1899, when he copyrighted a number of images of celebrity homes. An advertisement in a 1902 Boston directory promoted Marr's services in landscape and marine photography and noted specialties in interiors and magazine illustration. Among his clients were Boston art collector and patron Isabella Stewart Gardner and Christian Science founder Mary Baker Eddy.

In 1901, Dr. William Seward Webb, wealthy railroad entrepreneur and husband of William H. Vanderbilt's daughter Eliza, commissioned Marr to capture in more than seventy-five images the camp buildings and Webb family at their 115,000-acre Long Lake preserve: Nehasane Park. (Marr also documented Shelburne Farms, Webb's model agricultural property in Shelburne, Vermont.) His business continued as Thomas E. Marr & Son from 1910.[1]

1. Riley, "Self Assembled," 53; email from Ron Polito, Boston photographic historian, to the author, May 12, 1919.

MARVIN, EDGAR A. (1855–1910)
Active Port Henry, Essex County, 1873–1874; Ticonderoga, Essex County, 1874–1878

A younger brother of **George Fred Marvin**, who had a more extended Adirondack photographic career, Edgar (Ned) Marvin was born and educated in Elizabethtown, Essex County. In 1873 he and **William H. Bigalow** purchased the photographic business of **George W. Baldwin** in the Moriah hamlet of Port Henry and established Marvin & Bigalow, a partnership from which Marvin resigned after a March 1874 fire destroyed their studio. Not long thereafter it was announced that he had fitted up photographic rooms, described in effusive detail, in Ticonderoga.[1]

Marvin relocated to Plymouth, Wayne County, Michigan, by 1879; operated a portrait studio in Grand Ledge, Eaton County, between circa 1882 and 1892; and settled as a photographer in Detroit in 1892. He died there of heart disease at the age of fifty-four.[2]

1. *Plattsburgh Republican*, April 4, 1874; *Ticonderoga Sentinel*, June 20, 1874; July 18, 1874.

2. Tinder, *Directory of Early Michigan Photographers.*

MARVIN, GEORGE FRED (1850–1897)
Active Mineville, Essex County, 1882–1883; Keeseville, Clinton and Essex Counties, 1883–1892

Born and raised in Elizabethtown, Essex County, George Marvin was the eldest of eight children of Edgar Manly Marvin, a cabinetmaker and founder of a local dynasty in undertaking and furniture manufacture. He appears to have followed his younger brother **Edgar A. Marvin** into photography; an obituary identified him as a teacher during his early adulthood. By 1883 Marvin was living in the Moriah hamlet of Mineville, whence it was announced he would be "starting on his summer tour" on about June 1. "He is," noted the *Elizabethtown Post and Gazette* that year, "unquestionably, the second, if not the first, best artist in the county." Marvin's Mineville career was brief, although a number of portrait photographs survive from this period. In the fall of 1883 he relocated to Keeseville, where he remained for nine years. An advertisement in the 1892 edition of S. R. Stoddard's *Adirondacks: Illustrated* noted that Marvin was a "photographer and publisher of Adirondack and Ausable Chasm Views," executed "portraits in all the popular sizes and styles," worked "in any part of the region," and would that summer be spending time in Keene Valley and Lake Placid" (dates provided).[1]

Marvin sold his photographic outfit to **Frank A. Kirk** in November 1892, and in April 1894 left on what he intended to be a short tour of the Midwest as a "canvassing" photographer. He went first to Michigan, where his brother Edgar was a photographer, then on to Minnesota and to Wisconsin, where he died of a heart attack in Oshkosh in 1897. He is buried in Keeseville.[2]

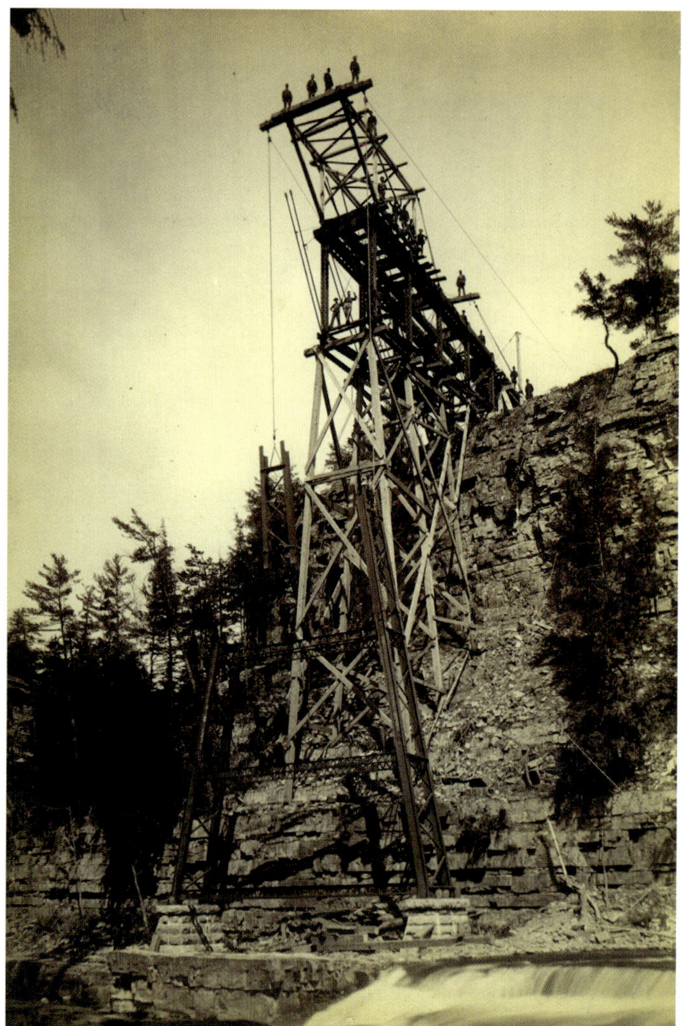

44. G. F. Marvin, construction of railroad bridge over Ausable Chasm, Keeseville, 1889. Courtesy of Adirondack Experience.

1. George Levi Brown, *Pleasant Valley*, 322; *Elizabethtown Post*, November 11, 1897; *Elizabethtown Post and Gazette*, May 10, 1883; *Essex County Republican*, October 25, 1883; S. R. Stoddard, *Adirondacks: Illustrated* (1892 ed.), 248.

2. *Elizabethtown Post*, November 24, 1892; Justice's Court, Town of Chesterfield, "Anna P. Doughty vs. Adelbert W. Boynton," State of New York Supreme Court, *General Court Appeal Book* (1895), 12, 19, 51.

MAXWELL, HAMILTON KEITH (1886–1939)
Active Lake George and Resort Areas of Essex and Franklin Counties, 1921–1922

Hamilton Maxwell was a photographic specialist, known for aerial images and detailed aerial

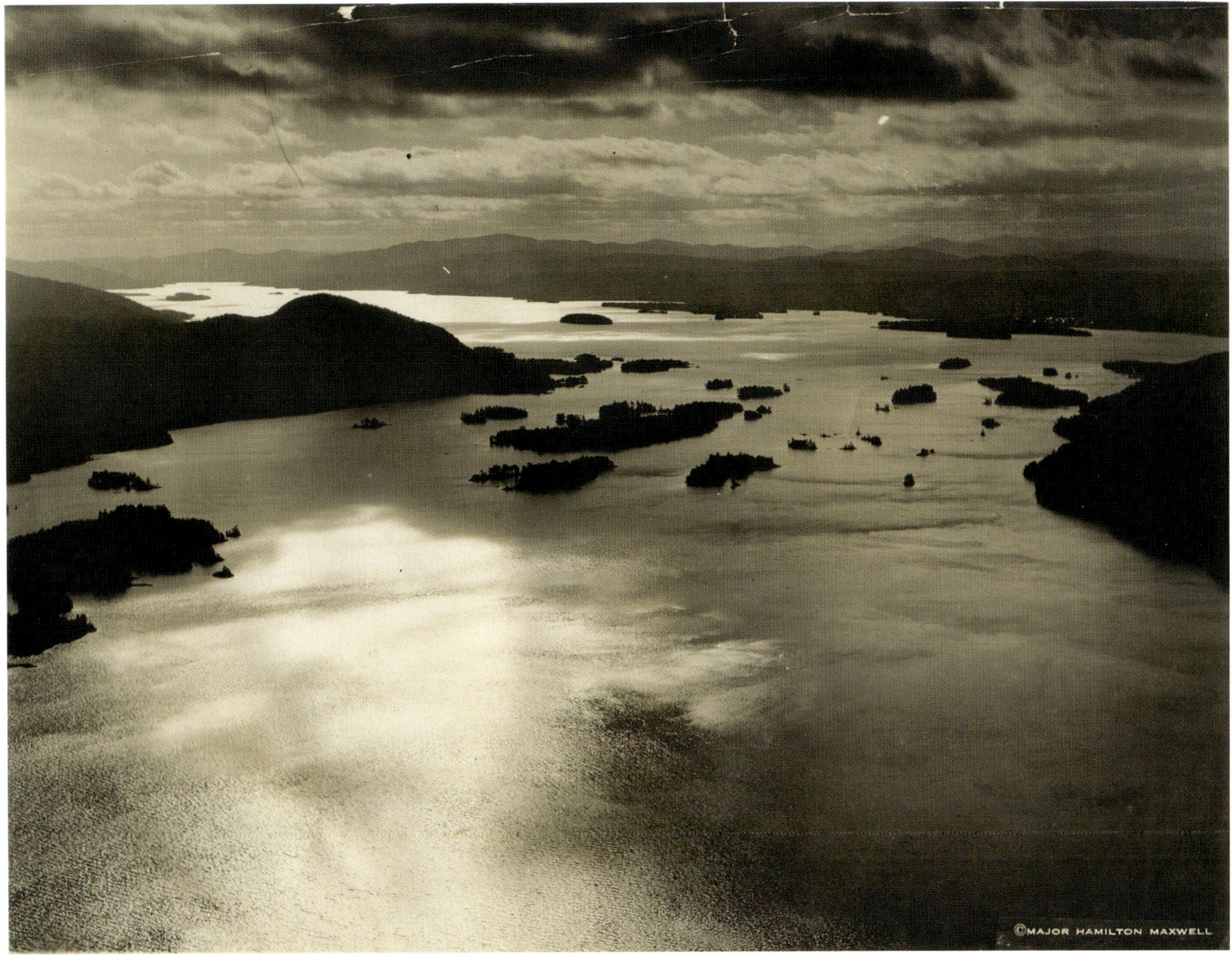

45. H. K. Maxwell, Lake George from the air, 1921–1922.

mapping work. He was born in Sydney, New South Wales, Australia, and removed to England around 1900. One of the first photographic officers to enter the Royal Air Force, he was placed in charge of photographic training during World War I and rose to the rank of major. Arriving in New York in 1919, Maxwell set about advancing aerial photography as a commercial enterprise. Of a 1920 assignment to photograph Niagara Falls and Niagara Gorge, he later recalled taking 140 images in a twenty-five-minute period, being violently ill in the course of the rough ride, and passing out when the pilot "decided to finish the job by flying under" the bridge spanning the gorge. A November 1922 Adirondack-related article in *New York Central Lines Magazine* featured a Maxwell oblique (bird's-eye view) of the Franklin County resort of Paul Smith's. The news photo firm of Underwood and Underwood distributed a number of early copyrighted Maxwell images.[1]

Maxwell's business, Hamilton Maxwell Inc., launched circa 1921, became one of two companies to dominate the American aerial photographic field during the next several years. As a company advertisement read: "Aerial photography of all descriptions; obliques of factories, estates, plants, etc.; mosaic maps of any size to scale." A 1927 mapping project of Manhattan was a notable commission. After leasing space in the elegant French Building on New York City's Fifth Avenue in late

1928, the firm abruptly dissolved eleven months later. By 1930 Maxwell was based in Stamford, Connecticut. A classified ad placed in *Popular Mechanics* that year read: "Learn how to make aerial surveys. Course includes flying, photography and engineering." Maxwell left the United States in the mid-1930s. He died in England.[2]

1. *New York Times*, January 22, 1928. Maxwell discussed technical aspects of aerial photography and mapping in the *Aircraft Year Book*, 1921, 57–59; Bruno, "A Job for One in a Million," 104; M. Frank Wooley, "Adirondacks Charm Potent in Early Fall," 38.

2. *Aircraft Year Book*, 1922, 11, 249; *New York Times*, December 13, 1928; November 21, 1929; advertisement, *Popular Mechanics*, February 1930, 66.

MCCLELLAN, KATHERINE ELIZABETH (1859–1934)

Active Clinton, Essex, and Franklin Counties, 1895–1912, Early 1920s

Born and raised in Paterson, New Jersey, Katherine McClellan was a member of the fourth graduating class of Smith College in Northampton, Massachusetts, in 1882. She spent the following eight years as, successively, a private school principal, an instructor in Latin and English, and a private tutor. As a "spinster" living in her parents' home, McClellan relocated with them circa 1893 to Saranac Lake in pursuit of improved health for her younger sister, Daisietta, who had tuberculosis. Her physician father became Saranac Lake's first public health officer and the supervisor of St. Armand, the town in which a portion of the village of Saranac Lake lies and where he developed an exclusive residential enclave, Highland Park.[1]

Finding "time hanging heavily on her hands," McClellan began in Saranac Lake to seriously pursue photography, a subject she had flirted with as a member of the Photography Committee in college. Her hobby became a career as friends asked for copies of her images and hotels began to exhibit and sell prints of her work. She gave lessons in "Kodakery" at her Highland Park studio.[2]

Although it was reported in 1898 that she had "done at the request of friends some very clever portrait work," McClellan's photographic specialty in the Adirondacks was sweeping landscapes, noted for their "correct composition" and painterly quality. In 1896 she published a souvenir booklet featuring her own text and illustrations: *John Brown, or A Hero's Grave in the Adirondacks.* Caroline

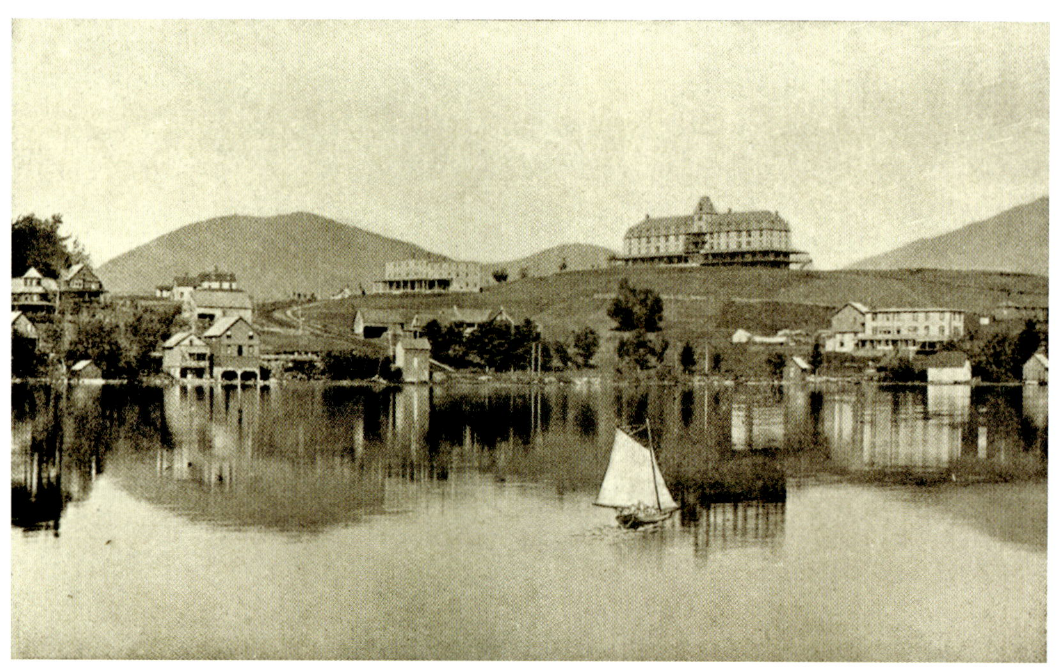

46. K. E. McClellan, *Lake Placid*. From Rockwood, *An Adirondack Romance*, 1897. Courtesy of Adirondack Experience.

Washburn Rockwood's 1897 novel, *An Adirondack Romance*, incorporated nineteen of her landscape images, and a second McClellan souvenir booklet, *Keene Valley*, appeared in 1898. She also produced a few calendars and offered developing and printing services for amateurs. In 1897 McClellan's extended visit as a photographer to the exclusive seasonal Hotel Champlain south of Plattsburgh led to a relationship that lasted for several years. In 1899 she oversaw the hotel's "department for the sale of art goods and photographs" in a new building on its campus, and in 1900 advertised the availability at the hotel of her "artistic studio portraiture, and out-of-door poses, miniatures, and tinted photographs."[3]

Family contacts led to several private shows outside of the Adirondacks where McClellan's work was warmly received; the *New York Herald* described her photographs as "high art" and the *Philadelphia Public Ledger* noted that McClellan showed "herself master of a very difficult art." In 1903 she opened a part-time studio in Northampton, where she was appointed senior photographer for the Smith College yearbook and announced herself in the college *Monthly* as "ready to take all orders for photographs." She settled permanently in Northampton in 1912 and became Smith's official photographer, documenting campus life for college files and publications. She also undertook commissions for portraits of visiting dignitaries to the town: Henry James, Helen Keller, Julia Ward Howe. As her reputation grew, McClellan was profiled in *Good Housekeeping* and *New Idea Women's Magazine*. In 1915 her works were prominently displayed at the Panama-Pacific Exposition in San Francisco.[4]

Leaving Northampton, and Smith, in 1918, McClellan relocated with her sister to Sarasota, Florida, where they owned a fifty-six-acre tract of bayfront property they had begun to develop as McClellan Park: "A high class place of residence" with curving streets; meticulous, environmentally sensitive landscaping; and a yacht basin, bathhouse, and clubhouse. In 1923 they sold the development and remaining lots to a corporation, but later opened a tearoom in the McClellan Park Clubhouse and then a gift shop in Sarasota. McClellan gave up neither her Adirondack connection nor photography. She continued to oversee building in her father's Highland Park development into the 1920s and in 1922 built a summer home, Kath-E-Mac, in Saranac Lake. Her last Adirondack images were of one of her first subjects, the John Brown Farm in North Elba, Essex County.[5]

1. Biographical overview, Katherine Elizabeth McClellan Papers; *Elizabethtown Post*, November 24, 1904.

2. Hines, "Women in Photography," 140; advertisement for McClellan Studio, *Saranac Lake Directory*, 1902, 60.

3. "Workshop of an Artist," *Adirondack Enterprise*, 1898 Souvenir Edition, 11; *Elizabethtown Post*, September 2, 1897; *Plattsburgh Sentinel*, July 7, 1899; Hines, "Women in Photography," 140; Folwell, "Straight Shooter," 44; Rockwood, *An Adirondack Romance*, passim. Images from *John Brown* appeared in the *Second Annual Report of the Commissioners of Fisheries, Game and Forest of the State of New York*, 1897.

4. Folwell, "Straight Shooter," 45, 47; Biographical overview, Smith College; *Elizabethtown Post*, November 24, 1904.

5. "McClellan Park," Sarasota History Alive!"; Folwell, "Straight Shooter," 47.

MCCORMICK, FRANK J. (1872–1942)
Active Tupper Lake, Franklin County, 1901–1942

Frank McCormick grew up in a farming family in Jingleville, a St. Lawrence County hamlet several miles outside of downtown Canton. After high school he apprenticed in Canton's Wells Gallery before opening a photographic studio in his Jingleville home in 1894. Relocating to Tupper Lake by 1900, he was listed in that year's federal census as a sawmill laborer. By late 1901 he had established himself as a photographer, placing an ad in the 1902–3 Saranac Lake directory offering "High Grade Artistic Work in All the Latest Styles of Photography," "enlargements," "Adirondack Views and Amateur Supplies," "Kodaks for sale or to rent," "Developing and Printing for Amateurs," and "Lessons in Kodakery."[1]

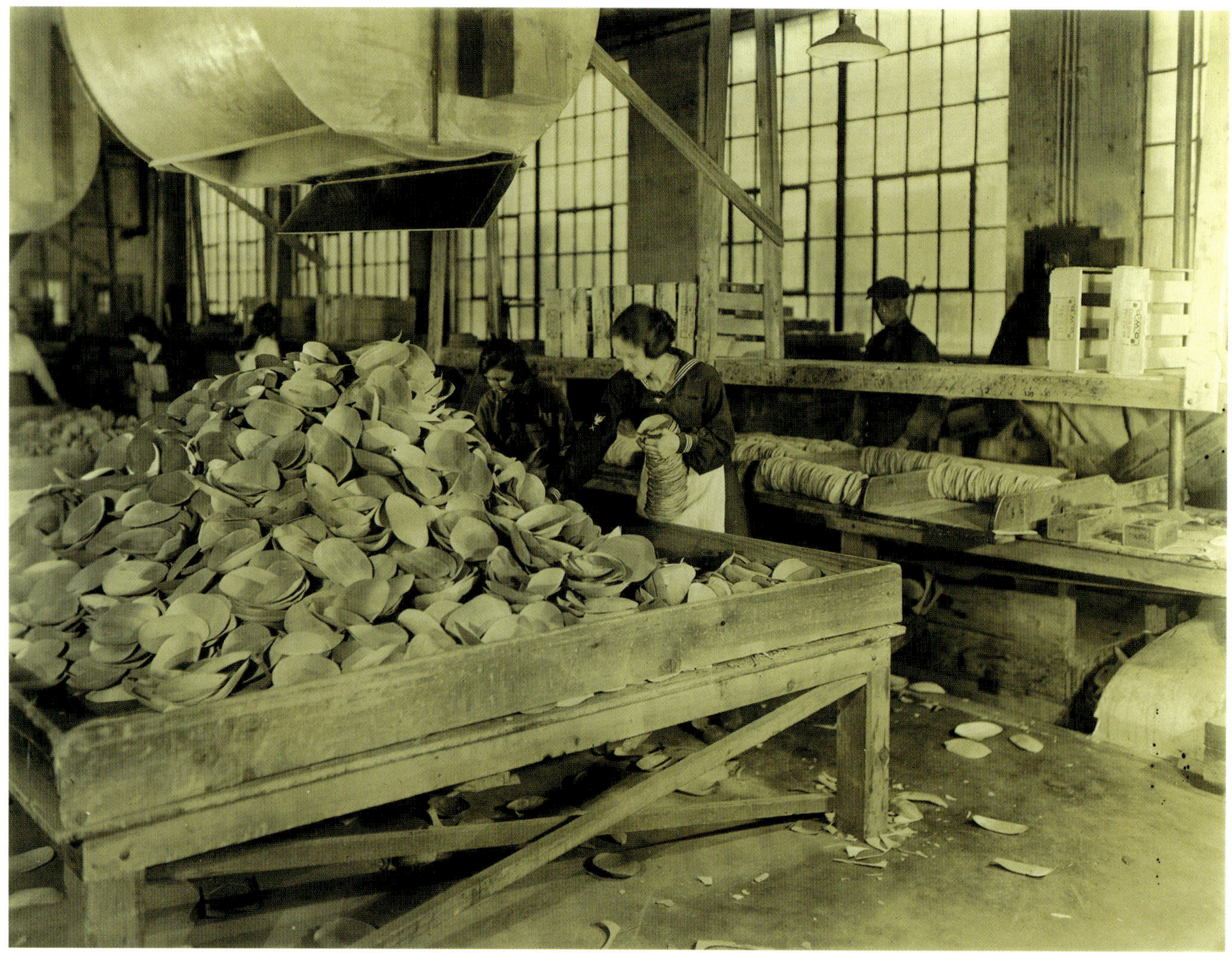

47. F. J. McCormick, women at Oval Wood Dish factory, 1920. Courtesy of Adirondack Experience.

McCormick documented the life of his and nearby communities to the west, advertising his business as McCormick's Studio from about 1913. He participated actively in that life himself, serving as treasurer of the Tupper Lake Fire Department for twenty-five years. Proximity to logging operations provided him with many opportunities to record aspects of the lumber industry. In 1920, two years after the Oval Wood Dish Company opened a lumbering and factory operation in and near Tupper Lake, McCormick was commissioned to take a series of pictures for the company's use in lobby displays, advertising pamphlets, newspapers, and magazines. McCormick died of a heart attack in the workroom of his studio while engaged in developing film for clients. His son James F. McCormick (1913–2008), who worked with him from the mid-1930s, became an employee of Tupper Lake's Veteran's Hospital after his father's death and eventually its chief medical photographer.[2]

1. *Potsdam Junction Commercial Advertiser*, August 22, 1894.

2. *Tupper Lake Herald*, April 16, 1920; *Tupper Lake Free Press and Tupper Lake Herald*, May 21, 1942; July 19, 1978.

MCINTOSH, BURR (1862–1942)
Active Raquette Lake, Hamilton County and Vicinity, 1903–1904

Born in Cleveland, Ohio, and raised in Pennsylvania where his father was president of a Pittsburgh coal-mining company, Burr McIntosh had an eclectic career: actor (theater and movies, both silent and sound), journalist, photographer, author, publisher, film studio owner, lecturer, celebrity. He was a member of the class of 1884 at Princeton but left in 1883, debuted as an actor in 1885, and then began working as a journalist for several Philadelphia and Pittsburgh newspapers. He took pictures for *Leslie's Weekly* during the Spanish American War in 1898 while also representing Hearst and other news outlets as a reporter. In 1901 he opened a New York City photo studio and in 1903 founded *Burr McIntosh Monthly*. The magazine was novel in concept. Short on text, it was largely devoted to photographs, among them portraits of social and theatrical luminaries who posed in Burr's studio; images of socially popular sports such as hunting, polo, golf, yachting, Ivy League athletics; and picturesque scenery. Bound in string, *Monthly* was meant to be disassembled so that individual images could be removed for hanging as home wall décor. McIntosh declared bankruptcy in 1908, and in 1910 his periodical ceased publication. Despite financial and other setbacks during his long career, McIntosh was outgoing and optimistic. His nickname was the "Cheerful Philosopher."[1]

Between July 1903 and February 1904 a number of images appeared in McIntosh's *Monthly* of landscapes and the second homes and recreational pursuits of wealthy property owners in and near Raquette Lake. The August 1903 issue included views of the stylish camps of J. P. Morgan, Timothy L. Woodruff, and Alfred Gwynne Vanderbilt, in whose circle McIntosh comfortably moved. McIntosh was the (unattributed) author of and photographer for a November 1903 *Monthly* article detailing a September house party at Woodruff's Kamp Kill Kare as well as the photographer of unpublished images of a Christmas house party at Vanderbilt's Camp Sagamore.[2]

1. "Burr McIntosh, Class of 1884, and the *Burr McIntosh Monthly*."

2. McIntosh, "Sir Thomas in the Mountains."

MCINTOSH, REUBEN M. (1823–1902)
Active Ausable Chasm, Clinton and Essex Counties, Mid-1870s

The first photographer in Northfield, Vermont, Reuben McIntosh was born on a hilltop farm in Bethel, some twenty miles to the south. He began experimenting as a teenager with the new daguerreotype process and in 1853 relocated to rapidly expanding Northfield, where he focused on studio portraiture before taking up stereoscopic landscape photography. His images, according to a history of the town published in 1878, were "of a high order and possess the charm of being clear and distinct, reminding one of those taken in Switzerland, where the air is ambient and the sky clear and beautiful."[1]

Most of McIntosh's stereoscopic output recorded Vermont scenery, but he also photographed Ausable Chasm. The verso of a stereograph from his *Gems of Ausable Chasm* series listed forty-six views of "this remarkable natural wonder." A number of attributed views were published by the Ausable Company, owner of the chasm operation.

1. "Reuben M. McIntosh," 6–11.

MILLER, RUSSELL A. (1824–1909)
Active Franklin County, 1868

Russell Miller, born in Chichester, New Hampshire, was an early daguerrian, employed in 1845 as a studio operative in Lowell, Massachusetts. By 1853 he was a working for his own Lowell account and advertising the "largest and best daguerreotypes in the city." In 1860 he embarked for Madeira and the Azores, returning with what stereograph specialist William Darrah called "fine, probably the best, views of" both. Settling in Boston, Miller entered into a series of portrait-oriented photographic partnerships during the next several years.[1]

Miller accompanied a September 1868 excursion of the Webber Club, a party of eight Boston men, to Round Pond near Loon Lake, Franklin

County, to document their two-week camping trip. The resulting series, *Adirondac Views, N.Y.*, included at least twenty stereoviews. A Malone newspaper reported that the club members, who passed through town after their outing, "appeared to have had a jolly good time and were feeling gay enough. They brought out of the woods four splendid antlers, that sometime belonged to as many noble bucks. We suppose they came by them honestly enough." Miller also produced a few individual Adirondack landscape stereoviews.[2]

Working largely on his own in the 1870s, Miller published stereograph series of scenes and buildings in and close to Boston: *Boston Views*, *Boston Winter Views*, *South Shore Views*. He was listed as a solar printer (printing and enlarging from negatives by use of a special "solar" camera) in an 1886 Boston directory.

1. *Boston Daily Advertiser*, June 1, 1860; Steele and Polito, *Directory of Massachusetts Photographers*, 98–99; Darrah, *World of Stereographs*, 144.

2. "Home Again," *Malone Palladium*, September 24, 1868.

MIX, ALONZO L. (1845–1915)
Active Johnsburg, Warren County, 1885–93; Warrensburg, Warren County, 1893–1910

Alonzo Mix was the eldest of four children born into a farming family in Long Lake, Hamilton County. He went on to farm himself, but in the winter of 1869–70, at the age of twenty-four, spent a term at Warrensburg Academy, a private, fee-paying school that offered teacher training. "There was no other boy in the school who made better use of his time than Alonzo Mix," recalled a schoolmate. "Serious and thoughtful in disposition and of a deeply religious nature, he worked hard and made rapid progress. He had a pleasing manner which won him the respect and esteem of everyone" and was thought to be "destined for the ministry." Mix did not, however, become a clergyman. He returned to farming in Long Lake and was elected town supervisor in 1873 and 1874. In 1874 he appeared in the first edition of S. R. Stoddard's guide to the Adirondack region, *Adirondacks: Illustrated*, as one of the "superior guides" of Long Lake who could be hired to accompany sportsmen into the woods.[1]

Marrying in 1874, Mix relocated the following year to a farm in Johnsburg, his wife's hometown. His was a typical Adirondack subsistence farming operation, with land planted in meadow, buckwheat, corn, and oats, and small holdings of milch cows, sheep, and chickens. It was in Johnsburg that Mix eased into photography as an occupation; a few of his Johnsburg photographs included the word *amateur* in their imprint. Mix appeared for the first time as a photographer in the New York

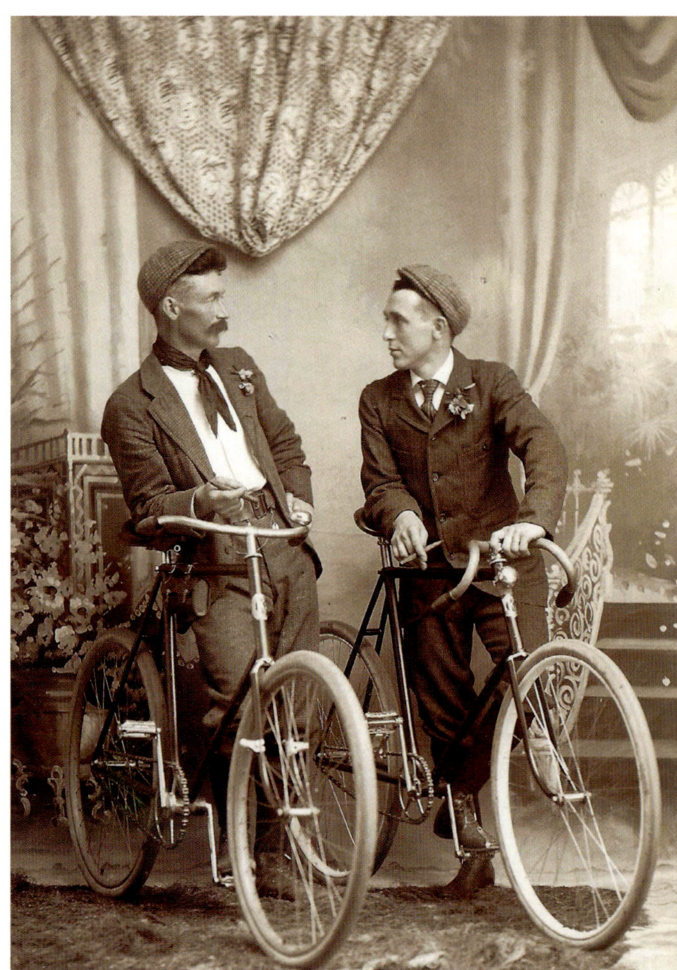

48. A. L. Mix, double portrait, 1890s. Courtesy of Warrensburgh Museum of Local History, Warrensburg, NY.

state census of 1892; in 1893 he moved to nearby Warrensburg to take over the photographic studio of **James T. Betts**. The space, above Hammond's Drug Store, was destroyed by fire in 1895, after which Mix took on another studio. According to an 1898 journal article: "While all classes of photographic art are in the province of Mr. Mix," he has three "special lines": "First, external views; second; family reproductions; third, individual photographs." Mix and his wife spent many consecutive summers from 1888 as seasonal employees at Echo Camp, the Raquette Lake, Hamilton County, summer retreat of former Connecticut governor Phineas C. Lounsbury. A large body of Mix's photographic work records the camp life of the Lounsburys and their neighbors.[2]

1. Ward, "Reminiscences of the Old Academy"; Aber and King, *History of Hamilton County*, 781; S. R. Stoddard, *Adirondacks: Illustrated* (1874 ed.), 153.

2. *Warrensburgh News*, March 22, 1894; July 29, 1897; 1898 souvenir ed.; "Alonzo L. Mix," *Warrensburgh News*, October 12, 1905.

MOLLOY, SARAH MALLORY (MRS. WILLIAM P.) (1832–1892)
Announced but Did Not Open a Photographic Studio in Plattsburgh, Clinton County, 1858

Fascinating as a would-be professional woman photographer some twenty-five years before women entered the field in any number, one wonders what led Sarah Molloy to consider opening a photographic studio in Plattsburgh, what kind of training she had and how she obtained it, and why she abandoned her career plans.

Daughter of John Mallory, a Plattsburgh pioneer who secured the first rights to providing water in the village, Sarah Mallory was commended at the age of eleven for the "very creditable" drawings she displayed at the 1843 Clinton County Agricultural Fair. In 1856 she married William P. Molloy, also of Plattsburgh, and in 1857 gave birth to a son in New York City. In September 1858 she was back in Plattsburgh, where, as Mrs. W. P. Molloy, she won first prizes for the "best colored crayon drawing" and "best pencil sketch" at that year's county fair. A month earlier she had begun advertising her Gallery of Art, to open shortly "over Col. Stone's Printing office" and offer "well executed pictures in Phototypes, Daguerreotypes, Ambrotypes, Sphereotypes, and Hillotypes in oils, India Ink, or plain, at reasonable prices. Mrs. M.," noted the advertisement, "possessing the acquirements of an Artist in painting will furnish Photographs in a very elegant style of finish." The announcement ran for two months in the *Plattsburgh Republican* and then vanished. Molloy was never again mentioned as a photographer. She lived much of her subsequent life in Brooklyn, but summered from 1881 at Echo Lodge, a Lake Placid camp of which she was part owner. A landscape artist specializing in Lake Placid views, she maintained a painting studio in a log cabin on the property.[1]

1. Palmer, *History of Plattsburgh, N.Y.*, 65; *Plattsburgh Republican*, November 20, 1841; October 28, 1843; March 15, 1856; December 19, 1857; August 7, 1858; unknown September date, 1858; Mallory, "Some Glimpses of Old Plattsburgh"; *Plattsburgh Sentinel*, May 2, 1890; MacKenzie, *Plains of Abraham*, 260–61. *Hillotypes* referred to a color process claimed to have been invented by a Catskills minister in 1851, *sphereotypes* to a photographic process on glass patented in 1856.

MONAHAN, ODIE ROBERT (1909–1980)
Active Lake Placid, Essex County, Late 1930s–1943

Odie Monahan first appeared on the Adirondack scene, not behind a camera, but in front of one, as he executed a buck turn on skis at Lake Placid in 1930. (He was the central figure three months later in a *New York Times* photograph titled *Part of the Fine Art of Skiing: Odie Monahan Taking a Cross Jump at Lake Placid*.) Monahan's background is difficult to trace, but he appears to have led a nomadic life. The 1930 image listed his residence as Aiken, South Carolina; at the time of his marriage in 1936, he was based in Miami, Florida. Monahan was later credited with a number of images (generally through photo services: R. I. Nesmith, Triangle), in the *New York Times*, *Life* magazine, and elsewhere. Sports-related images often referenced Lake Placid.[1]

Monahan was in Lake Placid from the late 1930s until 1943, producing real photo postcards and taking photographs of winter sports figures and sporting events (including photos for Otto Scniebs's 1939 book, *American Skiing*) until drafted at the close of 1943. He served in the Public Relations Section of the Fourth Marine Regiment as a combat news and aerial photographer until late 1945. (As a colleague remarked of their shared war service in Japan, Monahan was often "the ringleader of the correspondents . . . He had a way of getting things done and getting us into places, some maybe we should not have gone.") Monahan did not return to Lake Placid after the war, but settled in the San Francisco area, worked for the Oakland Better Business Bureau, and went into public relations. He died in San Diego.[2]

1. *Olean Times Herald*, December 29, 1930; *New York Times*, March 31, 1931; *Wilmington (DE) Morning News*, July 29, 1936.

2. *New York Sun*, November 22, 1937; Schniebs, *American Skiing*, passim; *Lake Placid News*, March 3, 1944; February 2, 1945. Canup, *War Is Not Just for Heroes*, 213, 225; "Mary Ross to Open Publicist Offices Today," *San Francisco Chronicle*, October 17, 1949.

MOORE, FREDERICK A. (1862–1912)
Active Moose River and Little Long Lake, Oneida County, 1895–1906

Frederick Moore was a Utica, Oneida County, clerk in 1890, and a photographer in nearby Rome in early 1893 before relocating later that year to Boonville. He was primarily a portrait photographer, with "special attention given to children," and maintained part-time studios in Remsen and nearby Turin, Lewis County. His preferred stalking ground as a hunter, and the subject of his Adirondack scenic photographs, was the southwestern Adirondacks. He sold his Boonville studio to **George H. Pollard** in 1909 and died "after a long illness" in 1912.[1]

1. *Boonville Herald*, October 19, 1893; *Lowville Journal and Republican*, June 18, 1908; *Rome Sentinel*, September 1912; "News and Notes," *Bulletin of Photography* 11, no. 269 (October 1912): 528.

MOORE, ROGER L. (1905–1997)
Active Lake Placid, Essex County, 1931–1937

Born and raised in Saratoga Springs, Saratoga County, Roger Moore was the son of an engineer active in the development of the early carbonic gas industry in the Saratoga region. He was listed as a Ballston Spa photographer in the 1924 Saratoga Springs directory. Relocating not long afterward to Albany, he worked as a news photographer with the *Albany Evening News* and, from 1929, with the *Knickerbocker Press*. In the summer of 1931, perhaps in anticipation of Lake Placid's hosting of the 1932 Olympic Games, he purchased the studio and novelty shop of **George T. Rabineau**, announcing that he would "continue the business of taking, enlarging and framing pictures, and developing and printing for amateurs." A 1933 advertisement offered "Photographs of Camps and Cottages; Special Post Card Offer."[1]

Moore's career bent was not really toward running a village photography shop. He was "particularly interested in action pictures," and once took a hundred images of a skier making a stem turn in order to capture a perfect shot. Many of his photographs of the Olympics were published, but he lost interest in Lake Placid when the event was over. He spent the winter of 1936–37 at Tuckerman's Ravine, a New Hampshire ski center, and after one more summer in Lake Placid returned to Albany, where he was employed by Empire State News Photos before serving in World War II as an Air Force photographer in the southwestern Pacific. After the war he worked for the New York State Department of Commerce, providing photographs for many tourist publications. In 1940 the Albany

Institute of History and Art mounted an exhibition of thirty of Moore's photographic prints.[2]

1. *Saratogian*, November 30, 1928; August 4, 1931; "G. T. Rabineau Sells Business to Albany Man," *Lake Placid News*, August 7, 1931; May 26, 1933; "Walter R. Moore Dies at Saratoga," *Lake Placid News*, August 3, 1948.

2. *Lake Placid News*, May 28, 1937; *Saratogian*, November 14, 1939; "Albanian's Photo Exhibit is Opened," *Knickerbocker Press*, April 5, 1940.

MOREHOUSE, MILES ALDEN (1847–1912)
Active Wevertown, Warren County, Mid-1870s–1895, 1908–1910

Miles Morehouse was a man of many talents. He spent the better part of his sixty-five years in Wevertown, the hamlet of Johnsburg in which he had been born, and appeared in federal and state censuses as a carpenter in 1870, a photographer in 1875, and a watchmaker in 1880. His small shop variously housed his clock, watch, jewelry, and musical instrument business, the town post office during a brief tenure as hamlet postmaster, and from 1892 to 1895, a drug store. "His quick, receptive business faculty," it was noted upon his appointment to postmaster, "together with the kindly, gentlemanly manner of Mr. Morehouse, will insure him the esteem of all."[1]

Morehouse's photographic output included a stereoview series titled *Adirondack Views* taken in the vicinity of Wevertown and bearing the imprint of Morehouse as "amateur photographer." As he observed in an 1884 photographic journal article on darkroom ventilation, he had "followed photography for several years, and found great pleasure in the art, but for good reasons sold my interest in the business, and have since engaged in another calling. Notwithstanding this change of occupation, I keep a good dry-plate outfit, and make pictures as an amateur, solely for the pleasure thereof, and feel much better repaid." In 1886 Morehouse submitted several 5 x 8 inch prints to *Anthony's Photographic Bulletin* for critical assessment, soliciting the editorial opinion that they were "charming," if sometimes exhibiting "a lack of artistic feeling in the selection of the points of view." Circa 1890 he began presenting a transcontinental stereopticon lecture, "Maine to Alaska," at local schools and churches, at rooms of the Independent Order of Odd Fellows, and once, at the Lake View House in Bolton on Lake George. Among Morehouse's outside enthusiasms were fishing and fox hunting. (He was recorded as trapping a forty-seven-pound skunk in 1906.)[2]

In 1887 Morehouse offered for sale his patent for the "only improvement ever made in plated knives; in 1894 he was awarded a patent for a "telephone transmitter" that projected sound some thirty feet into a room. "Wishing to engage quite extensively in the manufacture of proprietary preparations known as 'Crystal Remedies,'" Morehouse closed his shop in April 1895. The following year he headed west, where he was recorded in the 1900 US Census as a physician in St. Lawrence, Waupaca County, Wisconsin. His new title was undoubtedly useful in promoting his patent medicine for the treatment of hemorrhoids: "A pile cure that CURES."[3]

In mid-1905 it was announced that "Dr. M. A. Morehouse" had returned from the West after a nine-year absence and would again make his home in Wevertown. He reestablished his earlier business, expanding the operation with "a medical laboratory in addition to his work as goldsmith," and advertised for agents "to introduce a new line of family medicines from the favorite prescriptions of an old family physician now retired from practice." In 1908 he added a "small gallery for photographic work" to provide "truthful portraits of yourself, the children—and all your folks" as well as "cattle and houses . . . for a short time only." Morehouse was recorded in the 1910 US Census as a physician (although the Vermont chapter of the American Medical Association had decertified him in 1908 on the grounds that his license had been "fraudulently obtained").[4]

1. *Warrensburgh News*, December 24, 1891; April 21, 1892.

2. Morehouse, "Ventilation for the Dark-Room," 477; *Anthony's Photographic Bulletin* 18, no. 20 (October 23, 1886): 618; *Warrensburgh News*, September 4, 1890; November 29, 1906.

3. *Scientific American*, May 28, 1887, 347; *Geneva Gazette*, December 21, 1894; *Warrensburgh News*, September 17, 1896; September 22, 1898; May 28, 1908.

4. *Warrensburgh News*, September 28, 1905; August 24(?), 1905; May 28, 1908; *Glens Falls Times*, September 15, 1905; "Medical News: Vermont," *Journal of the American Medical Association* 50, pt. 1 (February 1, 1908): 375.

MOSES, CHESTER D. (1874–1950)
Active Lake Placid, Essex County, 1898–1905

Chester Moses was born in Worcester, Massachusetts, the son of a carpenter and Civil War veteran. His father died in 1881, and in 1889 his mother married Edwin C. Cleaves, for more than thirty years the head of the Department of Industrial Drawing and Art at Cornell University. The Cleaveses made their home in Cortland, Cortland County. Moses graduated from Cornell University in 1897 with a degree in engineering and from Long Island Medical College in 1902. He entered general medical practice in Buffalo in 1903 and became a specialist in X-ray technique and treatment at Buffalo's Deaconess Hospital.[1]

Moses was introduced to the seasonal community of Lake Placid by the Cleaveses, members of the Lake Placid Club and owners of Camp Herbert at the head of Mirror Lake. (They became full-time village residents in 1905.) Photography, which had begun for Moses as a hobby, became a paying summer enterprise. He was hired as the Lake Placid Club's first official photographer and copyrighted his first photograph (*Lake Placid from Eagle's Eyrie*) in August 1899. His work appeared in an article, "America's Playground in the Adirondacks," published in 1900 in *Puritan*, "a journal for gentlewomen."[2]

The Chester D. Moses Co. marketed "General Views," "Panoramas," and "Colored Landscapes" through the summer of 1903 from its "Art Photography" headquarters at Camp Herbert Photographic

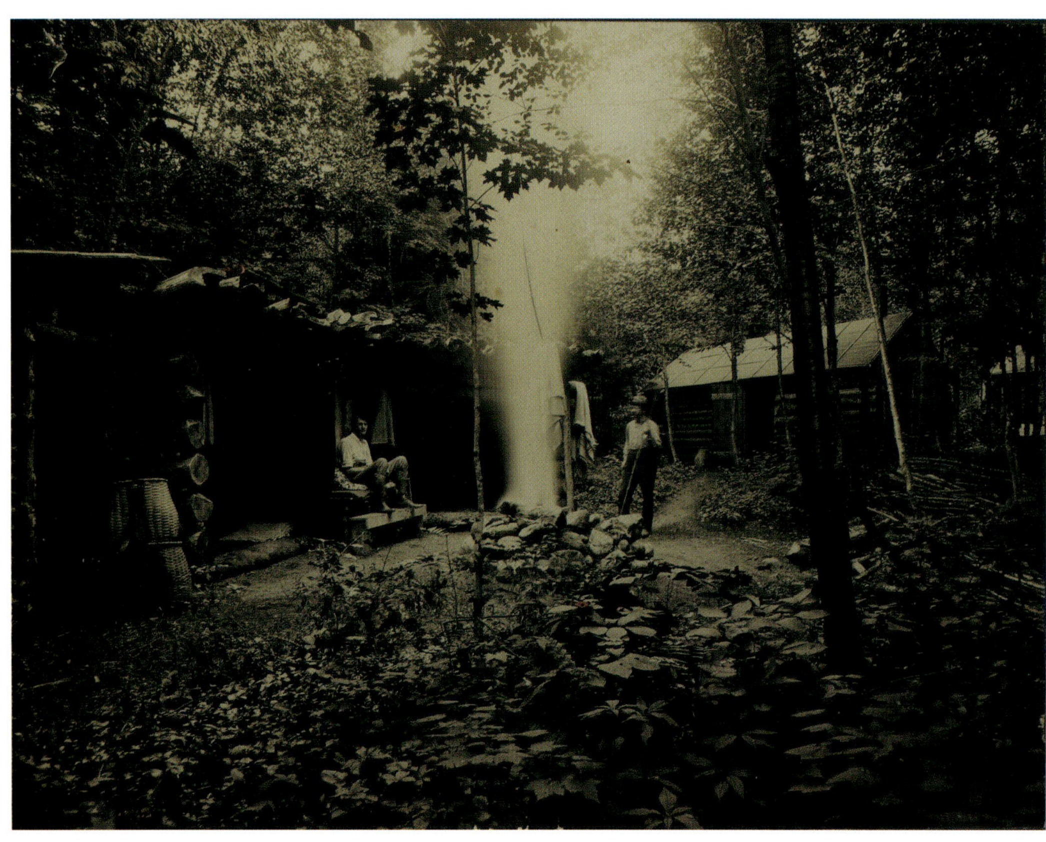

49. C. D. Moses, guides' camp, Upper Ausable Lake, circa 1901.

Lodge. "Why not continue," Moses queried in an advertising brochure, "the pleasures of the summer by having your camp or cottage artistically photographed, and a panoramic view of the outlook from your piazza?" After his relocation to Buffalo the business was managed by Moses's stepfather, who, according to an obituary, "devoted his time" in Lake Placid "to photography and art."[3]

Despite Moses's physical absence from Lake Placid, Moses & Co. had expansionist plans. In 1905 it signed a contractual agreement with the Silver Bay Association, owned by the YMCA and operated from 1904 as a semireligious resort and conference center in the Hague hamlet of Silver Bay, Warren County. The contract laid out the parties' respective responsibilities for the 1906 season, with the company, as "Photographers at Silver Bay," to provide camera equipment, furnish a photographer between mid-June and mid-September, sell Silver Bay photographs "through other stores now established by Chester D. Moses & Co.," and pay to the association 20 percent of gross receipts on sales. On its part, the association was committed to providing a darkroom with running water, store display space for photograph sales, room and board at the same rate given to convention delegates, and reimbursement of up to one hundred dollars for travel expenses between Lake Placid and Silver Bay. The contract was not executed, and there are no photographs in the Silver Bay Association archives attributed to Moses & Co. The business continued advertising through 1909 before it was leased and then sold to **Irving L. Stedman** and a partner in 1911.[4]

1. "Prof. Edwin C. Cleaves," *Cortland Standard*, August 11, 1913; "Dr. Moses, 75, Dies, X-Ray Specialist Here," *Buffalo Courier-Express*, March 18, 1950.

2. *Cortland Standard*, June 30, 1899; Maximilian Foster, "America's Playground in the Adirondacks," 81–95.

3. Advertising pamphlet in collection of Lake Placid Historian; "Cleaves," *Cortland Standard*, August 11, 1913.

4. Silver Bay Association, Board Minutes, November 3, 1905, on file in Silver Bay Association archives; *Troy Times*, October 19, 1911.

MOULD, W., & SON (1869–1878)

A Drug and Stationery Store in Keeseville, Clinton and Essex Counties, that Published Adirondack Views

W. Mould & Son was established in 1869 when Willis Mould (1823–1883) took his son, Henry M. Mould (1843–1910), into partnership in the store he had purchased in 1857. Although the imprint MOULD & SON PHOTOGRAPHERS appeared on some images it offered, the enterprise advertised itself in 1870 only as a "Dealer in Drugs & Medicines, Books & Stationery, Fancy Goods, Fishing Tackle, &c."[1]

The most popular of Mould & Son's photographic offerings were two stereograph series (*Adirondack Series* and *Ausable Series*) taken in 1865–67 by **Frank Robbins** of Keene, New Hampshire. Robbins had sold the negatives of these images to the Moulds before or not long after relocating to Oil City, Pennsylvania, in the late 1860s. The Moulds, in keeping with photographic tradition, published them under their own business name, but retained Robbins's series titles, image numbers, and image wording. **George W. Baldwin**, whose portrait studio was in the Moulds's building, has been suggested as the possible processor of their photographic stock. The business name disappeared in 1878 with the retirement of Willis Mould.[2]

1. *Essex County Republican*, August 18, 1870.

2. Bauer, "George W. Baldwin, Adirondack Photographer," 12.

MOULTON, JOSEPH CARR (1824–1914)

Active Ausable Chasm, Clinton and Essex Counties, and North Elba, Essex County, 1866–1870

In the 1840s Joseph Moulton relocated from his birthplace, Sandwich, New Hampshire, to Fitchburg, Massachusetts, where he spent some sixty years as a photographer. His output was prolific: estimated at more than 40,000 portrait and stereograph images over the course of his career. His meticulously kept journals recorded 10,350 portraits taken between 1887 and 1897.[1]

In September 1866 the *Fitchburg Sentinel* noted that Moulton has "recently been engaged in taking stereoscopic views in various localities. Among others are 12 views of the 'Chasm,' on the Ausable River in the town of Keeseville, N. Y. These views, we learn, have had a large sale in Keeseville and vicinity, and many in this vicinity who have visited the place, have not neglected to provide themselves with a set of these valuable pictures." Moulton's Ausable Chasm series eventually ran to at least nineteen views. The abolitionist John Brown's North Elba, Essex County, home and gravesite was another Moulton subject. In 1914 the *Bulletin of Photography* dubbed Moulton, then ninety, "the oldest photographer in America."[2]

1. Edsall, *Handbook of Fitchburg Photographers*, 133–34; Steele and Polito, *Directory of Massachusetts Photographers, 1839–1900*, 249.

2. *Fitchburg Sentinel*, September 14, 1866; Edsall, *Handbook of Fitchburg Photographers*, 133, 135.

MYERS, CARL EDGAR (1842–1925)
Active Central Adirondacks, 1871

Born on a farm in the German Flatts, Herkimer County, hamlet of Fort Herkimer, Carl Myers was raised in the hamlet of Mohawk. He went to work for the Mohawk Valley Bank in 1861 and was a teller and acting cashier until 1867, when he resigned to open a photograph gallery in the rapidly expanding village of Hornellsville, Steuben County.[1]

Myers was one of seven "lively chaps . . . all full to overflowing with good nature and fun" who spent a summer holiday camping in 1871 in the central Adirondacks—a vacation written up in humorous detail the following year by H. Perry Smith as *Modern Babes in the Wood: Or Summer Wanderings in the Wilderness*. Myers, "the philosopher, the artist," delineated as "striding" along "with his camera on his shoulder," was prone to the occasional "spasm" of "appetite for experiments of some kind." According to an 1893 history of Herkimer County, he published a series of stereoviews based on images taken on this excursion, of "the Old John Brown Tract, or Arnold House, the Forge, Fulton Chain of Lakes, the Raquette, Eagle, and Blue Mountain Lake, and the northern wilderness." He did not sign his work.[2]

In 1875 Myers sold his Hornellsville studio and returned to Mohawk. He spent the next several years in the study of hydrogen gas balloons before becoming an aeronautical engineer and devoting the rest of his professional life to ballooning and airship inventions. In 1889 Myers and his aeronaut wife, Mary Hawley, established a "Balloon Farm" in Frankfort, Herkimer County, where they conducted balloon-related scientific experiments and oversaw the manufacture of passenger balloons (including those flown at the St. Louis World's Fair). Their specialty balloons, among them weather and military balloons, were used by the US government.

1. Hardin, *History of Herkimer County*, 501–3.

2. Hardin, *History of Herkimer County*, 501–3; H. P. Smith, *Modern Babes in the Wood*, 18, 97, 107.

NEW YORK STEREOSCOPIC COMPANY (1857–1860)
Producers and Distributors of Views of Lake George Region, 1859

The New York Stereoscopic Company, of which the proprietorship is unknown, first advertised its "assortment" of views, "with and without color," in February 1858. In September 1859, under the exclusive agency of D. Appleton and Company, it announced "a great variety of entirely new stereographs of the most beautiful and noted scenes in the United States." Included in the more than three hundred views on offer, taken by anonymous photographers, were six views of Lake George (at least some copies of which were delicately hand-tinted).

These were among the earliest representations of the Adirondack landscape. The New York Stereoscopic Company ceased advertising in 1860, and dissolved in 1864.[1]

1. Darrah, *World of Stereographs*, 26; advertisement, *American Publishers' Circular and Literary Gazette* 4, no. 8 (February 20, 1858): 94; *American Publishers' Circular and Literary Gazette* 5, no. 39 (September 24, 1859): 481.

NICKERSON, AMOS STODDARD (1846–1912)
Active Ticonderoga, Essex County, 1874–1910

Amos Nickerson was the youngest son of a Manchester, Vermont, physician, who settled in Ticonderoga around 1839. He was listed as a Ticonderoga photographer in a New York State business directory in 1874. Primarily a portrait specialist, Nickerson advertised "all the new styles, both fancy and plain, large and small. Also first-class Ferreotypes made and finished to order." He produced a small body of stereoviews before entering in 1877 into a short-lived association with **Lavius H. Fillmore**; the two photographers were "prepared to do work in their line to suit customers." He partnered again, this time with photographer **Julius A. Thatcher**, at Thatcher's studio in 1884.[1]

Nickerson maintained satellite studios in other population centers for short periods: Chateaugay, Clinton County, in 1874; Warrensburg, Warren County, in 1890 and 1910. During summers he toured the Lake George region, taking individual and group portraits as well as landscape views. He supplemented his income as a justice of the peace and, according to the 1900 US Census, an insurance agent. Nickerson was recorded as a photographer working out of his own studio in the 1910 US Census.[2]

1. *Ticonderoga Sentinel*, July 18, 1874; June 11, 1875; February 23, 1877; November 30, 1877; November 21, 1884.
2. *Malone Palladium*, March 12, 1874; *Ticonderoga Sentinel*, March 3, 1892; October 27, 1910.

NORTON, JOHN A. (1874–1963)
Active Otter Lake, Oneida County, 1914–1963

John Norton was the longtime proprietor of as well as the photographer for the Standard Supply Company, a souvenir wholesale business and store, for which he produced nearly six hundred images for postcards in a span of over forty years. Born and raised in Boonville, Oneida County, the son of a lumber dealer, he graduated from the University of Buffalo with a degree in pharmacy and in 1900 became a druggist in Lyons, Wayne County. In 1914 he was lured to Otter Lake, a hamlet of Forestport, by his older brother, Roscoe, owner of the Otter Lake Hotel, who was striving to realize Otter Lake's potential as a summer community and resort.[1]

Norton opened the Standard Photo Supply Company (renamed the Standard Supply Company in 1918) shortly after his arrival in Otter Lake. He "has worked up quite a business in photographs, colored postcards and pennants," it was reported in 1916. He "has an established trade on the eastern side of the Adirondacks and finds his business opportunity growing." The 1920s and 1930s were Standard Supply's peak years, when the company offered more than eight thousand novelties, gifts, and souvenirs from a variety of sources.[2]

Norton's eventual territory for taking photos and selling postcards was broad: from the Black River region west of the Adirondack Park to the city of Rome, Oneida County, in the southwest, and as far east and north as Chestertown, Warren County, and Lake Placid, Essex County. In a region in which retail sales volumes were modest, the company relied on personal relationships with wholesale customers to turn a profit. As the proprietor of a store in Chestertown wrote in 1924: "Received the postcard. We were very much pleased with it. Sending money order for $7.50 for 1000 colored pictures. Will send other orders when business picks up."[3]

Wholesaling postcards in the Adirondack market became more difficult in the 1950s, when it was necessary to order the printing of from ten to fifteen thousand copies per view to assure a respectable return. From 5 to 15 percent of Standard Supply's later postcards were stock images provided by publishers, but the bulk of the firm's output continued to be based on Norton's original photographs, many of which had a long shelf life. Norton retired shortly before his death in 1963 at the age of ninety.[4]

1. Folwell, "Wish You Were Here," 61–62.

2. *Newark (NY) Arcadian Weekly Gazette*, May 9, 1900; "Ready for Guests at Otter Lake," *Boonville Herald*, May 4, 1916; author interview with John G. Norton, John P. Norton's grandson, July 24, 2016.

3. Author interview with John G. Norton, July 24, 2016; "Standard Supply Company Records," Adirondack Experience Library.

4. Author interview with John G. Norton, July 24, 2016.

ORR, ALEXANDER, JR. (1837–1906)
Active Warren County, 1868–1878

Born in Queens, New York, Alexander Orr was the oldest child of parents who moved their family to Queensbury, Warren County, around 1841 to join other Scots Presbyterian immigrants like themselves settling in the town's French Mountain area.[1]

Recorded in the New York state census of 1855 as a farmer living in his parents' home, by 1860 Orr was a laborer in nearby Hebron, Washington County. Not long thereafter he returned to Queensbury, where between 1861 and 1868 he was employed to maintain the town's cemetery as its sexton. Orr is likely to have trained with photographer **George W. Conkey** in Glens Falls, then the largest village in Queensbury, for the two men partnered briefly in the late 1860s as "Conkey and Orr, Portrait and Landscape Photographers." An 1871 Saratoga County directory listed Orr as a Glens Falls photographer. His output included portraits and views. While only his name appeared on portrait images, a series of Imperial (taller than standard) stereoviews of local scenery was published by "A. Orr & Son," Glens Falls. These would have dated to a brief period close to the completion of his son, Fred's, schooling in 1874 or 1875.[2]

By 1880 Orr had sold his business to C. L. Lovejoy and relocated to Wilmington, North Carolina, where he continued his career as a photographer. He was still based in Wilmington in 1882, but his activities for the remainder of the decade are uncertain. Orr appeared again in regional records in 1890, when he opened a studio in Sandy Hill, Washington County (renamed Hudson Falls in 1910). In 1897 he moved his studio to Fort Edward, where he died "after a long illness."[3]

1. Warren County, NY, "Historic Buildings, The First 100 Years: Bay Road Presbyterian Church."

2. Holden, *History of the Town of Queensbury*, 112.

3. *Glens Falls Times*, August 18, 1882; December 8, 1897; *Glens Falls Star*, March 9, 1898; December 4, 1896; *Saratogian*, December 28, 1906.

OVITT, GORDON DAVID (1893–1961)
Active Corinth, Saratoga County, 1944–1959

The son of a factory worker in the Day, Saratoga County, hamlet of Conklingville, Gordon Ovitt passed his life in Corinth, save for army service during World War I and brief stints in Detroit, Michigan, as a shipping clerk before and after the war. He ran a Corinth newsstand, stationery store, and ice cream parlor from 1926 to 1933, but was enumerated as a clerk in the 1940 US Census. His Ovitt's Studio offered photographic portraits.[1]

1. *Saratogian*, September 16, 1919; April 3, 1933; November 17, 1944; February 4, 1959.

PAGE, EDWARD HILEY LYTLE (1874–1932)
Active along the Route of the Fonda, Johnstown and Gloversville Railroad, Fulton County, 1903

The Fonda, Johnstown and Gloversville Railroad traversed a 132-mile interurban route between Schenectady and Northville, Fulton County, from

1870. Its owners counted on a summer surge in passenger traffic over a branch line from the early twentieth century, when as many as ninety thousand visitors descended on the railroad's popular Sacandaga Park.

Edward Page was in the Adirondacks in the summer of 1903 in connection with the preparation of a promotional viewbook produced by the FJ&G the following year. Titled *Camera Sketches of Sacandaga Park*, the publication was printed on heavy 9 x 12 inch stock and prefaced with a brief introduction from the railroad's Passenger Department. Its eighty-four pages, filled primarily with large-format photographs and one-line descriptors, was designed to "give the reader a most enjoyable mental trip through the park."[1]

Page was welcomed back to upstate New York by a regional newspaper "for the season" in late May 1904. (The piece noted that he had spent the winter taking pictures for a steamboat line on Florida's Tomoka River and contributing illustrated articles on Florida to New York newspapers.) Referring to the railroad's publication, the paper added that Page would "take active charge of an immediate general canvass for the sale of the volume of views." The role of *Camera Sketches* as a marketing vehicle was explicit: "Hundreds of these volumes are to be mailed and carried by enthusiastic admirers to every part of the Union, and we may expect to have the good fortune of welcoming many new comers to this section, who will abide with us and have a good time, and spend their money with us, and who will come again and bring still other desirable friends with them." PHOTOGRAPHS BY EDWARD H. L. PAGE was hand-stamped after publication on the title page of some but not all copies of *Camera Sketches*; other copies were stamped in the same location as "Copyrighted 1904 by Edward H. L. Page."[2]

It is possible that Page did not take all of the viewbook's photographs, or he may have subsequently sold the negatives to Northville photographers, for several of them—namely **Isaac E. Bowman, Joseph K. Dunlop**, and **George W. Stevens**—published images from the book at one time or another under their names. Page's other photographic efforts were scant: a prize-winning amateur image in a 1902 issue of *Leslie's Weekly*; an illustrated article about an abandoned Pennsylvania railroad published that year in the *Buffalo Courier* and again in *Scientific American* in 1905. By 1910 Page was an Altoona, Pennsylvania, real estate salesman.[3]

1. *Camera Sketches of Sacandaga Park*; "Sacandaga Park Pictures—Beautiful Book of Summer Resort Sketches," *Amsterdam Evening Recorder*, May 16, 1904.

2. *Amsterdam Evening Recorder*, May 20, 1904.

3. "Edward H. L. Page," *Altoona Tribune*, November 5, 1932; *Leslie's Weekly*, November 6, 1902, 447; Edward H. L. Page, "Old Portage Railroad," *Buffalo Courier*, November 30, 1902; Page, "The Old Portage Railroad in Pennsylvania," 74–76.

PARKS, JAMES GEORGE (1836–1895)
Active Lake George Region; Ausable Chasm, Clinton and Essex Counties, 1870s–1890

A leading Montreal photographer from the 1870s into the early 1890s, James (George) Parks was born in Saratoga County to English immigrant parents. Following his father in his first choice of occupation, he appeared as a Fort Edwards, Washington County, blacksmith in the 1860 US Census. "His artistic ideas, however, led him to take up the study of photography," and after apprenticing in an unknown studio, in 1864 he relocated to Montreal, where he opened his own business. Parks offered both portraits and landscape images. An 1878 advertisement promoted "1200 stereographs"—a majority of them of Montreal and other Canadian cities, but including views of Lake George and Niagara Falls. The verso of an 1890 stereoview referenced available views of Lake George, the Adirondacks, and Ausable Chasm.[1]

An 1893 advertisement provided details of Parks's photographic operation. He was, it noted, "the first artist, in Montreal, to retouch negatives, to enlarge pictures, by the solar camera, and to make dry-plates." He owned forty lenses "to suit all occasions," ranging "from microscopic size to the 'mammoth,' which cost over $500 and a journey to New York," and took photos of "nervous children, before they can move." His work was "accredited by 21 first prizes."[2]

1. *Men of Canada; or Success by Example*, 496; *Canada Spectator*, October 5, 1878, 1.

2. Advertisement, Terrill, *Chronology of Montreal and of Canada*, 257.

PEABODY, HENRY GREENWOOD (1855–1951)
Active Eastern Adirondacks, 1900–1908

Born a minister's son in St. Louis, Missouri, Henry Peabody graduated from Dartmouth College in 1876. After another academic year spent at the Massachusetts Institute of Technology studying architecture, electricity, and physics, he worked for several years for the Western Electric Company. He then took up photography, at first in Chicago, but from 1886 in his own Boston studio. Early specialties included marine, landscape, and architectural photography. Peabody was the official photographer for the Boston and Maine Railroad and self-published tourist brochures and a standard-setting folio of Maine coast scenic views in the late 1880s.[1]

Peabody's wife died in 1898, leaving him with a young daughter to support. To guarantee his income, he worked from 1900 into 1908 as a photographer on both the East and West Coasts for the **Detroit Publishing Company**. The company's postcard images were unattributed, but Peabody was responsible for a number of its Adirondack views. Eighty-five of over one hundred images mounted in an album of his eastern New York views depict the eastern Adirondacks, most of them unpeopled scenic landscapes of Lake George and its major hotels; the ruins of Forts Ticonderoga and Crown Point; and Ausable Chasm. Images in the album published by Detroit bear the company's imprint and a copyright date between 1902 and 1908. Those not published by the company are hand-labeled and undated.[2]

In the early 1900s Peabody shifted his area of concentration to the American West, settling in Pasadena, California. After leaving the Detroit Publishing Company he published several series of lantern slides and films for educational use, generally related to national parks. By the 1930s he was producing audio recordings to synchronize with these presentations. Peabody has been recognized as an artist who "exerted a vital influence on the profession and on the acceptance of photographs in the public interest."[3]

1. Andrews, *Photographers of the Frontier West*, 169; Bischof, Danly, and Shettleworth, *Maine Photography*, 47.

2. Peabody, "Album 2: Views of Eastern New York."

3. Andrews, *Photographers of the Frontier West*, 169.

PEASE, CHARLES S. (1855–1896)
Active Adirondack Viewshed of the Delaware and Hudson Railroad, 1890–1895

"As an enthusiastic photographer and having an eye for the artistic," Charles Pease produced images as an amateur that did much to advance the fortunes of the Delaware and Hudson Railroad, where he was employed from the mid-1880s and eventually assumed the title of baggagemaster.[1]

Born in Thompsonville, Connecticut, Pease settled in Cohoes, Albany County, in 1866. There he learned the printer's trade and became the publisher of *Pease's People's Railway Guide*, a continually updated timetable providing information on all trains leaving Albany and "as necessary to a traveling man as a well-filled pocketbook." In 1883 he affiliated with the Delaware and Hudson's Albany headquarters.[2]

A founder of the Albany Camera Club, organized in 1887, Pease was one of its most prolific and prominent members; his photographs were regularly mounted in club exhibits and singled out as "particularly fine." One Pease image, *An*

Adirondack Corner, was used along with photographs by **Seneca Ray Stoddard** and **George W. Baldwin** to illustrate an 1890 *Troy Times* article titled "The Adirondacks." The accompanying text asserted that Pease's camera work ranked "with the best efforts of professional skill." Pease provided many images for Delaware and Hudson annual reports in the mid-1890s and was praised in late 1895 for introducing "a new kind of advertising which promises to be most popular." This entailed the public display of photographs of "picturesque spots in the Adirondacks," developed and "nicely mounted and framed" by Pease, in which the only suggestion of commercialism was the printing of the *D and H* coat of arms below the photograph, "in itself a neat conceit." Pease died young. His wife continued to publish *Pease's Guide* until her death in 1912.[3]

1. *Essex County Republican*, January 2, 1896, quoting *Albany Journal*.

2. *Albany Express*, December 2, 1896; *Albany Times Union*, February 1, 1896; *Troy Daily Times*, February 8, 1883.

3. *Albany Times Union*, January 7, 1893; *Troy Times*, September 20, 1890; *Essex County Republican*, January 2, 1896; *Semi-Weekly Troy Times*, August 6, 1912.

PIERSON, EUGENE H. (1896–1988)
Active Lake Placid, Essex County, 1927–1959

Eugene (Gene) Pierson was born in Hackensack, New Jersey, the son of a bank cashier; in 1920 he was living in East Orange, New Jersey, and engaged in clerical work at a brokerage house. Pierson may have arrived in Lake Placid in 1926 as a correspondent for the *New York Times*, and announced himself as a local photographer in 1927, advertising "pictures taken at your home, of your home, in your home." Early specialties of the Pierson Studio included enlargements from Kodak negatives, children's portraits, group photos, identification shots for chauffeurs' licenses, Lake Placid camp interiors and exteriors, postcard views, and sports images.[1]

Pierson swiftly established sport photography credentials in the Adirondack winter sports capital. An official photographer for the 1932 Winter Olympics, he was also employed by the Lake Placid Chamber of Commerce to take photos of sporting events. The magazine *Popular Photography* noted his expertise in "filming skaters on wind-blown Lake Placid" in 1951; his most famous action shot was a dramatic image of a skier, pulled by a horse, jumping over a wall of ice in a skijoring event. Pierson's work appeared in photography magazines, on calendars, and in Otto Schniebs's 1939 book, *American Skiing*. Known for sixteen-millimeter color filming, he captured an unusual event in the early World War II period: a sham battle or "winter maneuver" featuring skiers with rifles and machine guns on Lake Placid's ski slopes. This footage was edited into a twenty-minute film for presentation to the War Department as part of a Chamber of Commerce bid for a Lake Placid–based army training course for ski troopers (a course subsequently awarded to Colorado's Camp Hale). A segment was used by Pathé News, producer of movie theater newsreels.[2]

Pierson began wintering in the South in the mid-1940s, and bought a Florida home in 1953. His year was henceforth divided between Florida winters and summers in Lake Placid, where he focused on marketing souvenirs and photochrome postcards of local scenes to the summer trade. In December 1959 Pierson sold his photo shop to **David William Jones**. After spending two subsequent summers living in a mobile home in nearby Wilmington, he and his wife purchased a Clearwater, Florida, hardware business—to be called the Marina Gift Shop and Beach Hardware Store—and relocated permanently to Florida in 1961.[3]

1. *Lake Placid News*, December 24, 1926; April 1, 1927; April 29, 1927; May 13, 1927; July 8, 1927; June 28, 1928.

2. *Lake Placid News*, January 21, 1938; December 15, 1939; November 14, 1941; December 25, 1942; February 23, 1984; Ensworth, "Camera on the Ice," 90; Schniebs, *American Skiing*, passim; Hoy, *Heritage of the Adirondacks*, 80.

For footage from Pierson's war games film, see https://www.britishpathe.com//video/us-army-ski-manoeuvres-dublin-issue/query/binoculars.

3. *Lake Placid News*, April 10, 1953; December 11, 1959; *Adirondack Enterprise*, May 29, 1961; December 2, 1991; *Adirondack Record–Elizabethtown Post*, May 24, 1962; June 20, 1968.

POLLARD, GEORGE H. (1867–1946)
Active Fulton Chain of Lakes, Herkimer and Hamilton Counties, 1909–1910

George Pollard, born in Utica, Oneida County, was by the mid-1880s a Utica clerk. After attending the studio of landscape painter Edward McDowell in New York City, he took up photography and in 1889 worked briefly in Little Falls, Herkimer County, before heading back to Utica. In late 1909 he purchased the Boonville studio of Frederick A. Moore. Primarily a portrait photographer, he contributed uncredited images "taken especially for this work" to a 1910 *Guide to the Fulton Chain*. Some of these photographs were published as real photo postcards.[1]

1. *Malone Telegram*, December 15, 1906; *Guide to the Fulton Chain of Lakes, Including Big Moose Lake*; "Handsome Souvenir Book," *Boonville Herald*, July 28, 1910; *Rome Sentinel*, September 17, 1912; "G. H. Pollard Dies at Age 78," *Rome Sentinel*, June 1, 1946.

PURSELL, JAMES WALTON (1877–1984)
Active Fulton and Hamilton Counties, 1909–1920

A native of Gloversville, Fulton County, James Pursell followed his father's trade as a glovecutter before transitioning to photography around 1909, when his occupation in a Gloversville directory was recorded as "glover and photographer." Subsequent directories listed him as a photographer. He and his wife explored the nearby countryside for nearly a decade on a tandem bicycle—at first pulling behind them a small cart loaded with camping gear, a bulky camera, glass plates, and a tripod—while Pursell captured views around Caroga Lake and in the Sacandaga Valley. This camera was succeeded by a smaller model and the bicycle by an automobile, expanding the Pursells's picture-taking range further into Fulton County and to Hamilton County's Indian and Blue Mountain Lakes. Many finished landscape views were hand-colored in oils by Margaret Pursell.[1]

Pursell was primarily a portrait photographer. Other specialties included school and wedding photographs and accident and crime-scene records for the Fulton County Sheriff. He was still taking pictures in 1943.[2]

1. O'Brien, "J. Walton Pursell, Photographer 1877–1964," 17–18.

2. "Hand Cut by Fall into Showcase," *Gloversville and Johnstown Morning Herald*, July 26, 1943.

PURVIANCE, WILLIAM TANNER (1829–1905)
Active Ausable Chasm, Clinton and Essex Counties; St. Regis and Saranac Lakes, Franklin County; Lake George Region, 1873–1874

Born in Warren, Pennsylvania, William Purviance got his start as a daguerreian artist in Pittsburgh around 1850. Moving into railroad photography, he became the official photographer for the Penn Central Railroad with the merger of the Pennsylvania and New York Central lines in 1867 and relocated his family to Philadelphia shortly thereafter. He offered "Scenes of . . ." stereoviews for Penn Central and other rail lines he represented, which were distributed by agents working on his and their behalf. Hs work included landscapes as well as images of tracks, bridges, trestles, tunnels, rock cuts, and stations.

Mr. Purviance "of the Pennsylvania, Lehigh Valley, Northern Central, & Erie railroad Companies" was reported locally in October 1873 to be stopping in Essex County, where he would be visiting Ausable Chasm, opened to the public that year,

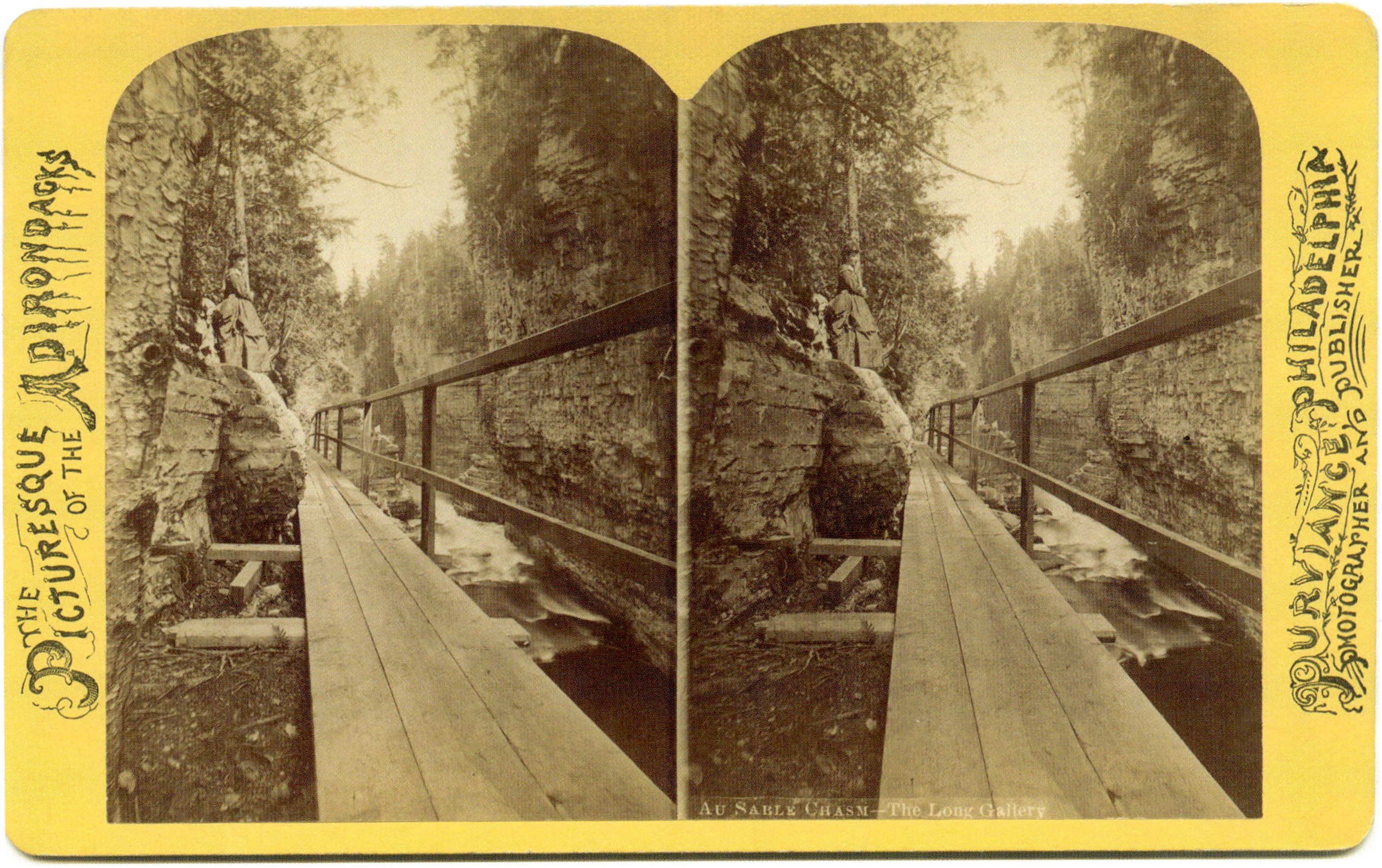

50. W. T. Purviance, *Au Sable Chasm—The Long Gallery*. Stereoview, 1873–1874.

to take "views, including stairs, &c. His work will be found first-class, and his pictures placed for sale on all the roads he is connected with. This will ensure large travel for next year."[1]

Purviance returned to take more Adirondack views the following June; he also provided stereographs for New York's Rensselaer and Saratoga Railroad. His series *The Picturesque of the Adirondacks* included views of Ausable Chasm and popular regional watering spots. Adirondack images also turned up in two other series: *Gems of American Scenery* and *American Scenery*. Purviance relocated his business and residence to New York City in the early 1880s, where he was listed as a photographer in local directories through at least 1888.[2]

1. *Essex County Republican*, October 23, 1873.

2. *Essex County Republican*, June 4, 1874; Darrah, *World of Stereographs*, 185.

PUTNAM, OSMOND DAVID (1861–1926)
Active Johnsburg, Warren County; Ironville, Essex County, 1885–1890

Osmond Putnam's photographic output was not large. Born in Johnsbury, Vermont, but moving with his parents and siblings to Johnsburg before 1880, he followed the career path of his father and grandfather in becoming simultaneously a farmer and a clergyman. To earn money to meet expenses at the Houghton Wesleyan Seminary in western New York, he canvassed during school vacations in the immediate region of Johnsburg, both on foot and by stagecoach, and talked families into having their pictures taken, usually with their homes, and often with their animals, in the background. Putnam was ordained in the Wesleyan Methodist Connection in 1890. He maintained a sideline in photography after taking up a pastorate that year

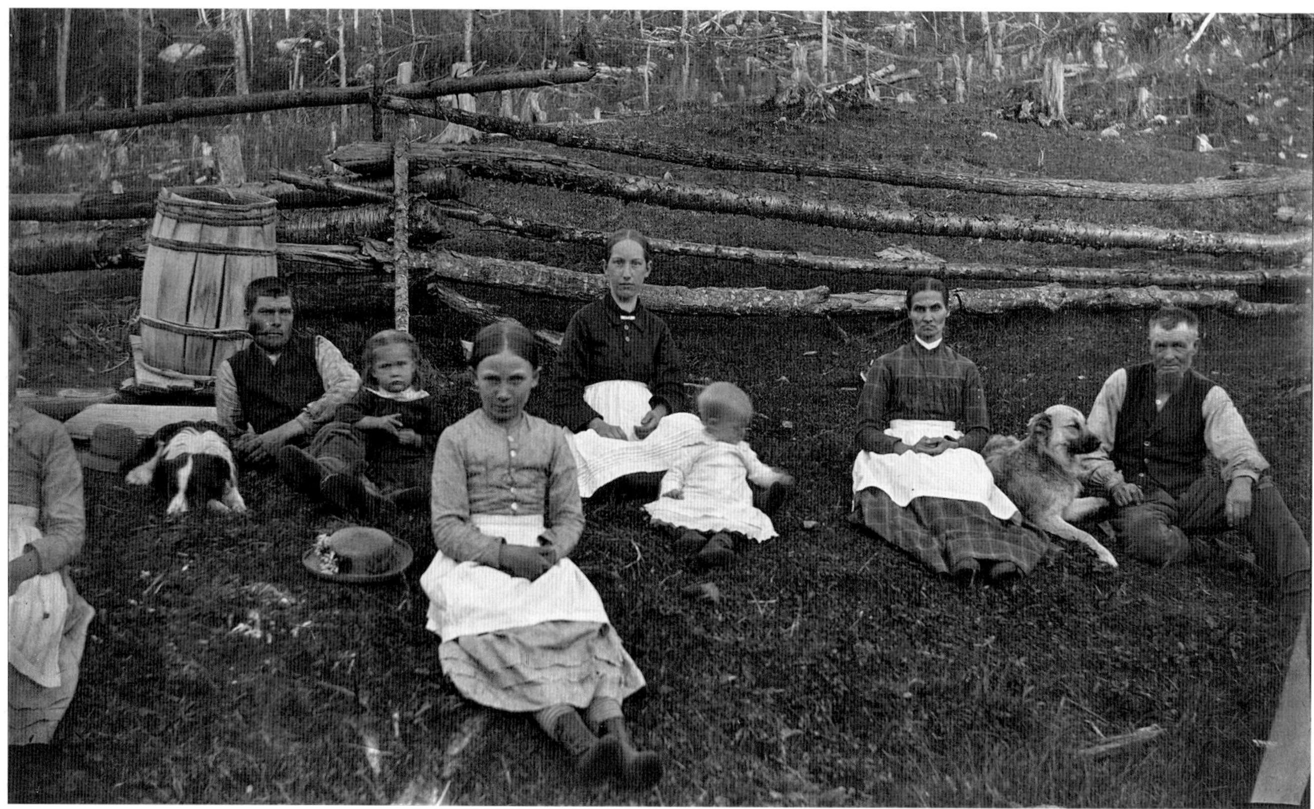

51. O. D. Putnam, Johnsburg family, 1886. Courtesy of the Adirondack Research Library of Union College.

in the Crown Point hamlet of Ironville. Subsequent ministerial assignments took him to South Albany and Readsboro, Vermont; to East Corinth and Hadley, Saratoga County; and to Stony Creek, Warren County, all before 1904. He settled not long thereafter in Wilton, Saratoga County, where he became an elder of the Methodist Church and continued to farm and preach.[1]

1. Jeanne Foster, *Adirondack Portraits*, xl, 63, 90; *Warrensburgh News*, May 22, 1890; Jean Hadden, "From Our Fields."

PUTNAM, TARRANT (1825–1906)
Active Keeseville, Clinton and Essex Counties, 1850–1851

A laborer and the eldest of six children living in 1850 with the "Widow Putnam" in Essex, Essex County, Tarrant Putnam was one of the Adirondacks' earliest photographers. According to an 1850 advertisement headed "Daguerreotypes!" in the *Essex County Republican*, he had "the pleasure of announcing to the Ladies of Gentlemen of Keeseville and vicinity, that he has opened rooms, for the practice of his art, in Prescott's Building, where he will be prepared, at all hours of the day, to receive calls. From the experience he has had in the art, he flatters himself that he can give entire satisfaction to all who may favor him with their patronage. Miniatures taken in all kinds of weather. Please call and examine specimens."[1]

Putnam did not advertise again. By 1857 he had relocated to Owatonna, Minnesota, where he was listed as a "Daguerreian Artist" in a Minnesota territorial census taken that year. Within the next five years he pursued opportunities as a US postmaster, an insurance agent, and a registrar of deeds. As a resident of Wilton, Minnesota, his occupation was listed in the 1880 US Census as "anything that's honest." Putnam died in Santa Clara County, California.[2]

1. *Essex County Republican*, June 8, 1850.
2. Palmquist and Kailbourn, *Pioneer Photographers*, 500.

RABINEAU, GEORGE T. (1873–1944)
Active Lake Placid, Essex County, 1917–1931

Born in Albany, Albany County, George Rabineau was the son of well-known Albany portrait photographer Charles S. Rabineau. He migrated to Lake Placid circa 1915 to work in the studio of **Irving L. Stedman**. During the winter of 1916–17 he leased the Main Street studio of **George A. Hand**, with whom he expected to enter into partnership when Hand returned from a winter spent elsewhere. Hand did not, however, live again in Lake Placid, and his premises became the Rabineau Studio, advertising specialties in "commercial and portrait photography," "summer and winter scenes," "sport post cards," and Kodak finishing.[1]

An occasional Rabineau image appeared in the *Lake Placid News*, but the photographer was best known for his large output of real photo postcards, including Lake Placid winter sporting scenes and winter landscapes. He also operated a "Photo, Art and Gift Shop" in the Palace Theater building, an extension of the trade in novelties he began in his photography studio. Rabineau was active in the Chamber of Commerce as well as a director of the Lake Placid Athletic Club and the Lake Placid–based New York State Sled Dog Club. In 1931 Rabineau sold his business to **Roger L. Moore** of Albany and left the village. In 1937 he entered the Essex County Home for Paupers in Whallonsburg. He is buried in the Old County Home Cemetery.[2]

1. *Lake Placid News*, January 7, 1916; January 5, 1917; March 21, 1919.

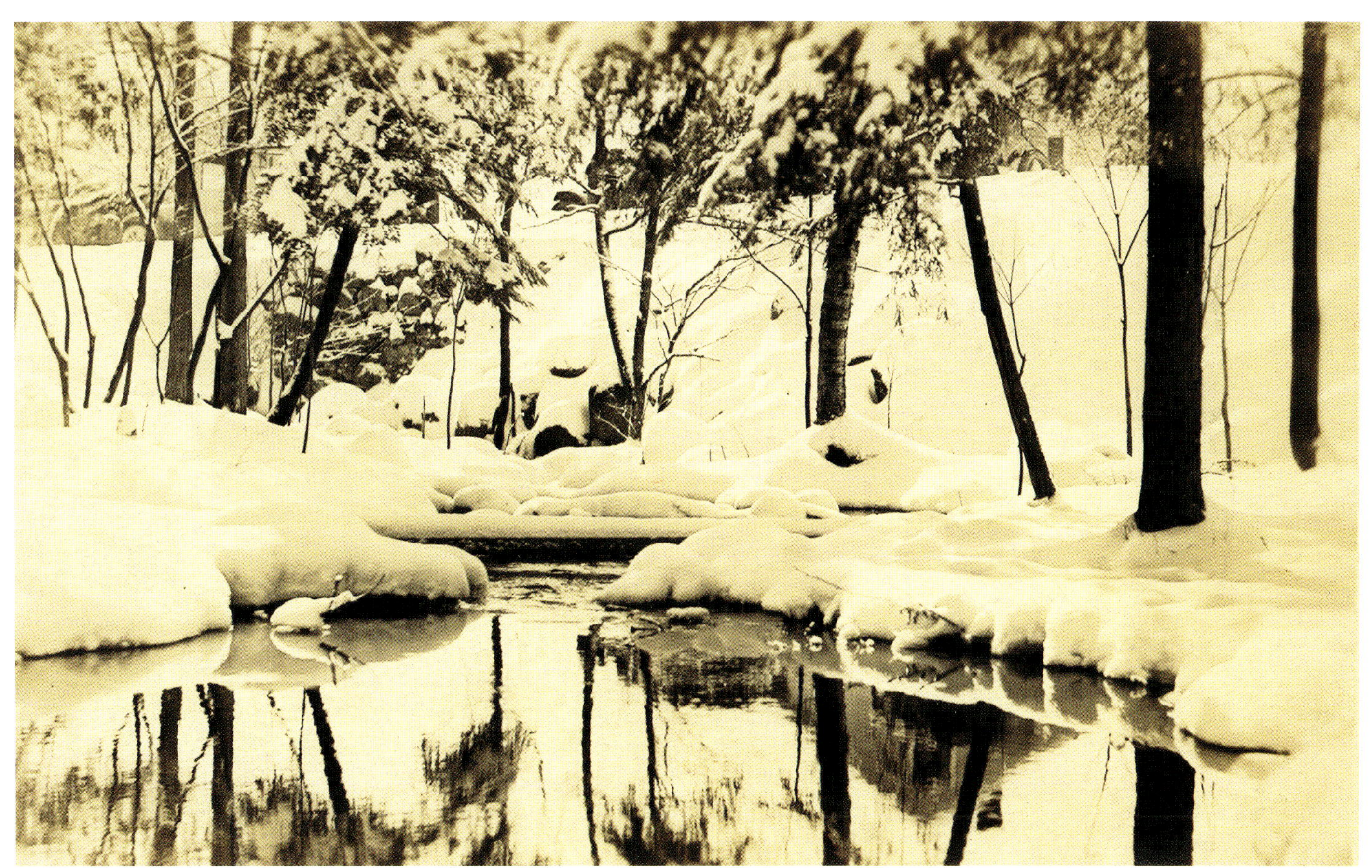

52. G. T. Rabineau, winter scene, Lake Placid, outlet to Mirror Lake. RPPC, 1917–1931.

2. *Lake Placid News*, April 18, 1924; September 23, 1927; April 13, 1928; January 10, 1930; June 3, 1932; August 7, 1931; May 26, 1944.

RANDALL, ELMER E. (1864–1931)
Active Keeseville, Essex and Clinton Counties, 1915–1931

The son of a Maine shoe manufacturer, Elmer Randall was the assistant manager of the *Haverill Massachusetts Gazette* in 1891 and a Boston photographer by 1902. In 1915 he took up residence in Keeseville, where he maintained an unobtrusive Adirondack presence as, primarily, a portrait photographer. His wife was the proprietor of a Keeseville millinery shop.[1]

1. *Essex County Republican*, November 20, 1931.

REISING, GROTUS H. (1852–1940), PSEUDONYM G. H. OR GEORGE H. RISON
Active Hamilton and Herkimer Counties, 1892–1901

The eldest of eight children, Grotus Reising was three years old when his parents immigrated from Germany to take up farming in Wilmurt, Herkimer County, a township that disappeared in 1918 with its division and reassignment to the adjoining towns of Ohio and Webb. He attended the Fairfield Seminary under the auspices of the Episcopal Church in Fairfield, Herkimer County, a school that offered both a classical academy for young men and a female collegiate institute. Between 1890 and 1894 he was the custodian of the Morehouse Lake Club, a proprietary sporting club founded in 1889 in the Morehouse, Hamilton County, hamlet of Hoffmeister for "social and recreative [i.e., hunting and fishing] purposes." He was entered in the New York state census of 1892 as a Morehouse guide.[1]

During his years with the Morehouse Lake Club, Reising took up photography. His work attracted outside attention in 1894, the year he left the club's employ, when several Reising photographs appeared under the pseudonym G. H. Rison in the first volumes of an intended multipart publication, *Camera Mosaics*, comprising "many hundred pictures made by leading members of American photographic societies." Images were reported to be "carefully selected" from "thousands of pictures," and some of the showcased photographers were well-known, among them **William Henry Jackson,** representing the Colorado Camera Club, and the celebrated Scottish-Canadian photographer William Notman for the Montreal Camera Club. Rison's accreditation was to the "Morehouse Lake Club," of which he was identified in the text as custodian. Rison images also appeared sporadically in the annual

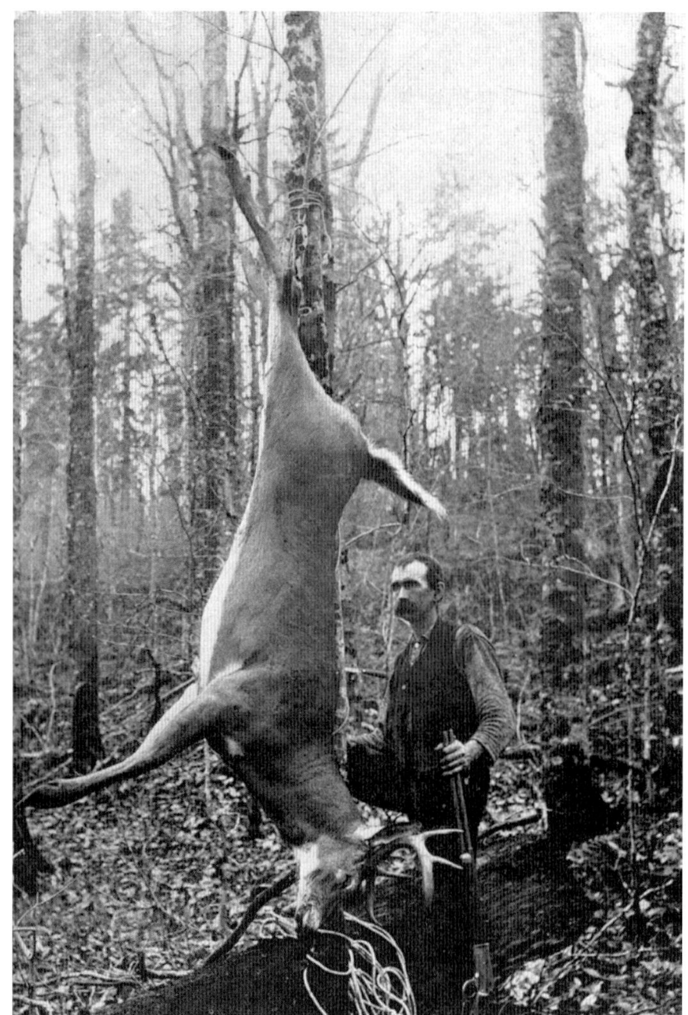

53. G. H. Reising (as G. H. Rison), self-portrait. From Jones, *Camera Mosaics*, 1894.

reports of the New York State Forest Commission and its successors between 1894 and 1901.[2]

Returning to Wilmurt at the conclusion of his Morehouse Lake Club employment, Reising followed a variety of occupations: forester, carpenter, town assessor, laborer. By 1930 he was retired. He never claimed photography as a career, and his later camera work appears to have been confined to the environs of Wilmurt. Styled "the sage," "the philosopher," and "one of the most informed men" in Wilmurt, he was called upon by neighbors to interpret and draw up legal documents, acted as the town's correspondent for the *Ilion Citizen* and the *Herkimer Telegram*, and maintained a lively interest in the community: serving as master of Ohio's North Star Grange, school trustee for Wilmurt's Reising and Star School Districts, and member of the committee to incorporate the Ohio cemetery. Reising developed a sideline as a disc jockey and carried his Edison phonograph and several hundred records to nearby lumber camps and church and village meetings, taking up collections to recompense his services. Never married, Reising generally lived as a boarder in someone else's home.[3]

1. *One Hundred Fifty Years, 1823–1973*, 17; Morehouse Lake Club records.

2. Jones, *Camera Mosaics*, part 1: title page, 133, 149; part 2: 190, 194, 237.

3. *One Hundred Fifty Years*, 17; *Ilion Citizen*, February 20, 1908; *Herkimer Citizen*, November 21, 1905; *Herkimer Democrat*, December 17, 1902; *Richfield Springs Mercury*, July 3, 1924; O'Hern, *Adirondack Characters and Campfire Yarns*, 138.

RICE, FREDERICK WILLIAM (1852–1934)

Active Saranac Lake, Essex and Franklin Counties, 1885–1904

Frederick (Fred) Rice was born in Connecticut and spent his early adulthood in Essex, Essex County, as a sailboat builder. Marrying in 1872, he relocated to Saranac Lake in 1876, becoming a builder of the specialized watercraft known as the Adirondack guideboat. He developed a second career as a photographer, focusing on local landscapes, outdoor groups, and photofinishing in a studio above his boat shop on the shores of Lower Saranac Lake. One group of Rice images has become well known: a series depicting Samuel Clemens (Mark Twain) and family, who spent the summer of 1901 vacationing in a lakeside cottage close to the Rice home.[1]

Rice's father, Caleb Hall Rice, had been one of ten children and a brother of William Marsh

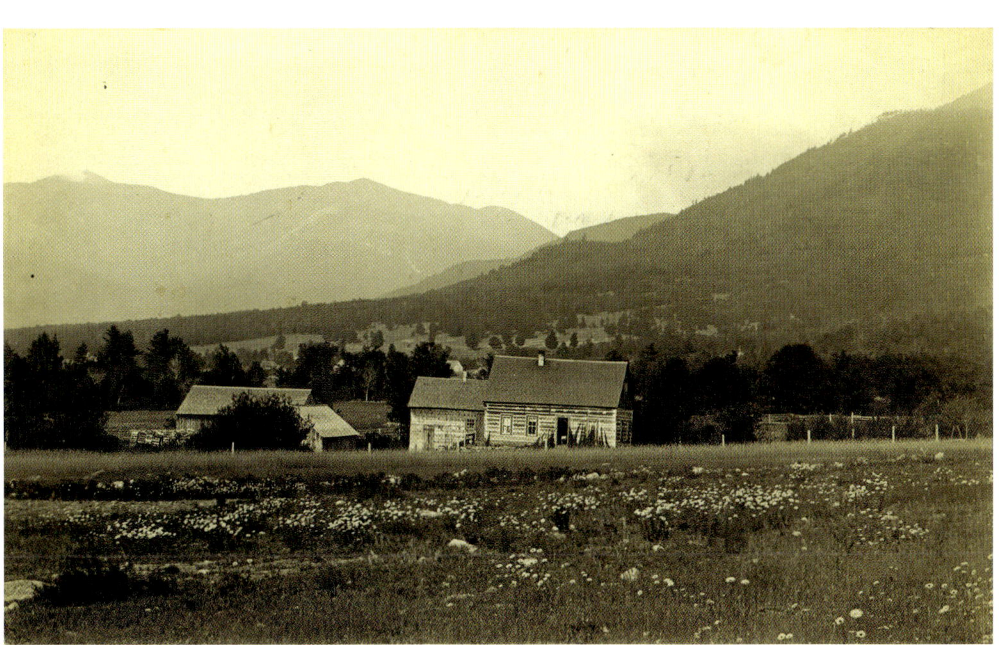

54. F. W. Rice, Wilmington landscape, circa 1896. Courtesy of Adirondack Experience.

Rice, who accumulated a fortune from investments in real estate and other ventures in Texas and Louisiana. William Rice was the victim of a sensational murder in 1900, and in the spring of 1904 Fred Rice, one of his childless uncle's many collateral descendants, was awarded $75,000 in the settlement of the William Marsh Rice estate that also financed the launch of Houston's Rice Institute, later Rice University. (The eldest ten of Fred's eleven children each received one thousand dollars in the distribution.) In late 1904 the Rices and their younger offspring moved to Mercer Island, Washington, where Rice became a Seattle businessman, dealing in loans and real estate for his own account. His wife and some of the children returned to Saranac Lake in 1906, and the Rices divorced in 1907, "the only difficulty" in the couple's long marriage having been, it was reported, "the aversion of the wife to living in Seattle." Rice married again, and fathered at least two more children. He is buried in Tracy, California.[2]

1. DeSormo, *Summer on the Saranacs*, 120.

2. "Saranac Lake Man Gets $75,000," *Ogdensburg Journal*, May 23, 1904; DeSormo, *Summers on the Saranacs*, 121; *Leavenworth (WA) Echo*, June 21, 1907.

RICHARDSON, THOMAS GOODHUE (1832–1880)
Active Ausable Chasm, Clinton and Essex Counties, 1873

Thomas Richardson was born in Jericho, Vermont, the son of a millwright. Recorded as an artist in 1863 Civil War draft records, in September 1864 he was reported to have "enlarged, refitted, and refurnished" his "Photograph Rooms" in St. Albans. While he did not serve in the war, Richardson gained modest fame as one of perhaps twelve hostages held briefly on the town green during the St. Albans Raid of October 19, 1864, when Confederate soldiers swooped down from Canada and robbed three St. Albans banks. This foray, the northernmost land action of the conflict, was part of a plan to raise money for the Confederate army and divert Union troops to defend its northern border.[1]

In May 1874 the journal *Photographer's Friend* noted the receipt from Richardson of a number of "superior views of Vermont and New York," including "many first class ones both in interesting subjects and workmanship." Among his stereographs bearing the general title *Vermont and Other Scenery* were forty-eight views of Ausable Chasm. These were in all likelihood taken in 1873, the year that the chasm first opened to the public. Richardson produced no other known Adirondack work. He appeared in the 1880 US Census as a merchant, but was identified as a photographer on his death certificate later that year.[2]

1. *(St. Albans) Vermont Transcript*, September 16, 1864; "An Illustrated Timeline [of the St. Alban's Raid]," http://www.stalbansraid.com/history/an-illustrated-timeline/.

2. "The Editor's Album," *Photographer's Friend* 4, no. 3 (May 1874): 96.

ROBBINS, FRANK (1846–1924)
Active Franklin, Essex, and Clinton Counties, 1865–1867

Frank Robbins, a native and resident of Keene, New Hampshire, did not have a Keene business address when he offered two stereoview series of Adirondack subjects via catalog in 1867. One of them, *Adirondack Series*, included thirty-eight Franklin and Essex County scenes of touristic interest. The other, *Ausable Series*, comprising thirty-three views of Ausable Chasm, was described on card versos as "the most complete series of Views ever published of this novel locality. Great care has been taken to get the choicest points of view, regardless of labor or danger. Many of the most beautiful views are entirely new, having never been visited before."

Robbins determined that his photographic future lay elsewhere than New Hampshire. By mid-1868 he relocated to Oil City, Pennsylvania, the principal shipping point in the heart of western Pennsylvania's petroleum-extraction industry. This region had grown rapidly since the sinking

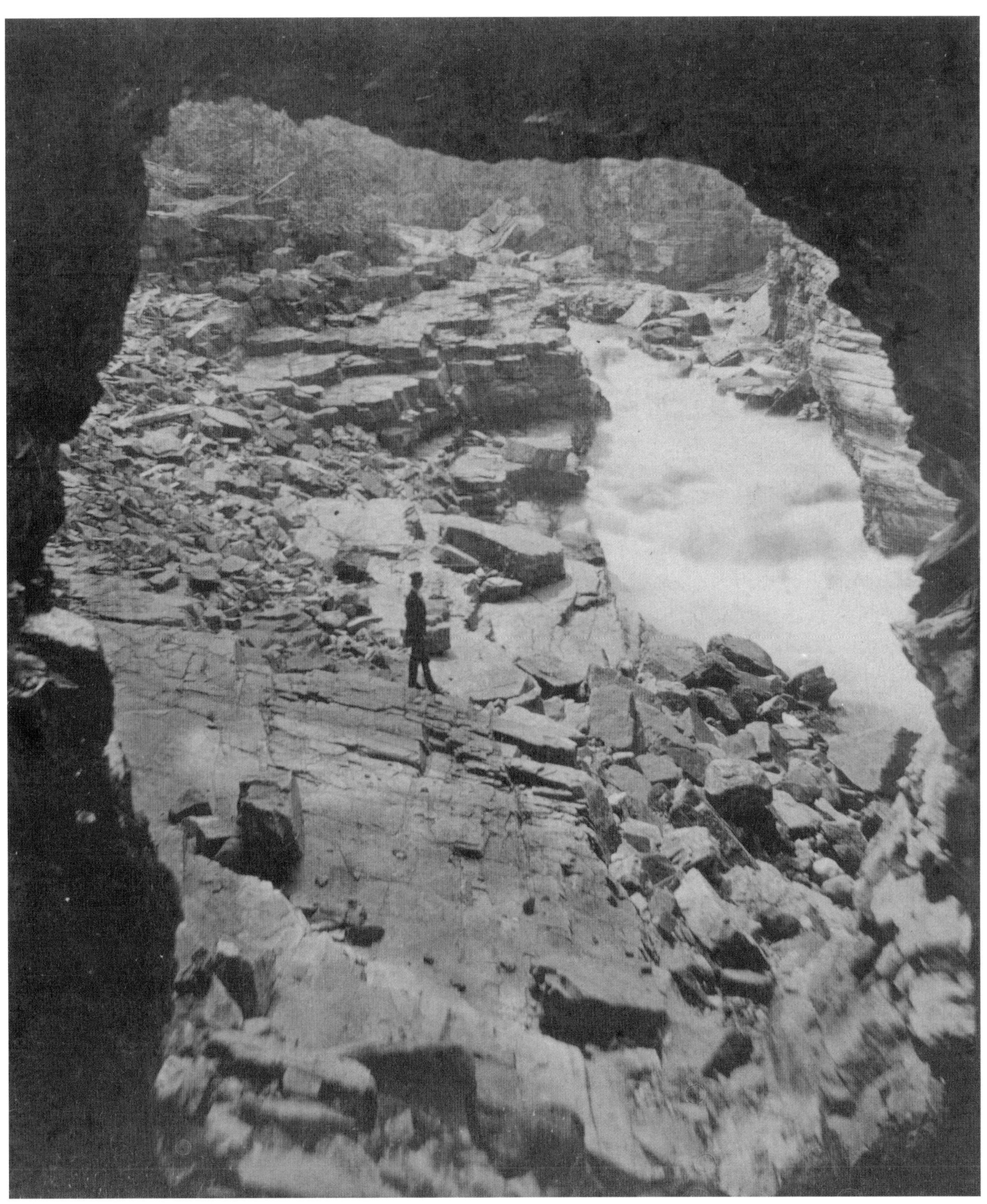

55. F. Robbins, *Ausable Series: From Devil's Oven, Looking Out*. One-half stereoview, 1865–1867.

there of the first commercially successful oil well in 1859, and Oil City, founded in 1860, claimed a population of from eight to ten thousand people and a public library by 1865. In conjunction with the move, Robbins sold the negatives of his Adirondack views to **W. Mould & Son** of Keeseville.[1]

Robbins became the foremost visual recorder of Pennsylvania's oil boom. His earliest Pennsylvania stereoview series, *Large Stereoscopic Views of the Oil Region*, contained images dating to 1868 and 1869. In 1879 he followed the boom some eighty miles northeast to Bradford, incorporated as a city that year and on its way to becoming the center of "America's first billion dollar oilfield." Robbins is estimated to have produced at least 250 oilfield-related stereographs. Many of his images were recycled in the early twentieth century as postcards. The boom ended in 1901 as oil was struck in areas of the West, but Robbins stayed on in Bradford. He, alone, in partnership with his son, then his son alone, occupied the same second-story studio on Main Street for fifty years.[2]

1. Cone and Johns, *Petrolia*, 562–63; email from Gordon C. Pollard to the author, July 18, 2017.

2. Spencer, "Oilfield Photographers," 46–47; "Derricks of Triumph Hill"; Hatch, *Illustrated History of Bradford*, 225; *Bradford Evening Star and Bradford Daily Record*, September 7, 1939.

ROBERTS, HOBART VOSBURG (1874–1959)
Active Ohio, Herkimer County,
1906–Early 1950s

Hobart Roberts was the eldest of four children born to well-heeled parents in Utica, Oneida County, where his father owned a department store, the John A. Roberts Company. Upon graduating in 1893 as class valedictorian from the Peekskill Military Academy, Roberts joined his father and spent his working life in the store's management. In 1903 he married Florence Stratton, daughter of Utica photographer **Robert T. Stratton**. Stratton is thought to have been instrumental in his son-in-law's taking up photography as a hobby.[1]

Roberts became well known as an amateur wildlife photographer, developing an explicit focus on photographing animals at night. His method was borrowed from jacklighting, the popular hunting practice (banned in New York State in 1897) of shining a light into a forest, thus blinding an animal caught in its beam so that it would stand still long enough to be shot. "This sport-for-sport it seemed to me then," wrote Roberts in 1936, "led to the idea of using Kodak and flash-powder instead of a gun, shooting for a picture instead of for a kill."[2]

Roberts's favorite hunting grounds were the shorelines of Little Woodhull and South Lakes in the town of Ohio, where his family owned a camp. Many of his nocturnal photographs were taken from a flat-bottomed boat on which were mounted cameras and two flash stands, with one flash used to startle an animal into action after it had been located with the jacklight and the second to freeze the action for the photograph. Other nighttime images, taken in the woods, were generated by moisture-proof cameras attached to baited tripwires that encouraged animals to take their own "self-portraits" as they foraged. Roberts's painstaking sport required patience, with two or three sets of flashes considered a good "dark-room bag" for a night's effort.[3]

One of Roberts's most famous images, a 1907 deer caught *In the Stillness of the Night*, garnered a silver medal in the Scientific Photography category at the first International Exposition of Photographic Arts and Industries in New York in 1915. By late 1939 his images, not all of them of wildlife or taken at night, had appeared in important salons and exhibitions in twenty-three cities in fourteen states as well as in six European countries. Roberts's animal photographs were reproduced in numerous publications over the years: *National Geographic*, *Audubon*, *Country Life*, *Field and Stream*, *Outdoor Life*, the *London News*, the *New York Times*, and *U.S. Camera 1940*, a volume spotlighting work of well-known contemporary photographers. The book's contents were selected by photographer Edward Steichen.[4]

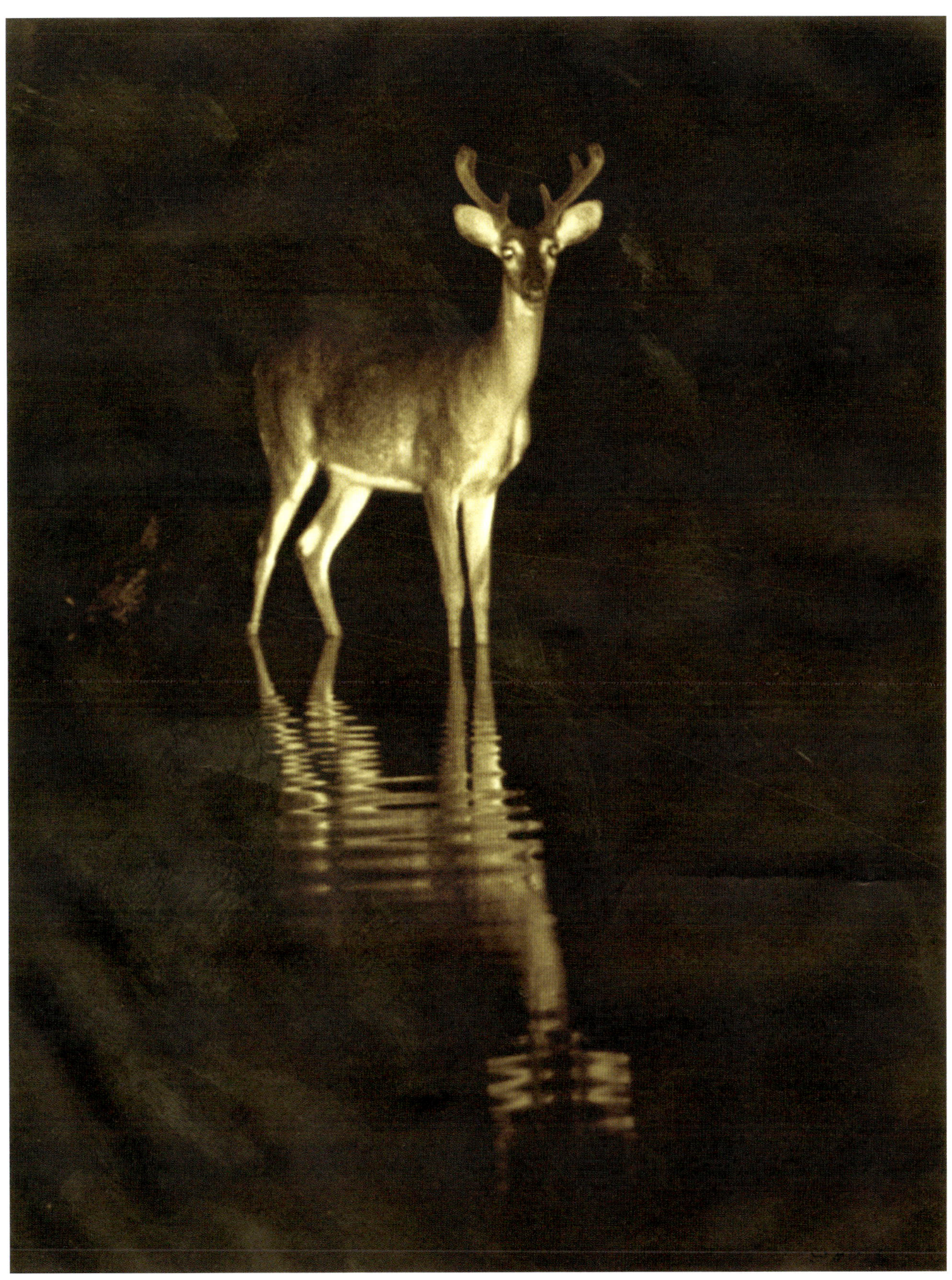

56. H. V. Roberts, *In the Stillness of the Night*, 1907. Courtesy of Adirondack Experience.

1. Biographical sheet from unknown source, Photographers' File, Adirondack Experience.

2. Roberts, "Blazing a Path through the Darkness," 558.

3. Sinnott, "The Pioneering Photography of Hobart Roberts," 21; Lee, "Shooting Wild Life with the Camera at Night," 13.

4. Roberts, "Camera Hunting with a Flashlight," 42; "News and Notes," *Photographic Journal of America*, May 1915, 257; "Hobart V. Roberts' Nature Photographs Go on Display," *North Tonawanda Evening News*, October 25, 1939.

ROBIDEAU, ELI (1880–1949) AND NORBERT E. (1913–1987)

Active Malone, Franklin County, 1905–1987

Eli Robideau was born one of eleven children on a farm in Ellenburg, Clinton County. He studied at Albany Business College and worked for the General Electric Company in Schenectady before taking up photography in the early 1900s. In 1905 he acquired the one-time Malone studio of **Christopher R. Fay**, whose negatives he absorbed in the purchase along with those of Fay's successors, Eugene Clair and Copeland & Kipp. The portrait-oriented Robideau Studio briefly maintained branch operations in the early 1920s in Tupper Lake and Chateaugay, Franklin County, and Huntingdon County, Quebec. It was responsible for class pictures in regional schools, documented accident and crime scenes, and undertook occasional commercial work, such as photographing all the properties belonging to the Sheffield Farms Company between Lake Champlain and Ogdensburg, St. Lawrence County.[1]

The entrepreneurial Robideau erected a filling station and confectionary and tobacco shop on a corner of a Malone residential property where he operated a summer tourist camp for a few years, and developed his historic home as a club with a nine-hole golf course that became the Colonial Inn. He received two patents, one for an adjustable automobile headrest for Ford cars (1915), and another for a Sanitary Dust Remover (1920) widely used in conjunction with mops for homes, hospitals, and public buildings. He was joined in the photograph studio by his son, Norbert, around 1933.[2]

Norbert Robideau prefaced his photographic career in 1931 with attendance at the Scott Carbee Art School in Boston, dedicated to the training of fine and commercial artists (a school briefly attended by artist Arshile Gorky). Returning to work in his father's studio during the Great Depression, he was listed as a photographer in the town directory of Saranac Lake, Essex and Franklin Counties, between 1933 and 1937. He gradually took over the studio, operating it until his retirement in 1986. Like his father, he focused on portraiture, and was known for his success in capturing the best in children. He photographed a number of public figures: Babe Ruth, New York governor Thomas E. Dewey, and Dutch Schultz, a Prohibition Era gangster tried in Malone in 1935 on income tax evasion. Robideau is honored today through Malone's annual Robideau/Lamitie-King Juried Art Exhibit for area school students.[3]

1. "Eli Robideau, Native of Ellenburg, 69, Dies," *Plattsburgh Press-Republican*, February 28, 1949; *Malone Farmer*, April 18, 1923; October 16, 1918; March 19, 1919; April 21, 1926.

2. *Malone Farmer*, July 2, 1924; June 16, 1926; *Massena Observer*, April 13, 1937.

3. Whitaker, "Photographer Chronicled Life in Malone"; *Malone Farmer*, September 30, 1931; *Malone Telegram*, unknown day, May 1987; "17th Annual Robideau/Lamitie-King Exhibit Award Winners," *Malone Telegram*, April 26, 2018. Lamitie-King was a Malone art teacher.

ROSS, HAROLD D. (1876–1912)

Active Fulton Chain of Lakes, Hamilton and Herkimer Counties, 1892–1910

Harold Ross, born in Ilion, Herkimer County, took up photography as a teenager summering with his family on the nearby Fulton Chain, his only Adirondack subject. According to an 1896 news item, he had established photographic headquarters for the past "several seasons" at the town of Webb's Forge House; his "collection of views" was said to take "in about every point of interest along the lakes." He produced a few images of the Adirondack League

Club in Old Forge as a partner in Ilion's Ross & Royle in 1899, and was listed in the 1900 US Census as an artist living in his parents' home.[1]

Ross conducted two Fulton Chain photograph galleries in 1902: one in Old Forge and another at the head of Fourth Lake. A postcard imprint announced his specialty as "Views of All Summer Resorts." He was responsible for a number of Adirondack views for the American Museum of Natural History's series of illustrated lectures for teachers in 1902 and placed in a 1905 competition sponsored by *Field and Stream* magazine with his image of "an old Indian guide living in the Adirondacks." In 1908 Ross relocated his business to Utica, Oneida County. He left behind a wife and young son at his early death from typhoid fever.[2]

1. *Ilion Citizen*, July 23, 1896.

2. *Syracuse Journal*, July 19, 1902; Harold D. Ross file, box 25, Albert S. Bickmore Papers, American Museum of Natural History, New York; *Herkimer Citizen*, April 25, 1905; *Utica Herald-Dispatch*, October 26, 1912.

RUNIONS, CHARLES E. (1865–1923)
Active Cranberry and Star Lakes, St. Lawrence County, 1910–1912

A native of Lisbon, St. Lawrence County, Charles Runions was the youngest of eight children of Canadian-born John Runions and his Irish wife. His father managed a business that built carriages, buggies, and sleighs while running a Lisbon store and farm. In 1887 Runions's older brother Alva established himself as a Canton, St. Lawrence County, portrait photographer from a homemade horse-drawn gallery. This marked the beginning of Runions Brothers, a loosely constructed enterprise in which Alva and three brothers occasionally partnered to operate portable, section-built "branch photograph parlor[s]" from a central Canton headquarters in some forty-three villages and hamlets across St. Lawrence, Jefferson, Franklin, and Lewis Counties. (A Runions Brothers studio was lost to fire in Tupper Lake, Franklin County, in 1899.) Two of the brothers headed west, leaving

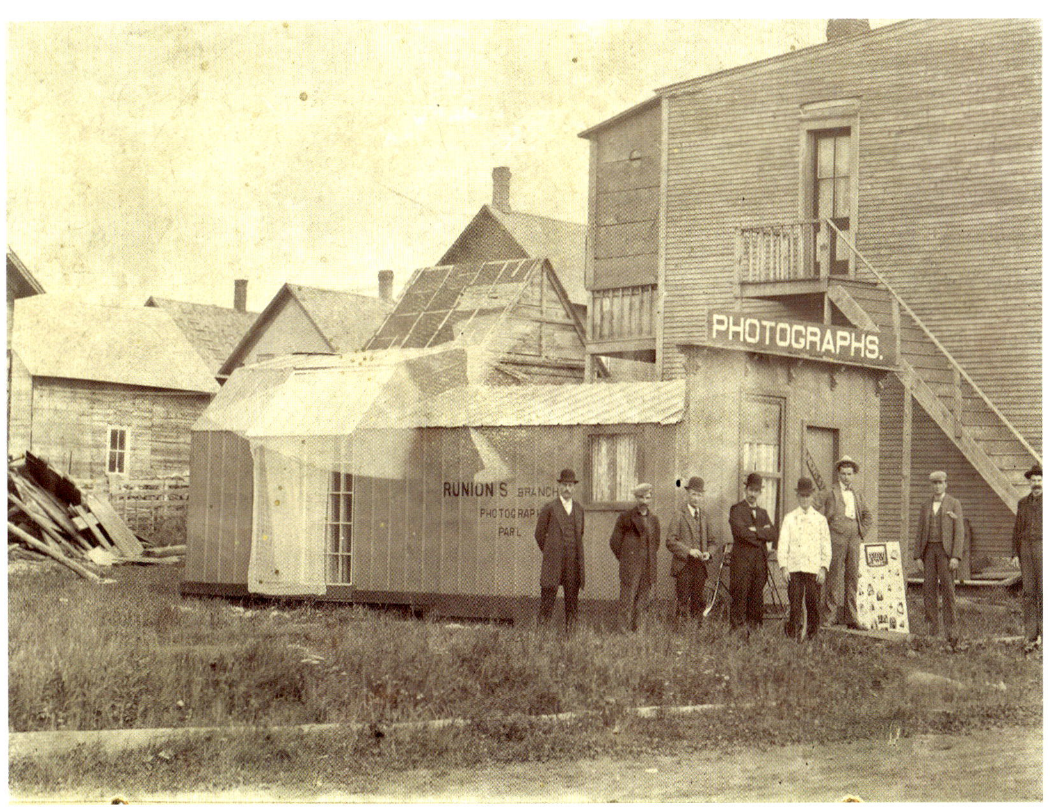

57. Runions Brothers, portable photographic gallery, Tupper Lake, 1890s. Courtesy of Goff-Nelson Memorial Library Archive, Tupper Lake.

only Charles and Alva behind. Sister Zerua made a career in the developing rooms.[1]

Runions, while overseeing Runions studios elsewhere, used stamped imprints bearing his own name in the early twentieth century on real photo postcards from both Star and Cranberry Lakes, primarily in the St. Lawrence County town of Clifton, where family members sometimes summered. After Alva's death in 1922, Charles took over the portrait business and what was then estimated to be ten satellite studios. At the same time, he personally worked a dairy farm belonging to his wife in Philadelphia, Jefferson County. Runions's life ended badly. In 1923 he shot and killed a hired man on the farm before turning the gun on himself. The murder-suicide was thought to have been caused by the pressures of Runions's multiple responsibilities but also brought to mind what others later recalled as instances of apparent mental instability.[2]

1. "Runions Painting Goes to Iowa," *St. Lawrence Plaindealer*, March 26, 1935; *Potsdam Herald*, August 4, 1899; *Potsdam Junction Commercial Advertiser*, November 21, 1922; August 15, 1939.

2. *Watertown Herald*, April 22, 1911; "District Attorney Probes for Motive for Runions' Act," *Ogdensburg Republican-Journal*, July 25, 1923.

SANTWAY, ALFRED W. (1887–1975)
Active throughout the Adirondacks, 1911–1924

Born into a French-Canadian farming family in Russell, St. Lawrence County, in 1907 Alfred Santway graduated from the Potsdam Normal School, the precursor to SUNY Potsdam and known for its teacher-training program. That fall he enrolled at the University of Michigan with the goal of a career in chemical research, but, upon contracting tuberculosis, was forced to withdraw from the university in 1910 at the end of his junior year. He spent nine months at the Adirondack Cottage Sanitarium in Saranac Lake and learned photographic skills in its occupational/recreational therapy program. In 1911 he took up residence in the isolated Adirondack hamlet of Star Lake in Clifton and Fine, St. Lawrence County, to continue his convalescence, opening a photography studio and producing real photo, and, early on, a few mechanically printed, colored postcards. In 1917 he published two viewbooks, one featuring photographs of the Adirondacks and the other images of the Thousand Islands.[1]

Regaining his health, by mid-1918 Santway relocated to Watertown, some fifty miles west of Star Lake and the county seat of Jefferson County. He bought a small print shop and continued his photographic work during the next three years as he managed the office of the Watertown Business Men's Association. In 1920, following the career direction in which he had begun to move in Star Lake, Santway founded Kamargo Press, a publisher and distributor of advertising brochures promoting northern New York's tourist industry. He expanded the business in 1924, and folded the postcard business into Kamargo as a subsidiary. Many of the company's key employees entered military service after the 1940 passage of selective service legislation, tourism dried up, and Kamargo Press was liquidated in 1941. A former sideline in plastic molding henceforth became Santway's primary business interest, with the Alfred W. Santway Company, Inc., creating plastic products for gift stores.[2]

Santway's earliest real photo images from the "Santway Photo-Craft Shop, Star Lake" were hand-titled on negatives, appearing as white on finished postcards of the central and western Adirondacks. From about 1914, still hand-labeled images bore the imprint SANTWAY PHOTO-CRAFT COMPANY, INC., STAR LAKE. His final Star Lake work, dating from circa 1916–17, featured machine-printed titles in small capital letters. Although work with original labeling was republished by the "Santway Photo-Craft Company, Watertown," most post-1920 Santway images were likelier to have been purchased from unattributed photographers than taken by Santway himself.

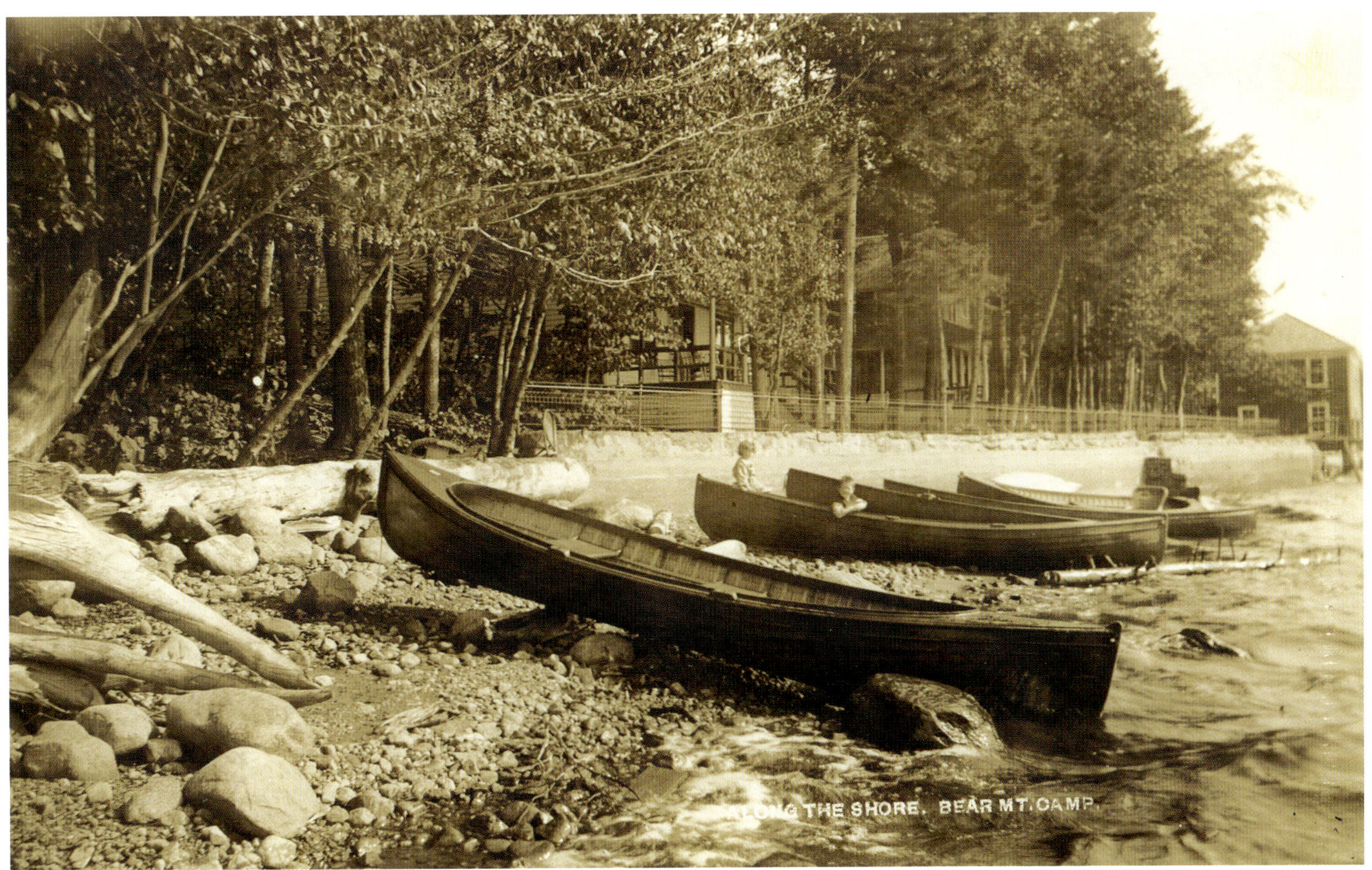

58. A. W. Santway, *Along the Shore, Bear Mt. Camp*, Cranberry Lake. RPPC, 1916–17.

1. Santway, "From Little Red Schoolhouse to the University of Michigan," 6; "A. W. Santway Dies; Karmargo Press Owner," *Watertown Daily Times*, August 29, 1975.

2. Santway, "From Little Red School House to the University of Michigan," 6–7; *Watertown Daily Times*, October 15, 1924; "A. W. Santway Dies," *Watertown Daily Times*, August 29, 1975.

SATTERLEE, ALBERT (1827–1901)
Active Northville, Fulton County, 1870–1875

Born in Hamilton County, Albert Satterlee appeared in the 1850 US Census as a shoemaker in Edinburg, Saratoga County. During the following decade he relocated to Northville, a hamlet of Northampton, where, by 1870, he was a local photographer. In April 1872 he took over the second-story, Main Street, rooms of photographer T. B. Warner, announcing a specialty in "baby pictures."[1]

Satterlee departed Northville for Illinois around 1875, where he appeared as a Sandwich photographer in an 1876 compendium of DeKalb County voters and taxpayers as well as in the 1880 US Census. He died in Streator, Illinois.

1. *Gloversville Intelligencer*, April 18, 1872.

SAWYER, CHARLES HENRY (1868–1954)
Active Eastern and Central Adirondacks, early 1920s

"C. H. Sawyer, of the Sawyer Pictures, Concord, N. H., arrived here on Tuesday to make pictures of the Adirondack scenery," the *Lake Placid News* announced in August 1922. Sawyer, the article continued, is "well-known for his photographs of White Mountain scenery." He was also among the most successful of a number of photographers who carved out a photographic specialty as the heads of commercial enterprises producing hand-colored photographs suitable for hanging in middle-class American homes.[1]

Born in southern Maine, Charles Sawyer established himself as a portrait photographer in Providence, Rhode Island, in the late 1890s. His sojourn in the city coincided with that of Wallace Nutting (1861–1941), a Congregational minister who took pictures as an amateur and shortly after retiring from the ministry issued a catalog of his photographic work. Nutting's signed, hand-colored images—of which he claimed to have produced some ten million by 1936—were central to a career that established him as a household name in the field of traditional decorative arts.[2]

Sawyer, often referred to as a "Nutting-like photographer," closely followed Nutting's occupational model. He returned to Maine in 1902 and worked briefly for Nutting before setting up on his own in Farmington the following year. In 1920 he relocated to Concord, New Hampshire, where the Sawyer Company henceforth produced hand-colored scenic photographs of popular vacation spots from Sawyer's negatives. Signed prints were generally matted and available for sale in various sizes in hotels and jewelry, gift, stationery, drug, and department stores. The company's focus was on New England, but offered a substantial body of Adirondack views, listing thirty-nine titled and twenty-one untitled photographs of the region in a January 1924 catalog. The Ausable Chasm Company was a longtime customer, and an "immense," hand-colored Sawyer photograph of the Lake George Narrows attracted widespread attention when exhibited in a New York City window display sponsored by the Lake George Board of Trade in 1926.[3]

Sawyer's son, Harold, took over management of the company in the early 1930s. Although commercial availability of color film from mid-decade meant that hand-colored photographs were no longer exceptional, the Sawyer Company continued offering images for another forty years.[4]

1. *Lake Placid News*, August 25, 1922.

2. Denenberg, *Wallace Nutting*, 23, 48, 195n6, 199n9.

3. Ivankovich, "Guide to Wallace Nutting-like Photographers"; Gray, Ivankovich, and Peters, *The Hand-Painted Photographs of Charles Henry Sawyer*, 3–4, 5, 6, 19, 49–53; *Lake George Mirror*, July 31, 1926.

4. Gray, Ivankovich, and Peters, *Hand-Painted Photographs*, 7, 8–9, 22.

SCHOOLEY, CHARLES M. (1879–1940)
Active Forestport, Oneida County, 1905–1918

Charles Schooley, son of a Candor, Tioga County, farmer, was listed in the 1900 US Census as a Candor watchmaker. Five years later he was a photographer working for his own account. At about this time he began taking landscape photographs in Forestport hamlets popular during the summer season that he published as real photo postcards. By 1915 he was a Forestport photographer and jeweler. He relocated his family to Old Forge, Webb, Herkimer County, not long thereafter, where he appeared in the 1920 US Census as a watchmaker and jewelry store proprietor. ("Let me supply your needs in jewelry or timepieces; 23 years experience," a 1921 journal advertisement proclaimed.) During his years in Forestport and Old Forge, Schooley was reportedly "a well-known guide," holding "the record for long distance snowshoe tramps in the lower Adirondacks." He returned to Candor in 1926, but continued to sell real estate lots in an eleven-acre Forestport tract he owned from 1921 into the early 1930s.[1]

1. *Syracuse Post-Standard*, June 5, 1921; *Utica Observer Dispatch*, November 28, 1926; *Rome Sentinel*, April 21, 1921; February 14, 1931; "Former Guide Dies in Candor," *Ithaca Journal*, December 3, 1940.

SEXTON, FLORA DELL (1877–1953) AND THERESA A. (1860–1941)
Active Hague, Warren County, 1905–1917

The Sexton sisters took dozens of photographs about Hague in the first decades of the twentieth century. While the sisters are said to have worked in tandem, prints and the many exposed Sexton glass plates now in the collection of the Hague Historical Society are attributed to Flora, who outlived her sister.

Flora and Theresa Sexton were the daughters of a Hague farmer. Their surviving brother, Smith Sexton, became a builder and local hotel proprietor. The sisters took over the two-hundred-acre family farm around 1900, raising cows, horses, goats, sheep, pigs, chickens, and vegetables. As a way to supplement their meager farm income, the women set up a summer tent in the middle of the village for several years from which they offered photographic portraits and marketed images of local interest to residents and seasonal tourists. A darkroom was maintained at home, but no identifying imprint was connected with their work.[1]

Flora Sexton appeared as a farmer and the head of household in the New York state census of 1925; Theresa's occupation was recorded as housework. The sisters became eccentric and reclusive over the years, said to threaten anyone setting foot on their property with guns. (Flora was charged with first degree assault at the age of sixty-nine for shooting a rider-bearing horse in its flank as it passed her home. She spent several days in jail.) They lived their last years in poverty. Flora deeded her real estate in two parcels in 1949 and 1952 to the Warren County Department of Public Welfare in exchange for its commitment to her ongoing support. The photo albums she left behind were labeled after her death as the property of the Warren County Welfare Department.[2]

1. McKinstry, "The Shooting Sexton Sisters," 30.

2. *Ticonderoga Sentinel*, September 26, 1946; *North Creek News Enterprise*, May 27, 1953.

SIPPERLY, WILLIAM H. (1835–1920)
Active Eastern Adirondacks, 1871–1880, 1892–1902

William Sipperly, born in 1835 in Rensselaer County, spent the better part of his working life in Saratoga County. Appearing in the 1860 US Census as a farmer in the town of Clifton Park, by 1865 he was located in Schuylerville, where his "Daguerrian Rooms" were destroyed by fire in 1868. His occupation was given in the 1870 and 1880 US Censuses as a Mechanicville photographer, and at one point during the decade he maintained studios in Mechanicville, Schuylerville, and Saratoga. Portraiture was the backbone of his business, but Sipperly is also known for his stereoviews. A number of them were of the Adirondacks, where he often summered.[1]

Sipperly spent most of the 1880s in Vermont, owned a gallery in Bennington in mid-decade, and visited many nearby towns and villages as a traveling photographer in his "photograph saloon." In 1892 he returned to Saratoga County and opened a Ballston Spa studio in which he remained for more than twenty-five years. Sipperly was spotted spending "a few weeks" in Saranac Lake in 1898 and taking portraits in "his tent in the yard of Sunnyside Cottage," a tuberculosis cure cottage close to the rail station. By 1910 he had largely given up photography.[2]

1. *Saratogian*, March 12, 1868; May 11, 1871; May 25, 1871.

2. *Industries and Wealth of the Principal Points in Vermont*, 205; *(Brattleboro) Vermont Phoenix*, October 9, 1885; *Londonderry Sifter*, October 8, 1885; *Schuylerville Standard*, February 21, 1892; *Plattsburgh Press*, July 19, 1898.

SISSON, HENRY W. (1878–1946)
Active Lake George Region, 1897–1904

A socially and politically well-connected native of Caldwell, later Lake George, Henry Sisson began taking pictures at an early age and copyrighted two photographs in 1891, when he was thirteen. In 1897, at the nineteen, he published a sixteen-page *Lake George Book of Views*.

In 1900 Sisson issued a more ambitious viewbook: the fifty-eight-page *Lake George Scenery: A Book of Gems*. (One photograph from this volume, *Moonlight on Lake George*, was selected for publishing in the journal *Photographic Times* in 1901.) The seasonal weekly newspaper *Lake George Mirror* ran a standing advertisement in 1903 for "Henry W. Sisson, Landscape Photography." The photographer's views, it noted, were "on sale at all news stands."[1]

In 1904 Sisson gave up photography and accepted a job as deputy county clerk for Warren County after his father's election to the post of county clerk in 1903. He resigned the office in 1917 and moved into real estate and insurance, developing his own property: a garage and, in the 1920s, a bungalow court for tourists, reputed to be the first of its kind outside of California. Sisson was an active citizen of Caldwell, serving as village president and on numerous civic committees.[2]

1. *Photographic Times* 33, no. 5 (May 1901): 200; *Lake George Mirror*, July 18, 1902.

2. *Ticonderoga Sentinel*, July 19, 1917; *Glens Falls Post-Star*, May 20, 1921; *Warrensburg–Lake George News*, June 6, 1963.

SLAYTON, HERMAN EDWARD (1856–1940)
Active Ausable Chasm, Clinton and Essex Counties, Late 1870s

A Vermont native, Herman Slayton was a student at the Vermont Methodist Seminary in 1874. By 1880 he was a photographer in the state capitol of Montpelier. He appears to have given up photography around 1882, having produced a number of stereographs, most of them of Montpelier, but including a few of Ausable Chasm. Slayton's later years were spent as a merchant, selling products from stationery to groceries to washing machines.

SLOCUM, FRANK EUGENE (1856–1950)
Active Central and Western Adirondacks, 1882–1897

Born into a farming family in Greig, Lewis County, Frank Slocum and older brother Arnold were by 1880 boarding together in Oneonta, Otsego County, and "photographing." Settling in Lowville, Lewis County, his wife's hometown, in 1882, Slocum advertised a ten-month-old "Portable Photograph Building" for sale that year before becoming proprietor of a local portrait studio.[1]

In 1884 Slocum announced that he would be traveling to Saranac Lake, Essex and Franklin Counties, and planned to "take views upon fifteen or twenty lakes which will be visited on the route." An 1889 Adirondack guidebook carried an advertisement for the Lowville "artist," reading: "Photographic Views of the Adirondacks . . . Views of CAMPS and SPECIAL SCENERY taken to order. Appropriate Scenery at the Gallery for Photographing Camping Parties." But Slocum, whose wife died in 1888, had by the time the guide was published left Lowville, selling his studio to **William G. Mandeville** in late 1888 and moving with his two young children to nearby Copenhagen, where he combined photography with a two-year stint as village postmaster. The verso of mounts from a Copenhagen series of fourteen *Views of Star Lake and Vicinity* noted, "Will visit the lake each month during the season. Orders left at the hotel will be promptly executed." In 1897 Slocum issued a view booklet, *Souvenir of Fulton Chain from Recent Photographs.*[2]

Slocum relocated his photography business to Gouverneur, St. Lawrence County, around 1900. In 1901 he was in Watertown, Jefferson County, where a 1903 regional compendium of notable men of central New York recorded him as the city's "official photographer." Declaring bankruptcy in late 1901, Slocum moved with his second wife and young daughter to Peoria, Illinois, in 1903 or 1904. He appeared irregularly as a photographer in Peoria directories through 1928 and also, according to federal census data, followed the occupation of "button coverer" and "button maker" in his "own shop." He was referred to in an Illinois obituary as a "pioneer photographer" of Illinois.[3]

1. *Lewis County Democrat*, August 16, 1882

2. *Lewis County Democrat*, July 16, 1884; *Lowville Journal and Republican*, March 10, 1887; June 30, 1887; May 10, 1888; December 20, 1888; March 19, 1898; *Utica*

Herald, December 8, 1888; Wallace, *Descriptive Guide to the Adirondacks*, 1889 ed., unpaged addenda.

3. Dwight J. Stoddard, *Notable Men of Central New York*, 302; *Decatur (IL) Herald*, February 21, 1950.

SMITH, GEORGE J. (1853–1920)
Active Ausable Chasm, Clinton and Essex Counties, 1885–1889

"Mr. G. J. Smith," reported the *Burlington Free Press* in 1889, "an enthusiastic group and view photographer, recently received from London, England, a handsome bronze medal, taken in a stereoscopic competition, for his views in Ausable Chasm, N. Y., Charles river, Mass., and Prospect park, Brooklyn, N.Y." Except for images of these subjects and one of a "man cleaning fish," no other Smith stereographs have come to light.[1]

Born in England, George Smith immigrated with his wife and the first of his four children to Burlington, Vermont, via Canada in the early 1880s. By 1888 he was a private secretary at the Baldwin Manufacturing Company, later serving as secretary, then secretary and manager, of its successor, the Baldwin Refrigerator Company. He maintained an interest in photography, giving a series of stereopticon lectures in the parish house of St. Paul's Church for its "young people" in 1906. Naturalized in 1892, Smith retired and relocated to Los Angeles, California, in 1912.[2]

1. *Burlington (VT) Free Press*, August 6, 1889; Treadwell and Darrah, *Photographers of the United States of America*, 643.

2. *Burlington Free Press*, June 11, 1906.

SMITH, MASON CHARLES (1903–1992)
Active Ticonderoga, Essex County, 1932–1943, 1945–Mid-1980s

Mason Smith was the eldest of eleven children of a laborer and a native of Ticonderoga. After high school he apprenticed in the photographic studio of **Burnell F. Dandurand** before enrolling in a course at the Illinois College of Photography in 1924. There, he and townmate **Lyman Paul Grover** captured between them five out of nine prizes awarded at a monthly Camera Club competition. Upon completion of the program, Smith went to work in Bayonne, New Jersey, as a photographer for the Babcock and Wilcox Company, boilermakers, and also took on commissions from fraternal orders, the YMCA, fight promoters, and local newspapers.[1]

Babcock and Wilcox moved its plant to Ohio in 1932, and Smith returned to Ticonderoga. He opened the Colonial Studio (the name *colonial* chosen because of the town's connection with historic Fort Ticonderoga). But starting a new business in the early years of the Great Depression was not easy. The Smiths lived for a while in the studio, which Smith shuttered for five months in late 1935, citing "poor business during winter months and position in New York City" as reasons for the closure.[2]

Enlisting in the navy in 1943, Smith served for twenty-six months as a photographer with the Seabees in the Pacific and earned four bronze stars. His wife, Henrietta, and children joined her mother in New York City, where the two women found jobs with wealthy families: Henrietta as a lady's maid and her mother as a cook.

Returning home in October 1945, Smith reopened his studio, calling it henceforth simply the Mason Smith Studio. For the next forty-plus years he was Ticonderoga's principal photographer, responsible for thousands of individual, family, summer camp, and school portraits; commissions from local enterprises; newspaper photography for the *Ticonderoga Sentinel*; and developing and finishing work for amateurs. An 11 x 13 foot Smith image of the Beech Hill ski area in Schroon Lake was displayed in New York City's Grand Central Terminal in 1947 under the sponsorship of the New York State Department of Commerce. Henrietta worked alongside her husband as his receptionist and bookkeeper until her death in 1980. Smith gradually gave up photography in the mid-1980s.[3]

1. Kenneth F. Smith, "Mason Smith—Professional Biography," undated, unpublished manuscript; email from Smith's daughter, Moira Smith Park, to the author, March 7, 2018; *Ticonderoga Sentinel*, March 19, 1925.

2. Moira Smith Park email; *Ticonderoga Sentinel*, October 31, 1935; April 9, 1936.

3. Smith, "Mason Smith—Professional Biography"; *Ticonderoga Sentinel*, February 13, 1947.

SPENCER, FRANK T. (1862–1905)
Active Malone, Franklin County, 1892–1905

Frank Spencer, born in the agricultural community of Westville, Franklin County, was identified in the 1880 US Census as a seventeen-year-old artist living on his parents' farm. In the mid-1880s he apprenticed with portrait photographer **Christopher R. Fay** in Malone, "where he was for a long time employed and where he became a first-class photographer." In 1893 he took over the portrait studio of **Charles J. Ferris**. Despite a devastating fire in 1902, which destroyed his workplace and his negatives, Spencer persevered, spending, it was said, some one thousand dollars in fitting out a "convenient and elegant" new studio with a camera that cost "nearly $300" and "handsome new backgrounds painted in New York City."[1]

Spencer was a well-known violinist, his orchestra furnishing "the music at Malone opera house and at dances throughout the county for many years." He also taught dance, conducting ballroom classes in the small communities around Malone. Having "accumulated quite a little property," in 1897 he purchased the "old" armory building (superseded in 1892 by a new facility). "It was his ambition and purpose to eventually rebuild it and convert it into a popular amusement house." Spencer died, apparently of a heart attack, at the age of forty-three.[2]

1. *Malone Palladium*, September 29, 1887; January 22, 1902; May 21, 1902; October 4, 1905; *Franklin Gazette* (Fort Covington, NY), July 1, 1893.

2. *Malone Farmer*, October 4, 1905.

START, EDWARD THOMAS (1867–1952)
Active Saranac Lake, Essex and Franklin Counties, 1898–1915; Bolton, Warren County, 1906–1913

Born in Ashby-de-la-Zouch, a small market town in Leicestershire County, England, Edward Start was the son of a master butcher and grew up in nearby Loughborough before emigrating alone in 1884 to the United States. He joined the household of an uncle in Providence, Rhode Island, and was recorded as an eighteen-year-old grocery clerk in the Rhode Island state census of 1885. By 1887 Start was a hairdresser, an occupation he followed throughout the remainder of his Providence residency.

Start must have begun taking pictures in Providence. He visited Saranac Lake in the mid-1890s (and was credited with village photographs in 1898), but continued to reside in Providence, where he became a naturalized US citizen in 1899. He relocated to Saranac Lake shortly thereafter, possibly in response to an offer by T. Edmund Krumbholz, the ebullient manager of the Ruisseaumont Hotel in nearby Lake Placid, to work for him as the hotel's staff photographer during its open summer season. Start continued, however, to support his family primarily by hairdressing, and was recorded as a Saranac Lake barber in the New York state census of 1905 and a 1908 village directory. It was not until 1910 that his occupation was noted in census data as photographer, although he had by then been recording Saranac Lake life under his own name for more than a decade. A photograph of the village's annual winter carnival can be dated to 1901; other local images from the first decades of the twentieth century chronicled community life and warm-weather gatherings at nearby camps.[1]

In 1903 Start became the staff photographer at the Kirkwood, a winter-season hotel managed by Krumbholz, in Camden, South Carolina, a position he held for forty years. In 1906, when Krumbholz left the Ruisseaumont to manage the seasonal

Sagamore Hotel in Bolton, Warren County, Start became the Sagamore's staff photographer. He worked with Krumbholz again at the Buckwood Hotel in Shawnee on Delaware, Pennsylvania, after the Sagamore burned to the ground in early 1914. Few images link Start directly with his hotel work, but according to a mid-1930s Camden newspaper article, "His pictures of lake scenes, by-way scenes and mountain views have been used in many of the leading newspapers which carry rotogravure sections." Start's work for his own Saranac Lake account appears to have ended around 1915. A Saranac Lake obituary noted his long association with **William F. Kollecker**, suggesting that Start was responsible for unattributed work for Kollecker when not professionally engaged elsewhere.[2]

Start maintained a winter home in Camden from 1930 until his retirement from the Kirkwood in the mid-1940s. Despite his long absences, he called Saranac Lake home.[3]

1. "Our Illustrations," *Adirondack Enterprise*, 1898 souvenir edition; "Edward Start Funeral Here," *Adirondack Enterprise*, February 5, 1952.

2. *Camden (SC) Chronicle Independent*, August 29, 2014; email from Mary Hotaling to the author, April 22, 2019; unsourced partial newspaper clipping from mid-1930s article on Start in the City of Camden Archives; "Edward Start Funeral Here," *Adirondack Enterprise*, February 5, 1952.

3. *Camden (SC) Chronicle Independent*, August 29, 2014.

STEDMAN, IRVING LYNN (1874–1957)
Active Lake Placid, Essex County, 1909–1950

Irving Stedman was born in Homer, Cortland County, where his father was a carriage blacksmith. A graduate of Cornell University, from which he earned a degree in engineering in 1901, he first appeared in Lake Placid during the summer of 1903 as an operator for photographer **Chester D. Moses,** a fellow Cornell graduate whose hometown adjoined Stedman's. He continued to work off and on for Moses & Co. over the next several years and occasionally operated a Homer photographic shop before leasing around 1909 and, with partner Homer Lockwood, buying Moses's business in 1911. The partnership ended in 1913. A 1914 advertisement for Stedman's Photographic Shop offered "everything photographic," including "1000 Adirondack Views" (many of them possibly

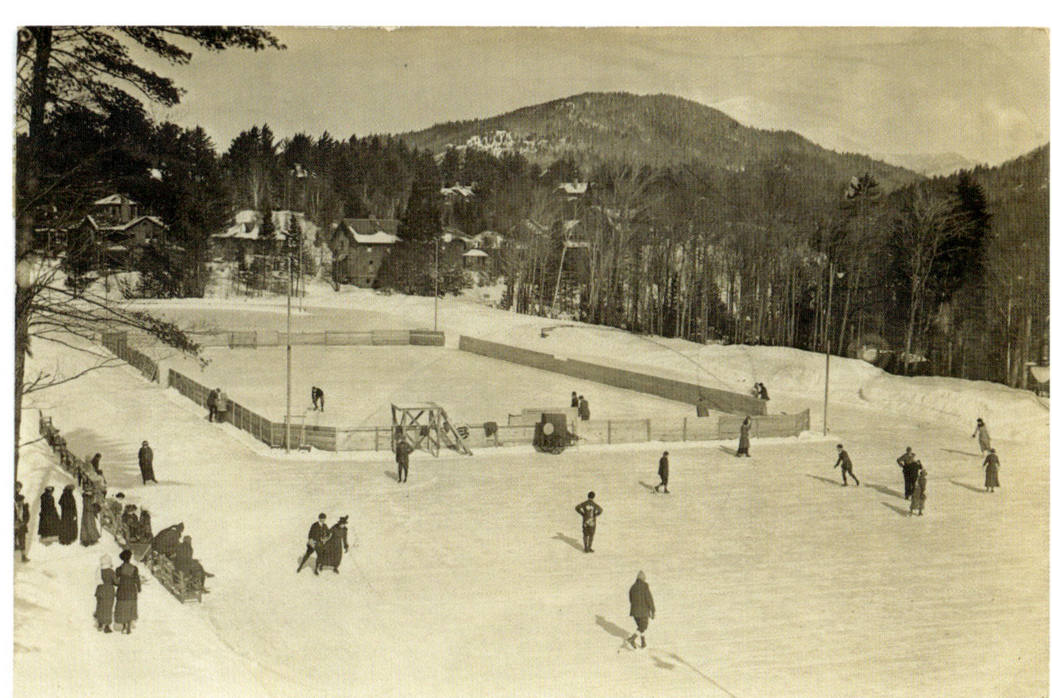

59. I. L. Stedman, skating on Mirror Lake, Lake Placid. RPPC, 1910–1920.

acquired as part of the Moses purchase), "Hand Colored Photographs in Oil," "A Fine Line of Dennison Quality Goods," "Columbia Grafanolas [phonographs] and 100 New Records." "Amateur Work" was a specialty.[1]

Like Moses, Stedman became the official photographer for the Lake Placid Club and maintained a club "stand" as well as his Main Street shop. As club photographer he recorded its activities and marketed the organization, in part through the provision of picture postcards "of scenery, buildings, and club life worthy to be sent to friends as the quickest way to give a partial idea of the beautiful and distinctiv [*sic*] features of the club." He photographed village events and sold scenic postcards and images of sporting figures and events at both his outlets.[2]

Distinguished visitors to Lake Placid provided Stedman with photographic opportunities far from home. Lake Placid Club member Bert Underwood was a founding brother of Underwood and Underwood, the first American firm to enter the field of news bureau photography. A US army major in charge of the photographic section of its Signal Corps during World War II, after the war Underwood hired Stedman to photograph battlefields in France and Germany for the company, a commission that took him abroad from May 1919 until July 1920. President Franklin D. Roosevelt, who visited Lake Placid in 1929 and 1932, called upon Stedman to take one of the first series of photographs of his Warm Springs Foundation polio treatment center in Georgia. From the late 1920s on Stedman spent occasional winters in South Carolina and Florida, finding employment as a hotel photographer.[3]

1. *Ithaca News*, March 21, 1900; *Homer Republican*, December 3, 1903; July 12, 1906; December 21, 1911; *Essex County Republican*, October 10, 1913; *Lake Placid News*, November 20, 1914; *Cortland Standard*, May 5, 1929; *Adirondack Enterprise*, September 13, 1963.

2. Lake Placid Club, *Handbook*, unpaged preface, 87. The spelling peculiarities in the handbook reflected club founder Melville Dewey's promotion of "simplified spelling."

3. *Cortland Standard*, May 6, 1919; *Au Sable Forks–Adirondack Record*, July 23, 1920; obituary from unidentified newspaper in files of Lake Placid historian.

STEFFEL, JOSEPH J. (1901–1976)
Active Schroon Lake, Essex County, Mid-1920s–1976

Joseph (Joe) Steffel arrived in the Adirondack region "on assignment." Born in New York City, he was a photographer by the age of nineteen. As an operator in the mid-1920s with the portrait division of the White Studio, known for capturing the images of hundreds of Broadway performers, Steffel was dispatched to take pictures at children's summer camps around Essex County's Schroon, Paradox, and Pyramid Lakes. By 1932 he was manager of the College Annual Department of the Arthur Studios, specializing in "school and college photography." He took pictures at Princeton, Fordham, and other universities for their annual yearbooks, and in June 1942 reported that he had worked on seventy-four high school yearbooks during the previous winter.[1]

Steffel's summer headquarters was Schroon Lake, a community of which he became a part for nearly fifty summers. In the late 1930s his wife and daughter began joining him for vacations from their home in the Bronx. He later bought a Schroon Lake residence in which he installed his "Summer Studio."[2]

"We wonder," remarked the *Ticonderoga Sentinel*'s Schroon Lake correspondent in 1941, "if the town realizes how fortunate we are in having Mr. Steffel, a photographer with his experience, come to Schroon each summer." In addition to his work for hotels and children's camps, Steffel served as photographer for the town's Chamber of Commerce and its Central School (whose senior students twice dedicated the yearbook to him). He took Christmas card photographs for local families and drove north out of season to chronicle weddings, sometimes returning to photograph the silver anniversaries of the same couples whose weddings he had covered. He served on committees, acted as judge for various sponsored competitions, and could be counted on for small checks in support of local fund drives—even delivering a box of tinfoil from New York for a wartime salvage campaign. As a *Ticonderoga Sentinel* correspondent quoted from a January 1947 Steffel letter, "'Got me a couple new rods and reels . . . Can't wait for June and Schroon.' Doesn't that just sound like Joe?" Steffel died in Schroon Lake.[3]

1. "Steffel Back on Campus," *Notre Dame Scholastic* (Univ. of Notre Dame student paper), April 15, 1932; *Suffolk County News*, July 7, 1933; *Ticonderoga Sentinel*, June 19, 1941; June 18, 1942; August 15, 1978.

2. "Steffel Award," *Ticonderoga Sentinel*, August 15, 1978.

3. *Ticonderoga Sentinel*, August 28, 1941; July 1, 1943; August 24, 1944; January 30, 1947; August 15, 1978.

STEVENS, GEORGE W. (1867–1937)
Active Northville, Fulton County 1900–1912

George Stevens was known in his Mohawk Valley hometown of Little Falls, Herkimer County, as a "balloonist and photographer" in the mid-1890s. Between 1895 and 1897 he attracted attention as the former, when "Prof. Stevens" made a number of ascensions and "managed" other balloonists in central New York: Auburn, Ithaca, Syracuse. In 1897 he opened a job-printing office in St. Johnsville, Montgomery County.[1]

Stevens became a photographer in the Northampton village of Northville around 1900, where he was still resident in 1910. He owned a home in Sacandaga Park and specialized in souvenir tintypes, while also publishing scenic postcards of its amusement facilities. Around 1912 he returned to the Mohawk Valley and opened the George W. Stevens Studio in Amsterdam, Montgomery County. By 1920 he had given up photography and was working for wages as a wagonmaker in Volney, Oswego County; by 1930 he was a retired widower living in Mayfield, Fulton County. "Ill for a long time" before his death, Stevens died in Ogdensburg, St. Lawrence County, as a resident of Pythian House, a home maintained for its elderly members by the nonsectarian fraternal order Knights of Pythias.[2]

1. *Herkimer Democrat*, May 16, 1894; *Auburn Bulletin*, July 19, 1895; *Waterloo Observer*, June 26, 1895; *Little Falls Journal Courier*, July 20, 1897; December 23, 1897.

2. *Schenectady Gazette*, May 3, 1912; *Amsterdam Recorder*, November 17, 1937.

STIEGLITZ, ALFRED (1864–1946)
Active Caldwell, Warren County, Intermittently from 1890s–1918, and Seasonally Thereafter into the Late 1930s

Alfred Stieglitz was the eldest of six siblings, born in Hoboken, New Jersey, to well-to-do German-Jewish immigrants Hedwig and Edward Stieglitz, a woolen merchant. In 1871 the family relocated to Manhattan, and in 1872 began spending summers as hotel guests in Caldwell, later Lake George.

Stieglitz took a boyhood interest in photography. Family members often had their likenesses taken by professional photographers, and Stieglitz gravitated to their darkrooms: recalled by him as "mysterious places" where he watched them work and "learned how a properly developed negative should look." A photographer remembered from his Adirondack childhood was **George S. Irish**, "a tintyper at Lake George" who became his "friend."[1]

The Stieglitzes moved to Germany for an extended stay in 1881, where Alfred studied engineering from 1882 to 1885 at the Polytechnikum in Berlin. Purchasing his first camera in 1883, he won a silver medal in London for photography in 1887. His family returned to the United State in mid-decade, but Stieglitz stayed on until 1890: seeing Europe, taking pictures, organizing photographic exhibitions, and continuing to win competitions with his work. In 1886, during Stieglitz's absence, his father purchased Oaklawn, an elegant lakeside summer cottage in Caldwell. In 1891, "to rid the family retreat of the pungent smell of livestock"

60. A. Stieglitz, *Music—A Sequence of Ten Cloud Photographs, No. II*, 1922. Courtesy of Adirondack Experience.

raised on a thirty-seven-acre farm across the road, he bought the farm without lake access and added it to the family holding. Oaklawn was sold in 1919. "The Hill," as the more modest farm property was called, became the home of the extended family and Stieglitz's beloved retreat.[2]

Much has been written about Stieglitz's career, during which his hands-on role behind the camera was often secondary to his prominent position as the leading American proponent of photography as art. He coined the term *Photo-Secession* for an American movement, of which he was a founder in 1902, that took its name from a term used by a German group of artists who supported a more naturalistic style than that embraced by traditional photographers.[3]

Stieglitz's road to photographic prominence began in 1892 with an editorship at the *American Amateur Photographer*. Five years later he became editor of the influential New York Camera Club's journal, *Camera Notes*, before announcing in 1902 his plan to publish and edit his own quarterly, the groundbreaking *Camera Work*, dedicated to the furthering of modern photography. The journal survived until 1917 and established Stieglitz as one of the most influential champions of the medium as fine art. He was concurrently a prominent art dealer, in 1905 opening 291 at 291 Fifth Avenue (at first called The Little Galleries of the Photo-Secession). The gallery promoted the work of contemporary American painters and photographers and produced the premiere US exhibitions of European artists Cezanne, Matisse, and Picasso. Stieglitz owned two more galleries during his career, but by the time 291 closed in 1917 his own photography had become central to his life.

Edward Steichen, renowned artist, photographer, and a co-founder of the Photo-Secession, later wrote of his close friend: "Stieglitz's greatest legacy to the world is his photographs, and the greatest of these are the things he began doing toward the end of the 291 days." This period predates by two years the sometimes long summers Stieglitz began spending at the Caldwell family farm—from 1919 to 1927 with his muse, lover, and later, second wife, Georgia O'Keeffe, and then often on his own. While many of Stieglitz's early photographs have been described as "narrative" and "painterly," his later work eliminated the storytelling element. He photographed mundane subjects: skyscrapers as seen from his New York City apartment, modest buildings (including his Caldwell darkroom, originally the entrance to a hothouse), servants at The Hill and friends who came to visit him there. A number of the photographs of Georgia O'Keeffe comprising his remarkable twenty-year compilation titled *Portrait of Georgia* were taken at the farm. *Equivalents*, a series of more than four hundred cloud configurations photographed between 1922 and the mid-1930s that reduced pictorial content to the abstract, was photographed there, as was a late series of aging poplar trees, some of which had been planted on the Stieglitz property by Alfred's father.[4]

One Caldwell landscape figured as a unique source of inspiration. In 1925 Stieglitz explained its importance to him in writing to Sherwood Anderson: "I have been looking for years—50 upwards—at a particular sky line of simple hills—how can I tell the world in words what that line is—changing as it does every moment. —I'd love to get down what 'that' line has done for me—May be I have—somewhat—in those snapshots I've been doing the last few years." Although his view from The Hill, encompassing the body of water that gave the Lake George region its name, was central to his artistic vision, the lake itself attracted little of Stieglitz's photographic attention.[5]

Stieglitz interacted with the Lake George community, although more often with its working class than the haute-bourgeoisie summer people whose company his parents had enjoyed. (He did, however, serve as a judge of the Second Annual Camera Exhibit at the Sagamore Hotel in Bolton in his mid-seventies.) The photographer's beloved farm is long gone, sold to a developer in the late 1950s and replaced by a suburban subdivision. Georgia O'Keeffe, who spent much of her time in New

Mexico after 1928, returned to Lake George after Stieglitz's death to bury his ashes beneath a pine tree on the shore of the lake. Thus the Adirondacks retains a physical token of the celebrated artist whose regional photographs enhanced his reputation and now grace the collections of premier museums throughout the United States.[6]

1. Norman, *Alfred Stieglitz*, 21.

2. International Center of Photography, *Reflections in a Glass Eye*, 228–29; Moore, "Leading Amateurs in Photography," 428; Mitchell, "Stieglitz in the Adirondacks," 67.

3. Szarkowski, *Alfred Stieglitz at Lake George*, 10; Doty, *Photo-Secession*, 24, 33.

4. Richter, *Georgia O'Keeffe and Alfred Stieglitz*, 67; Mitchell, "Stieglitz in the Adirondacks," 68; Edward Steichen, *A Life in Photography* (Garden City, NY: Doubleday & Company, 1963), quoted in Szarkowski, *Alfred Stieglitz at Lake George*, 10; "Mr. Alfred," 9.

5. Alfred Stieglitz to Sherwood Anderson, July 5, 1925, Alfred Stieglitz Archive, Yale University, quoted in Szarkowski, *Alfred Stieglitz at Lake George*, 29.

6. *Lake George Mirror*, August 18, 1939; Walsh, "Georgia in New York." The main house at Oaklawn still stands inside a modern skin as part of a Lake George condominium time-share development.

STILLMAN, WILLIAM JAMES (1828–1901)

Active Harrietstown, Franklin County, 1859

A painter, art critic, journalist, and photographer, William Stillman was the first artist to photographically record close-ups of Adirondack landscape features. The youngest of nine children born to a machine shop operator in Schenectady, Schenectady County, he attended Union College. After graduating in 1848, Stillman announced his intention to take up landscape painting and went to New York City to study briefly under Frederick Church, emerging leader of the Hudson River School of painting. Venturing to Europe in 1850, Stillman applied himself to painting in England for a year before returning to New York City, where he was elected an associate member of the National Academy of Design. His landscape paintings exhibited there received modest praise.[1]

In 1854 Stillman began to write professionally as the fine arts editor of the *New York Evening Post*. In 1855, in partnership with John Durand, son of Hudson River School painter Asher B. Durand, he founded the *Crayon*, the first commercially successful American journal devoted to the arts. Stillman was the publication's initial editor and principal writer. His professional reputation would derive from his long career as a distinguished art critic, and a photographer.[2]

Thanks to his childhood proximity to the Adirondacks, Stillman grew up a skilled woodsman and enthusiast of the region. He completed *Study on Upper Saranac Lake*, an oil painting on canvas now in the Boston Museum of Fine Arts, during a summer spent at the lake in 1854. In 1858 he invited eight men from his social circle, among them Boston-area poets James Russell Lowell and Ralph Waldo Emerson, on an expedition into the northern wilderness. The group's three-week sojourn on the shore of Follensby Pond, Harrietstown, at what they called Camp Maple but was dubbed by their local guides the Philosophers' Camp, has been extensively documented. The self-styled Adirondack Club, delighted with the success of its first outing, urged Stillman, club secretary, to return to the region the following winter to explore a 22,500-acre tract offered for sale on Ampersand Pond, not far from Follensby. While there, Stillman contracted pneumonia. Before being "ordered off" to Florida to recuperate, he made his first venture into photography in taking two half-hour lessons from James Wallace Black, a commercial photographer in Boston.[3]

In 1859 Stillman organized and presided over a visit by Adirondack Club members to their about-to-be acquired camp, bought at tax auction for $455.87. Carrying with him his "rude, inefficient and cumbersome" photographic equipment, he spent several months on his own at the site. The images Stillman took during his stay impart no sense of specific place, but depict tightly cropped elements from nature (trees, ferns) with meticulous attention to foreground details. He called these

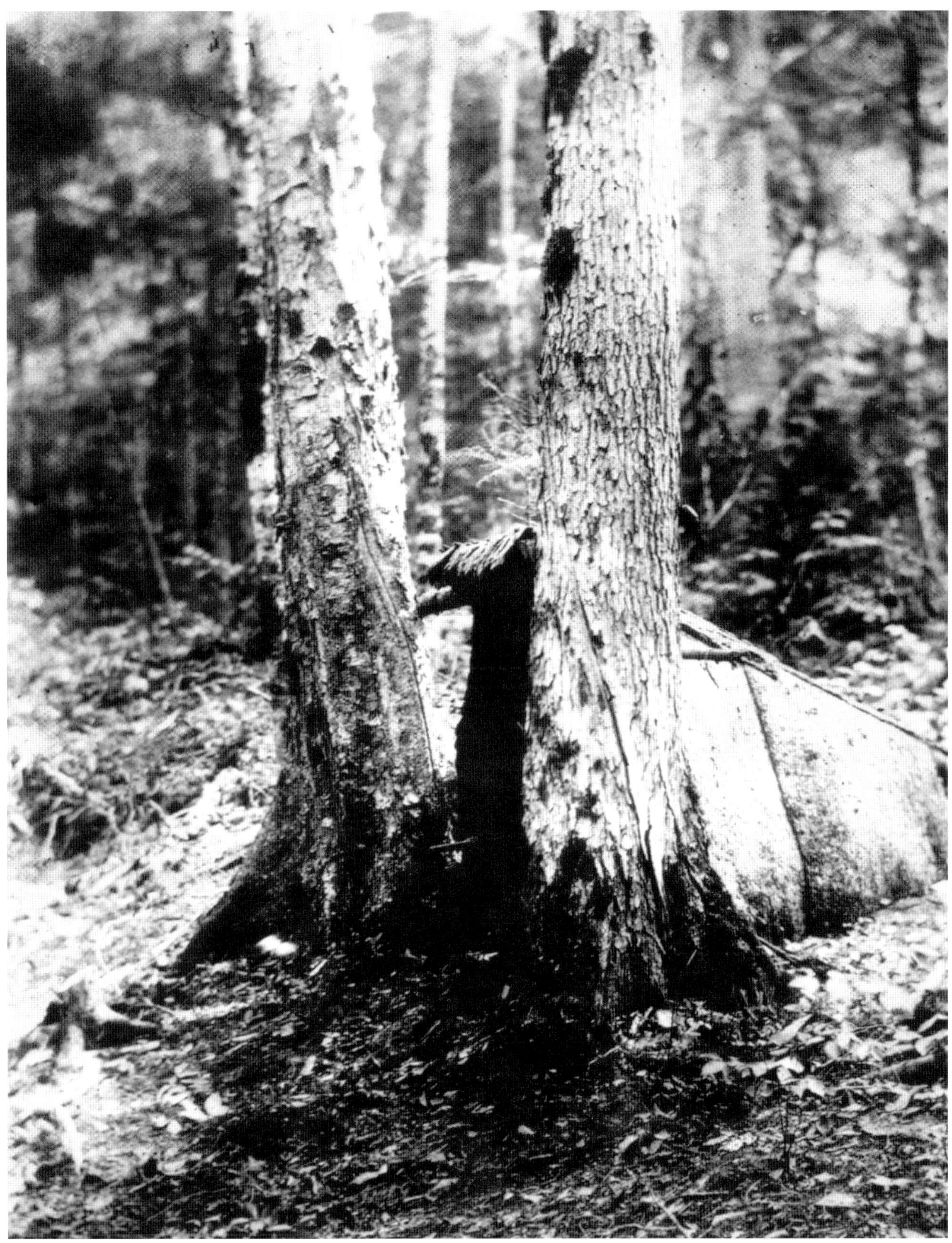

61. W. J. Stillman, untitled, from the portfolio *The Forest: Adirondack Woods*, 1859. Courtesy of Special Collections, Schaffer Library, Union College.

photographs "studies" rather than "views," representing an early use in photography of a term borrowed from the vocabulary of painting. Black published a small volume of prints from his images later that year as *Photographic Studies by W. J. Stillman. Part I. The Forest. Adirondac Woods.* The work was well received, with a reviewer for the *Atlantic* noting, "The points of view are chosen with the fine feeling of an artist, and the tangled profusion and grace of the forest, with the moment's whim of sunfleck and shadow, are given with exquisite delicacy . . . One may study these pictures til he becomes as familiar as a squirrel with fern and tree-bark and moosewood and lichen, til he knows every trunk and twig and leaf as intimately as a sunbeam."[4]

The summer of 1859, Stillman later wrote, "was my last serious experience of woodland life." He left for Europe later that year and, "without intention or prevision," returned only intermittently to the United States thereafter. Disappointed in his skill as a painter, Stillman gradually gave up painting, but continued to take photographs, using them in journal articles and illustrated books. He produced only one other series of American images: from photographs taken in and around Cambridge, Massachusetts, circa 1874. His most famous work is an 1870 series of the Acropolis of Athens. Other images were captured in Crete and Italy.[5]

Artists collected his work, but Stillman considered his involvement in photography no more than an exercise in scientific experimentation, writing in the *Crayon* in 1855 that neither "composition" nor "poetry" would "ever be attained by the photograph." "There is no small irony," noted an art scholar in reference to a 1988 exhibition of Stillman's photographs, "in the fact that the medium that contributed to his disillusion as a painter should challenge and inspire another body of work which stands today as Stillman's major achievement as an artist."[6]

1. Anne Ehrenkranz, cont., "William James Stillman: Painter, Critic, Photographer," in Stillman, *Poetic Localities*, 13.

2. Ehrenkranz, in Stillman, *Poetic Localities*, 14–15.

3. Stillman, *Autobiography of a Journalist*, 199, 283.

4. Schlett, *A Not Too Greatly Changed Eden*, 133–34; Stillman, *Autobiography of a Journalist*, 283; Ehrenkranz, in Stillman, *Poetic Localities*, 18; Waggoner, *East of the Mississippi*, 102; Stillman, *Poetic Localities*, 116n1, quoting from the *Atlantic*, January 1860.

5. Stillman, *Autobiography of a Journalist*, 291–92; Ehrenkranz, in Stillman, *Poetic Localities*, 22–24.

6. Linda S. Ferber, cont., "'The Clearest Lens': William J. Stillman and American Landscape Painting," in Stillman, *Poetic Localities*, 101.

STODDARD, SENECA RAY (1843–1917)
Active Primarily in the Eastern and Central Adirondacks, 1867–1910

The Adirondack region's most prolific landscape photographer as well as one of its finest, Seneca Ray Stoddard has been called "the Eastern counterpart to the great camera image-makers of the West like **William Henry Jackson** and Carleton Watkins." He was also a writer, a lecturer, a publisher, a cartographer, an entrepreneur, and an environmentalist.[1]

Stoddard was born in Wilton, Saratoga County, just outside the border of what became the Adirondack Park. His father was a farmer and moved often. Not long after the death of his first wife in 1851, he relocated his family to the town of Burke, Franklin County, and later to the environs of Troy, Rensselaer County. In 1862 Stoddard began working as a painter of decorative wall panels, among them landscape views, at Troy's Eaton, Gilbert & Company, a manufacturer of railcars and omnibuses. In 1864 he advertised as a Glens Falls, Warren County, "House, Sign, and Ornamental" painter, and in 1865, in partnership with G. E. Norris, as "prepared to do all kinds of Carriage, House, Sign, Banner, and Ornamental Painting in the best style and at reasonable prices."[2]

Stoddard appeared in the 1870 US Census as a Glens Falls landscape painter. Several dozen of his paintings survive (most of them held by the Adirondack Experience, Blue Mountain Lake). But

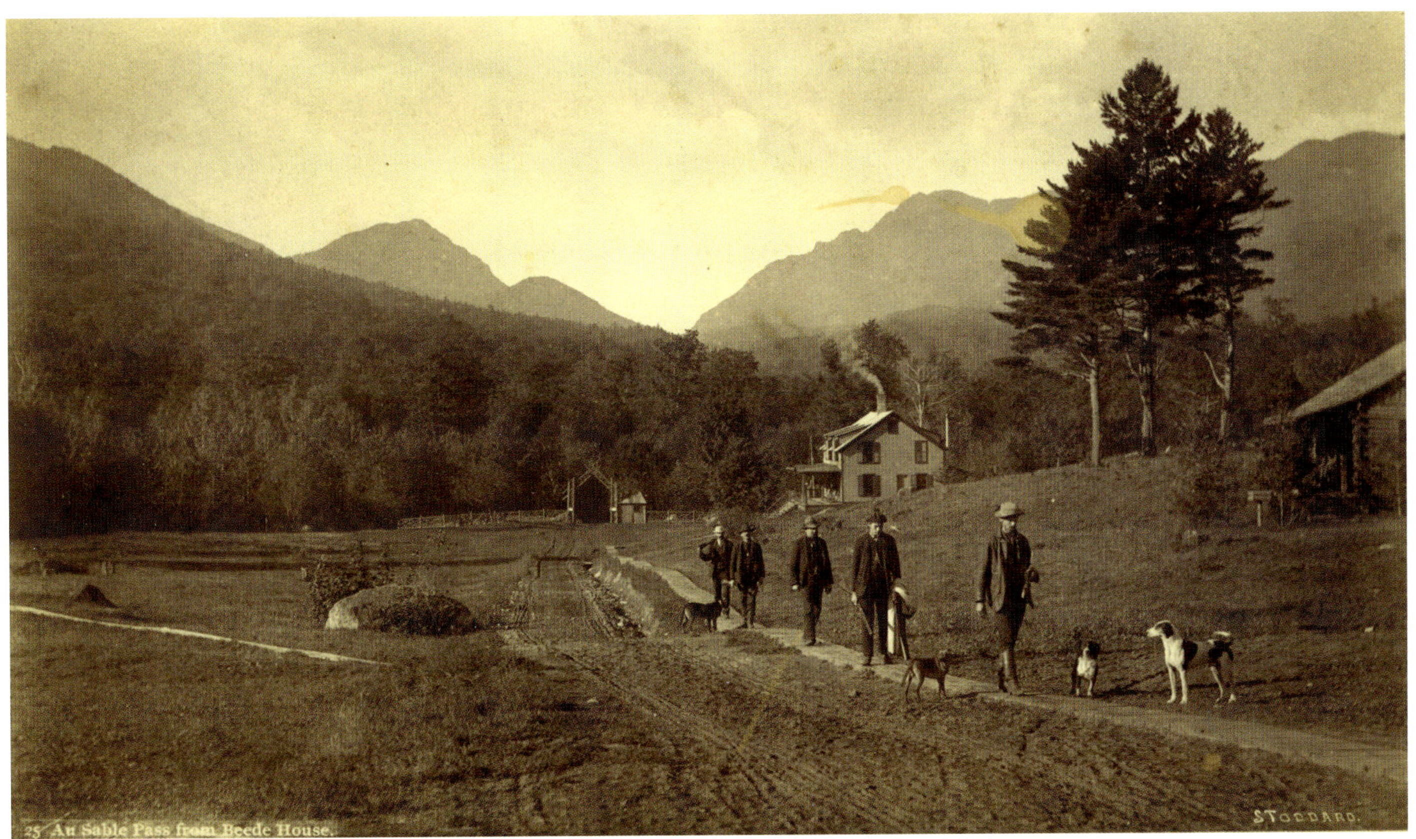

62. S. R. Stoddard, Au Sable Pass from Beede House, Keene Valley, 1887. Courtesy of Adirondack Experience.

sometime in the mid-1860s he had taken up landscape photography, an art that became the cornerstone of his varied professional life. He is thought to have learned the wet collodion process from Glens Falls photographer **George W. Conkey** before entering into a brief photographic partnership with Warrensburg photographer **James H. Carpenter** as Carpenter & Stoddard to produce a small group of Lake George stereographs. His earliest images—of Glens Falls—created as an independent photographer date to 1867.[3]

Photographs of the Lake George region were credited as the basis for Stoddard wood engravings in the initial, 1868, edition of Benjamin Franklin DeCosta's tourist guide, *Lake George: Its Scenes and Characteristics*. Early stereoviews were offered by New York distributor **E. and H. T. Anthony and Company** as part of its Christmas selection in 1871. Stoddard made a first trip into the Adirondack interior in 1870 and a second in 1873. He published a descriptive guidebook to the region, *Adirondacks: Illustrated*, the following year, announcing in it the availability of six hundred stereographs, one hundred 8 x 10 inch photographs, and one hundred 11 x 14 inch photographs. In 1877 he detailed his working methods in an article in the *Philadelphia Photographer*. He continued to take photographs into the first years of the twentieth century.[4]

Focusing his camera and business on products with tourist appeal, Stoddard largely eschewed fields that held little interest for this genteel, resort-oriented market. His guidebook, annually revised and updated through 1914, became enormously successful. Written in a breezy, often self-deprecating, narrative style and illustrated with engravings and, later, photographs, it promoted the region's natural wonders, recreational opportunities, historic sites, and accommodations while also providing historical information, distance tables, train fares and schedules, route suggestions, and maps. Editions published from 1893 on dispensed with much of the narrative. Stoddard issued more than twenty other book titles from his Glens Falls studio over the course of his career, most of them souvenir photograph collections relating to specific locations. He also produced a short-lived magazine, *Stoddard's Northern Monthly* (1906–8), "dedicated to glorifying and preserving the Adirondacks," and undertook private photographic commissions from hotels, great camp owners, and railroads. (In 1880 the Delaware and Hudson Railroad equipped a special train to Stoddard's specifications so that he could photograph sites along its New York City to Montreal route through the Adirondacks.)[5]

By 1880 Stoddard was marketing his views as works of art in New York City, Boston, Philadelphia, Montreal, London, Paris, and Berlin. He sold them by mail and through bookstores. In 1884 he leased newsstands on two Lake George steamboats and retail space at several hotels. His Glens Falls studio was a family dominated venture in which his two wives, Helen Augusta Potter (married to Stoddard in 1868 and the mother of his two sons, who died in 1906) and Emily Doty, as well as a staff made up mostly of other women, handled details of production and marketing.[6]

What made Stoddard's photographs stand out? In 1876, *Philadelphia Photographer*, the most influential American journal in its field in the last decades of the nineteenth century, compared his work to that of fine European landscape photographers. "The stereos are perfect gems," it noted, "but the larger views captivate us most. They seem to be filled with the feeling and expression of the true artist. For choice of subjects, arrangement, and balance of lines, depth and beauty of perspective, well-chosen and effective foregrounds, and clearly defined yet subdued distance . . . we have rarely seen these views excelled."[7]

In 1888 Stoddard began providing negatives to the American Museum of Natural History for a series of magic lantern presentations given to public school teachers by its Department of Public Instruction. (Forty-seven of sixty-five slides for a March 1889 lecture on "Lakes and Glens of New York" were from Stoddard images.) In 1891 he began to offer illustrated lectures of his own. As a proselytizer on behalf of preserving the region's natural resources, his 1892 lecture on the Adirondacks, tendered across New York State and in the Assembly Chamber of the State Legislature, is thought to have influenced that year's passage of legislation establishing the Adirondack Park. "If the lecture as delivered by Mr. Stoddard," it was reported, "with the accompanying illustrations, could be attended generally throughout the state, it would do more in two months time to correct the abuses of the Adirondacks than all the surveys and commissions of the past twenty years." Later Stoddard lectures, presented along the East Coast to Florida and as far afield as Chicago and Nebraska, touched not only on the Adirondacks but also on his extensive travels in the United States, Alaska, Cuba, Nova Scotia, the Mediterranean, Northern Europe, and Russia.[8]

Stoddard's expansive, light-filled photographs have led some art scholars to classify a portion of Stoddard's output as *luminist*. This term, first used in connection with Hudson River School landscape painting from circa 1850 to 1875, characterized works with open foregrounds, deep, hazy backgrounds, "stillness of mood and flat balanced order." Silvery stretches of open water and "low sunlight faced centrally across the view" were other earmarks of the luminist approach. Among Stoddard's notable stylistic experiments were night and flash photography and a simulated lunar effect achieved in photographs taken during the day to create shadows capturing the effect of moonlight.[9]

Stoddard's total output of Adirondack stereographs, mounted prints, and magic lantern slides ran into the thousands and sold in the tens of thousands. The quality and quantity of his product were remarkable. So, too, was his ability to exploit the avenues available to promote his work. Intimately versed in the landscape of the region, Stoddard was remembered after his death as having "done as much to popularize the Adirondacks as any man who ever lived."[10]

1. Fuller, "Seneca Ray Stoddard," 3.

2. Adler, *Early Days in the Adirondacks*, 31, 33, 34, 38.

3. Crowley, *Seneca Ray Stoddard, Adirondack Illustrator*, 3; French, "The History of the Adirondacks in 3-D"; Waggoner, *East of the Mississippi*, 268.

4. DeCosta, *Lake George*, iv; S. R. Stoddard, *Old Times in the Adirondacks*, 45; S. R. Stoddard, "Landscape and Architectural Photography," 146–48.

5. Bauer and Bauer, "Seneca Ray Stoddard," 12; *Plattsburgh Sentinel*, June 4, 1880; November 11, 1892.

6. Bauer and Bauer, "Seneca Ray Stoddard," 8; Crowley, *Seneca Ray Stoddard, Adirondack Illustrator*, 5.

7. "Editor's Table," *Philadelphia Photographer* 13, no. 150 (June 1876): 192.

8. Seneca Ray Stoddard file, box 28, Albert S. Bickmore Papers, American Museum of Natural History, New York; Fuller, "Seneca Ray Stoddard," 3–4; *Glens Falls Times*, May 10, 1892, quoted in Bauer and Bauer, "Seneca Ray Stoddard," 10; *Red Cloud (NE) Chief*, July 26, 1901.

9. Horrell, *Seneca Ray Stoddard*, 45, 74, 106, 108–9; Wilmerding, *American Light*, 142–43.

10. "S. R. Stoddard at the End of Life's Journey," *Elizabethtown Post*, May 3, 1917.

STONE, NATHAN LEVI (1836–1907)
Active Potsdam, St. Lawrence County, 1872–1906

Nathan Stone was born into a farming family in Louisville, St. Lawrence County. After graduating from Potsdam's St. Lawrence Academy, he taught for two years before taking up photography, at first in Ogdensburg and then in the well-known New York City portrait house of Abraham Bogardus. After operating galleries in Carthage and Antwerp, Jefferson County, and Canton, St. Lawrence County, he returned to Potsdam in 1870 and opened his own studio in 1872. The holdings of historical societies in the northwestern Adirondacks suggest that his was the studio of choice for many families in the region.[1]

Stone ran two contiguous operations: the portrait studio, or the Great Northern Portrait House, and the Great Northern Copying House. (The two combined in some advertisements as the Great Northern Photograph and Copying House.) By 1894 the copying business was producing fifteen thousand copies of photographs annually for wholesale and retail customers across the United States. An 1880 newspaper article described unusual orders filled by the company: the isolating of a single girl's face from a group and fashioning from it a half-length portrait with arms and hands; the creation of "a pleasing picture of a man, erect, in health, his eyes open and sparkling with vigorous life" from careful notes provided by the sender along with the accompanying image of a dead body lying in a coffin. Common requests included the addition of ear and finger rings and glossy silk for dresses "with lace wherever it should properly appear" for women, and "an enlarged or a better trimmed whisker or mustache," watch chain, and/or "fine set of shirt studs" for men.[2]

Stone's son, N. Clark Stone, joined his father as a partner in the dual operation in 1887. The partnership dissolved ten years later, its "senior member" maintaining the portrait business while his son took over the copying venture. Stone continued to take pictures until shortly before his death. Among them were a few commissions for local corporations, including a set of photographs of the Hannawa Falls Power Company in Pierrepont, just outside the Adirondack Park, for the 1900 Paris Exposition.[3]

1. Curtis, *Our County and Its People*, pt. 3, "Personal Sketches," 133–34.

2. Curtis, *Our County and Its People*, pt. 1, "Historical," 480; "N. L. Stone's Photographic Establishment in Potsdam," *Potsdam Courier and Freeman*, July 22, 1880.

3. *Potsdam Courier and Freeman*, May 11, 1897; *Norwood News*, March 23, 1897; March 6, 1900.

STRATTON, ROBERT T. (1843–1920)
Active West-Central Adirondacks, 1890–1910

Robert Stratton was born in Pittsburgh, Canada, once a township at the eastern end of Lake Ontario and now part of the city of Kingston. By 1867 he immigrated to Utica, Oneida County, where he was employed for several years as a cotton mill overseer. By 1879 he was a photo artist, working at first from home. For nearly twenty years, from the late 1890s until his retirement circa 1918, he was the proprietor of a Utica photography shop. (In 1910 he was one of twenty-two photographers listed in the city directory.) His output included portraits, scenes of Utica (some of them produced as stereoviews), and images of camp and hotel life along the Fulton Chain of Lakes and around Old Forge, where many wealthy and influential Utica families summered. Stratton is thought to have shared his photographic knowledge with **Hobart V. Roberts**, a Utica resident who became his son-in-law upon his marriage in 1903 to Florence, one of Stratton's five children.[1]

1. "Robert T. Stratton," *Bulletin of Photography* 26, no. 667 (May 19, 1920): 474.

STYLES, ADIN FRENCH (1832–1910)
Active Lakes George and Champlain; Franklin and Essex Counties, 1865–1871

Born into a Jericho, Vermont, farming family, Adin Styles entered the field of photography by 1859, when he received a "second place of honor" at the Vermont State Fair for "plain photographs." His residence was listed as Burlington. A Burlington "daguerreian artist" in 1860, he entered that year into a partnership—Styles, Davis and Styles—that advertised itself as "prepared to execute any kind of Picture made by the photographic art" at three Vermont locations: Burlington, under the direction of Styles; Montpelier, under **Guy B. Davis**; and St. Albans, under Adin's younger brother, Adoniram. The partnership lasted only a year before Styles made "his bow" as an independent artist in 1861, asking friends "to call on him" at the Vermont Gallery of Art, Burlington, where he offered "photographs, plain and colored, portraits and views" of Vermont. In December he publicized the addition of new backgrounds, columns, and "other fixings" that would enable him to make portraits "more beautiful" and in "greater variety of attitudes than any other establishment in the State." During the next several years Styles trained many operators at his Church Street studio. **William Henry Jackson**, who hand finished photographs for Styles, described and sketched his operation.[1]

Stereoscopic landscape views took on increasing prominence in Styles's artistic output. Selling his gallery in 1866, he thereafter focused solely on the "View Business" and expanded his inventory of high-quality stereographs. By late 1868 he offered some eight hundred views, primarily of Vermont, but including nearly ninety views of the Adirondacks, many of them in a series titled *Adirondack Region*. Styles also produced a series of *Scenes in Florida* from his Burlington studio.[2]

In 1868 Styles married the recently widowed wife of a Burlington lawyer. She came with some property, and in 1872 Styles sold the Vermont Gallery of Art to **Sereno A. Bowers** and relocated to Florida. His views continued to be widely distributed, primarily by publisher J. Ward and Son of Boston, with later images sometimes unattributed as "American Scenery."[3]

Styles soon transitioned out of his early occupation. A venture as proprietor of the Riverside House in Jacksonville ("a very pleasant location, large rooms, first class table, courteous attendance and reasonable prices" for "Invalids and Tourists") was shortly displaced by farming. The "wonderful and satisfactory" display from Styles's Oak Bluff Farm near Jacksonville won "first premiums on some fifty varieties of vegetable, on best guinea grass hay, on best Sea Island cotton, best peanuts and for a superior starch" at the 1878 Florida State Fair. In 1892 his twenty-five-acre, citrus-producing Oak Bluff Orange Grove, reported to be "one of the handsomest in the state," produced nearly five thousand boxes of fruit. Styles is buried in Jericho Center Cemetery, Jericho, Vermont.[4]

1. *Burlington (VT) Free Press*, September 23, 1859 (as Adin Stiles); June 28, 1861; December 27, 1861; unpaged advertisement in *Vermont State School Journal and Family Visitor* 2, no. 1 (April 1860); the last ad for the partnership appeared in the *Montpelier (VT) Green-Mountain Freeman*, June 20, 1861; Jackson, *Time Exposure*, 73–76; Hales, *William Henry Jackson*, 13–14.

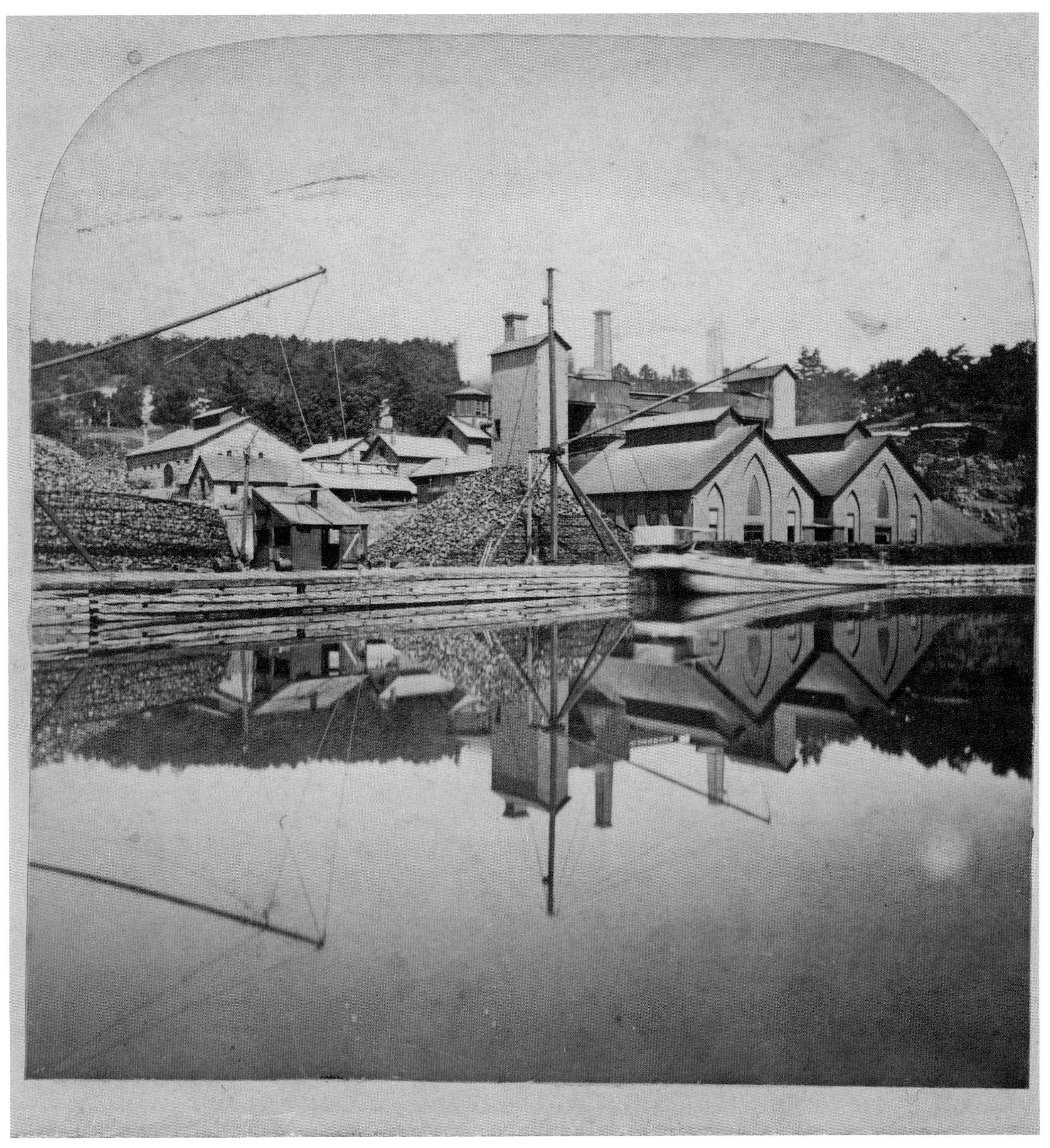

63. A. F. Styles, *Iron Works, Port Henry, N.Y.* One-half stereoview, 1865–1871. Digital image courtesy of the Getty's Open Content Program.

2. *Burlington (VT) Free Press*, December 17, 1866; October 30, 1868.

3. *Burlington (VT) Weekly Free Press*, September 15, 1876; Waldsmith, *Mementoes of Home*, 19.

4. *Albany Express*, November 13, 1873; "Florida Farming," *Burlington (VT) Free Press*, March 15, 1878, quoting undated item from *Jacksonville Sun*; "A Florida Thousand Hen Farm," *Poultry Keeper* 8, no. 2 (May 1892): 22.

SUMY, ITSUZO (1891–1970)
Active Chestertown, Warren County, 1933–1969

Born in Toba, a village on Japan's Pacific coast famous as the birthplace of cultured pearls, Itsuzo Sumy graduated from the University of Tokyo in 1915 with a degree in mining engineering. He practiced his profession in Manchuria for several years before immigrating in 1922 to the United States via Seattle, two years before the Immigration Act of 1924 limited the number of immigrants allowed into the United States and banned Arab and Asian immigrants altogether. He became part of New York City's Japanese community, estimated at around 4,600 in 1920. This cohort differed markedly in background from the immigrant Japanese population of the West Coast. Generally younger, better educated, and more urban-oriented, its members were primarily male and members of or aspirants to the middle class as students, businessmen, traders, and government officials; a few were industrial workers, artists, and writers. Sumy, like other Japanese settled in the East, did not have to contend with the virulent, ongoing hostility faced by his countrymen toiling as farmers, railroad workers, and miners in California, Oregon, and Washington.[1]

First employed at Nara Trading in New York City, a company that distributed Japanese souvenirs, in 1926 Sumy ventured to Lake George to join a former co-worker in the operation of a seasonal gift shop. In 1932 he took over a summer-only novelty shop in Chestertown launched by his brother and became a permanent Chestertown resident the following year. His shop and a second career as a self-taught photographer specializing in weddings and anniversaries, organizational meetings, chauffeur identity portraits, and postcard images provided a living. Sumy minutely recorded the life of Chestertown over a nearly forty-year period. The quantity, quality, and diversity of his images, it has been noted, suggested "that creating a body of work that could live on as an archive must have been a goal."[2]

Sumy lived quietly behind his rented store, never married (like many of his countrymen in a male-dominated immigrant population), and never learned to drive. He immersed himself in community life, bringing several Japanese friends up from New York City to play in a 1934 Chestertown-Pottersville tennis tournament sponsored by the Chamber of Commerce (won by one of Sumy's compatriots), and afterward taking part in a three-man demonstration of jujitsu, a martial art in which he held the highest degree achievable. His life, as was that of other Japanese immigrants living in the East, was disrupted only mildly by World War II. Restrictions included the impounding of images he took of a titanium mine in the Essex County village of Tahawus and confiscation of his cameras and film for the duration of the war. Sumy continued, however, to take pictures with equipment borrowed from friends. Becoming a US citizen in the early 1960s, he died after being hit by a car on an icy Chestertown winter road.[3]

1. Folwell, "Itsuzo Sumy," 61; Sawada, *Tokyo Life, New York Dreams*, 14–16.

2. Folwell, "Itsuzo Sumy, 61–62.

3. Folwell, "Itsuzo Sumy," 62, 64; Donna Lagoy, town of Chester historian, email to the author, March 26, 2017; *North Creek Enterprise*, August 16, 1934; *Chestertown Summer Sentinel*, September 1, 1950; "Sumy, Famed Photographer Killed by Car," *Warrensburg–Lake George News*, January 15, 1970.

TAFT, FRANK M. (1851–1938)
Active Lake George Region, 1883–1900

Frank Taft was a popular Glens Falls, Warren County, photographer. Born in Brattleboro, and

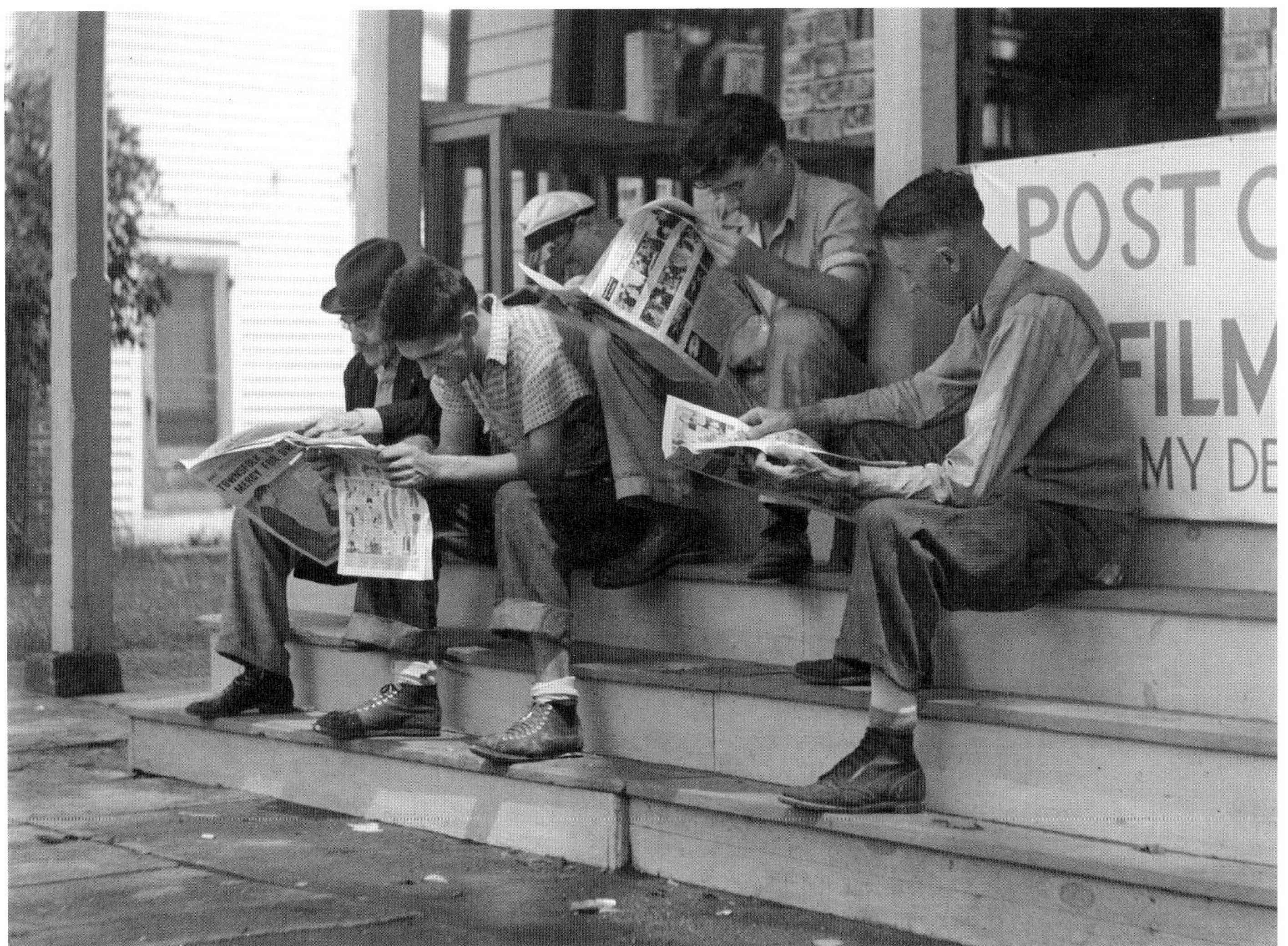

64. I. Sumy, newspaper readers on Chestertown post office steps, 1938. Courtesy of the Historical Society of the Town of Chester.

raised in Rockingham, Vermont, he entered the Bellows Falls portrait studio of his father, Preston W. Taft, at the age of fifteen. He later lived variously in the Vermont towns of Chester and Rockingham, producing images under his own imprint from both locations. In 1883 Taft relocated to Glens Falls, advertising "Brilliancy and Softness combined in a photograph make it what it should be. Give the new comer a trial." Most of his outdoor work centered on Glens Falls, but he captured a number of images of the hotels, residences, and boats of Lake George. He maintained his Glens Falls studio for thirty-one years, and purchased the studio and negatives of **George W. Conkey** in 1896. Retiring in 1914, Taft sold his business to George P. Sauter of Schenectady.[1]

1. "Frank M. Taft Retires," *Bulletin of Photography* 14, no. 359 (June 24, 1914): 788; *Bellows Falls Times*, August 22, 1873; *Glens Falls Times*, October 11, 1883; *Glens Falls Star*, October 9, 1896.

TEFFT, ARTHUR J. (1884–1956) AND LILA LINSLEY TEFFT (1896–1988)
Active Speculator, Hamilton County, 1930–1959

Born in Avon, Connecticut, Arthur Tefft appeared in the 1910 US Census as a Hartford photographer working for his own account. During the 1920s he produced images for linen postcards bearing his imprint from Hamden, Connecticut, a suburb of New Haven.

In 1930 Tefft accepted a summer job as official photographer at the Christian family Camp of the Woods in Speculator, a village in the town of Lake Pleasant, a position he held until his death twenty-six years later. During his early years at the camp, real photo postcards bore the imprint ARTHUR J. TEFFT, MT. CARMEL, CONN, but in 1935 he and his wife, Lila, moved permanently to Speculator. In addition to his Camp of the Woods output, Tefft recorded local community life and took pictures at nearby children's summer camps and schools; his Adirondack Studio sold his own work and Kodak products, provided services for amateurs, and produced the occasional real photo postcard for others.[1]

Lila Tefft worked with her husband from at least 1939, when she was reported to be in Wells taking photographs for the school yearbook when her husband was temporarily indisposed. For many years the chairman and paid executive secretary of the Hamilton County Tuberculosis and Health Association, she took over her husband's business after his death and was responsible as Lila Tefft for a number of photographs and articles in area newspapers. Her equipment and images were lost to fire in late 1959.[2]

1. "Tefft, Speculator Photographer, Dies in Hospital," *Gloversville Leader Herald*, December 31, 1956.

2. *Hamilton County Record*, May 11, 1939; *Gloversville Leader Herald*, December 2, 1960.

TERZIAN, WILLIAM (1912–1987)
Active Silver Bay, Warren County, 1933–1950

In flight from the atrocities of the Armenian genocide in the former Ottoman Empire, William (Bill) Terzian arrived in the United States with his parents and two younger brothers in 1923. The family settled in Brooklyn, where Terzian's father was identified in the 1930 US Census as a pharmacist, his mother as a dress operator. Terzian was then a student at Brooklyn Technical High School, a competitive public school specializing in science, technology, engineering, and mathematics.

In 1933 Terzian made his first visit to the Silver Bay Association, a family oriented spiritual, educational, and conference center in the Hague hamlet of Silver Bay operated from 1904 by the YMCA. He had been steered to Silver Bay by the executive secretary of the Brooklyn Central Branch of the YMCA, then known as the "largest YMCA in the world" and offering Americanization programs to immigrants. Terzian became Silver Bay's resident photographer for several seasons and presided over summer classes that transformed a number of Silver Bay youngsters into enthusiastic photo hobbyists. The main body of his association work dates from the summers of 1933 and 1936, but he took photographs of Silver Bay through the 1940s. Some of these appeared in the association's marketing materials. Others were reproduced by Terzian as postcards bearing his imprint.[1]

Terzian spent several years in Queens, where his occupation was recorded as photographer in a photo studio in the 1940 US Census. In 1943 he moved to Manhasset, Nassau County, and opened his own studio in early 1948. Terzian of Manhasset, specializing in children's portraits, school yearbooks, and weddings, remained a successful business venture until Terzian's retirement in 1985. He and his wife relocated to what had previously been their summer home, two miles south of Silver Bay, where Terzian died.[2]

1. Cole, "History of Photography," 2; Winship, "Silver Bay Postcards."

2. *Manhasset Press*, February 27, 1948; Winship, "Silver Bay Postcards."

THATCHER, FRED C. (1882–1969) AND J. GLENN (1911–1948)
Active Caldwell, Warren County, 1907–1948

Son of **Julius A. Thatcher**, Fred Thatcher showed an early inclination to follow in his father's photographic footsteps as teenage secretary of Ticonderoga's Golden Hours Photo Club. He was

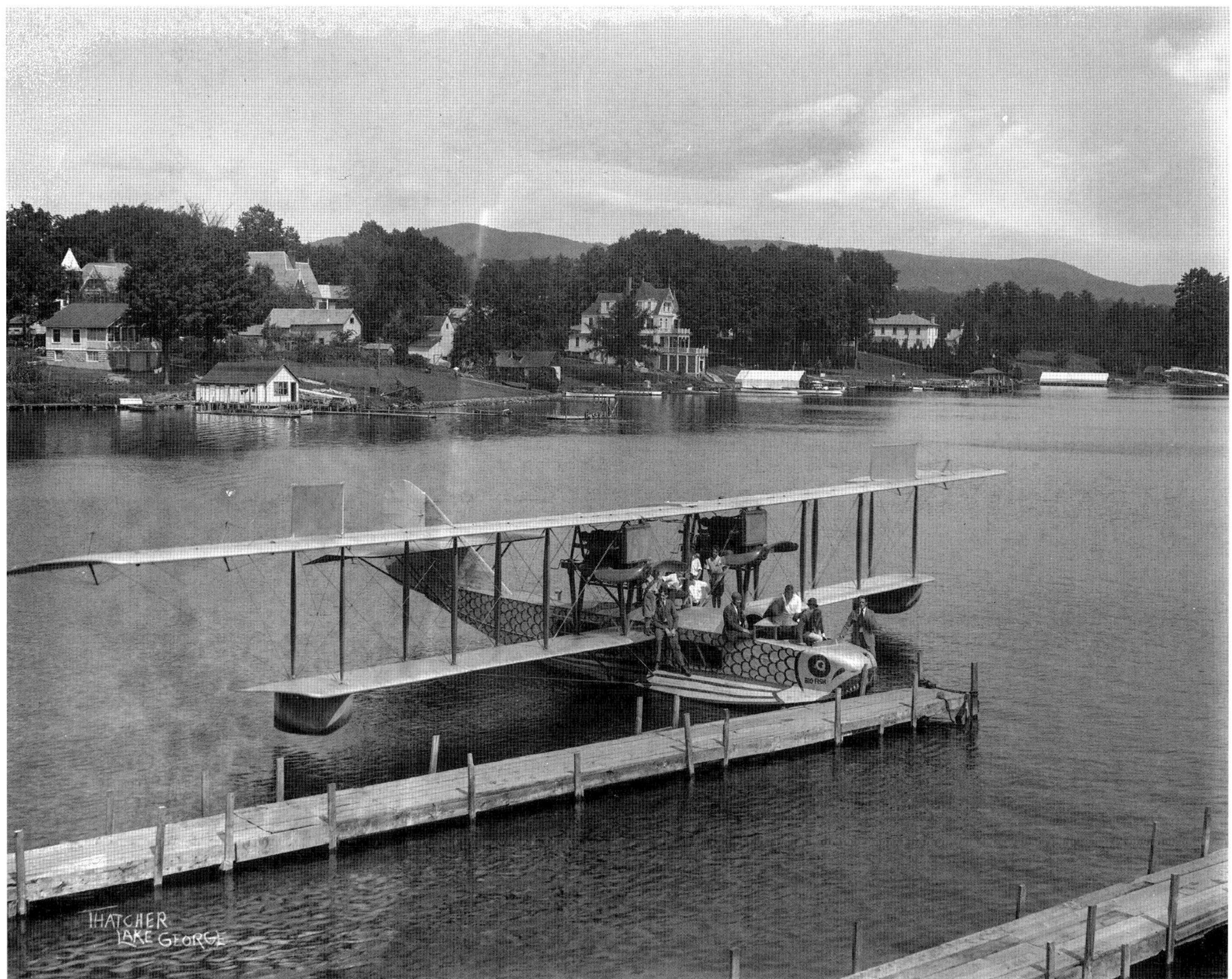

65. F. C. Thatcher, commercial flying boat *Big Fish* at Lake George, 1921. Courtesy of the Historical Society of the Town of Bolton and the Bolton Historical Museum.

employed by the General Electric Company as a machinist in Schenectady, Schenectady County, by early 1902, but returned to manage his father's Bolton Landing studio that summer and worked briefly in his Ticonderoga studio in the fall before gravitating back to Schenectady. He appeared in the New York state census of 1905 (with no listed occupation) as a Schenectady resident.[1]

Thatcher permanently located to Caldwell, later Lake George, in the summer of 1907, opening a seasonal photo studio on the grounds of the Fort William Henry Hotel. He and his father often ran competing advertisements for their respective studios in the *Lake George Mirror*, a newspaper catering to the lake's seasonal resort population. Fred's 1909 advertisement (similar to those of 1907 and 1908) read, "The New Studio: Cottages, Hotels, Camps photographed. Portraits, Groups and Views. Developing and Finishing for Amateurs. Also Tintypes that are sure to please." By 1911 he had fabricated a motorboat, *Snapshot*, which enabled him to "conveniently reach any point on the Lake." He purchased land in 1921 on which he built the Lake View Hotel, relocating his photography business, known as the Thatcher Studio from about 1920, to its premises.[2]

Thatcher recorded the Lake George summer scene for thirty years, produced thousands of postcard images, and was active in local affairs, serving in the early 1920s as Caldwell village president. He began to spend long winters with his family in Eau Gallie, Florida, in the mid-1920s (resigning from his position as village trustee in 1927, as it conflicted with his winter schedule). Retiring in 1937, he handed the Thatcher Studio over to his son the following year.[3]

Glenn Thatcher continued the seasonal operation. (His full-time job, according to the 1940 US Census, was truck driver for a laundry.) In 1942 he enlisted in the Naval Air Force and, after attending the Naval Training School of Photography at the US Naval Air Training Center in Pensacola, Florida, served for two years in the South Pacific as a chief photographer's mate. Demobilized in November 1945, he returned to Caldwell and the Thatcher Studio, managed during his absence by his wife, the former Justine Feaster. Thatcher died in 1948 of wounds received two years earlier in a motorcycle accident. The studio continued to be mentioned occasionally in newspapers until 1953, although under whose proprietorship it operated is uncertain.[4]

1. *Ticonderoga Sentinel*, May 17, 1900; January 2, 1902; July 31, 1902; October 30, 1902; November 3, 1904.

2. *Lake George Mirror*, August 13, 1909; July 18, 1914; *Glens Falls Post-Star*, June 18, 1923; "Snapshot" information from online summary of Thatcher records available for sale from Michael Brown Rare Books, Philadelphia, 2012.

3. *Glens Falls Post-Star*, March 17, 1920; January 11, 1927; "Thatcher Graduated," *Warrensburg News*, July 29, 1943.

4. "Thatcher Graduated," *Warrensburg News*, July 29, 1943; October 31, 1946; "J. Glenn Thatcher," *Warrensburg News*, December 30, 1948; *Glens Falls Post-Star*, November 17, 1945.

THATCHER, JULIUS A. (1856–1934)
Active Ticonderoga, Essex County, 1875–1918; Bolton Landing, Warren County, 1880–1922

Julius (Jule) Thatcher was the middle of nine children of a Ticonderoga-based teamster, boatman, and farmer, according to census data. In 1875 he opened his first Ticonderoga "Photograph Gallery" on "G. A. Gregory's lot," offering tintypes and portraits. The early years were difficult, and Thatcher supplemented his income with sidelines, including the sale of sewing machines, and entered into brief partnerships with Ticonderoga photographers **Amos S. Nickerson** (1884) and a Mr. Wells (1892). In 1895 he built the Brick House Studio next to his new brick home in the town's Weedville section.[1]

A large part of Thatcher's business derived from seasonal work in the Lake George resort community of Bolton Landing, a hamlet of Bolton, where in 1880 he leased a home and studio near the bridge leading to the imposing Sagamore Hotel. (He would purchase the property in 1897.) As of 1893 his specialties were "groups, steam yacht parties, natural scenery, etc." Thatcher provided nearly one hundred images for a 1901 advertising piece titled *Lake George, State of New York, Illustrated: The Queen of American Lakes*, published by William Henry Tippetts, publisher of the resort newspaper *Lake George Mirror*. He also made useful contacts that brought in rewarding assignments. Among these were a series of photographs taken in 1897 at two-week winter intervals of a Lake George house under construction so that its absentee owner could view progress without visiting the job site, and forty-six photographs taken in 1903 of all phases of industrial farm life, commissioned by Clinton Osborne of New York City's Ethical Culture School for use in city school textbooks but never published.[2]

Thatcher began spending more time in Bolton Landing around 1904, although he continued to pass at least part of most winters in Ticonderoga, operating a studio in the town's business center as well as the Brick House Studio in 1912. By 1920 he had eased up on his workload and was living full-time in Bolton Landing. A 1922 medical diagnosis of "chemical poison, induced in practicing his profession," led him to retire altogether. In 1930 he and his wife relocated to the village of Caldwell,

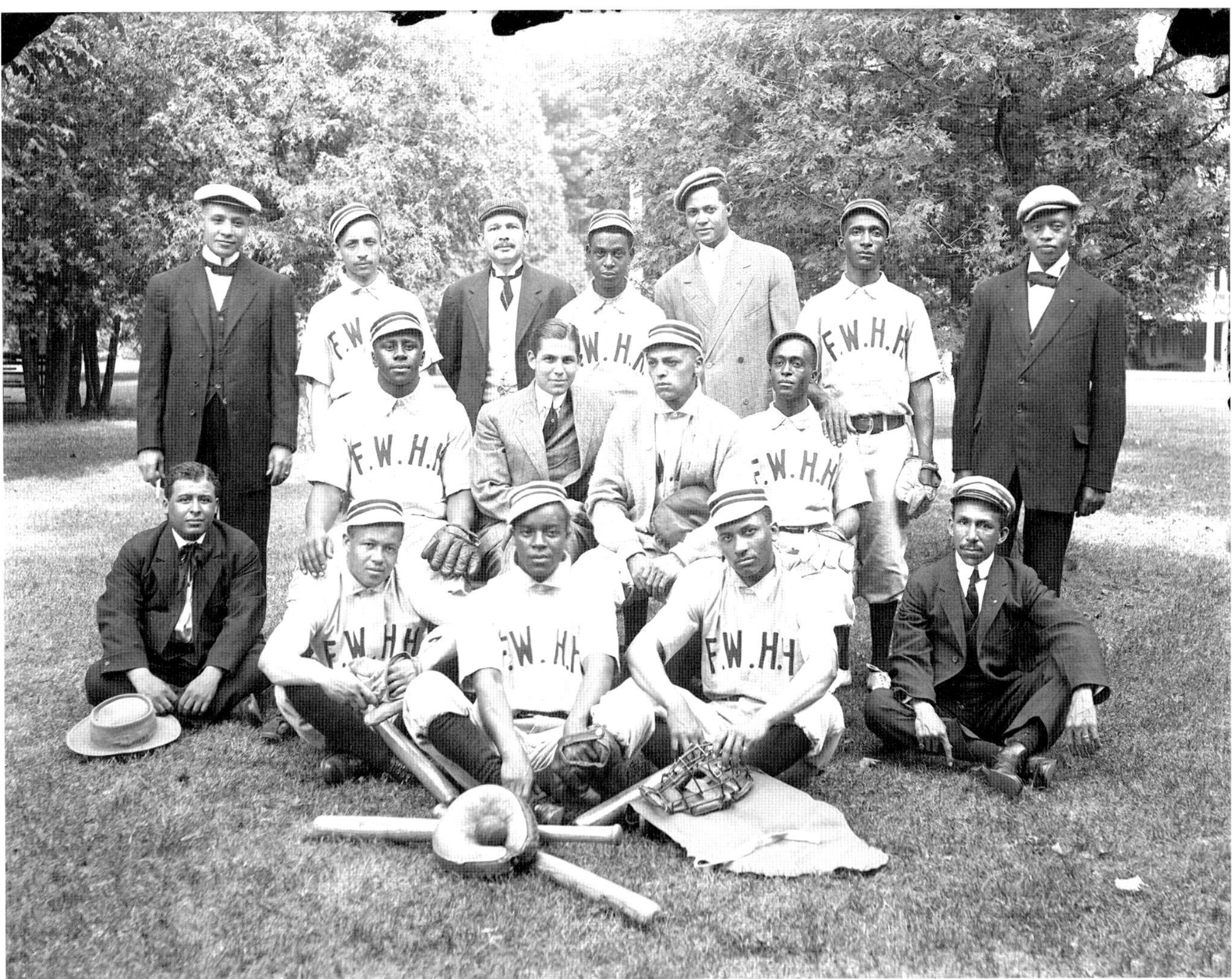

66. J. A. Thatcher, Fort William Henry Hotel baseball team, 1890s. Courtesy of the Historical Society of the Town of Bolton and the Bolton Historical Museum.

where their two children were established. His son, **Fred C. Thatcher**, and grandson **J. Glenn Thatcher** carried on the family tradition as photographers in Lake George.[3]

1. Online summary of Thatcher records available for sale from Michael Brown Rare Books, Philadelphia, in 2012; *Ticonderoga Sentinel*, January 23,1875; February 3, 1882; January 17, 1895.

2. *Lake George Mirror*, June 3, 1893; *Ticonderoga Sentinel*, November 21, 1884; February 3, 1892; December 23, 1897; November 30, 1899; July 31, 1902; January 1, 1903; *Glens Falls Daily Times*, May 5, 1897.

3. *Ticonderoga Sentinel*, Oct 31, 1912; *Lake Placid News*, October 13, 192

TOUSLEY, HORACE SMITH (1825–1895); EARLY SPELLING "TOWSLEY"

Active Keeseville, Essex and Clinton Counties, 1851–1883

Horace Tousley was among the early photographers to establish themselves in the Adirondacks. Born into a farming family in Jay, Essex County, he was, by the age of twenty-four, a photographer. He specialized, at first, in portraiture, and in 1851 opened Tousley's Sky-Light Daguerreotype Rooms above a jewelry store in Keeseville, a bustling village with a population of over five thousand in 1850. He could "be found, as usual," testified an

1853 advertisement, "in his rooms from sunrise until sunset, ready to supply patrons with Daguerreotypes, with or without colors."[1]

Living, as he did, close to Ausable Chasm, Tousley was among the pioneer photographers to lug their bulky cameras down into its depths (and was said to have had himself lowered on a rope to get the views he wanted.) By 1869 he was offering stereographs of the chasm as well as of "other home Localities." A list published perhaps five years later of views he kept "constantly on hand" included forty "Ausable River Chasm Views;" thirty-five "Adirondac Views," primarily of the Saranac and Tupper lake regions; and eight "Whiteface Mountain Views." Tousley's stereographs often included information on their reverse sides of value to tourists, such as routes and mileage to depicted sites and the names of hotel proprietors. His photographic gallery in Keeseville's Adirondack Hotel burned in an 1882 fire that destroyed fifty-nine buildings. Tousley retired shortly thereafter.[2]

1. *Essex County Republican*, July 30, 1853.

2. *Essex County Republican*, June 15, 1871, (advertisement dated December 3, 1869); Porter, "History of the Town of AuSable"; Tousley, "Adirondac and AuSable River Chasm Views"; Bauer, "George W. Baldwin's 'Gems,'" 30.

TRANQUILLE, DANTE O (1905–1981)[1]

Active throughout the Region, Particularly in the Western and Southwestern Adirondacks, 1929–1934, 1937–1972

Dan, or Danny, Tranquille was an award-winning newspaper photographer and longtime employee of sister newspapers *Utica Press* (mornings) and *Utica Observer-Dispatch* (afternoons). A Utica native, he took his first photograph for the papers in 1929. In the early years, he also provided sketches and cartoons, among them nationally acknowledged cartoon editorials related to the Lindbergh kidnapping in 1932. Leaving the papers in 1934 with the intent of setting himself up as a freelance artist and photographer, Tranquille returned in 1937 and was appointed chief photographer in 1944. His work, distributed via Associated Press Wirephoto, achieved widespread recognition. He won numerous professional prizes and was often called upon as a panelist and lecturer. His pictures traveled the world in exhibits sponsored by the National Press Photographers Association (of which he was a charter member) and *Encyclopedia Britannica*, and were frequently displayed at Utica's Munson Williams Proctor Art Institute. Two Tranquille images, *Remington Rand Strike-Breaker* and *Football Game*, were chosen for inclusion in a 1949 exhibition, *The Exact Instant—100 Years of News Photography*, assembled by Edward Steichen for the Museum of Modern Art.[2]

Tranquille photographed everything deemed newsworthy within his papers' catchment area and for many years provided a full page of photographs for the *Observer-Dispatch*'s Sunday edition. He was responsible for the images in two Adirondack-related compilations of articles originally published in serial form and authored by the popular *Observer-Dispatch* columnist David H. Beetle: *West Canada Creek* (1946), about the seventy-mile long tributary of the Mohawk River that drains the southern Adirondack Mountains; and *Up Old Forge Way* (1948). Many of the books' photographs were aerial views, a genre of photography to which Tranquille was devoted.

The *Press* shuttered in 1969, and in 1972 Tranquille was unexpectedly "retired" from his job at the *Observer-Dispatch*. He and his assistants, to most of whom Tranquille had been a mentor, packed up all of his negatives, slides, photos, and equipment and removed them from the newspaper premises. As an employee of the paper, Tranquille had no personal rights to this material, but the paper decided against mounting an expensive lawsuit to reclaim it. Tranquille negatives and prints have found their way into a number of archival photograph collections over the years.[3]

"Always moving at a trot and always moving in a cloud of cigar smoke," Tranquille was appreciated by his co-workers for his coolness under pressure, his empathy, and his wit. As one editor phrased it,

"Thirty-five years of taking news photographs hasn't dulled his sympathy, his personal sorrow for the underling, nor his ability to laugh with the fortunate. Dante just likes people, and it shows in his pictures."[4]

1. According to John R. Taibi, the initial O in Tranquille's name stood for nothing and should not be followed by a period. Letter from Taibi to the Town of Webb Historical Society, March 22, 2015.

2. *Utica Press*, July 12, 1934; "Mr. Dante O. Tranquille," *Utica Press*, April 10, 1981; Williams, "More than Photographer, Tranquille Was an Artist"; Museum of Modern Art, New York, master checklist (corrected) of works included in the exhibition *The Exact Instant—100 Years of News Photography*, February 1–May 1, 1949.

3. Email from John R. Taibi to the author, February 27, 2018.

4. "Dante O. Tranquille, Photographer, Dies," *Utica Press*, April 10, 1981.

TRUMBULL, ANNA C. (1853–1926); IMAGES PUBLISHED AS WORK OF MRS. E. E. TRUMBULL

Active Plattsburgh, Clinton County, and Northeastern Adirondacks, 1900–1916

Anna Trumbull was an amateur photographer. While her hobby did not interfere with her primary occupation—"housework in her own home," according to federal and state censuses—or with her charitable work (Women's Relief Corps of the Grand Army of the Republic, Methodist Episcopal Church), she nevertheless produced a substantial body of published work.

Born into a West Monroe, Oneida County, farming family, Anna L. Caldwell engaged in "the millinery business" in Pulaski, Oswego County,

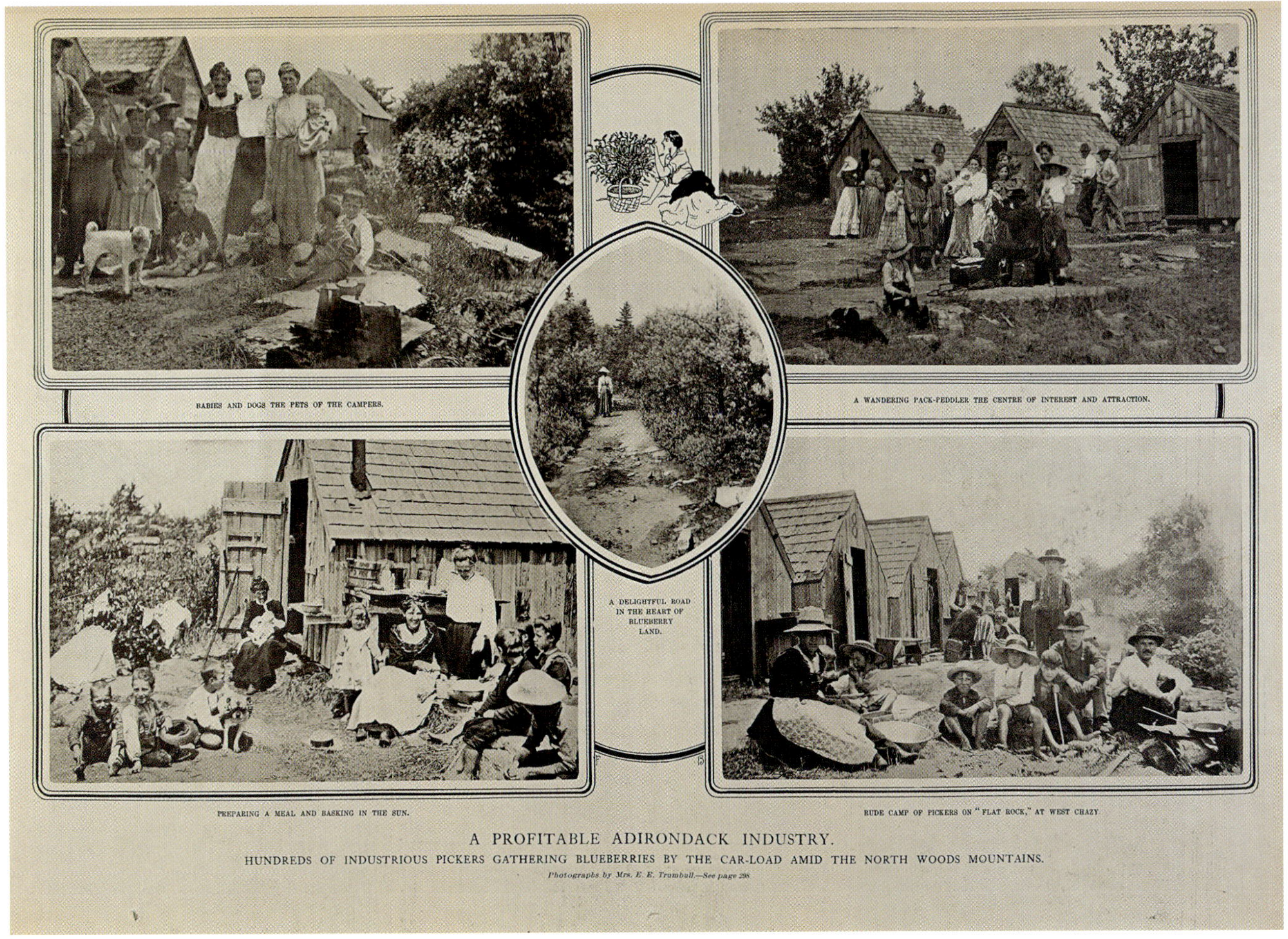

67. A. C. Trumbull, *A Profitable Adirondack Industry*. From *Leslie's Weekly*, September 25, 1902.

before marrying in 1887. Her husband, Egbert, a railway postal clerk, requested and received permission to transfer to the salubrious Adirondacks to improve his "enfeebled health." In 1890 the couple settled in Plattsburgh, from which Egbert accompanied a daily run on the Chateaugay branch of the Delaware and Hudson Railroad to and from Saranac Lake until his death in 1914.[1]

Around 1900 Trumbull's photographs began to win small cash prizes at the annual Clinton County Fair and to appear in journals devoted to or with columns given over to amateur work: *Photo Era*, *Amateur Photographic Advertiser*, *Paine's Photographic Magazine*, *Frank Leslie's Illustrated Newspaper*. Her subjects included snow scenes and other landscape subjects, children, flowers, and animals. Photographs of Saranac Lake's winter carnival featured in a 1905 issue of the *Illustrated Buffalo Express*; nine Trumbull images appeared in George Johnson's 1907 book, *Education by Plays and Games*.[2]

Trumbull's 1902 full-page, five-image spread of a Clinton County blueberry pickers' camp in the popular, large-format magazine *Leslie's Weekly* was a noteworthy achievement. A frequent officer of Plattsburgh's Garden Club, her later photographs of individual flowers and garden displays accompanied articles she wrote for such magazines as *Suburban Life* and *Garden*.[3]

1. *Ogdensburg Journal*, January 31, 1890; "Former Resident of Pulaski Dies in Plattsburg," *Pulaski Democrat*, May 26, 1926.

2. *Plattsburgh Sentinel*, March 22, 1901; *Illustrated Buffalo Express*, February 19, 1905; *Plattsburgh Republican*, November 7, 1908; George Ellsworth Johnson, *Education by Plays and Games*, passim.

3. "A Profitable Adirondack Industry," *Leslie's Weekly*, September 25, 1902, 298–99.

TUCKER, WILSON M. (1844–1910)
Active Piseco Lake and Lake Pleasant, Hamilton County, 1867–1877

Wilson Tucker, raised on a farm in Watson, Lewis County, opened a photograph gallery circa 1867 in the bustling cheese-manufacturing center of Little Falls, Herkimer County. Over the next ten years he produced more than two hundred stereoviews of Herkimer County scenery. An unusual series of twenty-six views, *Gems of the Adirondacks, Piseco and Lake Pleasant*, captured an as yet little photographed region of Hamilton County. "The waters of this locality," it was noted on the verso of a view card, "have long been deservedly popular for their supply of trout, the woodland for their game. A season spent in rambles, boating and camp life, leaves in the memory of the tourist a beautiful little chapter of the pleasures among the wilds of Piseco and Lake Pleasant."

Tucker gave up his studio around 1877 and entered the employ of the New York Central Railroad as a baggageman, eventually "in charge of many of the local baggage trains" on its Mohawk Division between Albany and Syracuse. He was with the railroad for thirty-two years, retiring in 1909. He may quietly have kept his hand in as a photographer, either as a hobbyist or an occasional operator in someone else's studio: in 1892 an exhibit was held of Tucker's landscape photographs ("equal to Jackson's famous pictures") in a Little Falls shop, while a 1908 Albany directory listed Tucker as a photographer at an Albany address, noting his home as Little Falls.[1]

1. *Little Falls Times*, September 5, 1892; "Wilson M. Tucker Dead," *Utica Observer*, September 9, 1910; "Wilson M. Tucker," *Little Falls Journal and Courier*, September 12, 1910.

UNDERWOOD, CLARENCE (1864–1935)
Active Wadhams Mills, Essex County, 1899–1903; Elizabethtown, Essex County, 1902–1935

Born in Westminster, Vermont, and raised by aunts after his parents' early death, Clarence Underwood apprenticed with photographer **Elbert M. Johnson** of Crown Point, Essex County, in the 1880s. After several years in the Midwest—working as a photographer in Chicago; marrying in St. Louis,

Missouri; and fathering two daughters, one in Illinois (1891) and the other in Kentucky (1892)—he returned to Essex County by 1899. He settled first in Wadhams Mills, a hamlet of Westport, and, after opening an Elizabethtown studio in 1902, relocated to the town in 1903. For the next thirty-two years he photographed local residents, buildings, landscapes, and events. Despite the loss of uninsured equipment and "a good many plates of small intrinsic value but irreplaceable from a historic standpoint" in a studio fire in 1932, Johnson launched a new studio above a beauty shop less than three months later. He was at the "daily work" he "loved" the day before he died of a heart attack at the age of seventy-four. The Underwood Studio was managed on behalf of his wife after her husband's death by photographer **Carl F. Huttig.**[1]

1. *Essex County Record*, December 23, 1932; *Adirondack Record–Elizabethtown Post*, March 9, 1933.

VAN AKEN, ELISHA M. (1829–1904)
Active Central and Western Adirondacks, 1859–1873

Elisha Van Aken, who in 1895 advertised himself as having followed the career of "practical photographer" since 1848, was born into a farming family in Rensselaerville, Albany County. He appeared in the 1850 US Census as a twenty-one-year-old artist in his parents' household. Relocating to Lowville, Lewis County, in 1856, he opened Van Aken's Picture Gallery in rooms above the post office. His eventual output included portraits, scenic views, and genre themes (live and stuffed animals, birds, plants). In 1871 Van Aken won a prize of thirty dollars in gold for best genre negative from *Photographer's Friend*; in 1872 a series of leaf prints with mottos was admired by the celebrated Berlin photographer Hermann Wilhelm Vogel, who exclaimed after seeing them that the forms of German "leaves are not so beautiful as those in America."[1]

In 1859 a regional newspaper conjectured that Van Aken, who photographed the region along the Beaver River from its Lake Lila source in Long Lake, Hamilton County, into Herkimer and Lewis Counties in August and September of that year, was "the first artist to take an instrument there." This speculation is likely to have been accurate. "We congratulate our friend Van Aken, upon the success of his enterprise," noted the newspaper. "The sporting world, who visit the North Woods, will recognize, in them, the scenes of their manly sports with rod and gun. We predict, for this artist, *profit*, as well as pleasure, from his pioneering." Van Aken's only known stereoview series of the region, *Views About "No. 4," John Brown's Tract, N.Y.*, may have been taken on this outing or somewhat later.[2]

Leaving Lowville in late 1873, Van Aken briefly operated a gallery in Watertown, Jefferson County, before settling circa 1876 in Elmira, Chemung County, where he was a well-known photographer for thirty years. **George W. Carter**, a former pupil, purchased his Lowville studio. Van Aken's son, Charles, followed in his father's footsteps as an Elmira photographer.[3]

1. *Elmira Telegram*, March 17, 1895; *Lewis County Banner*, September 10, 1856; *Lewis County Democrat*, September 20, 1871; "Good for Van Aken," *Lowville Journal and Republican*, January 17, 1872, quoting article from *Photographer's Friend*, January 1872; Treadwell and Darrah, *Photographers of the United States*, 708–9.
2. *Lewis County Banner*, August 24, 1859; September 7, 1859.
3. *Watertown Times*, November 29, 1875; "Fiftieth Wedding Anniversary," *Lowville Journal and Republican and Lowville Times*, November 30, 1922.

VAN SANT, FLORENCE ALLAIRE (1869–1933)
Active Jay, Essex County, 1898–1902

Florence Johnson was born in Philadelphia. Her father was a New Jersey teacher before becoming a real estate dealer in New Jersey and New York City. Married at her family's Brooklyn home in 1889 to Charles Van Sant, Florence accompanied her husband—a Methodist clergyman educated at New Jersey's Drew Theological Seminary—on his

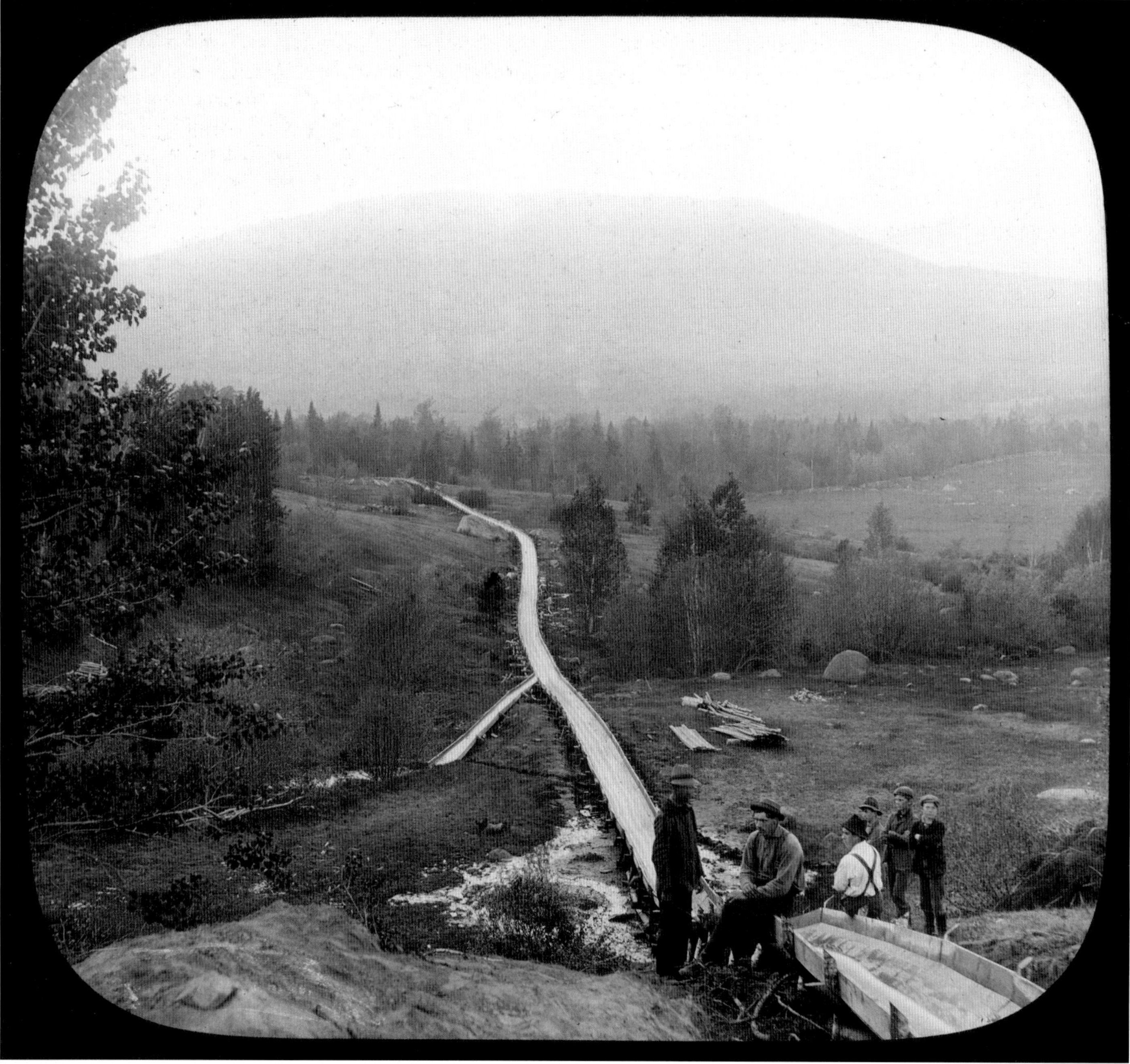

68. F. A. Van Sant, men at Rogers Company log slide, Ausable Valley. Lantern slide, 1900-1901. Courtesy of New York State Archives and New York State Education Department, Division of Visual Instruction.

1890 church assignment to Beekmantown, Clinton County. Subsequent postings took the couple to the Essex County villages of Essex in 1891 and Bloomingdale in 1894. Charles contracted tuberculosis not long after taking up his third appointment. He resigned his ministry, and in 1896 the Van Sants settled in Jay, where they lived with his chronic illness until Charles's death in 1908. During the long period of his retirement, noted an obituary in a regional Methodist publication, Florence, "whose many gifts and graces were very helpful to him during the years of his active ministry . . . struggled heroically to support herself and her husband. By teaching music, by photography, and by writing on bird and animal life she was able to keep their home together and to give him something of the comfort he had thought to afford her."[1]

Van Sant opened a Jay photographic gallery in 1898, but her most familiar images were taken in the field, primarily of nearby landscapes and the logging operations of the J. & J. Rogers Company in Au Sable Forks. She sold images to New York State for inclusion in the annual reports of its Forestry Commission and for lantern slides produced by the Education Department's Division of Public Instruction. The American Museum of Natural History purchased images from her in 1901–2 for use in magic lantern lectures. Charles Van Sant acted as his wife's assistant when well enough to do so, but, as he lost ground, Florence spent less time in the field and ceased taking pictures altogether in late 1902. She also gave up writing about local birds for the Audubon Society's magazine, *Bird-Lore*, although an early poem, "The Rev. Mr. Chickadee, D.D.," published in *Bird-Lore* in 1900, reappeared in print many times: in 1919 featured on the children's page of an issue of the *South Dakota Educator*, and in 1921 quoted in Inez McFee's *Little Friends in Feathers*. Van Sant was enumerated in the New York state census of 1905 as a music teacher; her husband died in 1908.[2]

Van Sant decamped to Westchester County following her husband's death, but returned to Jay two years after remarrying in 1913. Her second husband, Almon Henry Ward, was the son of a prominent local lumber dealer and twenty-three years younger than his bride. He was recorded as a farmer and she as a housekeeper in her own home in the 1920 US Census. Around this time the Wards developed a summer cottage colony, Heart's Desire Camps, on their dairy farm, leading the local newspaper to honor Mrs. Ward in her obituary as "one of the best known business women of Ausable Valley."[3]

1. "Vansant–Johnson," *Brooklyn Daily Eagle*, December 28, 1889; J. M. Cass, "Charles F. Van Sant," *Minutes of the Troy Annual Conference of the Methodist Episcopal Church held in Saratoga Springs, N.Y., April 15–20, 1908*, 141–42.

2. *Elizabethtown Post*, December 22, 1898; F. A. Van Sant file, 30, Albert S. Bickmore Papers, American Museum of Natural History, New York; *South Dakota Educator* 32, no. 10 (June 1919): 28; McFee, *Little Friends in Feathers*, 218.

3. Advertisement, *Brooklyn Daily Eagle*, May 15, 1921; *Adirondack Record–Elizabethtown Post*, August 20, 1931; "Florence Van Sant Ward," *Adirondack Record–Elizabethtown Post*, March 23, 1933.

VEEDER, AARON (1828–1906)
Active Ausable Chasm, Clinton and Essex Counties, 1875; Lake George Region, Pre-1881

A native of Albany, Albany County, Aaron Veeder was listed in local directories by the early 1870s as a "landscape photographer." In October 1875 it was reported that, despite "cold and rainy" weather, he was in the Adirondacks photographing Ausable Chasm, at least thirty views of which he issued in a series titled *Artistic Stereo Gems of Ausable Chasm*.[1]

Veeder's most popular landscape subject was the New York State Capitol, inaugurated in 1879. He photographed other Albany sites as well, and moved beyond the city to take pictures in Saratoga Springs, New York City, the Catskills, and along the Hudson River. He gave up landscape photography in 1881 and turned his attention to portraiture, becoming one of Albany's most celebrated portrait photographers. Actively involved, as was his wife, in the Prohibition movement, Veeder produced distinguished photographic portraits of Emma H. Willard, president of the Women's Christian Temperance Union, as well as suffragists Elizabeth Cady Stanton and Susan B. Anthony.

1. *Essex County Republican*, October 21, 1875.

WARDNER, SETH (1852–1921)
Active Bloomingdale, Essex County, Late 1870s–Mid-1880s

The son of a farmer, Seth Wardner was born in Fairfax, Vermont. He relocated before 1870 with his parents and five siblings to Wilmington, Essex

County, and was enumerated in the 1870 US Census as a farmhand. By 1877 he was in Bloomingdale, a hamlet of St. Armand, where, according to an obituary, "he was the first photographer in this section of the woods and one of the earliest guides." Wardner's stamped imprint on cabinet cards—primarily individual and group portraits—produced during the first several years after his arrival identified him as a Bloomingdale "photographer and jeweler"; he was recorded as a photographer in the 1880 US Census. Appearing in the New York state census of 1892 as a farmer, Wardner was also the proprietor of a boarding house during this decade. His Rest-A-While Cottage accommodated some twenty guests and was located one mile from Bloomingdale's railroad station.[1]

1. *Malone Farmer*, July 6, 1921; *Ticonderoga Sentinel*, July 7, 1921; Delaware and Hudson Company, *A Summer Paradise*, 1896 ed., 132. Wardner was cousin to another Seth Wardner (1823–98), an early settler of Brighton, Franklin County. The Bloomingdale Wardner was often recorded as Seth Wardner, 2nd.

WEBSTER, LOREN (1837–MID-1870S?)

Active Crown Point, Essex County, Mid-1860s; Schroon Lake, Essex County, and Johnsburg, Warren County, 1868–1873; Corinth, Saratoga County, 1873–?

Loren Webster, the son of a blacksmith, was raised in New Haven, Vermont. He appeared in Crown Point records as a photographer in 1865 and 1866, where he was assessed for taxes to support the Civil War effort. In 1870 he was an artist living in Schroon Lake and, according to a carte de visite imprint, was a portrait photographer specializing in "Ambrotypes, Ferrotypes, and Gem Pictures at the lowest rates." Another carte de visite imprint places him in Johnsburg, Warren County, at about the same time. In 1873 he opened a "photograph saloon" in Corinth, Saratoga County. Webster disappeared from local records around 1875.[1]

1. *Daily Saratogian*, October 15, 1873.

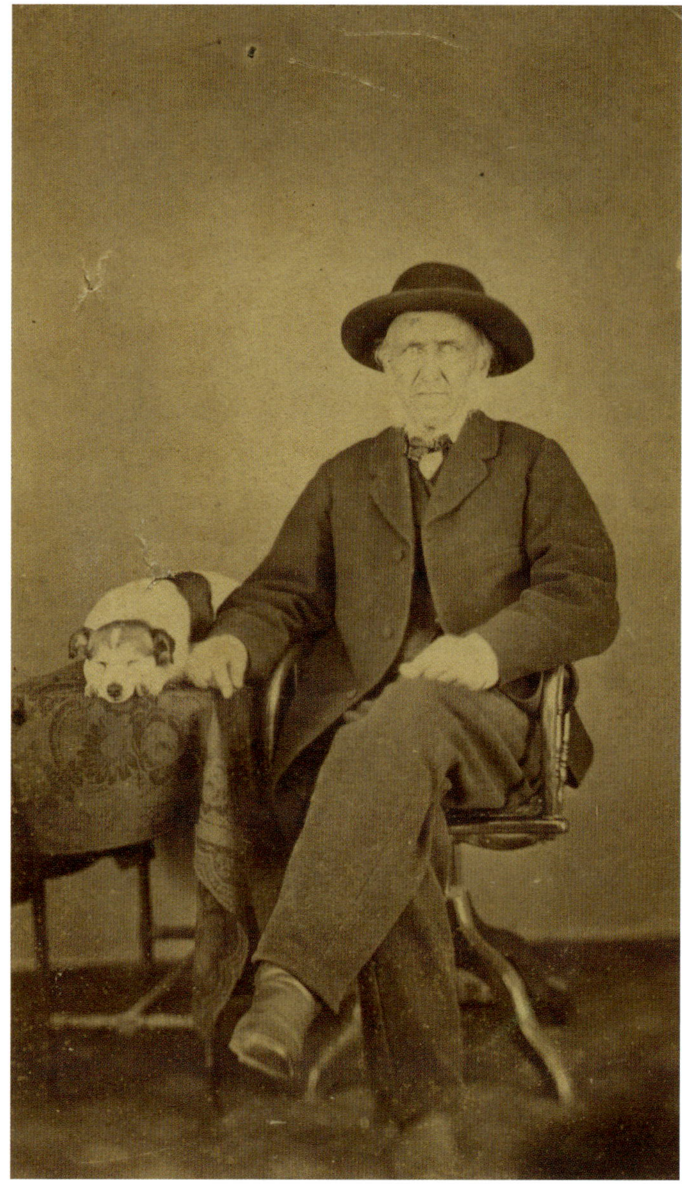

69. L. Webster, portrait, 1868–1870.

WEEDMARK, WILLIAM PORTER (1927–1999)

Active in Old Forge, Herkimer County, 1945–1980

Born in the Herkimer County town of Ilion, William Weedmark was raised after his mother's early death by his paternal grandparents in the Webb hamlet of Old Forge, where his grandfather, William H. Weedmark, was active in the Brown Tract Guides' Association. He began to take pictures before graduating as class valedictorian from the local high school in 1946, after which he opened a studio in his grandparents' home that became his lifelong base. He documented more than two hundred weddings, some of them planned around his dates of availability, and chronicled local events, large and small. He also recorded the wider region—the Fulton Chain of Lakes and Big Moose Lake—often from the air in the company of bush pilot friends. Hundreds of Weedmark's photographs are cataloged and housed at the Goodsell Museum in Old Forge.[1]

1. Masters, "Weedmark Family Legacy," 3; Peg Masters, email to the author, July 27, 2016.

WETMORE, AUGUSTUS, JR. (1832–1906)
Active in Essex and Franklin Counties, 1862–1863

Augustus (August) Wetmore was a socially well-connected New York City hobbyist. He appears in this compendium because several of his stereograph views landed in public collections, reflecting organized amateur enthusiasm associated with the early years of the medium's development.

A member of the Seventh Regiment New York State Militia, Wetmore served briefly in the Civil War. Not long after his discharge he was invited to join the Amateur Photographic Exchange Club, founded in New York City in 1861 by Henry T. Anthony (then engaged with his brother in what became the **E. and H. T. Anthony Company**). The country's first camera club, this was modeled on one established in England. The invitation list for membership was "formed from the best amateur photographers that Mr. Anthony with his means of judging could select," and was made up primarily of professional men. According to club rules, its roster could include only amateurs, to the extent of twenty (a maximum later relaxed). Each member was expected to send, on a bimonthly basis, "at least one stereoscopic print, a copy of which has not been sent before, or its equivalent mounted and finished," to every other club member. The exchange club was active through September 1863, when it disbanded, due in large part to the drafting of some of its members (including Henry Anthony) into the Civil War.[1]

Surviving Wetmore stereoviews from among those he shared with club members relate to Adirondack camping. Their titles were hand-entered on preprinted labels. Known examples number between 145 and 165 (one is dated June 2, 1863). Wetmore is also credited with a cabinet card portrait of author Mary Mapes Dodge in the collection of the Museum of the City of New York.

Wetmore held positions in a number of civic organizations in his later years. He was a member of the Board of Managers of the American Institute of the City of New York for the Encouragement of Science and Invention, as well as secretary of the Mercantile Library.

1. Sellers, "An Old Photographic Club," 339, 340, 358.

WILSON, STEWART (1844–1922)
Active Mayfield, Fulton County, 1868–1885; Northville, Fulton County, 1885–1915

Stewart Wilson spent his life in Fulton County. Of Scottish parentage, he first appeared in federal census records in 1850, the year in which his recently widowed mother won a battle for his custody in Johnstown against the boy's adult half-siblings from his father's first marriage. By 1855 Wilson was in Mayfield, where his mother was a dressmaker.

Wilson was listed as a Mayfield photographer and farmer in a Montgomery and Fulton County business directory for 1869–70. "He makes a good picture," it was reported upon his opening of a Mayfield gallery to cater to participants at a local 1873 camp meeting, "and is a very popular young man." Calling himself a "View Photographer" during the 1870s, Wilson advertised "Stereoscopic & Large Views made to order," and in January 1878 announced views of "Gloversville and Vicinity, from Burr's Hill." This may have been his "fine" series of winter scenes that received praise that month for bringing "out, in a clear and vivid manner, the beautiful frost work of the last few days of the old year."[1]

Remaining in Mayfield until the mid-1880s, Wilson took portrait and view photographs and engaged in minority politics as secretary of the state committee of the Greenback Labor Party. Mid-decade he relocated to Northville, a hamlet of Northampton, where he henceforth eked out a living as a maker of tintypes for funseekers in the bustling seasonal pleasure ground of Sacandaga Park. His home and studio during the summer months was a rude, portable hut surrounded by a fenced-in yard full of chickens. With his long beard and shabby clothing, Wilson became known as the "Sacandaga hermit." A number of winters were passed in the park's railroad station before he moved late in life to Osborne's Bridge, a Northampton hamlet two miles from the park where Wilson froze to death in an unheated cabin during the winter of 1921–22.[2]

1. *Gloversville Intelligencer*, July 31, 1873; January 10, 1878; *Johnstown Republican*, January 24, 1878.

2. *Newburgh Register*, September 22, 1886; "Hermit Freezes in Shack," *New York Times*, February 11, 1922; Decker, "'Sacandaga Hermit' Was Colorful, Often Frightening Character."

WINSLOW, ALBERT G. (1871–1936)
Active Keeseville, Clinton and Essex Counties, 1900–1910

Albert Winslow was born in Moriah, Essex County, the son of an iron miner. By 1900 he was a Keeseville photographer, specializing in portrait work, but copyrighting views of the Ausable River, the Ausable Valley, Keeseville, and Lake Champlain's Port Kent Bay in 1908. His occupation was listed in New York state and federal census records as forest ranger in 1920 and fire ranger in 1925 and 1930.

WOOD, GEORGE BACON, JR. (1832–1909)
Active Elizabethtown, Essex County, 1882–Mid-1890s

George Wood was a comfortably well-to-do Philadelphia landscape and genre painter of modest reputation. The third of ten children born in Philadelphia to Quaker parents, he studied at the Philadelphia Academy of Fine Arts despite his family's religious attitudes (among them an aversion to art), and worked as a painter for nearly thirty years. He exhibited his first canvas at the Pennsylvania Academy in 1858, his last in 1887. In 1867 he painted the first of many landscapes in the Adirondacks, where he and his family had begun spending summers around Elizabethtown and where Wood, "taking a guide with him . . . would sometimes be gone for several days . . . cutting and marking trails" in the mountains. The family passed the occasional winter in Elizabethtown in the early 1870s, where Wood's seventh and last child was born in November 1873.[1]

In 1882 Wood transferred his primary interest to photography. "He made a name for himself from the very start," noted a contemporary journalist, and in 1884 won four prizes at a Boston Society of Amateur Photographers' exhibition. His subjects remained the same as those in his old medium: landscapes and genre scenes of animals and children, often his own. His Adirondack stamping ground was Essex County, where Wood photographed around Elizabethtown and Beede's Hotel in Keene Heights, later known as St. Hubert's and the site of the Ausable Club. As the local newspaper recorded in 1886, Wood, "a former resident of this place, and an Artist well known among landscape painters, is visiting our village for a few days, making sketches and taking photographic views of many beautiful places in the Adirondack Mountains." Nearly twenty years later he was still making brief visits to Elizabethtown. As reported in 1903, Wood, "to-day world-famed as a photographer," is "again sojourning among us, making headquarters at the Windsor [Hotel]."[2]

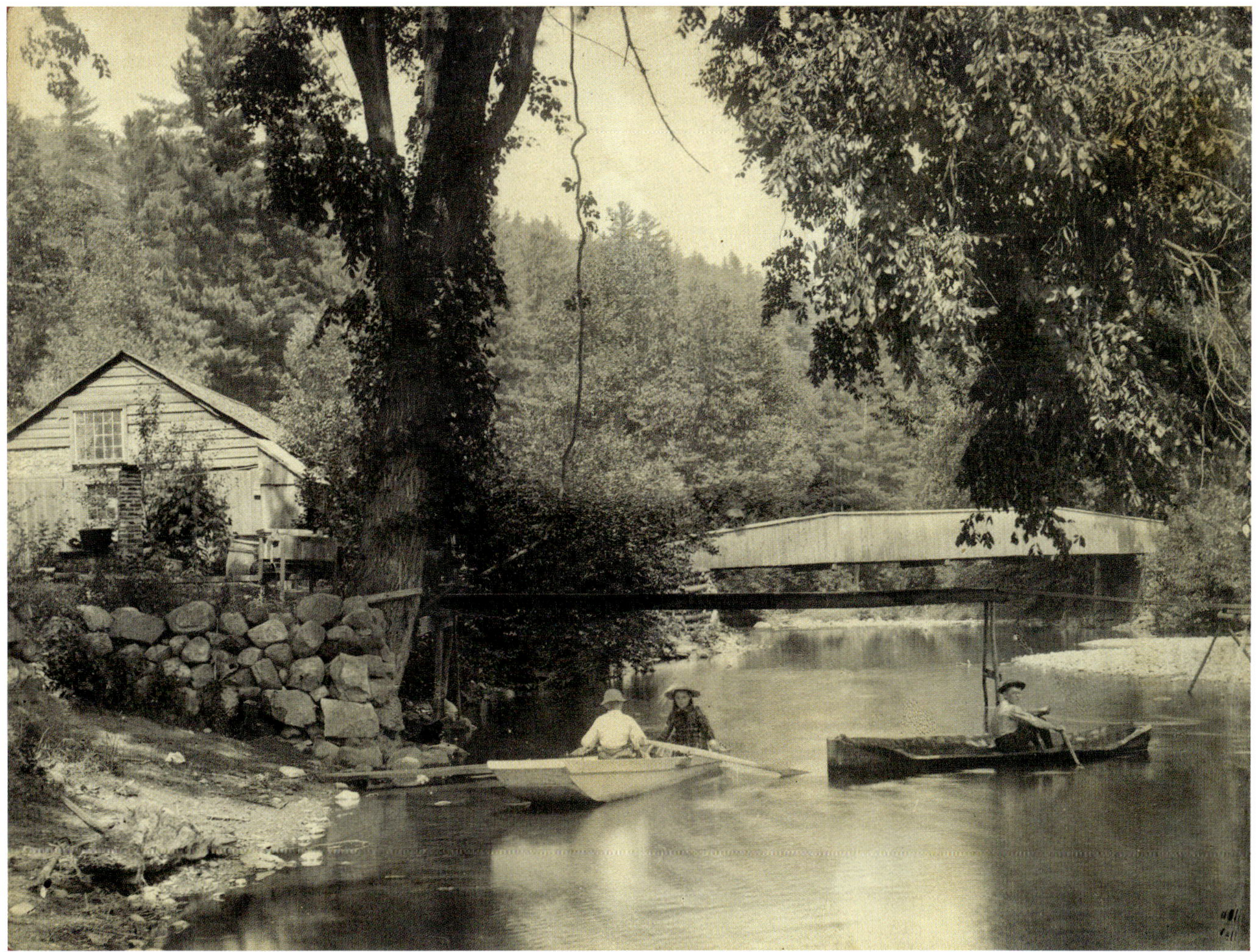

70. G. B. Wood Jr., The Boquet River, 1882–early 1890s. Courtesy of the Library Company of Philadelphia.

Wood continued to win competitive awards for his often lyrical photographic work—in London and Vienna (where he was awarded a "grand diploma" at the Vienna Salon in 1891) as well as in the United States. The last major show in which he participated was an 1893 juried event sponsored by the Photographic Society of Philadelphia and termed by **Alfred Stieglitz** "the finest exhibition of photographs ever seen in the United States." Wood took occasional photographs thereafter, but, for the most part, retired to "enjoy a life of comparative ease."[3]

1. Hoopes, "George B. Wood, Jr.," 120, 125; Coffin, *A Girl's Life in Germantown*, 1; *The New Path: Ruskin and the American Pre-Raphaelites*, 280.

2. Coffin, *A Girl's Life*, 7, 11, 12; Moore, "Leading Amateurs," 427; *Elizabethtown Post*, September 30, 1886; August 20, 1903.

3. Moore, "Leading Amateurs," 427; Finkel, *Philadelphia Revisions*, 41, 43; Hoopes, "George B. Wood, Jr.," 125.

WOODBURY, GEORGE F. (1861–1928)
Active Elizabethtown, Essex County, 1904–1908; Glens Falls, 1905–1909

An evangelistic Baptist clergyman born into a farming family in Bridgewater, Oneida County, the Colgate University- and Rochester Theological Seminary–educated George Woodbury became the Adirondacks' first and only Baptist "colporter missionary" in 1904. His position, financed by the American Baptist Publication Society and the New York State Baptist Convention, entailed preaching throughout the eastern Adirondacks both as an itinerant and in settled churches, attracting converts when he could. Woodbury was also charged with the selling of primarily denominational books and tracts. Based in Elizabethtown and then in Glens Falls (where he also served as pastor of the South Glens Falls Baptist church), Woodbury calculated in late 1909 that he had covered 21,167 miles by horse-drawn conveyance in the previous five years. He took nearly 700 photographs on his rounds, perhaps 150 of which were made into stereopticon slides for magic lantern lectures about his colporter work. These were presented some two hundred times to local audiences and at Baptist meetings in Philadelphia; Providence, Rhode Island; Dayton, Ohio; and elsewhere. He published a number of his photographs in an *Adirondack Colporter Missionary Series* of real photo postcards. In 1910 Woodbury left the Adirondacks for a family farm in Unadilla, Otsego County. He died in Clifton Springs, Ontario County.[1]

1. Woodbury, "How the Adirondack Colporter Missionary Does His Work"; Svenson, "Past Lives: Solitary Man," 16–17.

WOODWARD, CHARLES WARREN (1836–1894)
Active Rochester, Monroe County, 1873–1882

Charles Woodward was not a photographer, but a prolific publisher and distributor of stereographs, including Adirondack views, most of them pirated. The son of an Orange, Massachusetts, carpenter, he settled in Rochester in 1862 and launched a business selling picture frames. From its earliest days, the company offered a selection of paintings, engravings, and photographs for sale—items that might encourage the purchase of frames. In 1873 his State Street shop advertised "our own publications in stereoscopic views"; in 1876 it offered a worldwide selection of "views from 4,000 different Negatives," including images of "Hudson River and Lake George." The company floundered circa 1879; by early 1882 Woodward was selling views from his home address.[1]

In late 1882 Woodward became a partner in Rochester's reconstituted Union View Company, which from 1879 had sent photographic agents into communities to photograph residences, subsequently soliciting their owners to purchase the images. Woodward transferred some or all of his stereoscopic offerings to Union View. The company closed in 1883; later firm names with which Woodward was associated were Woodward & Albee and the Woodward Stereoscopic Company. An 1892 Rochester directory listed Woodward as a "travelling salesman."[2]

1. Fordyce, *Stereo Photography in Rochester*, 18–19; *Rochester Evening Express*, January 22, 1863; December 8, 1876; *Rochester Democrat and Chronicle*, September 1, 1873;

2. Fordyce, *Stereo Photography in Rochester*, 15, 17–18; *Oswego Daily Palladium*, July 5, 1880.

WOODWARD, GEORGE T. (1863–1919)
Active Plattsburgh, Clinton County, 1891–1909

Born in Ohio, George Woodward was a photographer in Columbus and Cincinnati before relocating to Plattsburgh circa 1891. The impetus for his arrival may have been the 1890 opening of the seasonal Hotel Champlain, for which he was reported in 1909 to have been the "official photographer . . . since it was built." His entry in Plattsburgh's 1892 directory advertised "Fine Photographs, Frames, Etchings, Engravings and Art Goods." Woodward maintained a summer studio in Plattsburgh's Cliff Haven, site of a Catholic summer school, and in 1906 offered sittings one day a week in leased space in Au Sable Forks.[1]

Woodward was primarily but not exclusively a portrait photographer. He immediately notified the public when one of his portraits was used in a

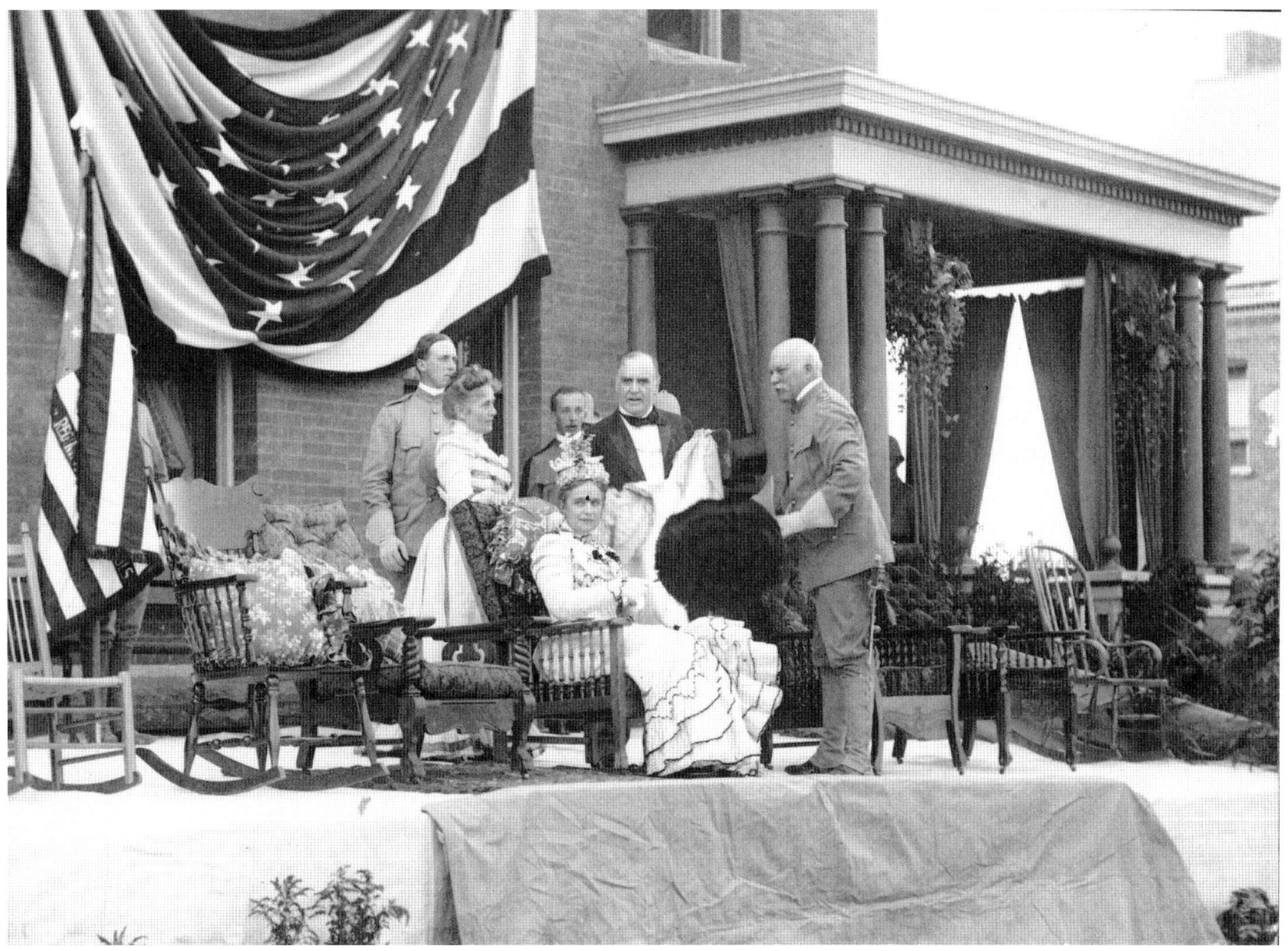

71. G. T. Woodward, President McKinley reviews the Twenty-Sixth Regiment, US Infantry, at Plattsburgh Barracks, August 1899. Courtesy of Library of Congress, LC-USZ62-100076.

major metropolitan paper in connection, perhaps, with an engagement announcement. He took pride in photographing three US presidents—McKinley, Roosevelt, and Taft—all of whom were guests at the Hotel Champlain and/or reviewed troops at Plattsburgh's army barracks. He was active outside of his profession in amateur theater as both an actor and director and was the drum major of the Plattsburgh City Band.[2]

In 1907 Woodward began spending winters in Jacksonville, Florida. In 1909 he expanded the small studio he had launched there, and in 1910 and 1911 was elected president of the Professional Photographers' Association of Florida. In 1912 he sold his Plattsburgh studio to **Daniel S. Brush**, an employee from 1904.[3]

1. *Plattsburgh Daily Press*, September 18, 1899; "Has Fine New Studio," *Plattsburgh Daily Press*, December 4, 1909, quoting *Jacksonville (FL) Times-Union*; *Elizabethtown Post*, April 12, 1906.

2. *Plattsburgh Sentinel*, August 30, 1901; *Plattsburgh Daily Press*, May 5, 1904; February 14, 1907; "Has Fine New Studio," *Plattsburgh Daily Press*, December 4, 1909.

3. *Elizabethtown Post*, May 9, 1912.

WOOLEY, JESSE SUMNER (1867–1943)
Active Lake George Region, 1887–1935;
Speculator, Hamilton County, 1921–1929

Jesse Wooley was born in Wilton, Saratoga County. In 1879 his farmer father moved his family to The Geysers, a settlement in Saratoga Springs, eventually becoming an oil dealer. The son centered his adult life in the village of Ballston Spa, some four miles south of The Geysers and the seat of Saratoga County government.

In 1880, at the age of thirteen, Wooley took a summer job as an errand boy for the Saratoga photographers Baker & Record. In 1881 he left school to work at the studio full time, became its assistant printer in 1883, and in 1885 relocated to Ballston Spa as printer for portrait and stereoview photographer T. J. Arnold. In 1887 Wooley purchased Arnold's third-floor business in a commercial building with borrowed money and set up on his own with specialties in "Portraits and Views."[1]

Wooley emulated in some respects the career path of photographer, writer, lecturer, and entrepreneur Seneca Ray Stoddard of Glens Falls, twenty-four years his senior and, like Wooley, born in Wilton. In 1893 Wooley began to travel occasionally with Stoddard as assistant, mentee, and enthusiastic photographic companion. His official assignment on most trips was to "manage the lantern" during Stoddard's illustrated lectures: in the Adirondacks (in 1893 and 1894); in winter resorts of Florida (1902); in Norfolk and Richmond, Virginia (1906). Wooley gave magic lantern lectures himself on vacation destinations from a combination of his own and purchased slides, the earliest of these in Ballston Spa in 1893. He traveled

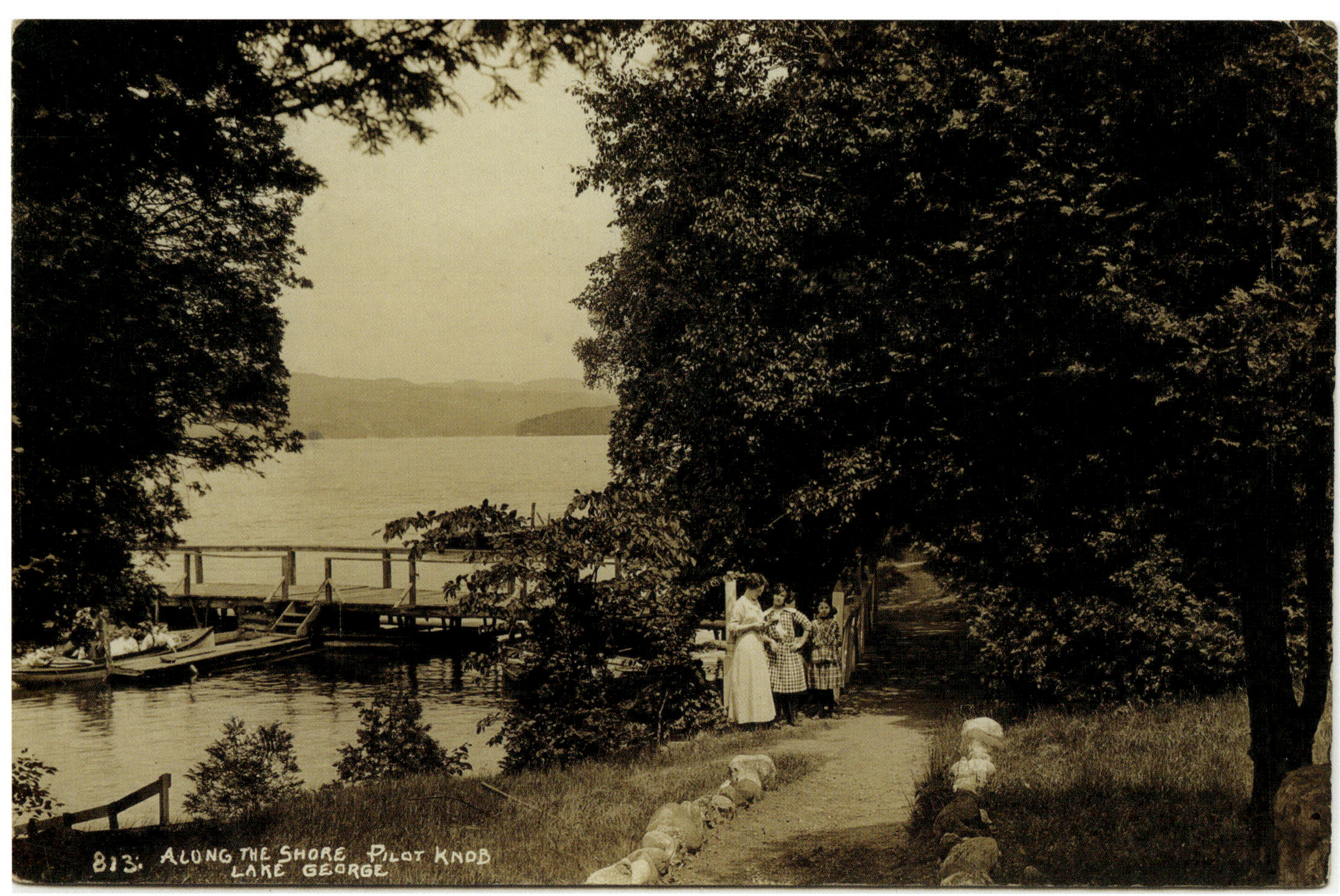

72. J. S. Wooley, *Along the Shore, Lake George, Pilot Knob.* RPPC, 1907–1920.

constantly during the following decade: to Florida, the West, and Europe. Each expedition provided new photographic subjects for his frequent lectures (and often a sizeable audience for the photographs he took among the organized groups that toured with him). Wooley's lecture circuit, unlike Stoddard's, was confined largely to nearby New York State communities and Florida, where he and his wife began spending part of their winters from the early 1920s. Lectures bore such titles as "A Summer Tour through the Adirondack Mountains and Lakes," "The Historic Hudson," "From Ice and Snow to Flowers and Fruit" (on Florida), "California and the Yellowstone," and "A Trip to Europe."[2]

Stoddard had established a steady income stream in supplying tourist venues with stereographs and single prints of various sizes. Wooley, while providing the same venues with a range of photographic images, offered the modern equivalent of stereoviews for tourist consumption: real photo postcards. In 1907 he secured contracts to supply souvenir postcards to Lake George steamboat companies and the Forest and Rensselaer amusement parks in Ballston and Troy, Rensselaer County. In 1908 he obtained a remunerative concession: taking photographs and selling photos and postcards at the Silver Bay Association, a WMCA-sponsored summer conference and family retreat center in Hague, Warren County. Details of his contract with Silver Bay are unknown, but may have been similar to those negotiated but not consummated between Silver Bay and photographer **Chester D. Moses** in 1906. The relationship ended in 1923. Wooley served as "official photographer for railroad and steamboat lines" on an extended trip through eastern Canada in 1914, made a two-week photographic tour through New York State on behalf of New York City's Valentine Postal Card Company in 1916, undertook assignments to photograph Lake George children's camps, and from 1921 through 1929 handled photography at Camp of the Woods, a Christian family camp in Lake Pleasant, Hamilton County, launched in 1914 by George Tibbitts, a founder of Silver Bay.[3]

Wooley regularly added new services and goods to his studio operation. He became an Eastman Kodak agent in 1895, took on developing and finishing work for amateurs, and increased stock to include frames, artist-illustrated postcards, stationery, Victrolas, records, art prints, and gift books. In 1915 he left the field of studio-based photography, selling his business to Howard L. Humes, an employee from 1903 who, as an operator, had "produced some really meritorious pictures" under Wooley's name. He hung on, however, to the store that he referred to as his "Art Shop" or "Little Gift Shop." In 1924 Wooley retired from retailing as well, handing his store over to his son while retaining and expanding his wholesale view business. He is known today for the several thousand images he left behind, including many panoramas, most of them of Lake George's scenic vistas, buildings, and summer life.[4]

1. Bogdan, *Exposing the Wilderness*, 169; Terrie, "Jessie S. Wooley," in Timberlake and Terrie, *J. S. Wooley, Adirondack Photographer*, 18; *Ballston Spa Journal*, September 27, 1924.

2. Terrie, "Jessie S. Wooley," in Timberlake and Terrie, *J. S. Wooley, Adirondack Photographer*, 27–28, 31–34; *Saratogian*, March 19, 1890; July 28, 1893; *Glens Falls Times*, June 18, 1894; February 28, 1906; *Troy Times*, March 1 1902; November 21, 1908.

3. *Saratogian*, July 20, 1907; May 23, 1908; September 17, 1910; *Troy Times*, September 15, 1914, *Schenectady Gazette*, August 20, 1921; *Ballston Spa Journal*, June 5, 1916; July 18, 1929; Bogdan, *Exposing the Wilderness*, 166.

4. *Saratogian*, August 29, 1906; *Ballston Spa Journal*, November 4, 1913; November 18, 1913; "Thirty Years of Business Life," August 7, 1915; September 3, 1915; December 12, 1916; August 5, 1920; "Father Retires Son Takes Hold," January 19, 1924; "Museum Adds to Wooley Exhibit," February 8, 1978.

YATES, ARTHUR P. (1841–1924)

Active along Adirondack Route of the New York Central and Hudson River Railroad, 1893–1907

Arthur Yates was born in Schenectady, Schenectady County, the son of a cabinetmaker. In 1861 he joined the Syracuse-based motor power department of the New York Central and Hudson River Railroad as a mechanical draftsman and remained with the line for nearly fifty years. He began taking railroad-related photographs in 1888. His most famous photograph, from 1891, was of the *Empire State Express* (a named passenger train and one-time flagship of the railroad) as it hurtled along at the speed of sixty miles an hour. This image was exhibited in 1893 at the World's Columbian Exposition in Chicago as a 5 x 8 foot enlargement (then called the largest photograph in the world) and served as the pictorial basis for a two-cent US postage stamp issued in 1901.[1]

Yates became the New York Central and Hudson River Railroad's first official photographer in 1893 and made a number of picture-taking forays into the Adirondacks on its behalf. Images from a trip taken in 1895 were used in the 1896 issue of *Health and Pleasure On "America's Greatest Railroad,"* a booklet marketing summer resorts accessible by the line. Unattributed work appeared in many other pre-1908 pamphlets, brochures, and booklets produced by the railroad. Yates retired in 1910, four years before the line was re-formed as part of the expanded New York Central Railroad.

1. Beauchamp, *Past and Present of Syracuse and Onondaga County*, 290–91; "Railroad Photography," *New York Railroad Men* 9, no. 5 (February 1896): 106–7.

Bibliography ❧ *Index*

Bibliography

Material readily available online (census data, city and town directories, military records, etc.) is not referenced in notes or in the bibliography.

Aber, Ted, and Stella King. *History of Hamilton County*. Lake Pleasant, NY: Great Wilderness Books, 1965.

"The Adirondack Mountains." *Harper's Weekly*, August 31, 1867, 548.

Adirondack Lifestyles, Vol. 1. n.p.: TEACH Services, 2008.

Adler, Jeanne Winston. *Early Days in the Adirondacks: The Photographs of Seneca Ray Stoddard*. New York: Harry N. Abrams, 1997.

Aircraft Year Book. Boston: Small, Maynard & Co., 1921.

Albrecht, Donald. *The Mythic City: Photographs of New York by Samuel H. Gottscho, 1925–1940*. New York: Museum of the City of New York and Princeton Architectural Press, 2005.

Alletag, Alfred. Employee File, 1949–1973. New York Foundation Records, Manuscript and Archives Division, New York Public Library.

Andrews, Ralph W. *Photographers of the Frontier West*. Seattle: Superior Publishing Company, 1965.

Averill, H. K., Jr. *A New Geography and History of Clinton County*. 2nd ed. Plattsburgh, NY: Telegram Printing House, 1885.

Bailey, Roger. "Dwight Church: The Flying Photographer and His Real Photo Postcards." *St. Lawrence County Historical Association Quarterly* 53, no. 4 (2008): 4–39.

Bassett, Samuel Clay. *Buffalo County, Nebraska and Its People: A Record of Settlement, Organization, Progress and Achievement*. Chicago: S. J. Clarke, 1916.

Bauer, Guenther. "George W. Baldwin, Adirondack Photographer." *Antiquarian*, Clinton County Historical Association (1999): 8–16.

———. "George. W. Baldwin's 'Gems of the Adirondacks.'" *Stereo World* 29, no. 4 (2002–3): 22–32, 37.

———. *The Stereoviews of George W. Baldwin, Keeseville, New York*. National Stereoscopic Association, View List Series no. 39, March 2007.

Bauer, Lois, and Guenther Bauer. "Seneca Ray Stoddard—Preserving the Adirondacks in Stereos and in Person." *Stereo World* 23, no. 2 (May/June 1996): 4–13.

Bayle, Bob. *An Adirondack Portfolio, 1902–1935: The Hiking Stories and Photographs of Francis Bayle*. Queensbury, NY: Published by the author, 2016.

Beauchamp, William M. *Past and Present of Syracuse and Onondaga from Prehistoric Times to the Beginning of 1908*. Vol. 2. New York: S. J. Clarke, 1908.

Beetle, David H. "Press Parade." *Utica Press*, June 22, 1936.

———. *Up Old Forge Way*. Utica, NY: *Utica Observer-Dispatch*, 1948.

———. *West Canada Creek*. Utica, NY: *Utica Observer-Dispatch*, 1946.

Bickmore, Albert S. Papers, 1854–1914. Special Collections, American Museum of Natural History Library, New York.

Bischof, Libby, Susan Danly, and Earle G. Shettleworth Jr. *Maine Photography: A History 1840–1915*. Portland: Maine Historical Society, 2016.

Bierstadt, Edward. *The Adirondacks: Artotype Views in the North Woods*. New York: Bierstadt, 1889.

Biographical Souvenir of the Counties of Buffalo, Kearney and Phelps, Nebraska. Chicago: F. A. Battey, 1890.

Bishop, Bainbridge. *A Souvenir of the Color Organ, with Some Suggestions in Regard to the Soul of the Rainbow and the Harmony of Light*. New Russia, NY: Published by the author, 1893.

Bjornland, Karen. "Rare Photos Reveal the Private Gardens of the Pruyn Family." *Schenectady Gazette*, July 8, 2008.

Bogdan, Robert. *Adirondack Vernacular: The Photography of Henry M. Beach*. Syracuse, NY: Syracuse Univ. Press, 2003.

———. *Exposing the Wilderness: Early Twentieth-Century Adirondack Postcard Photographers*. Syracuse, NY: Syracuse Univ. Press, 1999.

Bogdan, Robert, and Todd Weseloh. *Real Photo Postcard Guide: The People's Photography*. Syracuse, NY: Syracuse Univ. Press, 2006.

Bourke-White, Margaret. *Portrait of Myself*. New York: Simon & Schuster, 1963.

Bremer, Fredrika. *Homes of the New World; Impressions of America*. New York: Harper and Brothers, 1853.

Brown, Ellen Apperson. "ADK's Dramatic Beginning," *Adirondac*, January/February 2015, 28–31.

Brown, George Levi. *Pleasant Valley: A History of Elizabethtown, Essex County, New York*. Elizabethtown, NY: Post and Gazette Print, 1905.

Bruno, H. A. "A Job for One in a Million: Why Only a Few Men Can Photograph Cities, Chart Forests, Explore Jungles from Aircraft." *Popular Science*, April 1927, 11–13, 104.

Burdick, Neal, "A Wing and a Prayer." *Adirondack Life*, July/August, 1992, 52–57.

"Burr McIntosh, Class of 1884, and the *Burr McIntosh Monthly*." *Graphic Arts Collection* (blog), January 21, 2017. https://graphicarts.princeton.edu/2017/01/21/burr-mcintosh-monthly/.

California State Railroad Museum. "Beyond Shades of Gray: The Philip R. Hastings, M.D. Photograph Collection." *On Track* 6, no. 1 (Winter 1997): 1, 3.

Camera Sketches of Sacandaga Park. Gloversville, NY: Passenger Department, Fonda, Johnstown and Gloversville Railroad Company, 1904.

Campbell, Catherine H. "Albert Bierstadt and the White Mountains." *Archives of American Art Journal* 21, no. 3 (1981): 14–23.

"Campbell Mellis Douglas." *Canadian Encyclopedia*, http://www.thecanadianencyclopedia.ca/en/article/campbell-mellis-douglas.

Canup, Claude Richard. *War Is Not Just for Heroes*. Columbia: Univ. of South Carolina Press, 2012.

Carpenter, Warwick Stevens. "The Fine Art of Printing," Part 4 of "Saving All Parts of the Picture." *Outing*, May 1915, 151–61.

———. *The Summer Paradise in History: A Compilation of Fact and Tradition, Covering Lake George, Lake Champlain, the Adirondack Mountains, and Other Sections Reached by the Rail and Steamer Lines of the Delaware and Hudson Company*. Albany, NY: General Passenger Department, Delaware and Hudson, 1914.

———. *Winter Camping*. New York: Outing Publishing, 1913.

Child, Hamilton. *Gazetteer of Orange County, Vermont, 1762–1888*. Part 1. Syracuse, NY: Syracuse Journal Co., 1888.

Clark, Gary W. *19th Century Card Photos Kwik-Guide: A Step-by-Step Guide to Identifying and Dating Cartes de Visite and Cabinet Cards*. PhotoTree.com, 2013.

Coffin, Elizabeth W. *A Girl's Life in Germantown*. Boston: Sherman, French, 1916.

Cole, Robert M. "A History of Photography." *Hague Chronicle* 6, no. 7 (July 1977): 1–3.

Colvin, Verplanck. "The Helderbergs." *Harper's New Monthly Magazine*, October 1869, 652–67.

Cone, Andrew, and Walter R. Johns, *Petrolia: A Brief History of the Pennsylvania Petroleum Region, Its Development, Growth, Resources, Etc., from 1850 to 1869*. New York: D. Appleton, 1870.

Craig's Daguerreian Registry. http://craigcamera.com/dag/.

Crane, Galen. "The Dean of Photography." *Adirondack Life*, September/October 1997, 10–12, 15–16.

Crowley, William. *Seneca Ray Stoddard: Adirondack Illustrator*. Blue Mountain Lake, NY: Adirondack Museum, 1982.

Curtis, Gates. *Our County and Its People: A Memorial Record of St. Lawrence County, New York*. Syracuse, NY: D. Mason, 1894.

Darrah, William C. *Cartes de Visite in Nineteenth Century Photography*. Gettysburg, PA: Published by the author, 1981.

———. *The World of Stereographs*. Gettysburg, PA: Published by the author, 1977.

Davis, Keith F. *The Origins of American Photography, 1839–1885: From Daguerreotype to Dry-Plate*.

Kansas City, MO: Nelson-Atkins Museum of Art, 2007.

Decker, Lewis G. "'Sacandaga Hermit' Was Colorful, Often Frightening Character." *Gloversville Leader-Herald* (Gloversville, NY), October 2, 1970.

DeCosta, Benjamin Franklin. *Lake George: Its Scenes and Characteristics, with Glimpses of the Olden Times.* New York: Anson D. F. Randolph, 1868.

DeDe, Cathy. "He's the 'Dean' of GF Photographers." *Enterprise*, magazine of the *Glens Falls Chronicle*, 2001.

Delaware and Hudson Company. *A Summer Paradise: "The D & H," Manual of Excursion Fares, Hotels and Boarding Houses.* Albany, NY: Passenger Department, Delaware and Hudson. Title varies. Published annually from circa 1896–1930.

Denenberg, Thomas Andrew. *Wallace Nutting and the Invention of Old America.* New Haven, CT: Yale Univ. Press and Wadsworth Atheneum Museum of Art, 2003.

"Derricks of Triumph Hill." American Oil & Gas Historical Society, July 3, 2015. https://aoghs.org/oil-almanac/triumph-hill-oil.

DeSormo, Maitland C. *Heydays of the Adirondacks.* Saranac Lake, NY: Adirondack Yesteryears, 1974.

———. *Summers on the Saranacs.* Saranac Lake, NY: Adirondack Yesteryears, 1980.

Detroit Photographic Company. "Negative Registers." William Henry Jackson Collection, Mss. 341, 341-1, Box 1, History Colorado, Denver.

DiLaura, Mark A. "Niagara Falls." *Stereo World* 17, no. 4 (September/October 1990): 4–23.

Dilley, Butler F. *Biographical and Portrait Cyclopedia of Chautauqua County.* Philadelphia: John M. Gresham, 1891.

Donaldson, Alfred A. *Songs of My Violin.* New York: G. P. Putnam's Sons, 1901.

Doty, Robert. *Photo-Secession: Stieglitz and the Fine-Art Movement in Photography.* New York: Dover, 1960, 1978.

"Editor's Table: The 'Daguerreotype.'" *Knickerbocker*, December 1839, 560.

Edsall, Barbara. *Handbook of Fitchburg Photographers, A Biographical Guide, 1845–1945.* Hollis, NH: Hollis Publishers, 2012.

Ensworth, Bob. "Camera on the Ice." *Popular Photography*, March 1951, 38–41, 87–88, 90.

Fifty-Sixth Annual Catalogue of the Baltimore College of Dental Surgery. Baltimore: Baltimore College of Dental Surgery, 1895.

Finkel, Kenneth. *Philadelphia Revisions, The Print Department Collects.* Philadelphia: Library Company of Philadelphia, 1983.

Finn, Edna. "Behind the Lens: A Tribute to SL Photographers." *Adirondack Enterprise Weekender*, January 7, 1995.

Flynn, Andy. "North Country at Work: Grover Cleveland Captured the Early Days of Lake Placid Tourism in Photographs." North Country Public Radio, November 1, 2021.

Folwell, Elizabeth. "Itsuzo Sumy: Historian with a Camera." *Adirondack Life*, September/October 1996, 60–64.

———. "Straight Shooter." *Adirondack Life*, July/August 1993, 42–47.

———. "Wish You Were Here: Hand-Tinted Memories from Standard Supply." *Adirondack Life*, November/December 1989, 60–63.

Fordyce, Robert Penn. *Stereo Photography in Rochester, New York up to 1900.* Rochester, NY: Published by the author, 1975.

Foster, Jeanne Robert. *Adirondack Portraits: A Piece of Time.* Edited by Noel Riedinger-Johnson. Syracuse, NY: Syracuse Univ. Press, 1986.

Foster, Maximilian. "America's Playground in the Adirondacks." *Puritan*, October 1900, 81–95.

"Frank M. Taft Retires." *Bulletin of Photography*, June 24, 1914, 788.

French, Tom. "History of the Adirondacks in 3-D." *Watertown Times*, July 14, 2013.

Frothingham, Washington. *History of Fulton County.* Syracuse, NY: D. Mason, 1892.

Fuller, John. "Seneca Stoddard and Alfred Stieglitz: The Lake George Connection." *History of Photography* 19, no. 2 (Summer 1995): 150–58.

Fynmore, Jim. *The Central Adirondacks: A Picture Story.* Prospect, NY: Prospect Books, 1955.

Gagel, Diane Van Skiver. *Directory of Photographers in the United States 1888 & 1889 and Canada 1889.* Bowie, MD: Heritage Books, 2002.

Gallos, Philip L. *Cure Cottages of Saranac Lake: Architecture and History of a Pioneer Health Resort.* Saranac Lake, NY: Historic Saranac Lake, 1985.

Gibson, H. Louis. *Biological Photographic Association, Its Half Century.* n.p.: The Association, 1981.

Gillies, John Wallace. *Principles of Pictorial Photography.* 1923. Reprint, New York, Arno Press, 1973.

Glaberson, William. "50 Years of Wishing You Were Here." *New York Times*, March 2, 1996.

Goodyear, Frank H., III. "Constructing a National Landscape: Photography and Tourism in Nineteenth-Century America." PhD diss., Univ. of Texas at Austin, 1998.

Gottscho, Samuel. *Wildflowers: How to Identify and Enjoy Them.* New York: Pocket Books, 1951.

Gover, C. Jane. *The Positive Image: Women Photographers in Turn of the Century America.* Albany: State Univ. of New York Press, 1988.

Grady, Joseph F. *The Adirondacks: Fulton Chain-Big Moose Region: The Story of a Wilderness.* Little Falls, NY: Press of the Journal and Courier Company, 1933.

Gray, Carol Begley, Michael Ivankovich, and John Peters. *The Hand-Painted Photographs of Charles Henry Sawyer.* Detroit: Treasure Press, 2002.

Greene, Nelson, ed. *History of the Mohawk Valley: Gateway to the West 1614–1925.* Vol. 3. Chicago: S. J. Clarke, 1925.

Guide to the Fulton Chain of Lakes, Including Big Moose Lake. Boonville, NY: Willard Press, ca. 1910.

Hadden, Jean. "From Our Fields." *Warrensburg–Lake George News* (Warrensburg, NY), November 26, 1986.

Hales, Peter B. *William Henry Jackson and the Transformation of the American Landscape.* Philadelphia: Temple Univ. Press, 1988.

Haley, Althea. "Here and There: Schroon Lake." *Ticonderoga Sentinel*, July 3, 1952.

Hall, Henry. *America's Successful Men of Affairs: An Encyclopedia of Contemporaneous Biography.* Vol. 1. New York: *New York Tribune*, 1895.

Hardin, George A. *History of Herkimer County.* Syracuse, NY: D. Mason, 1893.

Harding, R. Brewster. *Roadside New England, 1900–1955: A Photographic Postcard Record of the Eastern Illustrating & Publishing Company of Belfast, Maine.* Portland, ME: Old Port Publishing, 1982.

Hastings, John T. "From the Sheep to the Man." *Warrensburgh Historical Association Quarterly* 17, no. 1 (Spring 2012): 1, 3–5.

Hatch, Vernelle A. *Illustrated History of Bradford, McKean County, Pennsylvania.* Bradford, PA: Burk Brothers, 1901.

Heiner, Albert P. *Henry J. Kaiser, Western Colossus: An Insider's View.* San Francisco: Halo Books, 1991.

Hines, Richard, Jr. "Women in Photography." *Wilson's Photographic Magazine*, March 1899, 137–41.

Holden, A. W. *History of the Town of Queensbury in the State of New York, with Biographical Sketches of Many of Its Distinguished Men.* Albany, NY: Joel Munsell, 1874.

Hoopes, Donelson F. "George B. Wood, Jr.: A Student of Nature." *American Art and Antiques*, September/October 1979, 118–25.

Horrell, Jeffrey L. *Seneca Ray Stoddard: Transforming the Adirondack Wilderness in Text and Image.* Syracuse, NY: Syracuse Univ. Press, 1999.

Hoy, Ralph L. *Heritage of the Adirondacks: Frosty Peaks—Warm Hearts.* Edited by Joanne H. O'Roark. Santa Barbara, CA: Mendicus Press, 1979.

Hudson, Henrietta. "The Direct Color Printer." In *Careers for Women*, edited by Catherine Filene, 60–63. Boston: Houghton Mifflin, 1920.

"The Hudson River." *Life*, October 2, 1939, 57–65.

Hungerford, Edward. "Our Summer Migration: A Social Study." *Century*, August 1891, 569–76.

Industries and Wealth of the Principal Points in Vermont. New York: American Publishing and Engraving, 1891.

International Center of Photography. *Reflections in a Glass Eye: Works from the International Center of Photography Collection.* New York: Bulfinch Press in association with the International Center of Photography, 1999.

Ivankovich, Michael. "Guide to Wallace Nutting-Like Photographers of the Early 20th Century." February 1, 2010, Ezine articles, http://ezinearticles.com/?Hand-Colored-Photographs-by-Wallace-Nutting-Like-Photographers&id=3677080.

Jackson, William Henry. "Field Work." *Philadelphia Photographer*, March 1, 1875, 91–93.

———. *Time Exposure*. New York: G. P. Putnam's, 1940.

"Jesse Sumner Wooley." http://scholar.library.miami.edu/wooley.

Johnson, George Ellsworth. *Education by Plays and Games*. Boston: Ginn, 1907.

Johnston, Frances Benjamin. "What a Woman Can Do with a Camera." *Ladies' Home Journal*, September 1897, 8–9.

Jones, Harry C. *Camera Mosaics: A Portrait of National Photography*. Parts 1 and 2. New York: Harry C. Jones, 1894.

Journal of the One Hundred and Fifteenth Convention of the Diocese of New York. New York: The Convention, 1898.

Journal of the Senate of the State of New York at Their One Hundred and Twenty-sixth Session. Vol. 2. Albany, NY: Argus Printers, 1903.

"Kamp Kill Kare: The Adirondack Lodge of Francis P. Garvan, Esq./Office of John Russell Pope, Architects/Photographs by John Wallace Gillies." *Country Life*, December 1923, 57–60.

Kasher, Steven. *America and the Tintype*. New York: International Center of Photography; Göttingen, Germany: Steidl, 2008.

Keller, Krista. "'A Great Variety of New and Fine Designs': Advertisements for Painted Backgrounds, 1856–1903." Master's thesis, Ryerson Univ., 2013.

Kollecker, William F., and Hannah Clark Collection. MS 88-003, Adirondack Experience Library.

Kostroff, Ellen. *Life in Sacandaga Park 1880 to 1935: The Photographs of Joseph K. Dunlop*. n.p.: Bradford Smith, 2010.

Lacayo, Richard, and George Russell. *Eyewitness: 150 Years of Photojournalism*. 2nd ed. New York: Time Books, 1995.

Lake Placid Club. *Handbook*. Lake Placid, NY: Lake Placid Club, 1914.

Lee, Mary. "Shooting Wild Life with the Camera at Night." *New York Times Magazine*, August 26, 1928, 12–13, 20.

Leonard, John W., ed. *Who's Who in New York City and State*. 3rd ed. New York: L. R. Hamersly, 1907.

Lyden, Anne M. *Railroad Vision: Photography, Travel, and Perception*. Los Angeles: J. Paul Getty Museum, 2003.

MacKenzie, Mary. "Henry Kaiser's Road to Worldwide Renown Began in Lake Placid." *Lake Placid News*, May 24, 1979.

———. *The Plains of Abraham: A History of North Elba and Lake Placid*. Utica, NY: Nicholas K. Burns Publishing, 2007.

Mallory, E. P. "Some Glimpses of Old Plattsburgh." *Plattsburgh Republican*, November 12, 1887.

Marder, William, and Estelle Marder. *Anthony, the Man, the Company, the Cameras: An American Pioneer*. Edited by Robert G. Duncan. Plantation, FL: Pine Ridge Publishing, 1982.

Marvel, Janet. "Dick Dean: Adirondacks Postcard Photographer." *Glens Falls Chronicle*, August 12–18, 1995.

Masters, Peg. "Weedmark Family Legacy." (Town of Webb) *Historical Association News* 2, no. 2 (Fall/Winter 2003): 3.

McClellan, Katherine Elizabeth. Papers. Special Collections, Smith College Library, Northampton, MA. https://findingaids.smith.edu/repositories/4/resources/48.

"McClellan Park." Sarasota History Alive! http://www.sarasotahistoryalive.com/history/articles/mcclellan-park/.

McFee, Inez N. *Little Friends in Feathers*. New York: Barse and Hopkins, 1921.

McIntosh, Burr. "Sir Thomas in the Mountains." *Burr McIntosh Monthly*, November 1903.

McKinstry, Lohr. "The Shooting Sexton Sisters." *Adirondack Life*, September/October 1997, 30–32.

McLaughlin, Bill. "Merely Local." *Adirondack Enterprise*, February 14, 1962.

McMartin, Barbara. *Caroga: An Adirondack Town Recalls Its Past*. 2nd ed. Caroga, NY: Town of Caroga, 1998.

Mellon, Robert H. "The Eyes of Francis Bayle." *Adirondack Life*, Fall 1973, 5–8.

Memorial Gift Book: Lake George and Vicinity. Lake George, NY: Press of Lake George Printing Co., 1929.

Men of Canada; or Success by Example in Religion, Patriotism, Business, Law, Medicine, Education and Agriculture. Vol. 4. Brantford, ONT: Bradley, Garretson, 1895.

Michigan Historical Commission. *Michigan Biographies, Including Members of Congress, Elective State Officers, Justices of the Supreme Court, Members of the Michigan Legislature, Board of Regents of the University of Michigan, State Board of Agriculture and State Board of Education*. Vol. 2. Lansing: Michigan Historical Commission, 1924.

Miller, George, and Dorothy Miller. *Picture Postcards in the United States, 1893–1918*. New York: Clarkson N. Potter, 1976.

"Mr. Alfred." *Adirondack Life*, Winter 1976, 6–10.

Mitchell, Stewart. "Stieglitz in the Adirondacks: The Photographer Found His Focus at Lake George." *Adirondack Life*, September/October 2006, 67–73.

Moore, Clarence B. "Leading Amateurs in Photography." *Cosmopolitan*, February 1892, 421–33.

Morehouse, M. A. "Ventilation for the Dark-Room." *Photographic Times and American Photographer*, September 1884, 477.

Morford, Henry. *Paris in '67, or The Grand Exposition, Its Side-Shows and Excursions*. New York: George W. Carleton, 1867.

Museum of Modern Art. "The Exact Instant—100 Years of News Photography." https://www.moma.org/documents/moma_master-checklist_325638.pdf.

———. "The Exact Instant: Events and Faces in 100 Years of News Photography, Opens at Museum February 9." https://www.moma.org/documents/moma_press-release_325640.pdf.

The New Path: Ruskin and the American Pre-Raphaelites. Brooklyn: Brooklyn Museum, 1985.

New York State. *Colvin Reports on the Topographical Survey of the Adirondack Wilderness*. Title varies. Albany: Weed, Parsons, 1873–96.

Newhall, Beaumont, and Diana E. Edkins. *William H. Jackson*. Fort Worth, TX: Amon Carter Museum of Western Art, 1974.

Norman, Dorothy. *Alfred Stieglitz: An American Seer*. New York: Random House, 1960, 1973.

The Northern Adirondack Guide. Copy at Adirondack Experience. Available through museum's online database.

O'Brien, Peggy. "J. Walton Pursell, Photographer, 1877–1964." *Adirondac*, July 1984, 16–19.

O'Hern, William J. *Adirondack Characters and Campfire Yarns*. Cleveland NY: Forager Press, 2005.

One Hundred Fifty Years, 1823–1973. Ohio, NY: Sesquicentennial Committee, 1973.

"Out-Door Photography." *Humphrey's Journal of Photography and the Allied Arts and Sciences*, June 15, 1860, 56–57.

Page, Edward, H. L. "The Old Portage Railroad in Pennsylvania." *Scientific American*, January 28, 1905, 74–76.

Palmer, Peter Sailly. *History of Plattsburgh, N.Y., from Its First Settlement to Jan. 1, 1876*. Plattsburgh, NY: n.p., 1877.

Palmquist, Peter E., and Thomas R. Kailbourn. *Pioneer Photographers from the Mississippi to the Continental Divide: A Biographical Dictionary, 1839–1865*. Stanford, CA: Stanford Univ. Press, 2005.

"Panoramic Views by Harroun and Bierstadt." *Photographic Times and American Photographer*, June 1881, 216–17.

Peabody, Henry. "Album 2: Views of Eastern New York." Photograph Albums Collection, Historic New England, Boston.

Perrottet, Tony. "Where Was the Birthplace of the American Vacation?" *Smithsonian Magazine*, April 2013. https://www.smithsonianmag.com/travel/where-was-the-birthplace-of-the-american-vacation-5520155/.

Pflane, Arthur E. "People Worth Knowing." *Utica Observer-Dispatch*, March 25, 1956.

Pollard, Gordon C. "Images of the 19th Century Adirondack Bloom Iron Industry." In *Iron in New York*, edited by Martin M. Pickands, 1–43. Albany: New York State Museum, 2018.

Porter, Marjorie Lansing. "History of the Town of AuSable." *Essex County Republican*, March 15, 1952.

Post, Paul. "Missing Historical Marker Resurrects Debate over Photographer's Birthplace." *New York Times*, August 13, 2015.

"The Present Condition of Photography as a Business: Answers to Questions to the Craft." *Wilson's Photographic Magazine*, February 1896, 87–92.

"A Profitable Adirondack Industry." *Leslie's Illustrated Weekly Newspaper*, September 25, 1902.

Prospect House Hotel Register, Receiving Book and Weather Report Book, 1881–88, 1915–17. Blue Mountain Lake, New York. MS 63-262, Adirondack Experience Library.

"Railroad Photography." *New York Railroad Men*, February 1896, 105–110.

Resser, Dr. Charles E. "The Evolution of Ausable Chasm." *York State Tradition* 19, no. 3 (Summer 1965): 2–5.

"Reuben M. McIntosh." *Dog River Crier: A Newsletter of the Northfield Historical Society, Northfield, Vermont* (Spring 2010): 6–11.

Richter, Peter-Cornell. *Georgia O'Keeffe and Alfred Stieglitz*. Munich: Prestel, 2016.

Riley, Casey. "Self Assembled: Isabella Stewart Gardner's Photographic Albums and the Development of Her Museum, 1902–24." In *Photographs, Museums, Collections: Between Art and Information*, edited by Elizabeth Edwards and Cristopher Morton, 47–63. London: Bloomsbury Academic, 2015.

"Robert T. Stratton." *Bulletin of Photography*, May 19, 1920, 474.

Roberts, Hobart V. "Blazing a Path through the Darkness." *Country Life*, May 1936, 558–61.

———. "Camera Hunting with a Flashlight." *Country Life*, September 1922, 40–43.

"Rochester Photographic Association." *Photographic Times and American Photographer*, February 1884, 88–91.

Rockwood, Caroline Washburn. *An Adirondack Romance*. New York: New Amsterdam Book Company, 1897.

Rosenblum, Naomi. *A History of Women Photographers*." New York: Abbeville Press, 1994.

Ryder, Ron, with Jim Fynmore. *Black Cotton Stockings*. Boonville, NY: Country Books, 1954.

Sandweiss, Martha A. *Print the Legend: Photography and the American West*. New Haven, CT: Yale Univ. Press, 2002.

Sante, Luc. *Folk Photography: The American Real-Photo Postcard, 1905–1930*. Portland, OR: Verse Chorus Press, 2009.

Santway, Alfred W. "From Little Red Schoolhouse to the University of Michigan." *Innovator*, August 28, 1975, 6–7.

Sawada, Mitziko. *Tokyo Life, New York Dreams: Urban Japanese Visions of America, 1890–1924*. Berkeley: Univ. of California Press, 1996.

Schlett, James. *A Not Too Greatly Changed Eden: The Story of the Philosophers' Camp in the Adirondacks*. Ithaca, NY: Cornell Univ. Press, 2015.

Schniebs, Otto Eugen. *American Skiing*. New York: E. P. Dutton, 1939.

Seaver, Frederick J. *Historical Sketches of Franklin County and Its Several Towns with Many Short Biographies*. Albany, NY: Lyon, 1918.

Sellers, Coleman. "An Old Photographic Club." By a founding member of New York City's Amateur Photographic Exchange Club and published in five parts in *Anthony's Photographic Bulletin* 19 (1888): 301–4, 338–41, 356–61, 403–6, 658–61.

"Selling Power of Pictures." *Kodak Salesman*, June 1919, 6–7.

Severa, Joan. *Dressed for the Photographer: Ordinary Americans and Fashion, 1840–1900*. Kent, OH: Kent State Univ. Press, 1995.

Shepard, Augustus D. *Camps in the Woods*. New York: Architectural Book Publishing, 1931.

Sinnott, Wilma. "The Pioneering Photography of Hobart Roberts." *Adirondac*, January 1986, 20–24.

Slattery, Arthur. "Personalities." *Adirondack Enterprise*, October 15, 1962.

Smith, H. P. *History of Essex County: With Illustrations and Biographical Sketches of Some of Its Prominent Men and Pioneers*. Syracuse, NY: D. Mason, 1885.

———. *History of Warren County: With Illustrations and Biographical Sketches of Some of Its Prominent Men and Pioneers*. Syracuse, NY: D. Mason, 1885.

———. *Modern Babes in the Wood: Or Summerings in the Wilderness*. Hartford, CT: Columbian Book Company; Syracuse, NY: Watson Gill, 1872.

Smith, H. P., and William S. Rann. *History of Rutland County, Vermont, with Illustrations and Biographical Sketches of Some of Its Prominent Men and Pioneers*. Syracuse, NY: D. Mason, 1886.

Smith, Nicola. "Bradford, Vt. Celebrates a Native Who Photographed Railroads." *Valley News* (Bradford, VT), August 27, 2018.

Southall, Thomas W. "The Kilburn Brothers Stereoscopic View Company." Master's thesis, Univ. of New Mexico, 1977.

Spencer, Jeff A. "Oilfield Photographers—Three Who Captured North American Oil Booms: Frank Robbins, Frank Trost, and Jack Nolan." *Oil-Industry History* 12, no. 1 (2011): 45–57.

Standard Supply Company Records. MS 91-002, Adirondack Experience Library.

Steele, Chris, and Ronald Polito. *A Directory of Massachusetts Photographers, 1839-1900*. Camden, ME: Picton Press, 1993.

Stevens, Scott. "Fixed by a Sunbeam: Daguerreotype Portraits in New York State." *Heritage: The Magazine of the New York State Historical Association*, March/April 1989.

Stickler, Joseph William. *The Adirondacks as a Health Resort*. New York: G. P. Putnam's, 1886.

Stiles, Henry R. *History of Ancient Wethersfield, Connecticut*. Vol. 2, *Genealogies and Biographies*. New York: Grafton Press, 1904.

Stillman, William James. *Autobiography of a Journalist*. Vol. 1. Boston: Houghton Mifflin, 1901.

———. *Poetic Localities: Photographs of Adirondacks, Cambridge, Crete, Italy, Athens*. With contributions by Anne Ehrenkranz, Colin T. Eisler, and Linda S. Ferber. New York: Aperture Foundation and the International Center of Photography, 1988.

Stoddard, Dwight J. *Notable Men of Central New York*. Syracuse, NY: D. J. Stoddard, 1903.

Stoddard, S. R. *Adirondacks: Illustrated*. Albany, NY: Weed Parsons, 1874 and later editions.

———. *Catalogue of Photographs of New York Scenery*. Glens Falls, NY: S. R. Stoddard, 1877. Copy at Adirondack Experience Library.

———. *Lake George (Illustrated) and Lake Champlain. A Book of To-day*. 18th ed. Glens Falls, NY: S. R. Stoddard, 1888.

———. "Landscape and Architectural Photography." *Philadelphia Photographer*, May 1877, 146–48.

———. *Old Times in the Adirondacks: The Narrative of a Trip into the Wilderness*. Edited and with a biographical sketch by Maitland DeSormo. Saranac Lake, NY: Published by the editor, 1971.

Svenson, Sally E. "Past Lives: Solitary Man." *Adirondack Life*, July/August 2002, 16–17.

Szarkowski, John. *Alfred Stieglitz at Lake George*. New York: Museum of Modern Art, 1995.

Taft, Robert. *Photography and the American Scene: A Social History, 1839–1889*. 1938. Reprint, New York: Dover, 1964.

Talbot, Frederick A. "The Ice Carnival of Saranac." *Strand Magazine*, June 1901, 508–13.

Ter-centenary of Lake Champlain, 1609–1909. Ticonderoga, NY: n.p., n.d.

Terrell, John Upton. *The Man Who Rediscovered America; A Biography of John Wesley Powell*. New York: Weybright and Talley, 1969.

Terrill, Frederick William. *A Chronology of Montreal and of Canada from A.D. 1752 to A.D. 1893*. Montreal: John Lovell and Son, 1893.

Timberlake, Richard, and Philip Terrie, eds. *J. S. Wooley, Adirondack Photographer*. Syracuse, NY: Syracuse Univ. Press, 2018.

Tinder, David V. *Directory of Early Michigan Photographers*. Edited by Clayton A. Lewis. Ann Arbor: William L. Clements Library, Univ. of Michigan, 2013. https://clements.umich.edu/files/tinder_directory.pdf.

Tippetts, William Henry. *Lake George, State of New York, Illustrated: The Queen of American Lakes*. Lake George, NY: Tippetts, 1901.

Tousley, H. S. "Adirondac and AuSable River Chasm Views Constantly on Hand." Keeseville, NY: H. S. Tousley, ca. 1875. Copy at Special Collections, Feinberg Library, SUNY Plattsburgh.

Townsend, George Alfred. "Still Taking Pictures: Brady, the Grand Old Man of American Photography." *New York World*, April 12, 1891.

Treadwell, T. K. "A Perspective: Comments on Kilburn." *Stereo World* 1, no. 1 (March/April 1974): 1, 3, 12.

———. "The Stereoscopic Views Issued by the Anthony Company." National Stereoscopic Association, Institute for Photographic Research, Monograph no. 6, 5th ed., January 2002. https://stereoworld.org/wp-content/uploads/2016/03/anthonybook-1.pdf.

Treadwell, T. K., and William C. Darrah, compilers. *Photographers of the United States of America*. Portland, OR: National Stereoscopic Association, 1994.

US National Archives. Civil War Pension Files.

Vaule, Rosamond B. *As We Were: American Photographic Postcards 1905–1930*. Boston: David R. Godine, 2004.

Vermont: Its Resources and Industries, Embracing Historical and Descriptive Sketches of the Green Mountain State, and the Principal Cities and Towns Therein. Glens Falls, NY: C. H. Possons, 1889.

Verner, William K. "Edward Bierstadt's Adirondack Artotypes: A Preliminary Study." Unpublished manuscript, May 16, 1966, Adirondack Experience Library.

"Views Caught with the Drop Shutter." *Anthony's Photographic Bulletin*, September 28, 1889, 576.

Waggoner, Diane, with Russell Lord and Jennifer Raab. *East of the Mississippi: Nineteenth-Century American Landscape Photography*. Washington, DC: National Gallery of Art; New Haven, CT: Yale Univ. Press, 2017.

Waldsmith, John. *Mementoes of Home, the Photographic Legacy of A. F. Styles*. Columbus, OH: 1978. First draft typescript. Copy at Special Collections, Univ. of Vermont Library.

Wallace, E. R. *Descriptive Guide to the Adirondacks*. Several publishers, 1872 and later editions. First edition published with H. P. Smith's *Modern Babes in the Wood*.

Wallace, Frederic A. *Ancestors and Descendants of the Rice Brothers of Springfield, Mass*. Baltimore, MD: Gateway Press, 2005.

Walsh, Molly. "Georgia in New York." *Seven Days* (VT), June 24–30, 2015.

Ward, Spencer K. "Reminiscences of the Old Academy, Remembering 1870." *Warrensburgh News*, January 26, 1922.

Warrensburgh Historical Society and Sandi Parisi. *Warrensburg: 200 Years of People, Places and Events*. Warrensburg, NY: Warrensburgh Historical Society, 2014.

Watson, Elmo Scott. "Back-Tracking an Old Trail." *Coolidge (AZ) Examiner*, June 3, 1932.

Watson, Winslow Cossoul. *Descriptive and Historical Guide to the Valley of Lake Champlain and the Adirondacks*. Burlington, VT: R. S. Styles' Steam Printing House, 1871.

Webb, Nina H. *Footsteps through the Adirondacks: The Verplanck Colvin Story*. Utica, NY: North Country Books, 1996.

Wells, Frederic P. *History of Newbury, Vermont, From the Discovery of the Coös Country to Present Time*. St. Johnsbury, VT: Caledonian, 1902.

Whipple, Gurth. *Fifty Years of Conservation in New York State, 1885-1935*. Albany: Department of Conservation and New York State College of Forestry, 1935.

Whitaker, Robert. "Photographer Chronicled Life in Malone." *Plattsburgh Press-Republican*, May 6, 1988.

"William H. Jackson—Landscape Photographer." *Wilson's Photographic Magazine*, May 1893, 228–31.

Williams, Shirley. "More than Photographer, Tranquille Was an Artist." *Utica Observer-Dispatch*, April 10, 1981.

Wilmerding, John. *American Light: The Luminist Movement, 1850–1875: Paintings, Drawings, Photographs*. New York: Harper and Row, 1980.

Wilson, Edward L. *Wilson's Quarter Century in Photography*. New York: Edward L. Wilson, 1887.

Winship, Kihm. "Silver Bay Postcards." *Faithful Readers: The Writing of Kihm Winship* (blog), May 7, 2012. https://faithfulreaders.com.

Woodbury, Rev. G. F. "How the Adirondack Colporter Missionary Does His Work." *Elizabethtown Post*, June 8, 1905.

Wooden, Emily Beaman. *Beaman and Clark Genealogy: A History of the Descendants of Gamaliel Beaman and Sarah Clark of Dorchester and Lancaster, Mass., 1635–1909*. n.p.: Privately printed, 1909.

Wooley, M. Frank. "Adirondacks Charm Potent in Early Fall." *New York Central Lines Magazine*, November 1922, 38–39.

Worster, Donald. *A River Running West: The Life of John Wesley Powell*. New York: Oxford Univ. Press, 2001.

Index

Italic page numbers denote illustrations.

Acosta, Bernard M., 21, 67
Adirondacks, definition of, 3
Adirondack Survey (V. Colvin), 16, *37*, 38, 55, 56
Adirondack themes, 11–19
advertising images, 22, *53*, 97
aerial photography, 63, 77, 96, 104, 108–10
Agens, Ernest A., 21–22
Allen, Arthur N., 22, *22*, 74
Allen, Fannie, 22
Alletag, Albert, 22–23, *23*
ambrotypes, 6–7
Ameden, Ernest J., 23–24
American Museum of Natural History, 16, 137, 154, 155n8, 169
artotypes, 40
Ashley, George T., 25
Associated Press, 10, 164
Atherton, Lea E., 25
Ausable Chasm, Clinton and Essex Counties, 12–13, *12*, 28, 31, 42, 63, 77, 86, 100, 101, 108, *108*, 113, 119, 120, 123, 124, 126, 127, *127*, 132, *133*, 140, 142, 143, 164, 169
Au Sable Forks, Clinton and Essex Counties, 25, 31, 32, 51, 65, 75, 101, 105, 169, 174
Austin, Earl C., 25–26, *26*
Averill, Henry K., Jr., 13, 26–28, *27*, 63, 78

Bacon, Asa G., 28
Bacon, Charles G., 29
Bacon, William P., 29
Baldwin, Charles S. W. (Dr.), 29–30, 65
Baldwin, George C., 30, 62
Baldwin, George M., 30–31, 62
Baldwin, George W., 11–12, *11*, 13, 22, 31–33, *32*, 41, 48, 67, 107, 119, 125
Barker, B. Benton, 33
Barnum, Isaac D., 33–34, *33*
Barrett, Charles F., 34
Bayle, Francis, 34
Beach, Henry M., *14*, 34–36, *35*, 105
Beaman, Elias O., 3, 37–38, *37*, 55, 56
Beer, Sigismund, 2, 38–39
Beer Brothers, 2, 38–39
Beetle, David, 88n3, 164
Betts, James T., 39, 115
Bierstadt, Albert, 40
Bierstadt, Charles, 39, 40
Bierstadt, Edward, 39, 40
Bigalow, William H., 31, 40–41, 107
Bigelow, William A., 8, 41–42, 90
Bigelow Studio, 41
Billwiller, Henrietta. *See* Hudson, Henrietta
Bishop, Bainbridge, 42
Bixby, Marquis J., 42, 63
Blackburn, William, 8
Blue Mountain Lake, Hamilton County, *37*, 39, 40, 44, 87, 88, 99, *99*, 120, 152
Bogdan, Robert, 35
Bolton, Warren County, 34, 88, 90–91, 117, 144–45, 149, 161, 162
Boonville, Oneida County, 44, 52, 76–77, 116, 121, 126
Bourke-White, Margaret, 42–44, *43*
Bowdish, Robert F., 44
Bowers, Sereno A., 44–45, 156
Bowman, Isaac E., 45, 123
Brady, Matthew B., 3, 45–46
Brick House Studio. *See* Thatcher, Julius A.
Brown, Hobart J., 46, *46*
Brownell, W. Wallace, 46–48, *47*, 97
Brush, Daniel S., 32, 48, 175
Burlington, VT, 42, 44–45, 48, 63, 86, 90, 93, 101, 143, 156
business of photography, 7–8, *9*
Buttolph, Seymour E., 49, 71

cabinet cards, 6
Caldwell, Warren County, 1, 2, 49, 92–93, 141–42, 147–50, *148*, 160–62
camera clubs, 8, 21, 62, 95, 124, 131, 143, 171
Canada, 69, 71, 73, 74, 79, 95, 103, 123–24, 132, 143, 155, 172
Carpenter, James H., 49, 76, 153
Carpenter, Warwick S., 49–51, *50*
Carter, George W., 51, 106, 167
cartes de visite, 6
Cassens, Fred W., 70
Cassens, Harold, 70–71
C. C. Shop (or C. C. Studio). *See* Commo, Leo A.
Chandler, William D., 51
Chase, William Moody, 101
Cheeseman, William F. *See* Cheesman, William F.
Cheesman, William F., 51–52, 102, 103
Chestertown, Warren County, 24, 25, 34, 48, 60, 88, 121, 158, *159*
children's summer camps, 18, 77, 146
Church, Artemus M., 52
Church, Dwight P., 52–53, *53*

Civil War, 28, 29, 30, 42, 45–46, 49, 59, 71, 73, 89, 93, 95, 100, 132, 171
Civil War tax stamps, 8, 103, 170
Cleveland, Grover J., 54
collodion wet-plate process, 6, 7
collotype process, 40
Colonial Studio. *See* Smith, Mason C.
color photography, 9, 90–91
Colvin, Verplanck, 16, 28, 37, 38, 54–56, *55*
Commo, Leo A., 56–57
Cone, Leland D., 57
Conkey, George W., 57–58, 122, 153, 159
Conley, William A., 58
Coolidge, Calvin, 54
Coonrod, Arthur E., 58–59, *59*
Copeland, George T., 59–60
Cowan, William M. A., 60–61, 75
Cowen, William M. A. *See* Cowan, William M. A.
Crane, Edwin N., 61, *61*, 62
Crane, Frederick M., 31, 62
Crown Point, Essex County, 11, 28, 41, 57, 62, 95–96, 124, 128, 166, 170

Daguerre, Louis, 5
daguerreotypes, 5
Dandurand, Burnell F., 62–63, 82, 143
Davis, Guy B., 42, 63, 156
Dean, Richard K., 63–64
Dean Color Photo, 63–64
DeGraff, Esther H., 64, *64–65*
Delaware and Hudson Railroad, 58, 124–25, 154
Derby, Charles, 30, 65–66, *65*
Detroit Publishing Company, 66, 80, 94, 95, 124
Dewey, Guy C., 66
Distin, William L., 21, 32, 67
Dixon, George W., 67–68, *67*
Dodge, Franklin O., 68, *68*
Douglas, Evan C., 69
Dunlop, Joseph K., 8, 69–70, 123

E. and H. T. and Anthony Company, 2, 24–25, 37, 38, 153, 171
Eastern Illustrating and Publishing Company, 70–71, *70*
Eastman Kodak Company, 8–9, 21, 33, 54, 91, 177
Eby, Harold M., 71
Elizabethtown, Essex County, 31, 32, 41, 48, 58–59, *59*, 73, 74, 92, 107, 108, 167, 172–73, *173*
exaggeration postcards, 36

Fay, Christopher R., 49, 71–73, *72*, 74, 136, 144
Fell, William J., 73
Felt, Thomas C., 73
Ferris, Charles H., *72*, 73–74
Ferris, Charles J., 22, 74, 144
ferrotypes. *See* tintypes
Fillmore, Lavius H., 60, 74–75, *75*, 121
$5-Photo-Co. *See* Church, Dwight P.
Flanders, Martin P., 75
Fonda, Johnstown and Gloversville Railroad, 17, 122–23
Foote, Norman S., 76, *76*
Fort William Henry Hotel, 1, 2, 66, 95, 161, *163*
freak postcards, 36
Fry, Mr., 47, *47*
Fuller, James, 49, 76
Fulton Chain of Lakes, *ii*, 24, 44, 52, 80, 87, 120, 126, 136, 142, 156, 171
Fynmore, James F., 76–77

Galusha, Rae, 77
Gates, George F., 77–78
Gates, Philemon T., 6, 27, 78
Gates, Willis D., 78
gelatin dry-plate process, 7
Gibbon, Charles, 78–79, 98
Gillies, John W., 79
Gjersvik, Torleif, 79–80
Glens Falls, Warren County, 34, 57, 58, 60, 63–64, 88, 91, 92, 94, 107, 122, 152–54, 158–59, 174
Glover, Lycurgus S., 66, 80
Gockeler, Edward L., 80–81
Gottscho, Samuel H., 81, *81–82*
great camps, 16, *43*, 79, 84, 154
Great Northern Photograph and Copying House, 155
Grimes, Frank H., 75, 82
Grover, L. Paul, 82–83, 143
Guild, Jonathan F., 83

Hague, Warren County, *75*, 119, 140–41, 160, 177
Hamilton County, 7, 10, *14*, 21–22, 37–38, 39, 40, 42–43, *43*, 44, 48, 52, 55, 62, 68, *72*, 73, 76, 78–79, 84, 86, 87, 88, 95, 98–99, *99*, 107, 112–13, 115, 126, 130, 136, 159–60, 166, 167, 176–77
Hamilton Maxwell Inc., 109–10
Hand, George A., 83–84, 97, 98
hand-coloring, 9, 10, 34, 66, 69, 87, 107, 120, 126, 139–40, 146
Harris, David, 84
Hart, Harold J., 84
Hastings, Philip R., 84–86, *85*
Herkimer County, 21–22, 29, 34, 35, *50*, 51, 52, 54, 62, 64, 78–79, 80, *80*, 105, 120, 126, 130–31, 134, 136, 140, 147, 166, 170–71
Hewitt, Thaddeus E., 45, 86
Hibbard, Charles P., 9, 86
Hills, James H., 45
Hinckley, Harvey H., 86
Hodges, Frederick A., 87–88, *87*
Holley, J. Frank, 48, 88–89, *88*
hotels as clients/employers, 11–12, 30, 40, 51, 66, 111, 144–45, 146, 164, 174
Houghton, George H., 89, *89*
Howard, James J., 27, 41, 89–90
Howard, Leroy, 90
Hudson, Henrietta, 90–91
Huettig, Carlos or Charles. *See* Huttig, Carl F.
Huttig, Carl F., 84, 92, 167
Huttig, Emily D. (Mrs. Charles F. Huttig), 92

Illinois College of Photography, 57, 83, 143

imprints, 8
Irish, George S., 92–93, 147
Isaac, Abraham, 93

Jackson, William H., 3, 6, 66, 93–95, *94*, 130, 152, 156
Johnsburg, Warren County, 24, 45, 114, 127, 128, 170
Johnson, Elbert M., 41, 48, 57, 60, 95–96, 166
Jones, David W., 71, 96, 125

Kaiser, Henry J., 47–48, 79, 83, 96–98, *97*
Kaiser Photographic Stores, *97*, 98
Keene, Essex County, 25, 28, 31, 41, 48, 80, 101, 108, 111, *153*, 172
Keeseville, Clinton and Essex Counties, 5, 6, 12, 31, 79–80, 84, 93, 95, 101, 108, *108*, 119, 120, 128, 130, 134, 163–64, 172
Kellogg, Elmer E., 98–99, *99*
Kelly, Hugh A., 99–100
Kibbe, William H., 100
Kilburn Brothers, *15*, 100–101
Kirk, Frank A., 101, 108
Knechtel, A., *14*
Kodakery, 8–9, 19, 110, 111
Kollecker, William F., 101–3, *102*, 105, 145
Krumbholz, T. Edmund, 144–45

LaBarre, Isaac D., 103
Lake George (lake), 1, 2, 11, 16, 24, 33–34, 38, 45, 49, 57–58, 63, 74, 75, 78, 83, 89, 91, 92, 95, 108, *109*, 117, 120, 121, 123, 124, 126, 140, 141–42, 147–50, *148*, 153, 154, 158, 159, 160–63, *161*, *163*, 174, 176–77, *176*
Lake George, Town of. *See* Caldwell, Warren County
Lake Placid, Essex County, 17, 18, 30, 32, 46–48, *47*, 51–52, 54, 64, 71, 75, 79, 80, 83, 93, 95, 96–98, *97*, 101, 102, 105, 108, *110*, 115–16, 118–19, 121, 125, 129, *129*, 139, 144, 145–46, *145*
Lennon, Frederick P., 103–4
Lewis County, 21–22, 34–37, *35*, 44, 51, 52, 58, 98, 104, 116, 142, 166
Lincoln, Abraham, 45
Locke, Harris L., 104–5, *104*
loggers as clients, 13, 100, 103–4
Lowville, Lewis County, 21, 34–35, 51, 58, 106, 142, 167
Lyon, Harry W., 105

MacDowell, Winchester, 103, 105
magic lantern presentations, 9, 38, 154, 169, 174, 176
Maginley, Charles H., 106
Malone, Franklin County, 25, 30, 31, 49, 58, 66, 67, 71–73, 74, 86, 101, 136, 144
Mandeville, William G., Jr., 106, 142
Mann, James W., 107
Mann Brothers, 17, 106–7
Marr, Thomas Edgar, 107
Marvin, Edgar A., 31, 41, 107–8
Marvin, George F., 41, 101, 107, 108, *108*
Maxwell, Hamilton K., 108–10, *109*
McClellan, Katherine E., 110–11, *110*
McCormick, Frank J., 111–12
McGinley, Charles H. *See* Maginley, Charles H.
McIntosh, Burr, 112–13
McIntosh, Reuben M., 113
McKinley, William, 43–44, *175*
Miller, Russell A., 113–14
Mix, Alonzo L., 39, 114–15, *114*
Molloy, Sarah Mallory (Mrs. William P.), 115
Monahan, Odie R., 115–16
Montreal, Canada, 123–24
Moore, Frederick A., 116, 126
Moore, Roger L., 116–17, 129
Morehouse, Miles A., 117–18
Morse, Samuel F. B., 24, 45
Moses, Chester D., 118–19, *118*, 145–46, 177
Moulton, Joseph C., 119–20
Myers, Carl, 120

news photography, 10
New York State Conservation Commission, 16, 50
New York State Department of Education, 16, *168*, 169
New York State Forest Commission and successors, *14*, 16, 130–31, 169
New York Stereoscopic Company, 120–21
Nickerson, Amos S., 74, 121, 162
North Creek, Warren County, 24, 25, 77
North River Studio. *See* Ameden, Ernest J.
Northville, Fulton County, 17, 29, 45, 60, 70, 73, 86, 106, 123, 138, 147, 171–72
Norton, John A., 121–22
Nutting, Wallace, 140

oilgraph, 34, 36n1
O'Keeffe, Georgia, 149–50
Old Forge, Herkimer County, 52, 64, *64*, 79, 80, 105, 136–37, 140, 156, 164, 170–71
Old Homestead Studio. *See* Austin, Earl C.
Olympic Winter Games (Third, 1932), 18, 54, 116, 125
Olympic Winter Games (Thirteenth, 1980), 64
Orr, Alexander, Jr., 58, 122
outdoor recreation as subject, 15
Ovitt, Gordon D., 122

Page, Edward H. L., 122–23
Parks, James G., 123–24
Paul Smiths, Franklin County, 28, 32, 65, 106, 109
Peabody, Henry Greenwood, 66, 124
Pease, Charles S., 124–25
Philosophers' Camp, 150
picture postcards, 9–10
Pierson, Eugene H., 96, 125–26
Plattsburgh, Clinton County, 5, 6, 8, 26–28, 31–32, 41–42, 48, 56–57, 63, 65, 67, 74, 78, 80, 84, 89, 93, 107, 115, 166, 174–75, *175*

Pollard, George H., 116, 126
portrait accessories and backgrounds, 7–8
post–World War II shortages, 26
Private Mailing Card Act (1898), 9
Professional Photographers' Society of New York State, 21, 96
Pursell, James W., 126
Purviance, William T., 126–27, *127*
Putnam, Osmond D., 127–28, *128*
Putnam, Tarrant, 6, 128–29

Rabineau, George T., 54, 83, 116, 117n1, 129–30, *129*
railroads as clients/employers, 13, 94, 122–23, 124–25, 154, 178
Randall, Elmer E., 130
Raquette Lake, Hamilton County, 62, 84, 113, 154
real photo postcards (RPPC), 10
Reising, Grotus H., 130–31, *130*
Rice, Frederick W., 102, 131–32, *131*
Richardson, Thomas G., 132
Rison, George H. *See* Reising, Grotus H.
Robbins, Frank, 119, 132–34, *133*
Roberts, Hobart V., 134–36, *135*
Robideau, Eli, 73, 136
Robideau, Norbert E., 136
Rome, Oneida County, 29, 87, 116, 121
Roosevelt, Franklin D., 54, 146, 175
Ross, Harold D., *ii*, 136–37
RPPC. *See* real photo postcards
Runions, Charles E., 137–38
Runions Brothers, 137–38, *137*

Sacandaga Park, Fulton County, 17, *17*, 45, 69–70, 106, 122–23, 147, 172
Santway, Alfred W., 138–39, *139*
Saranac Lake, Franklin and Essex Counties, 3, 21, 22, 29–30, 31, 32, 36, 49, 54, 56–57, 64, 65, 67, 69, 71, 74, 79, 80, 95, 101–3, *102*, 105, 110, 111, 131–32, 136, 138, 141, 142, 144–45, 166
satellite studios, 7, 48, 58, 86, 90, 121, 137–38
Satterlee, Albert, 139
Sawyer, Charles H., 139–40
Schooley, Charles M., 140
Schroon Lake, Essex County, 18, 38, 41, 81, 143, 146–47, 170
Sexton, Flora D., 140–41
Sexton, Theresa A., 140–41
Silver Bay Association, 119, 160, 177
Sipperly, William H., 141
Sisson, Henry W., 141–42
Slayton, Herman E., 142
Slocum, Frank E., 106, 142–43
Smith, George J., 143
Smith, Mason C., 143–44
Spencer, Frank T., 144
spirit pictures, 44
sport photography, 116, 125, 129
Standard Supply Company. *See* Norton, John A.
Start, Edward T., 103, 144–45
Stedman, Irving L., 54, 119, 129, 145–46, *145*
Steffel, Joseph J., *18*, 146–47
Steichen, Edward, 134, 149, 164
stereograph or stereoview, 6–7
Stevens, George W., *17*, 123, 147
Stieglitz, Alfred, 4, 92–93, 147–50, *148*, 173
Stillman, William J., 49, 150–52, *151*
St. Lawrence County, 2, 5, 30, 49, 52, 58, 61, 62, 72, 73, 83, 84, 91, 104, 111, 137–38, 155
Stoddard, Seneca R., *12*, 13, 16, 31, 49, 56, 58, 114, 124–25, 152–55, *153*, 176, 177
Stone, Nathan L., 155
Stone, N. Clark, 155
Stratton, Robert T., 134, 155–56
Styles, Adin F., 44, 63, 93, 156–58, *157*
summer touring, 7, 25, 31, 41, 48, 65, 88, 96, 101, 108
Sumy, Itsuzo, 158, *159*

Taft, Frank M., 158–59
Taft, William H., 175
Tefft, Arthur J., 159–60
Tefft, Lila L., 159–60
Terzian, William, 160
Thatcher, Fred C., 160–62, *161*
Thatcher, J. Glenn, 160–62
Thatcher, Julius A., 160, 162–63, *163*
Thatcher Studio, 161, 162
Ticonderoga, Essex County, 11, 28, *33*, 48, 57, 60, 62–63, 74–75, 82–83, 101, 107, 121, 124, 143, 161, 162
tintypes, 6, *17*, *46*
tourism and photography, 1, 11–12, *11*, 138, 153, 178
Tousley, Horace S., 6, 163–64
Towsley. *See* Tousley, Horace S.
Tranquille, Dante O, 10, 164–65
Trumbull, Anna C. (Mrs. E. E. Trumbull), 165–66, *165*
Tucker, Wilson M., 166
Tupper Lake, Franklin County, 61, *61*, 62, 67, 99–100, 103–4, 111–12, *112*, 136, 137, *137*, 164
Twain, Mark (Samuel Clemens), 131

Underwood, Clarence, 92, 166–67
Underwood and Underwood, 10, 109, 146
Underwood Studio, 92, 167
Union View Company, 174
Upper Saranac Lake, Franklin County, 27, *89*, 150
Utica, Oneida County, 51, 62, 79, 84, 87, 97, 100, 116, 126, 134, 137, 155–56, 164

Van Aken, Elisha M., 7, 51, 167
Van Sant, Florence A., 167–69, *168*
Veeder, Aaron, 169

Wardner, Seth, 169–70, 170n1
Warner, T. B., 139
Warrensburg, Warren County, 25–26, *26*, 39, 49, 60, 63, 76, 114–15, 121, 153
Webster, Loren, 170, *170*
Weedmark, William P., 170–71
Wetmore, Augustus, Jr., 171

Wilmington, Essex County, 22–23, *23*, 31, 125, *131*, 169–70
Wilson, Stewart, 171–72
Winslow, Albert G., 172
W. Mould & Son, 119, 134
women in photography, 4, 22, 41, 154; Bourke-White, 42–44, *43*; DeGraff, 64–65, *64*; Hudson, 90–91; Huttig, 92; McClellan, *110*, 110–11; Molloy, 115; Sexton, 140–41; Tefft, 159–60; Trumbull, 165–66, *165*; Van Sant, 167–69, *168*
Wood, George B., Jr., 4, 172–73, *173*
Woodbury, George F., 173–74
wood engravings, 10, 38, 54, 56, 59, 72, *72*
Woodward, Charles W., 174
Woodward, George T., 48, 174–75
Wooley, Jesse S., 176–77, *176*
World War I, 10, 25, 54, 56, 62, 66, 83, 109, 122
World War II, 23, 63, 84, 96, 98, 116, 125, 125–26n2, 146, 158

Yates, Arthur P., 177–78

Sally E. Svenson is an independent scholar. A seasonal Adirondack resident for over twenty years, she has taken a special interest in researching unrecorded aspects of Adirondack history. Previous books on regional topics covered early church architecture and the history of Blacks in the Adirondacks. She has also contributed articles to *Adirondack Life* and *New York State Archives* magazines.

When not in the North Country, Svenson lives in New York City with her husband, Charles. She is a graduate of Cornell University and holds master's degrees from Columbia University and Columbia Teachers College.